The Race for the Rhine Bridges

The Race for the Rhine Bridges

ALEXANDER McKEE

DORSET PRESS
NEW YORK

This edition published by Dorset Press
by arrangement with Souvenir Press.

2001 Dorset Press

ISBN 0-7607-2318-4 *paperback*

Printed and bound in the United States of America

01 02 03 04 MP 9 8 7 6 5 4 3 2 1

RRD-H

CONTENTS

Part I FORTRESS HOLLAND 1940

Part II TARGET RUHR 1944

ILLUSTRATIONS

Facing page

ILLUSTRATIONS

Part I

FORTRESS HOLLAND
1940

CHAPTER ONE

RHINE AND RUHR

In front of me, Arnhem was burning. Against a blue backcloth of sky, on a sunny spring morning, immense columns of smoke poured up from the doomed town set on wooded hills behind a river, and drifted eastward towards the German border. The centre piece was a ruined church, one side of the tower still standing, with the sky bright behind the broken windows. The sound was continuous. Our shells poured overhead into the town with the noise of thousands of tons of water roaring over a waterfall. Above them rose the high, fluttering scream of German shells about to arrive and the unearthly moaning wail of the salvoes of 150-millimeter projectiles from the German multiple-barrel mortars. A battle is read through the ears, so that although the rolling rattle of machine-gun fire sounded like two crazy xylophonists trying to outdo each other on tin trays, the slower, sweeter note of the Bren was distinct from the sharp, angry, irregular rattle of the Spandau.

A rash of dust spurts kicked up along the wall of a riverfront house, accompanied by the heavy, drilling roar of a tank machine-gun; then the Canadian Sherman lets loose with its 75-millimeter turret gun and a cloud of grey-white smoke blossomed horizontally out from the wall. A second Canadian tank crawled along the Arnhem waterfront like an enormous insect, and both tanks blasted the house, which almost disappeared in the blossoms of spurting smoke and the irregular rashes of machine-gun fire.

The bridge—the great road bridge of Arnhem—dipped its shattered span into the Neder Rijn, the shorn-off girders reaching for the river like broken hands, or the hopes of its Dutch and German defenders.

The third—and last—Battle of Arnhem was at its height.

In its axis of advance it was almost an exact duplicate of the first battle, which had taken place there a month short of five years before. But because this was 1945 and not 1940, the forces engaged and the machines and weapons involved were immensely greater. And its objectives were different. They were a duplicate of the main intention behind the only Battle of Arnhem that is now remembered—the bitter British defeat of September, 1944, which was also the last outright German victory in the West during the Second World War.

The British victory at Arnhem in 1945 was not merely the third battle for that particular town in the space of less than five years, it was also the culmination of the third great Rhine campaign of the Second World War. In these three campaigns many key points—such as towns, airfields, and high ground situated at and around the vital crossing places—were assaulted twice or even three times. The soldiers who went forward to the attack or the counter-attack—or who dropped from the skies—were of many nationalities: Dutch, French, Germans, British, Canadians, Americans, approximately in that order.

All three campaigns featured the use of airborne troops and two of them involved the laying of an airborne "carpet" along a line of bridges deep inside enemy territory, with the hope that fast-moving armoured divisions would be able to link up in time before the lightly armed paratroopers were overwhelmed. This was a genuine innovation in the history of warfare, and few of these operations went exactly according to plan. Some were chaotic failures. Yet others were brilliantly successful.

Dominating them all was the Rhine. Linking them also, although to a lesser extent, was the Ruhr.

The commercial importance of a river lies not so much in its width as in its depth; and in the regularity of the water supply, which ensures adequate depth. The Rhine is unusual in that the primary fluctuations in its supply are governed by the Alpine icecap and the Atlantic rains, and only to a limited extent by the spring thaw. In Switzerland it is an Alpine torrent with a summer flow ten times as great as that in winter. On the plains between the Vosges and the Black Forest, the Rhine is up to two miles wide in summer but a meandering pattern of half-dry channels and banks in winter.

Here in 1940 the concrete fortifications of the Maginot and Siegfried lines faced each other directly across the river and, partially dismantled, still do. This is the disputed land of Alsace-Lorraine, part-German, part-French, with its capital at Strasbourg, where the Rhine as a commercially important navigable river really begins. This plain is a result of a lowering of the earth's surface by earthquake movements long ago. Because the river is easy to cross, Strasbourg has seen many invaders.

Beyond Strasbourg, the Rhine becomes more stable with the entry of major rivers that fluctuate also, but in different and therefore complementary patterns. Both the Neckar, flowing into the Rhine near Heidelberg, and the Main, which joins the main stream by way of Frankfurt and Mainz, are high in winter—when the Rhine is low; and low in summer —when the Rhine is high. There are still seasonal variations, but these range now from only 28,000 cubic feet of water a second in November to 70,000 cubic feet in July.

At this point also the character of the countryside changes completely, both geologically and historically. Historically, the atmosphere until now has been that of a settled Roman civilisation, as the main riverside towns testify—Speyer (*Augusta Nemetum*), Worms (*Borbetomagus*), Mainz (*Mogontiacum*).

But when the river enters what geologists call the Rhine "gorge" and the tourist agencies advertise as "the Romantic Rhine," the dominating atmosphere is German and mediaeval; and the scenery is unbelievable. Here the river has cut its way through the rock of the Rhenish uplands, so that for mile after mile great cliffs and hills rise on either side and on almost every one is perched the ruin of a mediaeval castle. To see any part of the Rhine between Bingen and Bonn, especially at sunset, is to feel oneself incorporated involuntarily in a fairy tale, and it is easy to understand why most of the Rhine legends are centred on this spectacular gorge.

The best-known legend concerns the Lorelei rock, which rises almost vertically 430 feet above the river, which at that point is 76 feet deep but a mere 650 feet wide. The restriction of so much water, the rocky and irregular channel, and the fast currents and eddies so caused would indeed make it dangerous for any boatman to take his eyes off the navigation to gaze even for a moment at any sun-bathing bikini-blonde, regardless of whether or not she had her transistor radio going.

It is true that the main towns by the river are still Roman in origin—Koblenz (*Confluentes*), Bonn (*Bonna*)—but here the Rhine was a Roman frontier and, as the ruined castles testify, a contested land for long years after the fall of Rome. And contested even more recently, as the broken piers of Remagen bridge proclaimed when I was there last, in 1952. In 1969, that is also history, already merging into the past with the Dragon Mountain and the legend of the Nibelungs among the Seven Hills across the river. Quite forgotten, at their foot, is the meeting place of Hitler and Chamberlain during the Czech crisis of 1938.

During its passage through the gorges towards the plain, the Rhine has collected additional water supplies from four more rivers—the Nahe and the Moselle from the west and the Lahn and the Sieg from the east. These rivers flow through wild and hilly country and in times of heavy rain are likely to flood, a fact to which I can testify from personal experience of living in the valley of the Sieg during the winter of 1945–46. I saved the unit's stocks of champagne from the drowned cellar only just in time.

The River Ruhr also rises in this mountainous country of dark pine forests full of deer and wild boar, which is also the country of the great artificial lakes and dams, some of them now well known, such as the Möhne.

From this river, the great industrial complex of the Ruhr takes its name, and from the Ruhr to the sea the river and the channels into which it diverges are embanked. This is the flood plain of the Rhine, where the river can at the same place, according to season, vary its width from 1,000 feet to three miles.

This area presents a particularly difficult military engineering problem to any army contemplating an assault crossing. Indeed, the state of the river governs the date of the assault, because no pontoon bridge can survive when the current, which flows at speeds between two and five and one-half knots, brings down the winter ice; nor can vehicles or heavy equipment cross the miles of flood plain until it has dried out.

Further, by blowing the embankments an enemy can

flood large areas with up to five or six feet of water at certain times of the year. Here, it is the river itself that is the main obstacle to a crossing, rather than the nature of the surrounding countryside.

On the other hand, once an army approaching from the west has closed up to the Rhine along most of its length, Germany is finished. This was not so in Roman times, when the legions were stationed on the west bank between Cologne (*Colonia Agrippina*), Xanten (*Castra*), and Nijmegen (*Noviomagus*). They too had to put military bridges across the Rhine when it became necessary to undertake a punitive expedition or "show the Eagles" to the Germanic barbarians, but they could never achieve decisive results because a loose tribal organisation offered no concentrated and vital targets to hit. Basically, it was the same problem sized up by the Duke of Wellington when he refused the command of the force designed to reconquer the lost British colonies in North America and not far different from the problems now faced by the United States in Vietnam.

The situation in modern Germany is almost the exact opposite, partly because of the exposed position of the great Ruhr concentration of industry, partly because the Rhine itself is Germany's major commercial highway, containing many of its major ports. It is a sea rather than a river and indeed is tidal in the lower reaches. Vessels of over 4,000 tons capacity can operate as far up as Duisburg, each one carrying four or five times the load of an average freight train. Consequently, in war it is vital for the Germans to push an enemy as far away as possible from the Ruhr and the lower reaches of the Rhine, while it is as equally vital for an enemy to close up to the Rhine in front of the Ruhr, or to outflank the entire river barrier from either north or south, preparatory to taking or encircling that huge industrial target.

Despite the prophecies and the theories of the air enthusiasts, the idea of producing a "third flank" by heavy air bombardment had disappointing practical results, except in terms of human suffering, and the Ruhr eventually succumbed only to ground attack. It had been a major factor in the calculations of the planners of the three Rhine campaigns of the Second World War.

The flood plain, from the Ruhr to the sea, was once the bottom of the sea. At another time, glaciers flowed across it; and at another time, enormous rivers. The seasonal fluctuations of modern times are very minor ones compared to those that have taken place in the past. The reason is that periodic alterations in relative sea and land levels affect the Rhine both at its source and its mouth. The river is itself part of the exchange mechanism by means of which either more or less water flows into the oceans and, being partly tidal, is directly affected by the results.

For instance, during the great flood of 1270—a time of inundations all round the coasts of northern Europe—Duisburg became virtually an island, a state of affairs that lasted for centuries. But by the seventeenth century the scales had tilted the other way; the River Ijssel, by means of which the Rhine fed the Ijsselmeer, or Zuyder Zee, dried up. Today, east of Arnhem in the area of the Dutch–German border an almost land-locked stretch of water marks the former course of the Rhine.

It is in this area between Arnhem in the north and Nijmegen in the south that the river wavers in its purpose through the flood plain, where the dykes rise up to 16 feet in height as a guard against the floods of a normal winter. The main body of water flows past Nijmegen towards its junction with the Maas near Moerdijk and the wide Hollandsch Diep and now has a Dutch name—the River Waal. But it is still the main torrent of the Rhine, 850 feet wide. Just inside Holland, however, a smaller waterway branches off north-west towards Arnhem—the Pannerden Canal.

When it reaches Arnhem, the waterflow divides at a spit into two more branches. The River Ijssel trends away north-east towards the Zuyder Zee, while the main stream, now called the Neder Rijn, passes under the walls of Arnhem westward to Rotterdam and the Hook of Holland. At Arnhem, the Neder Rijn, or Lower Rhine, is only 300 feet wide, although it spills over to the south to reach a width of 1,640 feet in winter, contained by a dyke. It was from this dyke that I watched the battle of 1945.

Between the Waal at Nijmegen and the Neder Rijn at Arnhem is a distance of about eight miles, and both towns are clearly in view of each other because, most unusual in Holland, they stand on high ground; the low-lying land between, being surrounded by rivers on three sides and a marsh to the west, is virtually an island. The "Island" was indeed what the British soldier was to call it during the exceptionally severe winter of 1944–45, and historically this may be correct as the area is probably that known to the Romans as the "Island of the Batavians."

Almost precisely 1,900 years ago—in A.D. 69—the Roman Second Legion fortified Nijmegen after suppressing the revolt of Julius Civilis, and were then replaced by the Tenth Legion. In A.D. 1944 the British Second Army was to fight bitterly for possession of the high ground in Nijmegen where the fort of the Roman Second Legion had stood, and where Roman remains are still dug up.

For the Dutch, however, the descendants of the Batavians, the fertile area between Nijmegen and Arnhem is the Over-Betuwe. In spring, it is a wonderland of blossoms, but in the spring of 1945 the scent of the blossoms mixed with the sickly sweet stench of death, as young men went forward to the last assault among the unburied corpses of a bitter winter of battle in the delta of the Rhine.

Conscious that they had been chosen to avenge the defeat at Arnhem seven months before, none realised that the war in the West had begun here, at Arnhem and Nijmegen, at 0355 hours on May 10, 1940, when many of them had still been at school, and none could foresee that history would turn full circle within five years and by the remorseless logic of geography lead them to attack the same objectives as the equally youthful German soldiers of 1940.

CHAPTER TWO

OPERATION YELLOW

Hitler had wanted war, but not war against the Western Powers, unless it was absolutely forced on him. On September 3, 1939, it was forced on him, as a result of his attack on Poland, when Britain and France declared war; all other nations remained neutral, with the single exception of the Soviet Union, which aided the Nazi State in the swift dismemberment of Poland.

On October 9, 1939, a little over a month later, Hitler issued his Directive No. 6 for the Conduct of the War. This was his blueprint for 1940.

Two estimates and a number of political facts are basic to its background. The first estimate concerned German war production, which, it was calculated, would not reach its peak until 1943. In 1940, the German armed forces would be comparatively weak when compared with the full German potential. Nevertheless, it was not advisable to wait, because of the second estimate, which concerned British war production. The resources of the British Empire, although they would gather more slowly, would in time exceed those of Germany. Therefore, Germany could not afford a long war with Britain. She had to strike immediately, if possible, in 1939.

The political facts must be somewhat brutally summarised. Hitler's ambitions, if that be the word to describe a mixture of ruthless logic combined with grandiose dreams of blood and power, lay in the East. The Franco-British declaration of war was a nuisance. He had hoped to avoid it. But now that it had come he judged his Western adversaries, actual and potential, to be weaker in will than in power. He might secure a negotiated peace after very little fighting, or perhaps none at all, as he had done for so many years on so many occasions. With this in mind, Hitler wrote Directive No. 6 for operation *Fall Gelb* ("Case Yellow"):

"1. Should it become evident in the near future that England, and, under her influence, France also, are not disposed to bring the war to an end, I have decided, without further loss of time, to go over to the offensive.

2. Any further delay will not only entail the end of Belgian and perhaps of Dutch neutrality, to the advantage of the allies; it will also increasingly strengthen the military power of the enemy, reduce the confidence of neutral nations in Germany's final victory, and make it more difficult to bring Italy into the war on our side as a full ally.

3. I therefore issue the following orders for the further conduct of military operations:

(a) An offensive will be planned on the northern flank of the Western front, through Luxembourg, Belgium, and Holland. . . .

(b) The purpose of this offensive will be to defeat as much as possible of the French Army and of the forces of the allies fighting on their side, and at the same time to win as much territory as possible in Holland, Belgium and Northern France, to serve as a base for the successful prosecution of the air and sea war against England and as a wide protective area for the economically vital Ruhr.

(c) The time of the attack will depend upon the readiness for action of the armoured and motorised units involved. . . . It will depend also upon the weather conditions. . . ."

There were five more paragraphs, but these were the vital ones. Later directives show this plan evolving. It was to be an on-off, on-off affair, capable of cancellation at any time up to five hours before the attack was due, and as it was cancelled on a number of occasions this greatly favoured the success of the actual operation when it finally was launched. For although many Germans blindly believed in their leader, and most considered that he had done well up to that time to achieve so much with so little trouble and bloodshed, senior officers in the German Army knew better. They regarded him as a common little guttersnipe, possessing in an extraordinary degree the ability to hypnotise the common people, who were now started on a reckless adventure that could lead in the long run only to catastrophe. Some of them were in a position to keep the Allies informed of the impending attack and so, each time the German Army was alerted for Operation Yellow, so too were the Allied armies and the neutral victims.

Regarding the neutral Dutch, Hitler's Directive No. 8 stated:

"The attitude of the Dutch forces cannot be foreseen. Where no resistance is offered the invasion will assume the character of a peaceful occupation. . . . Operations against the Dutch Navy will be undertaken only if the latter displays a hostile attitude. . . . Neither in Holland nor in Belgium-Luxembourg are centres of population, and in particular large open cities and industrial installations, to be attacked without compelling military necessity."

But the Dutch were to put up more than a mere show of resistance and, tragically, the "compelling military necessity" was to arise.

Directive No. 9, of November 29, 1939, dealt exclusively with the final objective of Operation Yellow—Great Britain.

"In our fight against the Western Powers, England has shown herself to be the animator of the fighting spirit of the enemy and the leading enemy power. The defeat of England is essential to final victory. The most effective means of ensuring this is to cripple the English economy by attacking it at decisive points. Early preparations must therefore be made . . . to deal an annihilating blow to the English economy. . . . Should the Army succeed in defeating the Anglo-French Armies in the field and seizing and holding a sector of the coast of the Continent opposite England, the task of the Navy and Air Force to carry the war to English industry becomes paramount."

On January 10, 1940, a German aircraft carrying detailed plans of Operation Yellow force-landed in Belgium, the pilot apparently having lost his way in fog. The major carrying the documents managed to burn most of them, but not all, before capture by Belgian soldiers. It was almost too good to be true. In any event, it was yet another cry of "Wolf! Wolf!" and served also to focus attention on Holland and Belgium, when later variants of the plan shifted the emphasis of the attack southward to the Ardennes, while the armies advancing into Belgium were to "divert to themselves the strongest possible Anglo-French forces." In short, the Allies' mobile force was to be drawn northward, away from the Maginot Line, while the main attack cut in behind them. Nevertheless, both Belgium and Holland were to be taken, but it would have to be done quickly, before the French and the British could come effectively to their aid.

All very well to direct this and that to be done, but how was it all to be actually achieved? The events of the First World War, still no less bitterly remembered in Germany than in France and Britain, had shown the superiority of the defence over the attack, even when the defenders had only mere trenches to protect them. Now, most of the French border was covered by the elaborate concrete forts of the Maginot Line, from which a small number of troops should be able to hold off much greater numbers of attackers, thus freeing many Allied formations for an unopposed advance into Belgium and Holland, where they would be welcomed in the event of invasion.

And in Holland itself the traditional water defences, plus the large areas of marsh, would impose a serious obstacle even to tanks and at the very least delay an attacker sufficiently for the Netherlands forces to retire from one waterline to another until they were safe behind the inner and very formidable lake and river obstacles surrounding the heart of the country, which they called "Fortress Holland."

The demolition of some half-dozen key bridges would be the modern equivalent of pulling up the drawbridge of a mediaeval castle. The castle might fall, but only after prolonged investment and assault, and long before that the Allied forces would have come to their relief, by both land and sea. This was indeed the Dutch plan, and in ordinary circumstances it would have been a good one.

Two facts were to destroy it. The first was that the Dutch defences were designed to cope in the manner of 1918 with an attack on the lines of 1918. That is to say, a heavy attack. A ponderous, slow-moving assault of masses of men covered by the fire of masses of guns, giving ample time for countermeasures. Even to small details, the Dutch defences were precisely 1918—the forts were small pillboxes armed mostly with heavy machine-guns, deadly to unprotected infantry, and these were extended by wooden-revetted trenches with fire-steps that would not have been out of place in *All Quiet on the Western Front.*

The second ominous fact was Hitler himself. Generalleutnant Kurt Student, commander of the German airborne forces, told the British military critic Captain B. H. Liddell Hart that all the basic ideas were Hitler's and that he, Student, merely worked them out in detail and then led the key assault. Even discounting something for modesty, this must have been true, for the plan bears an unmistakable political imprint at many points, and Hitler was probably the most consummate politician of his age. Here the word is used in its widest sense to mean a man accustomed to calculating and working on both the thought processes and the emotional reactions of people; the people of his own nation, and the people of other nations also.

Operation Yellow was not a traditional military stroke; and is best understood by studying Hitler's technique during that series of bloodless successes, from the reoccupation of the Rhineland to the invasion of Czechoslovakia, where everything turned on bluffing and bewildering an irresolute or unready opponent and calculating the extent of his reactions precisely.

The Dutch were expecting a heavy attack, whereas what was coming was an exceedingly light attack, which itself lent surprise, carried out with lightning speed and on unexpected lines, including that "Trojan Horse" element that Hitler had already used in both Poland and Norway. This was to be popularly called the "Fifth Column," implying a mass of local sympathisers and traitors, a panic belief that was to help Hitler considerably.

In fact, the greater part of the "Trojan Horse" element consisted of German soldiers, in or out of uniform, infiltrated into the enemy's fortress in an unusual way. In both Poland and Norway it had been largely a "Trojan Seahorse," consisting of ordinary soldiers concealed in merchant ships lying in harbours. A variant of this plan was intended for the Dutch waterways. Local helpers were not scorned, but there were fewer of them and they played a smaller active part than is generally believed.

The effect of surprise on individuals is bewilderment and indecision, purely temporary, lasting possibly for a few minutes only; and this can always be achieved, even if the troops to be attacked have been notified in advance of the attack, provided that it is the first attack they have ever sustained, the enemy the first enemy they have ever seen. Up to that moment, they do not really believe. This was what was to happen to the Dutch, as Hitler had calculated, an attack all the more effective because Holland had not been at war for over a century.

On May 2, 1940, Hitler ordered the commanders of his airborne forces to Berlin. They were Generalleutnant Kurt Student, commanding the 4,500 highly trained parachutists of 7 Flieger Division, and Generalleutnant Graf Sponeck, responsible for the 12,000 air-transportable infantry of 22 Airlanding Division.

Both divisions were not merely small in numbers, but lightly armed and equipped. Machine-guns and light mortars were the heaviest weapons that could be dropped with the parachutists, and although the infantry division had some air-transportable artillery, its ground transport (which had to be loaded into the aircraft) consisted of bicycles and small trailers. Theoretically, an ordinary infantry division could wipe them out in a short time, because of its much greater mobility and fire power.

On May 6, that is, in four days' time, they were to be launched into the heart of Holland to play a major role in the swift defeat of that country, and this conference was to finalise the details of what seemed to some German Generals an insane gamble.

The theme of the plan was speed, surprise, and disruption. Key points in the enemy's defences were to be occupied, in the first hour of hostilities, not by his own troops but by German troops. And to add to the confusion such a swift and unexpected series of moves would cause, the Dutch government itself was to be the target of a secondary attack by soldiers dropping out of the sky, again in the first hour of the war.

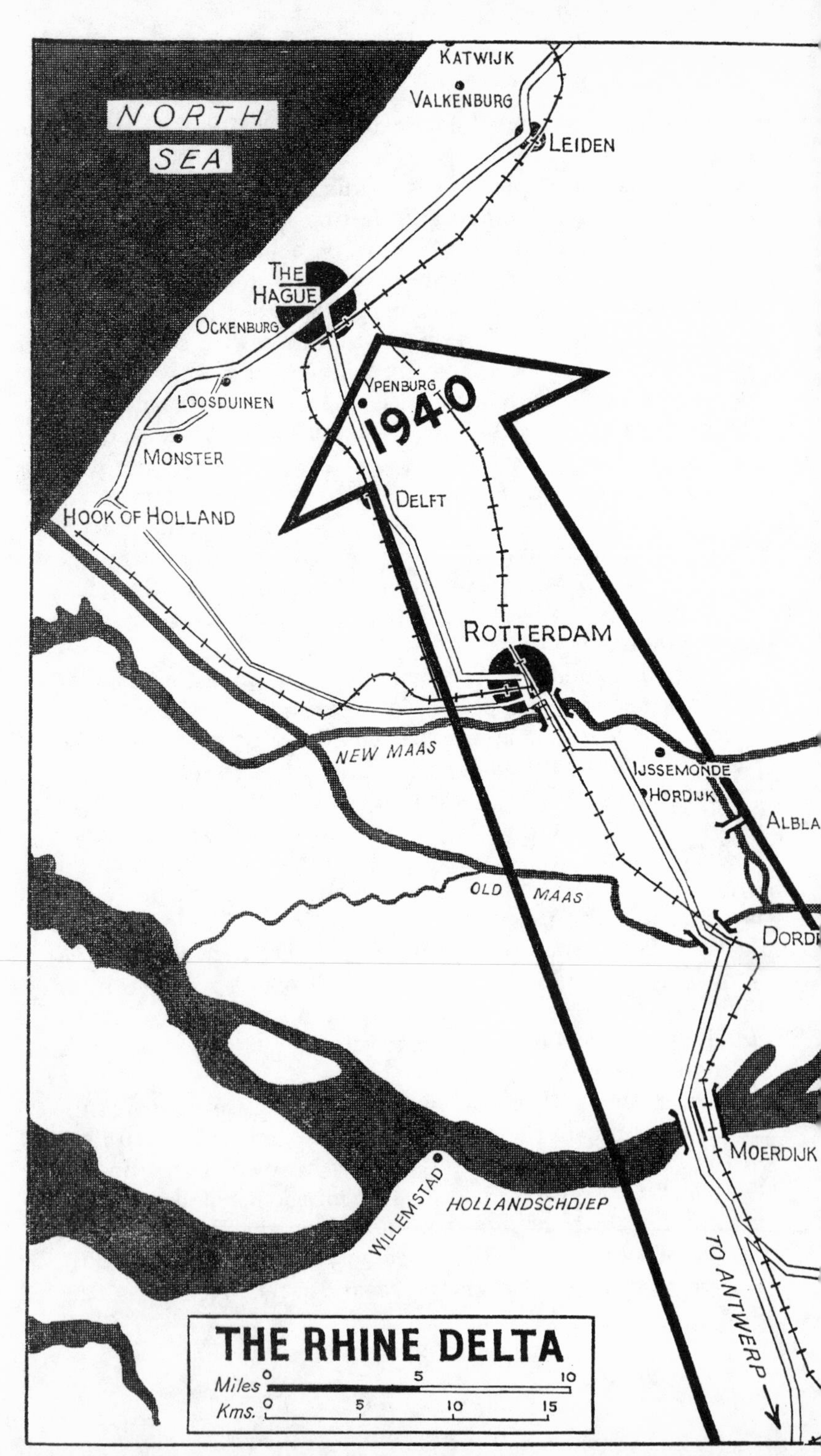
NORTH SEA
KATWIJK
VALKENBURG
LEIDEN
THE HAGUE
OCKENBURG
YPENBURG
1940
LOOSDUINEN
MONSTER
HOOK OF HOLLAND
DELFT
ROTTERDAM
NEW MAAS
IJSSEMONDE
HORDIJK
ALBLA
OLD MAAS
DORD
MOERDIJK
WILLEMSTAD
HOLLANDSCHDIEP
TO ANTWERP
THE RHINE DELTA
Miles 0 5 10
Kms. 0 5 10 15

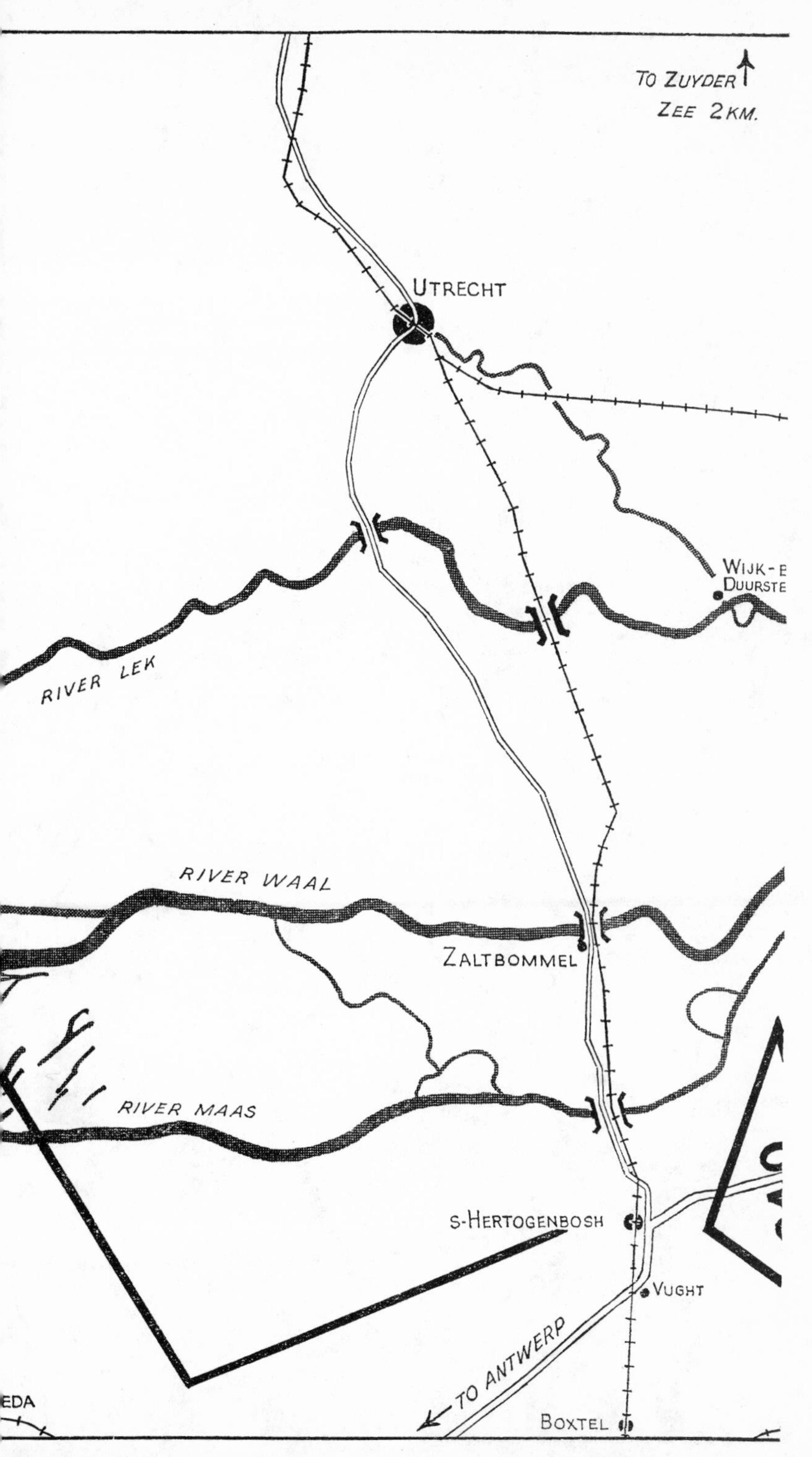
TO ZUYDER ZEE 2KM.
UTRECHT
WIJK-E
DUURSTE
RIVER LEK
RIVER WAAL
ZALTBOMMEL
RIVER MAAS
S-HERTOGENBOSH
VUGHT
TO ANTWERP
EDA
BOXTEL

TO ZUYDER ZEE 2 KM.

THE RHINE DELTA
CONTINUATION

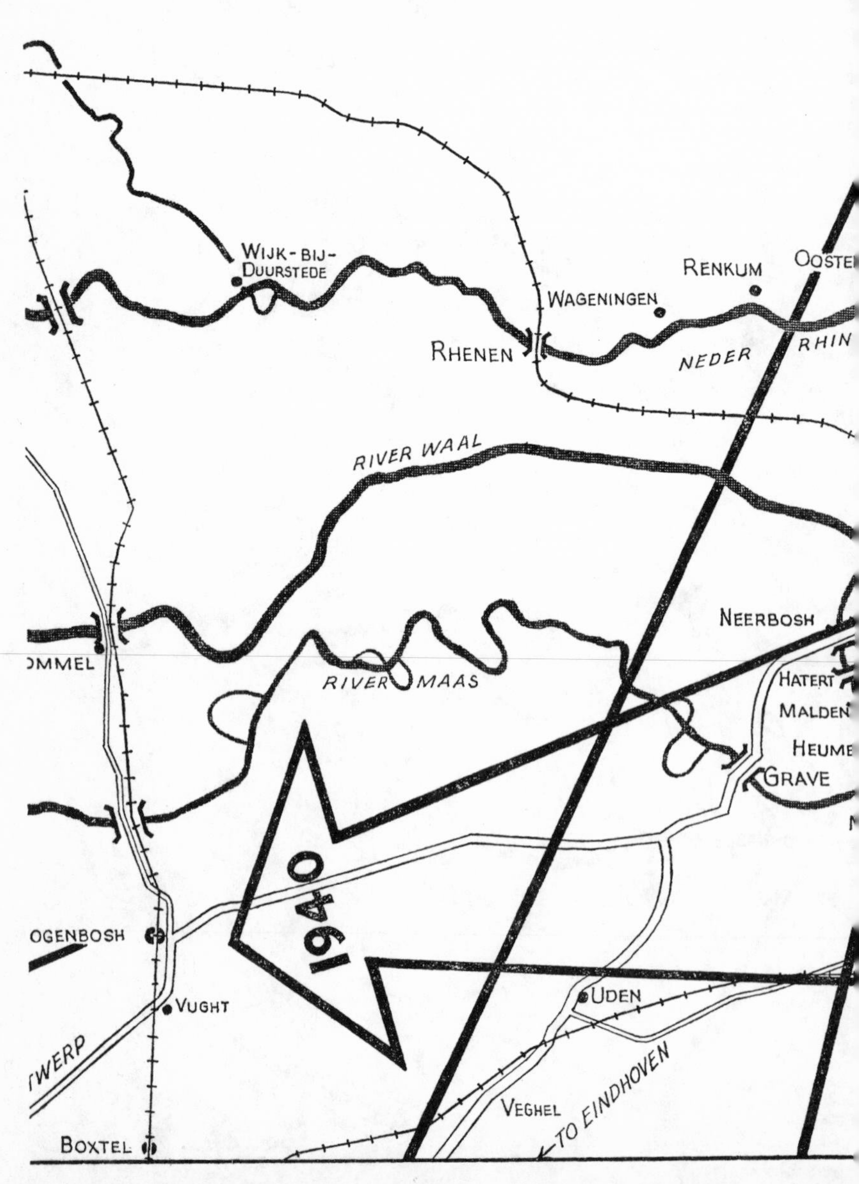

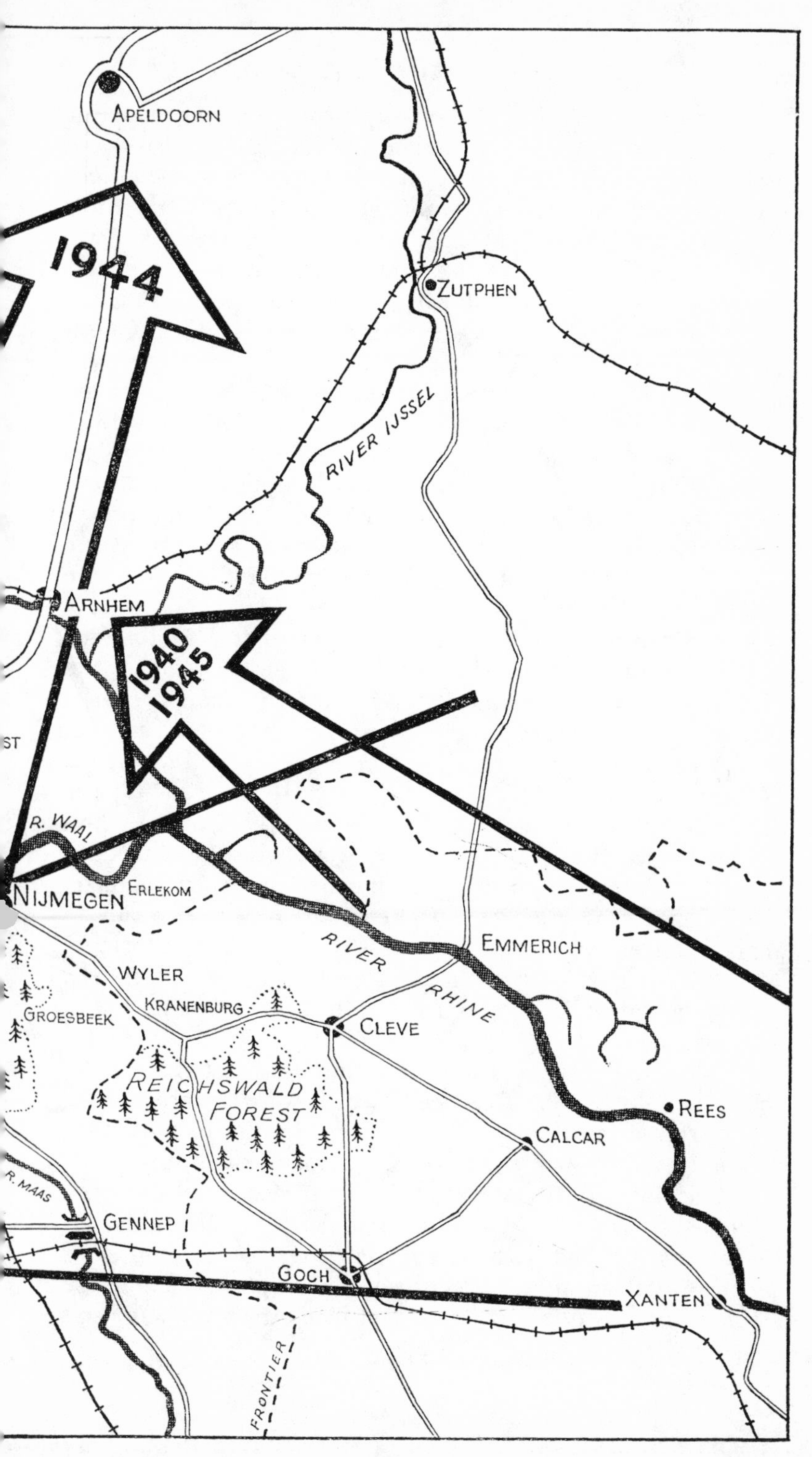

APELDOORN
1944
ZUTPHEN
RIVER IJSSEL
ARNHEM
1940
1945
R. WAAL
NIJMEGEN
ERLEKOM
RIVER
RHINE
EMMERICH
WYLER
KRANENBURG
GROESBEEK
CLEVE
REICHSWALD
FOREST
REES
CALCAR
R. MAAS
GENNEP
GOCH
XANTEN
FRONTIER

The political task, that of capturing the queen of the Netherlands and her government at The Hague, was given to Count Sponeck. He was to have two parachute battalions from Fallschirm Regiment 3 and with them capture the three airfields of Ypenburg, Ockenburg, and Valkenburg. After capture, two brigades of air-transported infantry—Regiments 47 and 65—were to be flown in and then advance on the Dutch capital, The Hague. Hitler stressed that Queen Wilhelmina was not to be harmed.

But the main military blow, the seizure of key bridges spanning the great waterways of the Rhine delta, was given to General Student, the paratroop expert. These bridges carried the main road and rail routes leading from Antwerp into the heart of Holland—the "fortress" that the German Army had to attack. In effect, they were drawbridges over a series of immense moats covering Fortress Holland from the south.

The first moat was the wide expanse of the Hollandsch Diep, a great waterway formed by the main stream of the Rhine (here known as the Waal) joining the main stream of the Meuse (here known as the Maas). The motor road and the railway crossed side by side at a little village called Moerdijk. After dive-bomber attack on the Dutch defences, one parachute battalion was to drop right on top of them, at both ends of the bridges simultaneously, and overwhelm the defenders.

This was what General Student called the "short method" —delivery of assault troops right on the objective, ready to fight at once, instead of a drop some distance away, a forming up, and then an approach to—by now—alerted defenders. Shock and surprise were to make up for the lack of weight in the assault.

The same principles were to be used against the bridges over the Old Maas at Dordrecht, which were a more formidable proposition because they were in a built-up area, with room only for a single company of parachutists to drop.

The third great waterway, the New Maas at Rotterdam, which also takes water from the Rhine via the Lek and Neder Rijn, was spanned over an artificial island by a complex of huge bridges in an almost entirely built-up area. Therefore Student proposed the bold stroke of using the waterway itself as a landing place—a dozen old seaplanes would fly in an infantry company and land on the Maas by the bridges—another example of the "short method." But because this force would be too weak to hold the bridges for long—in effect, they were in the centre of Rotterdam—Waalhaven airfield south of the river was to be captured simultaneously by parachutists who would be immediately reinforced by three battalions of air-transported troops—Regiment 16 from Sponeck's division. This regiment would reinforce not merely to the north, towards the Rotterdam bridges, but also to the south, towards the Dordrecht bridges.

With bridges across all three waterways in their hands, the Germans would in effect have laid an airborne "carpet" right across the Rhine delta, over which their tanks could roll forward into the heart of the country, to the seat of government itself.

The weak point of the German plan was that light airborne forces were to be dropped ahead of the armour for road distances varying from 60 to 100 miles, and would be required to hold their positions for many days against heavy odds. How many days? The swift relieving force was to consist of Generalleutnant Hubicki's 9 Panzer Division only. But before it could even get started, it had to cross a major river—the Maas—and possibly also the Maas–Waal Canal.

Bridges on both waterways were to be taken by guile; not by mass or weight, but by small groups of between ten and thirty men dressed as Dutch soldiers or civilians and already positioned inside the Dutch border beforehand. If any of these parties succeeded, they in turn would have to wait until relieved by regular units of the German Army advancing out of Germany; and these units also, although extremely fast-moving, had little fire power. In fact, the Germans had no overwhelming mass of troops anywhere; they were indeed somewhat inferior in numbers, overall, to their Dutch opponents, secure behind the water defences of the Rhine delta.

To orthodox tacticians, the plan seemed reckless to the point of madness. And maddest of all was the decision to divert 500 of the mere 4,500 paratroops available to an attack on the Albert Canal in Belgium. These 500 were to capture three bridges and the mighty modern fortress of Eben Emael, garrisoned by 1,200 men. To capture that concrete battleship, the Germans allotted 11 gliders made of wood and canvas, carrying 85 specially equipped assault engineers.

For the operation overall, there was no precedent. Although valuable lessons in air and tank warfare had been learned in Spain, and small bodies of paratroops had been used in the Norwegian campaign a month earlier (thus forfeiting the surprise their unheralded use might have achieved), the bold sweep of this conception by far exceeded even the imagination of tank enthusiasts. It was much more daring than the two previous plans, involving Belgian objectives, which had been worked out and then scrapped when a breach of security had revealed them to the potential enemy. Had Hitler known that some of the details of this third plan, and also the projected date of attack, May 6, had been communicated to the Dutch almost as soon as they had been finalised, the operation would have been cancelled also, as being probably too perilous.

Such was indeed the case, but Hitler did not know it. What the Germans were doing, consciously, was to reintroduce to the battlefields of Europe the Napoleonic concept of war, "that he who remains behind his entrenchments is beaten," but in the context of twentieth-century technology. The Russians, who first formed parachute forces, never did anything notable with them; the British, who invented and first used the tank, were strangely slow to grasp its potentialities. It was the Germans who were going to demonstrate, not only how to use air power, airborne forces, and armoured forces, but how to use them to their utmost effect—simultaneously, together, and where possible, concentrated.

CHAPTER THREE

"A—DAY" AT WAALHAVEN

Battles for the Bridges and Build-up of the Waalhaven "Airhead": May 10

What woke most people was the roar of aircraft, a steady but uneven droning that went on and on. Few people who heard it will ever forget the sound of those unsynchronised German aero engines, rising and falling like a menacing growl in the night. But on the night of May 9–10, 1940, the German side of the German border was still open. It was to be kept open until the last minute, in order to help achieve surprise. Only now was 9 Panzer Division crossing the Rhine at Wesel and coming into its forming-up area under cover of the Reichswald Forest, where the German border lances forward to Wyler among the hills south-east of Nijmegen.

On the Dutch side of the border there had been periodic alerts since May 7, the day after the German attack had been timed to start, originally. But nothing had happened, because bad flying weather had caused a temporary postponement. On May 8, the Dutch Army was ordered to be at immediate readiness for war. By 2200 hours on May 9—two hours before midnight—the Dutch had closed their frontiers, stopped telephone communications, closed the barriers on railway bridges, prepared road-blocks, and were ready to blow all bridges at a moment's notice. Units manning forward defences were ordered to "stand to" at 0300 hours on May 10. That is, one hour before the Germans were due to attack.

Dawn was at about 0400 hours, Dutch time, but this was not the only reason for the "stand to." Hitler had held his final conference with the airborne planners on May 2. On May 3 the Dutch military attaché in Berlin, Colonel Sas, learned that the invasion of Holland was imminent. His informant was a German intelligence officer—Oberst Hans Oster, head of Department Z of the Abwehr, controlled by the enigmatic Admiral Wilhelm Canaris. Both were later to pay with their lives for their opposition to Hitler's plans. The information received by the Dutch government from their military attaché in Berlin was reinforced by a similar message passed on to them from the Vatican in Rome. But nothing happened.

These warnings were from the German opposition led by General Ludwig Beck, who had stated: "If any offensive takes place without the Allies having received previous warning, we can hardly expect them to continue to make a distinction between the Hitler regime and the decent Germany."

The final, authentic warning came late in the evening of May 9. What the Anglo-Saxons call "D-Day," the Germans call "A-Day" (*Angriffstag*)—merely a method by which planning can take place without the exact date of an operation being known, the days being counted as "A plus" or "A minus" the key, unknown date. At 1900 hours on May 9, Colonel Sas was told by Hans Oster that A-Day was May 10, that Hitler was reported to have gone to the front, and that the chance of another cancellation was small. In any event, no cancellation could be made after 2300 hours that night—A-Day minus one—and that, even so, the decision would have to be taken earlier, in Berlin, at 2130 hours, to allow time for the message to reach the forward commanders.

When Oster passed his last message to the Dutch officer, he had obtained his facts by going personally into the High Command building. The information was authentic beyond doubt, and it was: "The orders have not been countermanded and that swine [Hitler] has really gone to the front. I hope we shall see each other again after the war."

The code-word *Danzig* had already been flashed to all units. 9 Panzer Division began to move forward into the Rhineland to take up springboard positions. On the Westphalian airfields of Delmenhorst, Fassberg, and Gutersloh the ground crews worked at high pressure to adjust for light-calibre bombs the racks of the Heinkels of Kampfgeschwader 4, which was to strike at the airfields of Rotterdam and The Hague.

"A stark black night camouflaged our preparations [wrote Oberleutnant Werner Baumbach]. The ground crews worked feverishly while the aircrews snatched a few hours of extra sleep. Then we assemble in the briefing room a few minutes before take-off. Targets are given out, the general situation explained. It is all so routine by now, that few words are necessary. Then we are driven out onto the field. The air is vibrating with the sound of engines being revved up and then idled. The flarepath is switched on briefly, eating a tunnel of light into the blackness of the night. Then the Gruppe Commander's heavily-loaded plane is rolling down the runway. One by one, we follow, making blind take-offs into the black night and assembling in loose formation, guided by the exhaust flames from the aircraft ahead. We are all climbing slowly, and it is getting lighter outside, although the earth below is still dark. Formation after formation emerges from the mist which hides the moors of the Ems Estuary."

The mass of planes, more than seventy bombers, droned slowly out over the North Sea before turning to port to fly parallel with the coast of Holland until they were opposite their targets. Then the formations slowly wheeled towards the Hague and Rotterdam, approaching now from the direction of England in the hope of achieving surprise. It was in vain. "Air raid alarm red! The sirens howled in city and harbour," wrote a Dutch officer stationed at Waalhaven, the airport of Rotterdam. "Through the misty dawn came the deep droning of many aircraft."

"We all munch biscuits and almost forget that there is a war on [wrote Baumbach]. Then we are called back to reality by the sight of puffs of smoke from heavy flak bursting all around us. The target is down there, but we cannot see it yet because of the mist. My gunner yells: 'Below—left—enemy fighter with twin fuselage!' It's a Dutch Koolhoven. I turn away and lead my formation down into the mist. We are flying blind, all eyes straining for a first glimpse of the target. Then we come through into the clear, the leading squadrons turning away already for the attack. In front and to one side, is the target aerodrome. Above it is what looks like a carpet suspended in mid-air—the smoke puffs of quick-firing anti-aircraft guns which we know so well from the British ships at Narvik. Our radio-operator yells: 'Fighters!' But it's a false alarm—they are ours, Messerschmitt 109s and 110s. In the same instant, my gunner and I spot our own particular target —a flak battery sited in a big farm on top of a little hill. We must destroy it, or our parachutists will be destroyed by it. I can see bombs exploding on the southern perimeter of the aerodrome as I make up my mind to come in low from the north, where the mist is still pretty thick. I want to surprise them. I put the nose down and the target seems to race towards me, the farm growing larger and larger in my bomb-sight, and dead centre. I press the button, and as the bombs fall away my gunner opens up to cover our getaway. We score a direct hit, and the walls of the farm building come down like playing cards."

As the bombers, somewhat scattered, began to stream back from the attack, individual Dutch aircraft made gallant but ineffectual sorties in machines as unsuitable as Lockheed Hudsons, which were easily picked off even by the twin-engined Messerschmitt 110s. Against the stream of returning aircraft, and passing them under the protection of the fighters, came the first waves of Junkers 52 transports carrying the parachutists, their sidedoors open and the men queuing up to jump at dawn into the boiling inferno of the bombed airfields.

The whole operation was under control of the Luftwaffe, to whom the parachutists also belonged, and the air organisation involved was considerable because of the many targets and the differing speeds and flight endurance of the various aircraft types involved. The streams of transport aircraft—430 triple-engined Junkers 52s—were very slow, taking nearly an hour to cross Holland; and these machines had to be marshalled in the correct tactical formations, according to their loads, so that military units would land more or less as units and not as groups of scattered soldiers. Unlike the bomber formations, the transports flew in one great wave direct from Westphalia, just to the north of Arnhem and the Neder Rijn, dividing into two separate streams only when nearing Rotterdam and The Hague. For the men in the machines, it was a tremendous spectacle.

Hauptmann Karl-Lothar Schultz commanded III Battalion of Fallschirmjäger Regiment 1, the unit that was to take Waalhaven airfield as a springboard for the assault on the Rotterdam bridges. In a narrative written soon afterwards, he described that dawn flight past Arnhem to Rotterdam.

"We're roaring along, still over German territory. Never before has any of us seen such a sight. Wherever one looks, around or above, there are transport planes carrying our parachutists; behind us the sun is climbing up the horizon, throwing a warm glow over the men behind me in the plane. Curious, they are peering out of the windows, their steel helmets buckled on firmly, ready for the jump. According to my map, we are almost at the border. There are no landmarks to make it obvious, but something down there makes it clear that we have crossed the Dutch frontier. Flashes everywhere on the ground. My men look puzzled, then one of them shouts: 'Dutch flak!' But the little bursting puffs of smoke, when they appear, are too far away to hurt us, and the boys are laughing. Last night, some of them told me they couldn't sleep, they were so happy at the thought of action. And now there's yet another sign that tells us we are over enemy territory. Ahead of us, parallel to our course, is a great waterway. Two bridges span it, a railway bridge and a road bridge. We have hardly glimpsed these bridges, when both disappear in a gigantic flash. Grey-black clouds of smoke come rolling up. The bridges are down, the Dutch have blown them. This display is repeated at nearly every bridge we pass. Down there, they seem at last to be aware that the war has begun. And what's that below, on our left? Once again, the lads are kneeling by the windows, one behind the other, bending forward to get a good view, and wondering if it is friend or foe. But they are ours—Heinkel 111s. Our hearts beat faster at the sight of them. We had thought the sky was full of planes, when we could see only our own transports, but now it is many times more crowded. Sparkling brightly in the sun, the Heinkels went past us as though drawn forward by rubber bands. And shortly after that, when the Messerschmitt fighters and destroyers literally zoom past us, I recall a remark made by one of the lads: 'If Hermann puts everything up, the birds will have to walk, there won't be room for them in the air!' "

Great clouds of oily black smoke were rising from the hangars at Waalhaven. Although the leader's machine had been shot down, the 28 Heinkels of II Gruppe of KG4 had bombed well and accurately. Forewarned, the Dutch had hidden an infantry battalion in the hangars in order to surprise the Germans when they landed; but now those reserves had been decimated, with many men trapped in the inferno. One Junkers 52, roaring low over the blazing shambles of the hangars, and possibly hit by flak, began to drop its "stick" of parachutists at exactly the wrong moment. The silken parachutes shrivelled instantly in the heat and the men hurtled helpless into the flaming wreckage like so many human bombs.

"Despite the noise of the engines [wrote Hauptmann Schultz], we can now clearly hear the explosions of shells beginning to burst uncomfortably close. We also hear little cracks and clacks inside our machine, and the lads look at each other, more than a little surprised. They aren't laughing any more. This seems to be in earnest. The plane is being turned into a sieve and the order to jump will be a relief to this tension. At last! We all dive out of the machine in no time."

A Dutch officer reported:

"As if by magic white dots suddenly appeared over the airfield like puffs of cottonwool. First there were twenty, then fifty, then over a hundred of them! And still they came popping out of the planes and began their slow, oscillating descent. . . . A hoarse command, then every machine-gun opened up . . . at the parachutes, at the planes. With so many targets, the men just did not know where to aim. . . ."

Wrote Schultz:

"While floating down, I establish my position and note the heavy fire coming from all round the perimeter of the airfield. That's where the defences are, and it looks as if they're strong. Even so, there are comic interludes. Some of my men land slap bang on the backs of cows which up to that moment had been peacefully grazing. . . ."

The drop had been a good one, most of the parachutists landing, as planned, around the outside perimeter of the airfield, and then pressing inwards with machine-pistols and grenades against the Dutch pillboxes and trenches. That forced the Dutch defenders—mostly from the Queen's Grenadiers—to take up positions firing outwards from the airfield perimeter. When they were thus pinned down by the parachutists, an unexpected event occurred. The next squadron of transport planes, instead of dropping more parachutists outside the airfield, roared in low over the airfield boundary—and landed. They were not carrying paratroops at all, but two platoons of airlanding infantry from Regiment 16. The great transports, touching down in the middle of the defences, were an easy target for the flak—one of them was streaming smoke and flame from two engines simultaneously—but land they did, all of them; and out of them poured the fieldgrey infantry to take the defending Queen's Grenadiers in the rear.

"Within thirty minutes of the start, the aerodrome is firmly in our hands" [wrote Hauptmann Schultz]. "Apart from a battery of four 7·5 cm Skoda guns, sited outside the perimeter and still spitting fire, the entire defence had been wiped out or taken prisoner. The Dutch had fought very bravely, harder in fact than one would expect from a people which had not waged war for over a hundred years. But the effect on the morale of the enemy had been so strong that his will to resist had been half-broken at the outset. First, the sky above him blossomed full of parachutes, then immediately afterwards he was attacked on the ground. I now learned that the airfields had been defended by an infantry battalion, four light-flak positions of four M.Gs. each, the Skoda battery, and last, but not least, four armoured cars."

The Skoda battery was soon dealt with. One of the landed transports that was still in flying condition took off again and made low-flying passes over the battery, forcing the gunners to take cover, while the nearest group of parachutists went in, firing as they ran. To the chattering of machine-pistols and the whiplike crack of exploding grenades, the battery fell. The way was clear for the bulk of Regiment 16—three battalions of airlanding infantry—to come in to the newly created Waalhaven "airhead." But where were they? There was no sign of them.

Then Hauptmann Schultz realised that his battalion's assault had gone faster than expected; that it was he who was early, not the reinforcements who were late. One of his men came running up to report: "Herr Hauptmann, the command post is ready, and the table laid!'

Schultz followed him into a building and then burst out laughing. An elaborate breakfast was ready on the table and the radio was on—the mayor of Amsterdam giving a propaganda speech. "Boys, where did you magic all this from?' asked Schultz.

"We didn't, Herr Hauptmann, the Dutch had it all ready for us."

But Schultz never finished his breakfast. He was interrupted by the drone of many motors, the transports carrying III Battalion. A continuous stream of aircraft came in to land, spilled out their men, guns, munitions, trollies, and motor cycles, and then took off again. It was like an airborne conveyor belt in operation.

In one of the leading aircraft was the battalion commander, Oberstleutnant Dietrich von Choltitz, who found that although the airfield was in German hands, the surviving Dutch infantry was trying to withdraw in an orderly manner under cover of mortar and long-range artillery fire. "The sound of conflict was deafening," he wrote later. "The howl of aero-engines and ammunition exploding in the hangars was joined by the crash of mortar fire and the rattle of machine-guns plugging the planes. Speed was the thing!"

Indeed it was. The capture of the airfield was only a preliminary to the crux of the operation—the capture of the bridges. It was to serve as a springboard, first for his battalion to drive north for Rotterdam, second for the two other battalions of the regiment to drive south for Dordrecht. III Battalion landed first, because their task was infinitely harder. Instead of open country, they had to advance for miles through a built-up area to the centre of Rotterdam, through streets where a handful of men with rifles and machine-guns could easily hold up superior numbers of advancing infantry. In the meantime, the bridges might have been blown.

To reduce this risk, the Germans gambled two tiny forces in an extremely bold manner. At the same time as the attack on Waalhaven began, 50 paratroops led by Oberleutnant Horst Kerfin dropped on a stadium in South Rotterdam, close to the southern end of the bridges, while 12 Heinkel 59 seaplanes carrying 120 infantrymen and engineers under Oberleutnant Schrader landed on the river on both sides of the great Willems bridge, before taxiing clumsily to the north bank. Then the soldiers had to inflate their rubber dinghies, board them, paddle to the wall, and climb up onto the river bank.

During this time, they were hopelessly vulnerable. But the very boldness of their arrival helped. "Workmen crossing the big bridge on their way to work had mistakenly decided that the seaplanes were English, and so they helped the soldiers to climb up the river bank," recorded the regimental historian, Oberstleutnant Diedrich Bruns.

Shortly afterwards, the 50 paratroops joined them, in an equally unorthodox manner—they simply commandeered some of the city's trams and, bells ringing madly, drove through the streets and across the complex of bridges, which were linked in mid-river by an artificial island, to the north bank. And here they were to remain for five days and four nights, completely cut off from the south bank, for although von Choltitz's battalion fought its way through the streets to the river, by then the bridges were being so swept by Dutch fire as to be impassable. On the other hand, the Dutch could not retake them, though they tried bitterly.

There was nothing slow about the Dutch reaction. Within hours, they had a fleet of patrol boats and small warships up the river, engaging the German parachutists and infantry on both banks, and had brought Waalhaven under fire from long-range guns sited in the suburbs and directed by observers watching from tall buildings or even from the tops of the cranes at the docks. So hard were the Germans pressed, and so precarious was their hold on the north bank of the Maas, that they considered abandoning their bridgehead. However, von

Choltitz refused to depart from his orders and continued to hold on stubbornly to what had been gained.

General Student had now arrived at Waalhaven and set up his command post there. As the heavy shells came howling in, sending up clouds of smoke and clods of flying earth, his only comment was: "Watch it, the English will soon be here as well."

At about noon, they came. Only six twin-engined fighter-Blenheims to machine-gun the airfield; no bombers, because the British War Cabinet was afraid that in the confusion friendly civilians might be killed by accident. Five out of the six were shot down, three crashing in sight of the airfield, the pilots obviously dead or badly wounded at the controls. From the first, on fire and out of control, a single airman bailed out, his parachute already on fire. Another, one engine blazing, flew right across Waalhaven before crashing into the Rotterdam motor road with a tremendous detonation.

On the river front, Dutch Marines trying to cross the Maas in boats to attack the German airhead were being beaten back by the murderous fire of heavy machine-guns, the Dutch torpedo-boat TM–51 was limping out of action, and the Dutch destroyer *Van Galen* was being dive-bombed by Stukas as she raced up-river towards Waalhaven. Unable to manœuvre in the narrow waterway, she was holed by near-misses and had to be grounded in the shallows to prevent her from sinking.

For many people in Holland May 10, 1940, was to be the end of an era, although they did not realise it that morning. Mr. W. Brugmans, who now lives in Garwood, New Jersey, was then a civil servant with his home near the Marine barracks in Rotterdam. He was awakened by the distant bombing on Waalhaven. He and his wife got out of bed and went to the window, from which they could clearly see the low-flying German aircraft being driven higher by the fire of Dutch anti-aircraft guns. He could not see what was happening at the bridges, but he knew intimately the area at the north end because it had been his favourite playground as a boy. Now it was a battlefield.

"At the north end of the Willemsbrug was a modern bank building, with layers of stone, like a fort," [he recollected].

"It gave the best possible view over the Willemsbrug and the elevated highway, and was guarded only by a watchman at night, so a group of storm troopers could easily get in. Once in, nobody could get them out again without blowing up the building. There was a delay because the Dutch Marines had to be gathered—some of them did not sleep in barracks, but at their homes in the town—and then they tried to retake the bank, the Maasbrug, and the White House, another high building nearby which the Germans had also occupied."

Mr. Brugmans reported for duty at the town hall, where there was good news. He learned that Waalhaven had previously been gridded for the heavy artillery that was hidden among the trees at Kralingen. With this grid-system, the artillery observers, who had a good view of the airfield from their lofty perches on cranes and buildings, could bring down fire on any part of it at will. Obviously, the Dutch authorities knew a good deal about the German attack and its objectives. The civilian population, naturally enough, did not.

This was the first, and probably the last, war in which radio played an important part. All over Holland people sat glued to their sets, tuning frantically from one station to another—from Hilversum to the London B.B.C. and back again—in order to find out what was happening.

Even the very young remembered that day for the rest of their lives. Maurits van Dongeren, who was only seven and a half years old at the time and was then living with his parents and his little sister Dieukwe in Rotterdam, has never forgotten it. "I remember it as if it was yesterday, because it was the day on which the break-up of our family life began," he explained to me at his present home in Poole, Dorset. "I stayed at home that morning and didn't go to school, but as it was nice weather I went out early and saw a lot of small planes circling in the air. Then I went back inside to listen to the radio. They were broadcasting a warning: "People of Rotterdam—stay in your houses."

Anxious waiting was not confined to the Dutch that day. There were not enough transport aircraft to bring in all the troops in one "lift," a feature that was to mark—and mar—most airborne operations of the Second World War. Diedrich

Bruns, who was then a company commander in I Battalion of Infantry Regiment 16, the unit responsible for building up and expanding the Waalhaven airhead as a base for capturing and controlling all main bridges across the waterways, spent all morning queuing at a German airfield with his motor bike, which he intended to smuggle aboard an aircraft.

Prior planning could not predict exactly how many gaps there would be in the formations of transport planes when they returned. There were many gaps, and as the Junkers 52s were refuelled, their crews talked of murderous flak. Losses had been so heavy that 5,000 men of the airlanding division were left stranded on German airfields and never took part in the battle at all. But Bruns managed to embark his company—and his motor cycle—on the afternoon of May 10.

They arrived over Waalhaven to find the airfield under intense and accurate fire from Dutch artillery. Several of the Junkers 52s were hit and began to blaze as soon as they touched down. Bruns did not wait even for the aircraft to stop rolling before he was disembarking his men. They jumped out while it was still bumping over the grass and ran for the perimeter, while shells howled down and fountains of smoke and dirt erupted around them. The motor cycle was last to leave, manhandled out by Bruns and his orderly. Then he rode off to find headquarters and get his orders.

The airhead was at the northern side of what was in effect an elongated island created by the New Maas flowing through Rotterdam in the north and the Old Maas flowing past Dordrecht to the south, and was secure only if main bridges and ferry sites could be held. To the south-east, both road and rail bridges at Dordrecht had been taken by a single company of parachutists led by Oberleutnant Freiherr von Brandis. But the Dutch had reacted vigorously, von Brandis had been killed, and the railway bridge recaptured.

I and II Battalions were directed towards Dordrecht to reinforce the precarious hold of the paratroops. Bruns piled his company into two Dutch trucks and led off early, driving down the motor road through Hordijk and Alblasserdam to one of the crossing sites at the Old Maas, where they took the 650 metre-long swing-bridge, but found the Dutch in possession of the ferry, having driven back the German platoon holding it. In failing light, and with the aid of two grenade-throwers and two machine-pistols, the Germans now retook it from about 100 Dutchmen equipped with heavy machine-guns as well as light machine-guns.

During the night the Dutch made four attacks against the German positions in Dordrecht, supported by suspiciously well-aimed artillery fire. It was being directed by a Dutch officer who was sitting at an undiscovered telephone in the middle of the German-held area. The most embarrassing discovery, however, was at Alblasserdam, where the Germans were astonished to find the river spanned by a major bridge that, although indisputably there, was not marked on their maps or listed among their objectives! They occupied it, all the same.

There was no news of the fate of the paratroops dropped near The Hague, north-west of Rotterdam and the rivers, nor of the airlanding infantry who were to support them. Nor was there any physical contact with Group South, consisting of Hauptmann Fritz Prager's reinforced II Fallschirmjäger Battalion, which had dropped at both ends of both bridges at Moerdijk, and swiftly captured them. These bridges carried the main road and rail communications over viaducts respectively 1,300 yards and 1,400 yards long. They were still intact. But what tanks would be the first to come roaring up the Antwerp road from Breda—German or French? Armoured divisions from the German and the French armies were both racing for the bridges over the Hollandsch Diep at Moerdijk, and with the same geographical objective—the German airhead at Waalhaven that was nourishing the entire bridge battle inside "Fortress Holland."

And over battered Waalhaven, parachute flares were drifting slowly down the night sky. In daylight, during the space of one day, the airfield had been attacked by German bombers, British fighters, British light bombers, and Dutch bombers. Now it was the turn of the British heavy night bombers. Thirty-six Wellingtons wandered overhead in a typical 1940-style individual-stream attack, one bomber every five minutes or so.

"They dropped their bombs any old where, and then from barely 50 metres up they fired their machine-guns at anything," [commented Hauptmann Karl-Lothar Schultz]. "The light flak soon drove them higher, but six of my men were wounded and a building full of ammunition received a direct hit. The whole lot blew up, together with stacks of signal flares, making a terrific firework display. Meanwhile, I was told to report to the Regimental Commander for orders. Here resided our Colonel,* with the sovereign calm of an old infantryman. In reply to each report that came in, that the Dutch were attacking here, there, and everywhere, he simply said: 'Rubbish. German paratroops are never attacked anywhere. It is simply a question of the Dutch making an appearance from time to time.' "

* Von Choltitz.

CHAPTER FOUR

THE "TROJAN HORSE" STRIKES AT DAWN

Arnhem, Nijmegen, and the Maas–Wall Canal: May 10

A little group of oddly assorted people were arguing and checking documents on the eastern side of the complicated lock-bridge at Heumen on the Maas–Waal Canal. It was only a small bridge over a small canal connecting the great waterways of the Meuse and the Rhine, and the landscape was rural and peaceful despite the pillboxes and casemates built along its western bank at frequent intervals. Nevertheless, it was the Dutch second line of defence, to which the units guarding the frontier with Germany five miles to the east would retire in due order in the event of attack. Consequently, there were Dutch sentries on the eastern end of the bridge, although their headquarters were on the western bank. Their unit, I Battalion of the 26th Regiment of Infantry, stationed along the southern half of the canal, had done very little during the winter to improve the defences.

It was about dawn when these sentries saw a small, disorderly crowd of some thirty men in civilian clothes, guarded by four others in the uniforms of Dutch field gendarmes, shambling down the road to the bridge from the east, the direction of the frontier. While three of the men dressed as military police kept the civilians corralled like prisoners, the fourth gendarme approached the sentry and, in native Dutch, explained that the men in civilian clothes were deserters from the German Army who had escaped across the border, and that his job was to hand them over to the nearest Dutch Army headquarters.

The sentry checked the man's documents, which seemed all right, and gave the order for the lock-bridge to be lowered for their crossing. A sergeant and two corporals of the bridge guard came out to assist the field gendarmes in controlling the mob of Germans in civilian clothes, and all this early morning stir and shouting by the bridge also began to draw a civilian audience. People living in nearby houses appeared at their front doors and then, curious, wandered over to see what it was all about.

The sergeant of the guard made a helpful suggestion that it might save time if he went with the field gendarmes and their prisoners to show them the way. The senior gendarme agreed—the other three men in military police uniform never spoke—and so they all moved off towards the west bank, followed by the more curious of the local inhabitants.

They had taken no more than a few steps when the "field gendarmes" and their "prisoners" suddenly acted in concert, like a well-drilled football team. The Dutch sentries were seized and overpowered in an instant. Then, spreading out and drawing machine-pistols and grenades from their clothing, the thirty men in civilian clothes stormed the three nearest casemates and the garrison office, making such skilful use of dead ground and covering fire that it was clear they were highly trained soldiers.

The Dutch sector commander, hearing shots in the distance, broke off the tour of inspection he was making and returned to his command post near the bridge. There he learned that the order to destroy the bridge had been received; so he sent off a cyclist, who quickly returned, having failed to deliver the message. The captain then mounted his own bicycle and pedalled down the road towards the bridge; just before he reached it, he was shot down.

In a matter of a few minutes, the bridge and its immediate defences had been captured, the senior Dutch officer killed, and two of the section leaders taken prisoner, thus making immediate counter-attack unlikely. It was a brilliant success, achieved by a German force numbering less than three dozen lightly-armed individuals.

At Malden, north of Heumen, there was another bridge, less important. Here, the German force consisted of eight men in civilian clothes and two more wearing some items of Dutch uniform. With machine-pistols and grenades they drove off the Dutch sentries, who were only armed with rifles, and occupied all the buildings before the Dutch had time to blow the structure. This bridge also was in German hands by dawn, but it did not long remain so.

The Dutch sector commander telephoned battalion headquarters for help, was refused it, and by mustering his clerks and cooks, found he had a further eight men, plus a light machine-gun. Using this to give covering fire, the Dutch rushed the building held by the Germans, and killed or captured them all, apart from one man in civilian clothes who sniped at them for some hours from cover in a field.

North of Malden was yet another bridge over the canal at Hatert. Just before dawn, a Dutch sentry noticed a number of men in civilian clothes loitering suspiciously by the bridge. Before he could check on them, one opened fire on him with a machine-gun, but missed. He was able to telephone the news to sector headquarters, who did not believe him; they did, however, shoot one of their own sentries as he tried to get away from the Germans by running across the bridge, and shortly afterwards fresh bursts of German machine-gun fire prompted them to fire the demolition charges. A cloud of black smoke rose up at the roar of the explosion, and after it had drifted away, the bridge was still there, damaged, but with the span unbroken.

With the Germans holding the far bank, it was impossible to lay fresh charges, and the captain of the Dutch garrison made for his casemate to organise a defence. The casemate, however, was well defended—by the Germans, who had got there first—and he was taken prisoner. Shortly after, the German follow-up force arrived, having driven hard across the border. This consisted of a small group of Waffen S.S. and a couple of tanks.

While the rest gave covering fire over the canal, four S.S. led by Obersturmführer Voght scrambled across the damaged structure and formed a small bridgehead on the west bank. The rest of the S.S. followed, stormed the two casemates by the bridge, then turned north along the canal bank, methodically rolling up the others and taking about 200 prisoners.

At Neerbosch, still further north towards the Waal, there were two bridges carrying the main road and rail links from Nijmegen to Antwerp. Here, the garrison commander acted on his own initiative. At 0417 he blew both bridges, some minutes before receiving the order to do so. He was only just in time, for almost immediately a German mobile force appeared on the far bank—an S.S. storm troop riding motor cycles and supported by two tanks. The Germans opened fire at once, and the Dutch replied, killing most of the motor-cyclists. One of the tanks blew up and the other began to burn. Into this smoke and confusion rolled a German armoured train; but this too was hit by Dutch fire and began to burn, before backing away towards Nijmegen.

But now it was around 0500 hours Dutch time, an hour after the bombing of The Hague, Waalhaven, Dordrecht, and Moerdijk had begun; an hour after the Germans had crossed the border into Holland; an hour after the initial assaults on the bridges of Maas–Waal Canal had been carried out. The tiny "Trojan Horse" units had been infiltrated across the frontier during the night, so that they were in position to strike at the bridges by 0355.

The result, reading from north to south, from the Waal to the Maas, was that the Germans had failed completely to secure the two important bridges at Neerbosch; that they had captured the bridge at Malden and lost it again; that they had captured the bridge at Hatert in a damaged but usable state; and that they had taken the locks and bridge at Huemen completely intact. But this was not enough.

The main water barrier south-west of Nijmegen was the great River Maas, where it looped west near the Waal to follow a parallel course to the sea; and the main highway to the west was carried over it by a great bridge at Grave, between Maas and Waal. This was the priority target, in theory, but the Germans had no paratroops to spare for its capture and the "Trojan Horse" units were thinly spread already. Everything depended on the speed with which the ground forces could exploit the successes on the Maas–Waal Canal.

The whole front southwards from Nijmegen down to Afferden, nearly 20 miles, was the responsibility of the German XXVI Corps, which attacked with only two divisions, the 254th in the north and the 256th to the south, with 9 Panzer Division behind them ready to advance over any bridges that were seized intact. The more bridges, the better, because an armoured advance goes faster when a number of routes are used than it does when everything has to go along one road only in one great traffic jam.

For their assault, 254 Division formed two special forces—the Gruppe Nijmegen and the Gruppe Grave. The former was to take the two great Waal bridges at Nijmegen, the latter to take the Maas–Waal Canal bridges as stepping stones to the main highway bridge over the 800-foot-wide Maas at Grave. Speed was essential, so that the Dutch would have no warning and fail to blow the bridge in time, but the Germans never even came near to achieving it. The Dutch blew it up by mistake at 0645, before any threat had actually developed.

If Gruppe Grave failed to get their Maas bridge, they were instead to turn south and assist in a crossing of the Maas at Mook, which was not screened by a forward canal line. But this, too, they failed to do, and 254 Division crossed without their aid; while farther south at Gennep a bridge was taken intact, and two German trains thundered over it, carrying guns and infantry to the rear of the Dutch positions.

Failure in the north and success in the south meant that 9 Panzer Division initially would have to advance along narrow, congested country roads, instead of breaking through onto the main east–west road route that runs from Nijmegen via Grave, 's Hertogenbosch. Tilburg, and Breda to the Antwerp–Rotterdam motorway. Ominously, none of the great bridges on that motorway—Moerdijk, Dordrecht, Rotterdam—were prepared for demolition. They were to be preserved for the use of the French Seventh Army, and if General Hubicki's 9 Panzer Division was too long delayed, the French General Henri Giraud might well ride into Rotterdam first.

What had gone wrong? For Nijmegen itself, General Franz Halder, chief of staff of the German Army General Staff, noted cryptically in his diary: "Trojan Horse did not get through, Nijmegen bridge destroyed." This scheme is believed to have involved planting Rhine barges with troops hidden below decks in the barge harbour at Nijmegen, and was probably frustrated by patrol boats or the mining of the Rhine by the Dutch at the last minute. But this was the only major failure on the Nijmegen front of what, following General Halder, I have called the "Trojan Horse" instead of the more spectacular but inaccurate term, "Fifth Column." Its actions were not mentioned in the German unit and formation war diaries at the time, presumably because the men wore civilian clothes or foreign uniforms, which rendered them liable to a summary death sentence.

In the main, however, they were German soldiers and not foreign sympathisers, although specially recruited for their task of seizing bridges over the Dutch waterways close to the frontier all along its length. Formed as Special Battalion No. 100, and recruited by the Abwehr, they numbered about 1,000 men. The majority were from Silesia in the east, but there was a useful minority of less than 200 men consisting of Germans who had lived in Holland or who had taken Dutch nationality, together with a few Dutchmen who were living in Germany.

During the winter they had been trained for their task in four secret camps located between the Rhine and the Dutch frontier. Their military training was thorough, but their disguises as Dutch military police, soldiers, or railwaymen were often very thin.

They left their camps during the night of May 9 in order to be in position at the bridges by dawn. If there had been any large and reliable body of pro-German sympathisers in Holland, this would not have been necessary. However, this type of attack combined with the use of parachutists had an unexpected bonus for the Germans, because it touched off a hectic "spy fever" among the Dutch that considerably hampered their military effort.

On the critical sector—the Maas–Waal Canal—these units had done their job well, initially capturing three of the bridges; but they had been let down by the follow-up formations. That day's verdict by XXVI Corps read: "The small success of the Gruppe Grave is disappointing. It can be traced to the unexpected strength of the Maas–Waal barrier. An impression that the leadership was sluggish and lacked foresight was confirmed by a personal visit from Ia of the Corps." This staff officer had found not only slack leadership, but one senior officer of the attacking force sound asleep on the afternoon of May 10.

A more basic reason, however, was the composition of the

Gruppe Grave. It had plenty of fire-power, developed from motor-cycle machine-gun companies, but these were extremely vulnerable even to small arms. The tanks, rationed out in packets of two at a time, did not really constitute a battering ram. A single machine-gun could separate them from their unprotected infantry riding along on motor cycles and bicycles. And their artillery was held up by the nature of the country south-east of Nijmegen, which was hilly, thickly wooded, and traversed only by small country roads or tracks.

The Germans had made good use of this terrain to seep forward across the frontier, unseen, in a stealthy infiltration, avoiding head-on attack on border posts and strongpoints. For the Dutch, it was as though the tide had come in behind them. At Groesbeek, which lay on the routes to Heumen and Malden, they fired a few shots, burnt their documents, and surrendered. At the border village of Wyler, the frontier guard post was first fired on from behind, and when the Dutch tried to get away, they found German tanks between them and the main Kleve–Kranenburg–Nijmegen road.

The task of the Gruppe Nijmegen was to advance along this road and also to the north of it, between Beek and the Rhine at Erlekom. The road ran direct to a traffic roundabout in Nijmegen just south of the river; from this, one road went north across the great Waal bridge to Arnhem, another led south-west to the bridges at Neerbosch and Grave. The defences were sited along the road from the frontier post at Beek, with the bulk of them north of the Waal, defending the route to Arnhem.

While German infantry pinched out the road-blocks, a mobile storm troop under Obersturmführer Weiss raced for the great road bridge over the Waal. Its single span, 244 metres long, was the largest of any bridge in Europe at that time. The storm troop was from the armoured reconnaissance battalion of the Waffen–S.S. Verfugungs Division, which did not operate as a division, but as corps troops for special missions such as this. Avoiding the main road, the handful of tanks and motor-cyclists slipped down country tracks over the 300-foot high hills near Berg en Dal and entered Nijmegen from the south.

At 0445 hours Dutch time, 50 minutes after crossing the

border, they had the bridge in front of them. But they were too late. The "Trojan Horse" unit that was to have attacked the bridge at dawn from Rhine barges moored in the nearby barge harbour had failed to arrive, and the Dutch had blown the great central span into the water at 0425, with a detonation that rocked the town.

A boy of fourteen, Phillip van Heerde, was thrown to the ground and cut by flying glass from broken windows. His home was on the Waalkade, the waterfront of Nijmegen between the road and rail bridges. Awakened by the noise of aeroplanes flying over the bridge and Dutch trucks roaring along the waterfront to get away from the advancing Germans, he had gone outside and walked up towards the road bridge just as it was destroyed. He picked himself up and, joined by his family, hurried along the quay and down the Grote Straat, which led towards the centre of Nijmegen.

They walked straight into the first of the storm troops, who were hurrying towards the Waalkade on foot, keeping close to the houses on either side of the road. They were shouting at all civilians, impatiently: "*Ins Hause, weg von der Strasse!*" ("Get off the streets!") When, almost at once, the Dutch infantry holding the north bank of the Waal opened fire on the leading Germans, the boy saw what they meant. "Our Dutch pillboxes held the whole day the Germans from Waalkade," he recalled, "but several civilians were hurt by Dutch fire. They tried to cross the Grote Straat and were shot down. The Germans were that Friday in our shop, a yacht chandlers and sailmakers; they were looking through our windows to the Dutch pillboxes near the bridge, but they could not pass the street!"

On the north bank of the Waal, the defences guarding the approaches to Arnhem were centred on the village of Lent. Two old forts served as barracks, being useless for modern warfare, and a few trenches had been dug during the winter, but the main fortifications overlooking the river consisted of three casemates, each equipped with an anti-tank gun and a heavy machine-gun. Casemate West covered the railway bridge. The road bridge was directly under the fire of Casemate Middle, which also held the demolition apparatus, and was flanked by Casemate East.

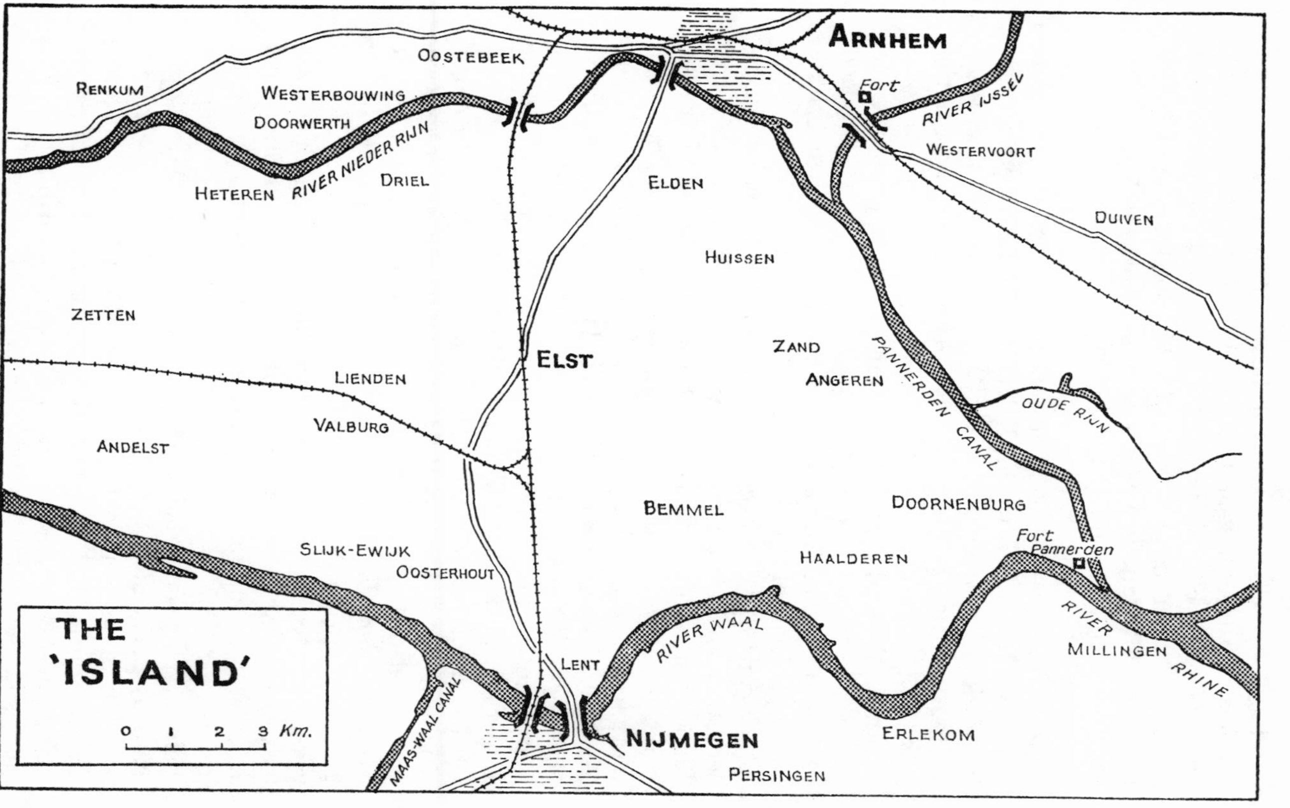
THE
'ISLAND'
0 1 2 3 Km.
ARNHEM
OOSTEBEEK
RENKUM
WESTERBOUWING
DOORWERTH
RIVER NIEDER RIJN
HETEREN
DRIEL
Fort
RIVER IJSSEL
WESTERVOORT
ELDEN
DUIVEN
HUISSEN
ZETTEN
ELST
ZAND
ANGEREN
PANNERDEN CANAL
LIENDEN
VALBURG
ANDELST
OUDE RIJN
BEMMEL
DOORNENBURG
SLIJK-EWIJK
OOSTERHOUT
HAALDEREN
Fort
Pannerden
RIVER WAAL
LENT
RIVER
MILLINGEN
RHINE
MAAS-WAAL CANAL
NIJMEGEN
ERLEKOM
PERSINGEN

The NCO commanding the heavy machine-gun team in Casemate East was Sergeant M. van Dijk, who lived at Arnhem and still does. He had been called up when he reached the age of nineteen, in October, 1938. He was now serving with 8 Frontier Battalion, which was responsible for holding the area between Beek and Nijmegen as well as the north bank of the Waal by the bridges. They were a reserve battalion attached to the 43rd Regiment of Infantry, which under the name of Group Betuwe held that marshy land between the Neder Rijn at Arnhem and the Waal at Nijmegen, and had its headquarters at Elst, midway between these two frontier towns.

In recalling those days, Sergeant van Dijk was blunt:

"I was going to tell you about how the defence of these bridges was organised, but perhaps I should really write: how it was *not* organised. We never got any information, not even the sergeants, and I can't remember that I ever saw an officer of higher rank than our captain. Of the three floors of our casemate, the lowest held the ammunition for the anti-tank gun and my heavy machine-gun; I was only inside it once before 10 May and was never told even how much ammunition there was. The middle floor was small and contained the ventilation system, which had to be worked by hand. In the upper floor, which was divided into two, were the guns. There we had a telephone line to HQ, but no telescope, no range-finder, not even a map of the area. During the winter the two-man steel pillboxes were built, forward of the dyke where we were; and they were underwater for a long time during the usual spring flooding of the Waal. The whole battalion was employed in digging trenches and building these pill-boxes, but the job was done very slowly, in a manner not calculated to improve the morale and low fighting power of the troops. This was a time of such idleness as I never saw before. There was hardly any preparation for a real war. Nobody believed in it.

"On the notorious night of 9/10 May we were awakened by the alarm and heard a tremendous regular buzzing of aeroplanes. But nobody thought it was a German attack, and just as in the solitary exercise we had held before, I went to my casemate wearing apart from my uniform only pistol belt and cap; I had not even my helmet with me. We just sat in the casemate, listening to the aeroplanes, and without receiving any information or orders, waited for dawn. The first instruction came through after dawn. It was for the military police in Casemate Middle to press the button to destroy the road bridge. Immediately after that telephone call the road bridge was blown up with a tremendous bang. The charge had been placed just behind the big pier on the northern side of the arch. Some minutes afterwards the railway bridge was similarly destroyed. But the first actual shot came from the Germans, and missed our casemate. Then we saw movement on top of the old Belvedere fortress in Nijmegen, and opened fire ourselves. But you could hardly call it heavy fighting. There were hours of silence, then suddenly a number of salvoes. Our casemate was hit seventeen times, probably by light shells from 2 or 3-inch calibre guns, and once a plane attacked us. Some of the 'clay fortresses'—the trenches we had dug—were completely obliterated; but our casualties were light. On the other hand, we were hemmed in by the enemy on three sides, for early that morning the Germans were already buying fruit, chocolate and so on in the shops at Arnhem."

Arnhem is protected by water on two sides—the Neder Rijn to the south and the Ijssel to the east, facing Germany, both rivers forming part of the Rhine delta. It is an extremely defensible position, with high ground to the north and west dominating the flat, low-lying delta plain. In the south, the road and railway from Nijmegen to North Holland and north-west Germany are carried across the Neder Rijn on two separate bridges some distance from each other, only the road bridge leading directly into the town of Arnhem. The latter is a single-span bridge carried high up over the flood plain and dykes on a viaduct and is of similar design to the other modern bridge across the Waal at Nijmegen.

To the east, the road and railway line leading from Germany into the heart of Holland were carried across the Ijssel side-by-side on a many-piered bridge of older design at a village called Westervoort. The old Fort Westervoort, now flanked by more modern casemates, guarded the Ijssel on the Arnhem side of the river. III Battalion of the 35th Regiment of Infantry held this position, with 22 Frontier Battalion forming a screen between the Ijssel and the German border.

On the night of May 9–10 the barricades were in place on all roads leading to the bridges. At about 0300 hours, when it was still dark, the sentries on a barricade at Didam, which barred a road route to Westervoort, saw a patrol of uniformed cyclists ride towards them out of the night. Their officer dismounted and produced a movement order apparently signed by a captain of the Dutch General Staff and directing him to carry out a march exercise through Didam to Apeldoorn via Westervoort.

The barricade commander, a lieutenant of 22 Frontier Battalion, noticed that although the uniforms worn by the military cyclists were apparently Dutch, their weapons were of an unfamiliar pattern. There was something odd about their helmets, too, although these were of familiar shape. In fact, the helmets were not made of steel, but fashioned out of cardboard in amateurish fashion. And, finally, he realised that out of the 28 military cyclists only one man—the leader—actually spoke Dutch! The lieutenant had them arrested and disarmed in front of the barricade, and eventually packed into a bus for despatch under guard to Fort Westervoort.

But in order to do this, the barricade had to be opened. Before it could be closed again behind the departing bus, the roar of engines could be heard on the frontier road. It was a storm troop detachment from the S.S. Standarte "Der Führer," a stream of motor-cyclists leading two tanks. They went straight through the conveniently opened barricade and on down the road towards the bridges. That was at about 0415 hours. It was an exceedingly light but unexpected form of attack, quite unlike a formal infantry assault behind an artillery barrage.

The weight in the German plan on this sector lay along the railway. Two regiments of the German 207 Infantry Division followed up the storm troop detachments, led by three trains—Armoured Train No. 7 carrying artillery and machine-guns followed by a troop train holding infantry, followed by yet another train carrying supplies, ammunition, and bridging equipment. The armoured train rolled into Westervoort Station, east of the Ijssel, at about 0440 and thundered on towards the bridge. As it pounded up the viaduct in full view of the defenders on the far bank, the demolition charges were fired from Fort Westervoort. At 0445 the bridges disappeared in spurting smoke, and subsided.

But although the structures were impassable now to vehicles, they still spanned the river and the marshy ground on both banks. Covered by the guns of the armoured train, the Germans set up a fire base on the east bank and swiftly mastered the guns of Fort Westervoort. One by one, these fell silent and eventually only two machine-guns were left, in positions so exposed that the Dutch dared not show themselves but fired by attaching a length of string to the triggers and blazing away blind by remote control. So completely did the Germans win this fire fight, that it took the Dutch garrison a full 15 minutes to surrender; no one dared show himself to put out the white flag.

The flanking casemates were similarly neutralised by fire, although they were able to stop the first attempt of the Germans, at 0800, to make an assault crossing in rubber boats. But a second attempt succeeded and together with storm troop detachments that had worked their way over the buckled girders of the bridges, these attackers succeeded in building up a bridgehead on the west bank around the battered fort. At 0920 the white flag was seen and by 0930 Fort Westervoort was in German hands. By 1600 hours they had a pontoon bridge across the Ijssel, and troops and vehicles were being pushed across to keep up the momentum of the advance.

Meanwhile, the leading troops had gone clean through Arnhem and by 1100 were making along the railway embankment for the outlying village of Oosterbeek. Here they divided, one force heading for Ede, the other striking for Wageningen, and pushing back the Dutch 4th Hussar Regiment, which had been brought up from reserve, until they were in sight of the main Dutch defensive position along the high ground called the Grebbeberg. This, the so-called Grebbe Line, was a strong position overlooking the valley of the River Grebbe and shielding "Fortress Holland" from the east.

As the Germans advanced westward parallel to the Neder Rijn, their progress was marked by the almost pointless destruction of the fine bridges across it. Both the road and rail bridges in southern Arnhem were demolished by previously prepared charges, while the railway bridge at Rhenen was destroyed by Dutch artillery after the charges had failed to explode. The Germans had even got across the Pannerden Canal and penetrated beyond Angeren in the Betuwe, the marshy land lying between Arnhem and Nijmegen.

The defenders of the north bank of the Waal were indeed "hemmed in on three sides," as Sergeant van Dijk had said. That evening they gave up their positions covering the ruined bridges over the Waal, dumping their heavy weapons and ammunition in a pond because there was no transport for them, and assembled by the walls of the old fort west of Lent. Because apparently no one was in control, Sergeant van Dijk personally led the retreat westward.

Next day, fourteen-year-old Philip van Heerde saw the Germans for the first time emerge freely onto the Nijmegen waterfront.

"There was no fire, most of the Dutch troops were gone, the the pillboxes empty. The Germans lay down with their Schmeissers, and then found a little boat belonging to Mr. Thull, which was moored there. When they used it to cross the river, a short burst of fire came from one of the pillboxes on the north bank near the railway bridge. But this did not stop them and in a few hours the first piers of a pontoon bridge were in place and the Waalkade seemed to belong to the Germans."

All that day the remnants of Group Betuwe retreated westward, eating when they could, snatching a few hours' sleep here and there in the fields, unhindered except for ineffective attacks by single German aircraft. On May 12 Sergeant van Dijk found himself sheltering with hundreds of other soldiers in a church at Vianer.

"Here we heard the news of the surrender on May 14th. It was a desperate situation, an awakening from an intoxication.

Four days seemed to be four years. One soldier started gathering pistols in order to continue the war off his own bat, but was discovered and stopped. Thoughts of home now predominated. Rumours that Arnhem was burned down made my best friend burst out in a fit of hysterical crying, and I had great trouble in calming him."

But in Arnhem, only the bridges had been destroyed; soon to be rebuilt, only to be blown again. The town had not been burnt to the ground—not yet.

CHAPTER FIVE

"COMPELLING MILITARY NECESSITY"

The Tragedy of Rotterdam

Moral courage is a rarer quality than physical bravery. The events of May 13 and 14, 1940, illustrated this exactly. On May 13, three contrasted groups of people passed through the Hook of Holland, the port at the mouth of the New Maas downstream from Rotterdam. The first party were visitors to Holland—the 2nd Battalion of the Irish Guards, sent to support the Dutch. They landed at dawn and received wildly contradictory orders from various Dutch sources—to go to The Hague, to go to Amsterdam, to go to Rotterdam.

At noon, a Dutch party passed them, outward bound for London; this consisted of various members of the royal family, some of whom wanted to go to Walcheren rather than England. The next party to arrive were also outward bound from the Hook for London. They came in at about 1800 hours, and when the Irish Guards saw who they were their decision to sit tight at the Hook was confirmed. For these last arrivals were members of the Netherlands government and diplomatic corps, setting an example that their troops generally did not follow.

If the Dutch government had tacitly admitted defeat in advance of the event, the German government—that is, Hitler—was, at the least, highly nervous and unsure. So much so that on the day following the flight of the Dutch politicians, Hitler issued his Directive No. 11. The third paragraph might have surprised the evacuees at the Hook. It read:

"On the northern flank the Dutch Army has shown itself capable of a stronger resistance than had been supposed. For political and military reasons, this resistance must be broken *quickly*. It is the task of the Army, by moving strong forces from the south in conjunction with an attack against the Eastern front, to bring about the speedy fall of Fortress Holland."

Hitler was worried about Holland because he was nervous about a French counter-offensive into the southern flank of his push through the Ardennes towards the coast of north-west France, the main aim of Operation Yellow. This pre-occupied him for a week. General Halder noted irritably: "The Führer has an incomprehensible anxiety about the southern flank. . . ."

To us now the fall of France seems inevitable; but it did not seem inevitable then, even to the Germans. Indeed, even Hitler's hope of gaining the coastline from Calais to the Zuyder Zee was essentially defensive. Six months previously, on November 23, 1939, Hitler had told his generals: "We have an Achilles heel—the Ruhr. . . . If Britain and France push through Belgium and Holland into the Ruhr, we shall be in the greatest danger. That could lead to a paralysis of German resistance."

Such an ambitious stroke was not to be contemplated by the Allies until 1944, but German fears of it in 1940 were real. The German blow into the Low Countries was a pre-emptive strike, but because Allied Plan D assumed that the main weight of the German attack would be there, the actual events in the north so hypnotised the Allied High Command that they did not recognise the massed panzer drive through the Ardennes as the main German effort until much too late, until they had all their mobile units committed far forward into Belgium and Holland, so that the thrust into France succeeded to an extent far beyond German ambitions.

It was on May 13 that von Rundstedt's armour crossed the Meuse near Sedan and broke through onto the plains of north-east France. In Belgium von Reichenau's Sixth Army had done so well in its drive to Brussels that as a reward for success its armoured corps was to be taken away to reinforce the Sedan breakthrough, leaving only the infantry. Von Reichenau protested angrily, because this would slow his advance, but the decision was undoubtedly correct; Sixth Army had completed its task of drawing the French armour away from Sedan.

Von Reichenau being a German general under German command, his protests were quite properly ignored, without repercussion. Four years later, the ambitious Allied attempt to take the Ruhr by an advance through Belgium and Holland was to be wrecked by a similar dispute, which, because it involved generals of two different nations, had international and political repercussions that prevented a clean-cut decision being taken on purely military and technical grounds.

The advance of the German Sixth Army had been facilitated by a swift crossing of the Albert Canal at the outset of the campaign. Some 400 parachutists had captured the two most important bridges at Vroenhaven and Veltwezelt, although failing to get the less vital bride at Canne; and an 85-strong force of glider-borne engineers had captured the great fortress of Eben Emael that commanded the canal.

Eleven gliders were used, developed directly from sport gliders, with a flat gliding angle of 1 in 12, which meant that they could be released by the tug aircraft many miles away and make a silent approach to the target; the skill of the pilots, coupled with the use of air-brakes, enabled absolutely "spot" landings to be made on the roof of the fort. Unlike the paratroop drops, the arrivals were absolutely accurate and there was no audible warning of the attack.

Using special charges, the engineers put the gun cupolas out of action and kept them out of action until the German ground forces arrived. There was very little the 1,200-strong garrison of Eben Emael could do about it, so unexpected were these tactics. Because the Germans kept quiet about them afterwards, the logicians of the British and American press were forced to postulate a mythical "Fifth Column" and the inevitable "Dutch officer" was trotted out to explain how German civilians growing chicory in underground caverns had blown up the whole fortress in an instant. Oddly enough, however, four years later the supposedly wrecked fortress was to be defended by the Germans against the Americans.

The overall situation on May 13 was that the German main effort (France) was showing all the signs of success; that the armour and some of the air power supporting the advance through Belgium was about to be taken away to support it;

and that therefore nothing would be available to help the assault on "Fortress Holland," which was apparently faltering on the brink of disaster. The flight of the Dutch government at this moment was largely coincidence, but not entirely. They had of course been the target of the airborne landings north of the New Maas, designed to take The Hague, and it was only the Germans who then understood how completely these had failed.

The force involved had been twice as strong as that which had succeeded at Waalhaven—two airlanding regiments instead of one. That is, it was twice as strong in theory —if it actually landed. But 5,000 men of Infantry Regiments 47 and 65, together with the bulk of the heavy weapons of 22 Airlanding Division, plus the medical services, waited all day on May 10 at the airfields in Westphalia. There were no aircraft to fly them in, because few of the Junkers 52s were coming back. Worse, some that did return were still loaded with the infantry who had embarked earlier. They had not even had a chance to land. What had gone wrong?

First, there had been technical errors peculiar to airborne warfare. The marshalling of the great streams of transport aircraft had been far from perfect, and units had become mixed in the air; therefore they were landed in a similarly scrambled state, losing much of their tactical effectiveness. Further scattering, particularly of the paratroop units, had occurred due to faulty navigation or inability to identify objectives from the air.

For instance, III Battalion of Fallschirmjäger Regiment 2, which should have dropped just south of The Hague, the Dutch capital, were in fact delivered to the Hook of Holland, the port of escape for the Dutch government three days later. About 100 infantrymen from two different companies of Regiment 65 were landed south-east of the Hook on the banks of the New Maas, miles from the nearest German unit, which anyway should not have been where in fact it was.

A further result was that some units were dropped in one place, and their ammunition in another; and that re-supply was therefore either difficult or outright impossible. The only consoling aspect was that where German troops came down in unscheduled places, they were hardly if at all opposed.

The really odd thing was that where German units were brought accurately to the right place at the right time, the Dutch were ready waiting for them. The historian of 22 Air-landing Division wrote:

"The element of surprise did not come into play because the Dutch had expected the air-landing operation since 2 May and both Regiments 47 and 65 found their intended landing places strongly garrisoned by troops and even partly mined. It is obvious that there was a fault in the security arrangements and our own picture of the enemy's dispositions was incomplete."

Not only the date and time of the attack, but details of the operational plans must have been betrayed to the Dutch. Although the refugee government of the Netherlands was to make much of the part played by a supposed "Fifth Column" in their defeat, they were perhaps naturally rather less free in advertising the advantages in that line that they themselves had enjoyed. In fact, they quite failed to mention it.

The assault by Count Sponeck's force on the Dutch government in its capital had depended on the capture by paratroops of three airfields situated in a rough triangle round The Hague that also gave control over three motorways leading into the city, followed by the landing of two infantry regiments in Junkers 52s on these airfields. They were Valkenburg to the north, near Katwijk-an-Zee; Ypenburg to the south-east on the main Rotterdam road; and Ockenburg (or Loosduinen) near the sea to the south-west.

At Valkenburg a well-dug-in enemy prevented the parachutists from clearing the airfield before the airborne troops arrived; but the pilots landed nevertheless, some with their aircraft on fire, and the infantry went straight into the attack without being able to form up. Against all odds, they took Valkenburg. But the airfield was muddy and, once down, the transports could not leave; soon it was quite blocked by grounded Junkers. When a reinforcing battalion arrived, it was unable to land and some pilots turned back; others made crash landings in fields or among the dunes by the shore. Back in Westphalia, the fly-in of the rest of Regiment 47 was stopped.

THE UPPER RHINE—1940
Pillbox of the Maginot Line on the French bank of the river, after the German Army had crossed. Original painting by a German soldier, Gefr. Hahn.

THE GERMAN ARMY CROSSES THE RHINE—May, 1940
Light bridge for marching troops constructed across the upper Rhine by German engineers.

NIJMEGEN ROAD BRIDGE—1934
Under construction, with the hous(where Philip van Heerde lived with hi family on the Waalkade shown arrowe((*left*). Two of the three churches visibl(were destroyed by American bombers ir 1943.

CASEMATE MIDDLE, NIJMEGEN
Situated near Lent, on the mai Nijmegen–Arnhem road, this pillbo: contained the apparatus for demolish ing the road bridge over the Waal. Not shell scars. *Photo:* M. van Dijk

DEFENDERS OF THE BETUWE—1940
Some of Sergeant M. van Dijk's com pany of 8 Frontier Battalion with heavy machine-gun.
Photo: M. van Dijk

At Ockenburg the first three Junkers carrying men from Regiment 65 found that they had the place all to themselves (the parachutists having been dropped wrongly at the Hook); but they attacked, with the gunners of the Junkers 52s giving them covering fire. And they also took their objective from an alerted Dutch enemy. But a British bomber attack completed the blocking of the runways, no build-up of an airhead was possible, and this force broke out towards Rotterdam.

At Ypenburg also, because of a faulty drop, there were no parachutists to take on the defenders before the first group of 13 transport planes arrived; 11 of those 13 planes were burning in the air before they touched down, and this airfield also was blocked. The attackers surrendered to the Dutch that evening, but a follow-up force of about 10 planes diverted and made cross-wind landings on the main Rotterdam motorway. From them, some 200 men commanded by the divisional medical officer fought their way towards Rotterdam.

Elsewhere, one of the successful fighting parties had been led by the head of the division's legal branch, and the commander of the artillery found himself commanding a single gun of the 5th Battery at Dordrecht. Worst of all, the divisional commander himself, Graf Sponeck, was forced to make an unscheduled emergency landing and, because the heavy wireless sets had been lost, was out of touch with his division. That night, however, he received orders by radio from General Albert Kesselring's Luftflotte 2 to abandon the Hague operation and break out towards Rotterdam. On May 13 his party reached Overschie, just north of the great port, and joined the divisional medical officer's party in blocking the Rotterdam road to Dutch reinforcements from the north. Now all roads led to Rotterdam and the tragedy began to unfold.

"The landing operations around The Hague must be regarded as a failure," wrote the historian of 22 Airlanding Division, "but nevertheless, simply by persevering, 2,000 men chained down three Dutch divisions and completely confused the high command of the Dutch Army." The division paid a high price for it. Overall, 42 percent of the officers and 28 percent of the NCOs and soldiers were killed and wounded in five days. Some units suffered particularly heavily. II

Battalion of Regiment 65 near The Hague and III Battalion of Regiment 16 at Waalhaven had losses of approximately 50 percent in all ranks. Further, roughly 90 percent of the Junkers 52s of the first wave never returned and so a large number of aircrews were lost as well.

While operations north of Rotterdam appeared to have collapsed in complete catastrophe, the vital airhead and airborne corridor between Rotterdam and Dordrecht, under continual attack by the Dutch, was only being held precariously. The area was approximately 17 kilometres long by 10 kilometres wide, and although much of it was bordered by the great waterways of the Old and New Maas, the German hold was tenuous.

At the north end, the defenders of the tiny German bridgehead over the New Maas in Rotterdam were being steadily whittled down by the Dutch Marines, until at length they had been reduced to only 60 men holding three buildings, some of them on fire. At the south end, the Dutch were also continually counter-attacking their lost bridges; as early as May 11, they succeeded in recapturing a bridge between Dordrecht and Moerdijk, and Hauptmann Schultz was twice wounded in a successful attempt to take it once again from the Dutch.

The bulk of the Luftwaffe was engaged elsewhere, so air support was increasingly restricted to supply drops of ammunition only; no food, no petrol, and few air strikes. The breakout by 9 Panzer Division had been delayed by the failure to get the bridge at Grave, and there was no sign of aid from powerful ground forces for three long, anxious days.

Then the first tanks rolled up from the south along the Antwerp road and on into Moerdijk, while Dutch artillery maintained heavy fire on the paratroop battalion holding the bridges over the Hollandsch Diep. The tanks were French. The spearhead of General Giraud's Seventh Army had crossed Belgium and made contact with the Dutch and were now about to roll up the German airborne "carpet" from the south.

In this crisis the Germans called up the Stukas, whose basic commitment was to aid the main effort far away in France. Although few in numbers, their great accuracy, combined with a method of radio communication that enabled them to be directed exactly at pin-point targets by the ground forces, made them worth their weight in gold. After their attack, a pall of smoke hung over Moerdijk and the remnants of the French armour that had penetrated it. A German witness recorded: "All that's left of the village is one house—not in enemy hands—and the church. A completely shattered French tank of the latest Panhard type, with a 3-centimeter gun and a machine-gun, blocks the main street, with all its crew dead."

Again, May 13 was the decisive date: The day the Germans broke out onto the plains of France, the day the Irish Guards landed at the Hook to reinforce the Marines, the day the Dutch government fled from Holland via the Hook, the day Count Sponeck's party reached the north of Rotterdam, was also the day that General Hubicki's 9 Panzer Division at last linked up with the Moerdijk paratroops.

That morning they rolled over the bridge across the Hollandsch Diep and drove down the airborne corridor towards Dordrecht and Rotterdam. By 1300 hours their spearheads had reached Hordijk, the centre of the hard-pressed airhead, and by evening they were in sight of the bridges over the New Maas at Rotterdam. But they could not cross them. The bridges were swept by Dutch artillery and small-arms fire from the north bank, and the 60 survivors of the tiny German bridgehead on the far side could neither be relieved nor withdrawn. It was now nearly four days since they had landed and they would have to endure yet one day more.

May 13 was also the first day of the dialogue between the two colonels—von Choltitz for the Germans, asking for the surrender of Rotterdam, and Scharroo for the Dutch, stubbornly refusing to give in to the weaker force. Undoubtedly, von Choltitz did his best to spare Rotterdam in 1940, as he was afterwards to save Paris in 1944; and Scharroo was equally right to resist him. In Rotterdam, the Dutch Army was not beaten and north of the New Maas the German airborne forces had virtually collapsed.

In his Directive No. 8 Hitler had written: "Neither in Holland nor in Belgium-Luxembourg are centres of population, and in particular large open cities and industrial installations, to be attacked without compelling military necessity." Up to now, as the R.A.F. official historian put it, "the Luftwaffe seemed to be operating against military targets in the narrowest sense." Had Hitler's "compelling military necessity" now arisen? Clearly it had, and on the evening of May 13 General von Küchler, commanding the Eighteenth Army, the German force attacking Holland, gave the order "to break the resistance at Rotterdam by every means." This was passed on to the Dutch by the panzer corps commander, Major-General Rudolf Schmidt, with a warning that failure to surrender "could result in the complete destruction of the city." This was a technical exaggeration, as no air force in the world then possessed the power to destroy a city with one blow, even a city as vulnerable as Rotterdam turned out to be. What was very carefully prepared was a "pattern" bombing raid by 100 Heinkels of Kampfgeschwader 54 operating in a tactical role.

The problem in such cases, as the Allies were to discover with much greater power at their disposal, is to lay down bomb lines that will ensure the safety of one's own troops. One answer is to arrange the flight paths parallel to one's own lines, so that if the aiming point moves back—as it tends to do, for human reasons—no disastrous consequences to one's own troops ensue. What happens to enemy—or even friendly—civilians in these cases never worries anyone very much; von Choltitz was an exception in this respect. The German plan in this case was neat, the bombers being split into two groups with their flight paths converging in a triangle with its apex just beyond the limits of the hard-pressed German bridgehead on the north bank of the New Maas. The "overs" and most of the "unders" would fall in Dutch-held Rotterdam, and not on the German positions.

Because of the possibility of the Dutch deciding after all to surrender Rotterdam at the last moment, a recall procedure was detailed. Oberst Lackner, commanding KG 54, reported: "On our approach we were to watch out for red Véry lights on the Maas island. Should they appear we had orders to attack not Rotterdam, but the alternative target of two English divisions at Antwerp." Red was an unfortunate colour, as it could be confused with tracer shells and bullets from light anti-aircraft guns, particularly in the dust and smoke haze of battle. The Heinkels were airborne from German bases at 1330 hours German time and due over target at 1500 hours German time on May 14.

Since 1040 hours that morning, the great Willems bridge had been the scene of an unofficial truce, with envoys of both sides crossing it; first two Germans who were taken through Rotterdam blindfolded to Colonel Scharroo, then Scharroo's adjutant to see von Choltitz. Sharroo appeared to be playing for time, but the Germans radioed to Kesselring's Luftflotte 2: "Attack postponed owing to parley." This meant the proposed tank attack across the Willems bridge, which was to be preceded by an artillery bombardment and the bombing raid at 1500. The recall signal was sent out to the bombers from German bases, but they were already over the Dutch–German border, entering hostile territory, and the radio operators had withdrawn the trailing aerials. This much reduced the range of the sets and the message was not received. The bomber force thundered on.

The Dutch official historian, Lieutenant-Commander F. C. van Oosten, recently stated:

"One of the Dutch army officers had the impression on May 14 that the German commander in south Rotterdam had done everything in his power to prevent this bombardment but that it had been decided in Germany—by Göring—that the attack had to be carried out and the city destroyed. Facts which have come up since the war tend to prove that this impression was correct."

The Dutch civil servant, Mr. W. Brugmans, had the same impression.

"Before the Dutch Government escaped to England, there was a radio call by Queen Wilhelmina saying: 'The right bank of Rotterdam is firm in our hands.' It was a challenge to Hitler, and he knew the answer. On the morning of May 14, I came home after having spent the whole night in the cellar of the Raadhuis. We heard the whole night through that so-and-so-many German bombers were in the air. So I went home early in the morning and told my wife, who was expecting our son number three, to pack the necessary things

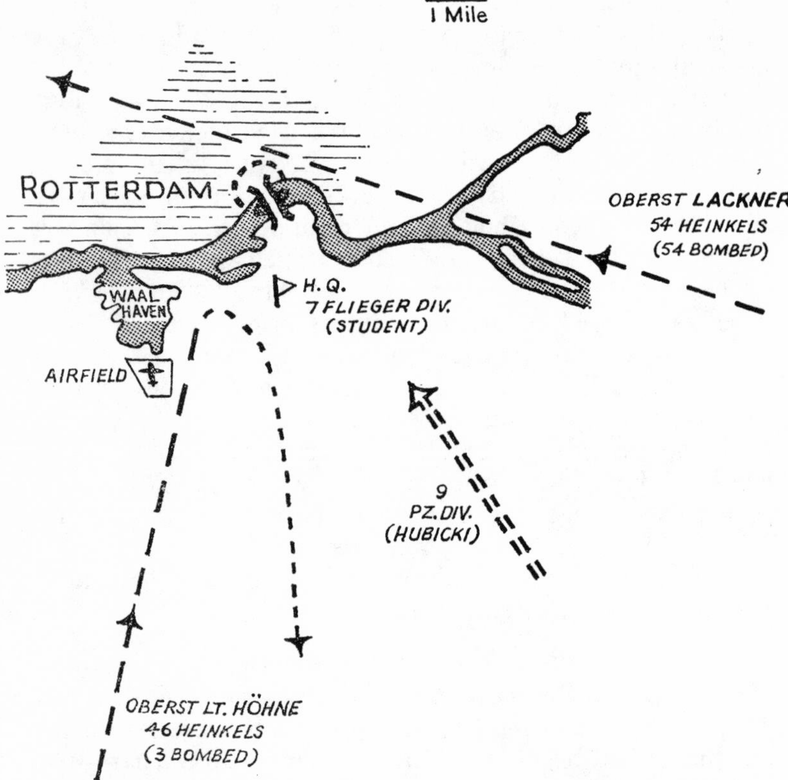

and we'd leave for my father's home on the outskirts of Rotterdam. I had a hell of a job to get a cab, nobody wanted to drive, but by promising a big fare I got one. The town was spookey. Every street corner had an infantry soldier, bayonet fixed, asking who we were, where we went. Some people were shooting at random, later on. There were big stories about the Fifth Column. I heard the Dutch infantry didn't even know the uniform of the Marines, and shot at them."

After seeing his family to safety, Mr. Brugmans returned to his work in the city and was on the Schiekade, near the Coolsingel, when the bombers came, flying low. He was dissatisfied with the defences.

"These German planes were slow, easy to get down, if one had the right guns or fighters. A day or two before, when the

Germans hit the barracks of the Marines, the 'Black Devils of Rotterdam,' with seven stukas, my house rocked back and forth. But compared with the English planes we saw later on, and the Flying Fortresses of the Yanks, the German planes were not so hot."

South of Rotterdam, the Geschwader split into two columns, Oberst Lackner's force of 54 Heinkels coming in from the east to form the right-hand stroke of the triangle, while Oberstleutnant Höhne's 46 Heinkels banked away to come in from the south-west, five minutes later, to form the left-hand stroke of the triangle. "They were very low," recalled Mr. Brugmans. "All of a sudden there were terrible explosions and fire bombs burning in the street and houses afire. Everything happened fast and all of a sudden the town was burning, and the streets were covered with glass."

A small boy staggered past Mr. Brugmans, carrying a suitcase and crying that his mother was buried under wreckage. People crowded into a store, which was a deathtrap because it had iron bars on all rear windows. Two or three soldiers were standing about with rifles in their hands, apparently with half a mind to fire at the bombers. "Don't shoot, don't shoot!" implored the civilians. "Go into the bomb shelter." And, meekly, the soldiers went. It seems the civilians thought that the bombers of Lackner's column might notice the rifle bullets and want revenge. "This wasn't war, it was senseless slaughter," said Mr. Brugmans.

"The bombing of Rotterdam was a mistake!" [wrote Diedrich Bruns]. "The Dutch had already capitulated and our liaison personnel were already in the town when the planes arrived. We tried desperately to make it clear by Véry light signals that the pilots were to return, but the pilots did not see them, and thus our commanders found themselves right in the middle of the German hail of bombs. Indeed our Kommandeur, Oberst von Choltitz (who later in the war, as a general, saved Paris from destruction by refusing to carry out Hitler's orders) was already in conversation with the Dutch in a hotel, when the 'magic' from the air started."

Then, at 1505 hours, flying at 2,300 feet, the 46 Heinkels of Höhne's group came roaring in from the south-west, flying much closer to the German positions on the Maas island. As the bombs fell away from Höhne's own aircraft and from the two immediately behind it, Höhne himself saw two Véry lights come up from the ground. It was not the clear and unmistakable barrage of lights that he had expected to see, if the raid was to be cancelled, and indeed Höhne was the only man in the formation to see them; but he ordered his radio operator to transmit the code-word for the rest of the formation to turn back. Slowly, the big Heinkels wheeled round, 43 of them still carrying their full bomb-load.

In all, only 57 out of the 100 bombers had released their loads on Rotterdam; these totalled 97 tons of 500-pound and 100-pound bombs, but the bulk had been delivered in a close-grouped pattern almost simultaneously, accurately, and from low level. The results were extraordinary.

Young Maurits van Dongeren, then not quite eight years old, who lived with his parents and baby sister near a main street called Speelmansstraat, recalled it:

"Some people were already leaving Rotterdam when, suddenly, the house was shaking, the doors moving, slates falling, and we heard the explosions of bombs. My father went out to look in the main street. He came back in ten minutes, and I never saw him so white as he was then. He said the town was 'All Fire.' We collected our belongings, but left my little sister's pram. You take only the things you can find quickly. I carried a roll of blankets on my shoulder. We walked down Speelmansstraat, where the road surface was broken open and the cobbles torn up. The fire was blazing out of the windows of houses and the curtains were blowing out also. The blankets I was carrying caught fire from the sparks drifting in the air. There was a lot of smoke, but I could see the sky. It was beautiful weather, but by now there was a lot of wind coming, and that seemed funny to me. I didn't realise it was from the fires.

"We walked round a corner to a bunker by the Oost Zee dyke, where my Mum had trouble with my sister—one man there said it was his child, and tried to take it away. It was very crowded, and we would have had to stand all night, so after about thirty minutes we left; after we had gone 50 yards the front wall of a burnt-out block of flats fell right on this bunker and I saw nobody come out. After that, we came to a small park. Crowded there were many people with dogs, cats, parrots, canaries, etc. Then buses came from many places outside Rotterdam to take these people away, but not their pets. 'No,' they said, 'I can't take your pussy cat.' We couldn't use our car, because Dad had lost his car key. We decided to walk along the road to Gouda and try to find accommodation in a farm, but all the buildings, including the churches, were full of refugees. My sister was crying all that night, but my Dad went back to our house, to save some things. People told my Mum, 'Your husband won't come back.' In the town, snipers shot at a door if it opened. Our house was burned later, when the wind blew the flames over towards it. There was a smell of burned bodies—a sweet smell. People had been trapped, while still at work, in shops and stores. My Mum became ill from the shock. She shook all the time when she walked. We went to relatives in Rotterdam south, and I saw the German soldiers; there was blood on their boots from the forced marching; they had marched all the way from Germany."

Meanwhile, Mr. Brugmans had reached his father's house on the outskirts and told him of the inferno in the centre of the city, adding: "They better give in before the whole town is bombed out." His father snapped back: "You're a traitor!" But they had given in. Colonel Scharroo came over the Willems bridge personally at 1700 hours to surrender; then the German troops marched over the bridge which up to now they had been unable to cross and on into the burning city.

From cellars and ditches and rubble on the north end, the 60 survivors of Oberleutnant Kerfin's force staggered out, dazed by their ordeal that had gone on for four nights and five days.

Von Choltitz described what he saw:

"A young paratrooper grasped the flag which he and his comrades had displayed on the foremost house to identify themselves to the bombers. He came up like a lost soul, the other warriors of the bridgehead behind him. Many were missing, and the survivors were dirty and worn, some without weapons other than hand grenades in their pockets."

With the surrender of the city went also the capitulation of Holland, which was announced at 2030 hours by the Dutch commander-in-chief, General H. G. Winkelmann. No doubt the flight of his government more than 24 hours before, influenced this decision. By itself, the air raid on Rotterdam, as Mr. Brugmans' father had spiritedly expressed it, was no argument for surrender; not even of the city, let alone of the nation.

Although the Dutch exiles in England were soon to spread the story that more than 26,000 people had been killed (*The Aeroplane*, November 15, 1940), the actual figure was under 900 out of a population of 600,000; but there were 78,000 homeless because the fire had gutted nearly 25,000 dwelling units (houses and flats) as well as many shops and other buildings in the city's centre. Although in absolute terms this was nothing at all (Hamburg was to have 277,000 buildings destroyed totally and an area of devastation measuring 15 miles by 12 miles), it was nevertheless quite extraordinary in comparison with the raiding force employed—57 twin-engined bombers carrying 97 tons of bombs. (For the tactical bombing of Caen in 1944 the R.A.F. was to use 450 four-engined heavy bombers carrying 2,560 tons of bombs.)

Subsequent experience of many raids by 50-plus Luftwaffe formations in daylight on English targets establishes that none achieved anything even approaching the destruction created in the Dutch city, and this disposes of the Dutch notion that Göring had planned to wipe out Rotterdam as an awful warning. On the contrary, these results could not even have been forecast before they actually happened, so unusual were they. With Hitler's anxiety to get the business of Holland over quickly, the generals on whom he put the pressure probably thought as the American general Omar Bradley did four years later, when he told a subordinate, brutally: "If it becomes necessary to save time, put 500 or 1,000 tons of air on Carentan and take the city apart. Then rush it and you'll get in."*

* For this and many other instances of American and British tactical bombing in Normandy, see *Caen: Anvil of Victory*, by Alexander

The nearest parallel as regards destruction achieved is probably the raid on the British aero-engine–production centre of Coventry, where 554 people were killed during a 10-hour night attack. But the force was much greater—449 bombers carrying 500 tons of high explosive and 900 incendiary cannisters actually reached the target.

That there was something very odd about the bombing of Rotterdam was obvious even to some of those without comparative experience. Young Maurits van Dongeren recalled: "There was a story going round that the Germans had poured oil on Rotterdam before bombing it, and that is why it burned so quickly." This was an obviously fanciful explanation of the mystery.

The Netherlands military attaché in London, Lieutenant Colonel C. Grootes, who supplied accurate figures of the damage, attributed it "to the fact that Rotterdam was in the front line right from the opening of hostilities. As a result public services such as fire brigade and the air attack warning systems were operating very poorly, if at all."

Diedrich Bruns, who went into the blazing city afterwards, also thought that inadequate fire-fighting played some part: "The houses were old and mostly made of timber. The *Flachenfeuer* was new in the war and the Dutch fire brigade was unable to cope with it. The Germans had many such fires later on. The air raid of the English on Hamburg was, in comparison to the insignificant attack on Rotterdam, an inferno; people got stuck with their shoes in the melted asphalt."

By *Flachenfeuer* Bruns meant a large, heavily built-up area, with very high buildings and narrow streets, with a high proportion set alight very rapidly. The effect was never experienced in England, because British cities are low-built, with fairly broad streets and a very high proportion of open space —as much as one-third of the area. The amount of combustible material per acre is small, compared to some continental cities.

McKee (Souvenir Press, 1964); for the effects of Luftwaffe raids during the Battle of Britain, see *Strike from the Sky*, by Alexander McKee (Souvenir Press, 1960). For 1943, Martin Caidin's *The Night Hamburg Died* and J. K. Dunlop's *Hamburg* are reliable guides.

It was not until 1943, when the three vital concentrations coincided—concentration of attack in time and space combined with a concentration of combustible material—that the terrible wind called the "fire storm" was first definitely identified. It is similar to placing a sheet of newspaper in front of an already blazing fire: It roars with immensely increased power. In certain circumstances, this effect can be achieved on the scale of an entire city, and it will be recalled that young van Dongeren had noticed, without at the time understanding, the strange wind that swept through the streets of Rotterdam. It may be that this was the first time the fire genie had got out of his bottle, but precisely because it was his first appearance in public, no one realised who he was or what he portended.

Rotterdam never came anywhere near rivalling the fame of Guernica, where the supposed results of a few bombs, dropped possibly by accident, had become a mandatory myth of the fellow-travellers. The Dutch were not Communists, and in 1940 the U.S.S.R. was an ally of Nazi Germany; therefore, Picasso was not inspired.

Further, parachutists and the "Fifth Column" had not only novelty value but political possibilities as well. As early as May 11, the Paris press reported that 200 parachutists had landed near The Hague in British uniform; on May 14, the Belgian premier, Pierlot, stated that parachutists were the most important German weapon (the Belgian Army having been assaulted by no less than 500 of them); on May 15, the Paris evening press had found German parachutists in Holland disguised as postmen, policemen and females; and on May 16, Mr. E. N. van Kleffens, minister for foreign affairs of the evacuee government of the Netherlands, informed the Paris press that parachutists had descended "by the thousand" in "French, Belgium and British uniforms, in the cassocks of priests and in the garb of nuns and nurses."*

The military reality was revealed by the capitulation. As

* See *The German Fifth Column in the Second World War*, by Luis de Jong, executive director of the Netherlands State Institute for War Documentation (Routledge & Kegan Paul, 1956). Dr. de Jong, who had originally believed in the existence of a "Fifth Column," discovered during his researches how very slight a basis it really had.

the men and weapons streamed in, it became obvious to both sides how great the disparity in strength had been. North of Rotterdam, three Dutch divisions found themselves surrendering to 2,000 airborne troops—in German uniform—who had no heavy equipment of any kind and were almost out of ammunition and food. In Rotterdam, Diedrich Bruns, holding a captain's command, had the embarrassing task of taking the surrender of a reinforced brigade. "A disarming is always depressing. Even then, I could not help sympathising with the bitterness my enemies must have felt. We took their best cars and drove around in them, and exactly five years later the Yugoslav Commissars were to drive away in my car."

The handful of betrayed airborne troops in the north had tied down the central Dutch reserves, greatly aided by Dutch rumours of a "Fifth Column." Bold and confident attacks would have exterminated them and probably led to the collapse of the German bridgehead in Rotterdam and a quite different conclusion to the war. But the casual shooting by inexperienced and trigger-happy Dutch soldiers had given the impression of many enemies on all sides. Inside Rotterdam, the shots fired at any door that moved—which had endangered Maurits van Dongeren's father when he returned to their house to save some belongings—were not from "Fifth Columnists" at all, but from nervous and credulous Dutch soldiers. The Dutch had in fact spent much of their time unproductively in firing at anything and at each other.

Such scattered and meaningless shooting is typical of inexperienced military units, and the Germans were not immune from the disease. In the late evening of May 14, with some random firing still going on and groups of Dutch soldiers coming in with their weapons to surrender at the German headquarters in Rotterdam, a roving detachment of storm troops from the S.S. Standarte "Adolph Hitler" panicked at the sight of armed Dutch infantry and opened up wildly with machine-guns.

It was General Student himself, the commander of the German parachute division, who leapt to a window to shout out at them to stop firing, and received a German machine-gun bullet through the head for his pains. It was a nasty wound, which put him out of action for many months, at the moment when his theories of a new type of warfare had triumphed. But Germany did not have the resources to develop them to any great extent. It was to be the British and Americans combined who were to train and equip complete airborne armies, and use them—in Holland.

The Van Dongeren family did not stay long with their relatives in south Rotterdam. Mrs. van Dongeren was still badly affected by the shock of the bombing, so they decided to move to the quiet country town where she had been born. It was set on the north bank of a river, with pleasantly wooded hills behind and fertile farms and orchards in front. In spring, the scent and sight of the blossoms turned the prospect into a haven of rural peace. Many rich Dutch people retired there to end their lives in the countryside quiet of the old town. The name of that town was Arnhem. And the house the family rented was on the south side of the Neder Rijn, a few hundred yards from the great road bridge that carried the highway north from Nijmegen. It had been demolished in the mad hours of May 10, 1940, but soon the span would be in place once more.

Part II

TARGET RUHR
1944

Maple Leaf Down

Normandy, focus of the world in summer,
All eyes, all thoughts upon you,
And a million men locked up in Calvados.
Your roads like deserts, deep in dust,
Dust that cloaked the fields and the blue
And rose-entwined meandering
Of trellis-work upon your cottages of stone.
A summer blue with skies, in Normandy,
And white with cumulus and dust,
And black with smoke of battle.
Like serpents, the armies crawled up from the sea,
And writhed upon your roads;
The vast armada lay, two-score mile of ships,
About your burning beaches, and the spires
Of Courseulles and Arromanches
Were but a prelude to the guns of Caen,
Of Villers Bocage, and the heights before Falaise.

All that is gone: down corridors of memory
I see the bullet-marks on white-clad walls,
And stone churches standing in the hills,
The windings of the Seulles and of the Orne,
The perfumed blue of Norman night,
And the stars, ragged in the trees.

All that is gone: buried at the end of all the years,
Beneath the weight of other memory.
But if I go back so far in time
That the Rhineland plain shall fade,
And the jagged towers of Arnhem,
The bleak and wintry Maas, and Antwerp
In her vale of pain; and stride down the years—
Past Ghent in autumn, and Calais
Standing at the last gate of summer,
By Abbéville and Beauvais, across the Seine,
I shall come at last to you. Again
You shall be mistress of my dreams,
The end, as once you were the beginning,
The gateway to Europe, of the path that leads us home.

CHAPTER SIX

FULL CIRCLE : 1940–1944

A British officer was carefully studying a map of the area where the van Dongerens now lived. Based on aerial photographs, it was not entirely accurate, but it would serve. He picked out the road bridge and below it wrote rapidly in pencil *Waterloo Br*, the lower stroke of the "W" nearly touching the van Dongerens' house. The date was September 13, 1944, and a final decision had been made. Taking a blank sheet of paper, he wrote on its right-hand corner TOPSEC, headed it OPERATION MARKET, and added below: 1 Para Bde O.O. No. 1. When he came to the critical paragraph 6 (INTENTION), he wrote:

"1 Para Bde will seize and hold the ARNHEM brs in the following priority:—

(a) Main br at 746768
(b) Pontoon br at 738774."

The officer was Tony Hibbert, brigade major of 1 Parachute Brigade of 1 British Airborne Division, which was part of 1 Airborne Corps, which in turn formed part of the First Allied Airborne Army. This force was the strategic reserve of the two army groups, one British, one American, which had broken the Germans in Normandy and were now driving forward some 250 miles beyond their beachhead base, towards the Rhine and the Rhine delta.

That strategic reserve was to be used to lay an "airborne carpet across the three main waterways of the Rhine delta—Maas, Waal, and Neder Rijn—over which a mobile corps spearheaded by an armoured division would advance to the Zuyder Zee and then turn right into Germany, to cut off the Ruhr, thereby bringing German resistance to an end at least by Christmas, 1944, it was hoped.

In essentials, it was a fairly close copy of Hitler's "Fortress Holland" gambit of 1940, and included many of the same objectives. The only difference was that the axis of the initial thrust was northwards, at right angles to the initial direction of the German axis in 1940; the early objectives were therefore to be approached from the south instead of the east.

The forces employed were to be very much greater, but the clear and logical German command structure of 1940 was lacking. Then, the airborne forces had been under the control of the Luftwaffe, which was directly responsible for the success of the resulting ground battle; hence they supported it to the hilt, taking staggering losses in transport aircraft and laying on Stuka or bomber strikes at the critical moments.

However, the Allied command structure was peculiar, in that the air forces bore sole responsibility when the force was in the air, the military when the force was on the ground. The air forces decided what risks they would run and what objectives they would or would not attack, with regard only to their own interests and not that of the customer, let alone of the battle as a whole.

Although the air forces consisted of British and American components under the command of an American, international rivalries played no visible part; it was the inter-service attitude that was to be disastrous. The inherent difficulties of an Allied command were plain, however, at the very top, with the proviso that this was also very much a matter of personalities and differing abilities.

There were three main bridges to be captured—all of them German objectives in 1940—and of these the Arnhem road bridge was the third, "the one bridge too far," as was predicted. The direct parallel lay with the Willems bridge at Rotterdam in 1940 and the precarious bridgehead held by a couple of companies and very nearly abandoned by the Germans as hopeless. The scaling up of airborne forces in the meantime is illustrated by the size of the force detailed to take Arnhem bridge in 1944—the three battalions of 1 Parachute Brigade. It was their Operations Order No. 1 that Major Hibbert was writing out on September 13.

There were also significant differences of doctrine between the German Army and the British Army at that time, and Major Hibbert was in an excellent position to assess them, as he had lived in Germany before the war, staying with a family that had two young sons in the Hitler Jugend. They were very keen on this youth movement, and when Hibbert began to help them with their "homework" he found that it was all military tactics—of a most interesting nature. He then had no thought of joining the Army, but the doctrine intrigued him—it stressed speed, mobility, aggression, flexibility, going round obstacles instead of pounding them head on. In effect, it said: "Weave, like a boxer. Don't just stand there, waiting to be hit, or you will be."

Shortly afterwards, Hibbert returned to England, joined the Royal Artillery, and was sent to Woolwich. Here, he found the same subject being taught, but in a very different way. This doctrine was almost static, stressing security, balance, and the use of prepared positions. If you did happen to advance, then you went forward cautiously, dug in, fixed careful lines of fire, and so on. In view of what Hibbert had just heard in Germany, this was merely asking to be attacked and cut off.

While the British doctrine stressed the importance of keeping your balance, so that the enemy could not catch you unprepared, the German doctrine stressed boldness and the deliberate acceptance of risks. Their idea was that by vigorous and constant attack the defender himself could be put off balance, thereby enabling the attacker to take risks and get away with it. The two doctrines were incompatible. They do, however, serve to explain exactly what happened in 1940, and nothing else does. Both sides fought strictly in accordance with their previously thought-out ideas; and the better idea won.

These contrasts remained to the end of the war, although in less exaggerated form, complicated by additional factors such as the immense amount of actual battle experience accumulated by the Germans, offset by the great material superiority of the Allies. In the air, the pendulum had swung completely. The Allied air forces were so powerful and efficient that the Germans were hardly able to move by day, while some Allied ground units went out of their way to make themselves conspicuous from the air because they feared a case of mistaken identity on the part of their own air force far more than they did an attack by the Luftwaffe; the results were so much worse, in the first case.

The situation regarding the "Fifth Column" was also reversed. Now it was the Allies who wielded this weapon. The emphasis, however, was on a body of armed and—with luck—Allied-directed sympathisers in the occupied countries, instead of the more traditional "Trojan Horse" consisting of organised and disciplined bodies of soldiers wearing disguise. But although the Germans did not rule out such scarifying events as a rising of the whole Dutch population, they did not allow this to distract them unduly from fighting the visible enemy.

The fact that there was to be a campaign at all in 1944 was due to one thing only—the successful defence of the British Isles in the summer and autumn of 1940—an unexpected defiance that brought nearly 2,000 Rhine barges into the English Channel and half-paralysed commercial traffic on the Rhine as a result. About half these vessels were German, the rest were Belgian and Dutch. Their appearance in open sea resulted from the fact that the Germans had not foreseen the collapse of France, let alone the invasion of England, and were not prepared.

Although the German Army was told that a cross-Channel invasion was basically only a large-scale river crossing, in which "Units of the Air Force will act as artillery, and units of the Navy as engineers" (Hitler's War Directive No. 16), it was not designed or organised to carry out seaborne invasions, and the German navy was too weak for its task. Further, the complicated equipment and techniques required had not been developed in Europe. Winston Churchill, who had failed to carry off a seaborne invasion at Gallipoli in the First World War, failed again on the Norwegian coast in April, 1940, became prime minister on May 10, and failed once more at Dakar in September.

Hitler's invasion preparations were similar—quite desperately improvised—but because he stood to lose all if he lost, he never actually attempted the final throw. A major part would have had to be played by the Rhine barges and tugs, none of them designed either to operate in open water or to land and discharge their cargoes onto open beaches. The Rhine goods traffic depended in large measure not so much on self-propelled barges as on "dumb" barges, that is, barges designed to be towed by tugs in fleets of anything up to eight or nine per tug. In sheltered waters, with a one-way current, the barges follow docilely enough. But not so in open water, with currents, eddies, and an aggravated wind-against-tide effect caused by the fetch of the winds, plus the wave effects experienced in shoaling water. One barge, sheering continually, is then a handful for a single tug. As assault craft, the barges were useless; as supply vessels, uneconomical, cumbersome, and vulnerable.

As for marshalling a fleet of them, tactically loaded, for a timed descent on the English coast, it was impossible. The distances varied and so too did the extremely rapid and complicated currents to be crossed; at times, some of the barges would have gone sideways as fast as they went ahead, even assuming a flat, calm sea, which is extremely rare in the Channel. In ordinary conditions of Force 4 or so, they might well have gone backwards as well as sideways.

Nevertheless, the German shipping plan for 13 divisions worked out at 155 small transport vessels and 1,722 barges, with 471 tugs and 1,161 motor-boats to act mainly as propulsion units for the bulk of the barges. This was the plan; the reality was somewhat less.

Looking back, it would have been in the best interests of all concerned if this amazing armada had been allowed to sail to the inevitable fiasco. Hitler would have been utterly discredited and the unnecessary war might have been ended before any real damage was done.

Of course, the Germans had planned to use airborne forces against England. But, like their navy, these had already been decimated in the spring campaigns. General Student himself had received a serious headwound at Rotterdam and was in hospital; and, as we have seen, the losses among the airlanding troops, transport aircraft, and aircrews had been high indeed. 7 Flieger Division was to take the high ground north of Folkstone in Kent, secure crossings over a small canal, and establish one road-block.

Although appropriate to the strength of the force available, such a modest plan would have astounded the English had they known of it at the time. The rapid and complete German success, which the Germans themselves had not expected, had created a worldwide impression of an irresistible force, overwhelming in numbers and superiority of equipment, which planned to the last detail and could not fail. In America and in France also, British resistance was written off already; only the date of the defeat had still to be settled.

In 1944, however, what had started as a European war had become a world conflict. The Allies had an airborne army totalling eight divisions in all—so many that airborne troops soon became a glut on the market and they could not be sold to ground force commanders at any price. In retrospect, the sparing German use of airborne troops seems appropriate; the Allied expansion of airborne forces a bloated monstrosity.

In 1944, airborne forces were also much less effective generally. In 1940, the possession by one side or the other, as we have seen, of one light machine-gun or two machine-pistols, was enough to turn the tide at a bridge or river crossing, circumstances which favoured the use of lightly armed airborne troops. But this was no longer the case. Although the support weapons of an airborne division had been scaled upwards to include 17-pounder anti-tank guns, the accompanying scaling-up of the ground forces had far exceeded this. Airborne forces could expect swift armoured counter-attack from tanks weighing more than 60 tons and carrying 88 millimeter guns, plus self-propelled artillery of up to 150 millimeters. Only the most heavily armed land forces could cope with this.

A clear but cruel verdict on the Allied airborne forces might be: too many, too late. The vast fleets of transport aircraft they required could have been put to better use supplying the armoured divisions and very often were taken away for that purpose.

As far as seaborne assault was concerned, however, the necessity for large, specially designed forces was inescapable. By 1944 the many daunting technical problems had been solved and although production still lagged behind requirement, the techniques of assault and supply over open beaches had been satisfactorily developed. Nevertheless, there were still limitations.

The main one was winter. A June "gale," which was hardly even a "yachtsman's gale," destroyed the American Mulberry Harbour on the Normandy coast and damaged the

British Mulberry. The winter Force 8s, 9s, and 10s would disrupt open beach discharge operations on the American supply sector for long periods and even hamper work inside the British Mulberry, which, more solidly constructed, still exists off Arromanches and now serves to protect extensive natural mussel beds. Marvellous ingenuity on a gigantic scale had created these artificial harbours on an enemy shore, and the beachhead battle could not have been fought, let alone won, without them. Nevertheless, they were merely the most spectacular part of what was largely a beach discharge operation, carried out partly under the protection of artificial breakwaters formed of sunken ships.

My own unit, having arrived off the Normandy coast on the evening of July 31, 1944, as part of a convoy of about 30 Liberty ships, took all next day to discharge. I was technically interested in this, because I was one of those who in 1940 had disbelieved in the possibility of a successful German invasion being mounted from freighters and Rhine barges. What it really did take to carry out such an operation was being demonstrated before my eyes. But it was still strictly a "mid-season" invasion.

The big ships of our convoy had to anchor miles out from that shallow-water shore. Then the vehicles and stores had to be transhipped to lighters and LCTs, which carried them into the beach or alongside jetties. The beach itself was encrusted by the great hulls of the LSTs, which carried tanks and other heavy vehicles on a number of decks and took so long to discharge that they had to be allowed to dry out. They lay there like stranded whales, waiting for the next tide to float them off.

My own unit, which was a British one attached to the headquarters of the newly formed First Canadian Army, boasted one staff car and two three-ton trucks. An LCT came alongside the Liberty ship and, wearing full marching gear, we lowered ourselves down rope-ladders, praying not to fall into the gap where the side of the LCT was intermittently banging against the side of the freighter. Then, as the staff car and the trucks were swung over the side, we got underneath and helped guide them into position on the rolling deck of the LCT.

It was a flat, calm, sunny day, the best possible conditions, and the water was literally oily from the many wrecked ships and sunken landing craft whose positions were marked by red flags sticking out of the waves. With a Force 4 onshore wind the affair would have been distinctly hazardous, and in much above Force 5, impossible. All this had to be done outside the protection of the British Mulberry on our right and the half-circle of the Courseulles blockships on our left. Once in the LCT, we still had to wait for the tide for some hours; then we all headed for the beach, the engines of our vehicles were started up, and as the bottom-plates nuzzled the sand the flat bows went down and we simply drove up the sand into the wreckage of the West Wall.

The sound of guns, audible far out across the Channel, seemed to run in a menacing half-circle girding the landward horizon. This was now an illusion because, although the front ran close to Courseulles, this was the extreme left flank of the Allied beachhead. Far away on our right, the Americans had at last broken out from Avranches, about three weeks later than planned. In holding the bulk of the German Army on their front for so long, the British and Canadians had taken casualties that amounted to about double those that had been expected and prepared for.

At the same time, their losses, and the very heavy losses of the American infantry divisions also, had in effect passed the ball to the American armour commanded by General George Patton, giving them an easy, spectacular ride through the German rear areas that conveyed a quite false impression as to who had done the actual fighting. This was shortly to have very serious consequences, because the supreme Allied commander, General Dwight D. Eisenhower, was a general in rank only and could not control his team, largely because he had no ideas of his own and generally held those of the last general he had talked to. Very shortly, a really critical decision between three major alternatives would have to be taken, and no decision was in fact taken. Events just happened.

The first event was a gift from the Führer. When the American armour broke out, instead of allowing his armies to retreat to the Seine in orderly fashion, Hitler ordered his own armour to cut it off and so seal the Allies in their tiny beachhead for the winter. Theoretically correct, the order bore no relation either to the situation on the ground or to the overwhelming Allied air superiority. The German armour was almost encircled and trapped at Falaise. This should have been the decisive battle and was in fact intended to be. All along, the Allied plan had been to smash the German Army between Normandy and the Seine, and then just motor into Germany. Falaise gave them an unexpectedly favourable opportunity. Ever since, the very name of that Norman town has been the epitome of carnage and annihilation. But in fact half the 100,000 Germans caught in the "pocket" managed to break out towards the Seine and then, evading yet another encircling move, to cross it.

Their losses in equipment were heavy and it was the remnants of units that got away; but necessarily it was the best led, best trained, and most determined who survived. I was only a minor cog, but better informed than many, and on August 28 noted in my diary:

"The Germans have got clear of the second trap now, despite the valiant efforts of the spectacular Sunday papers to destroy him. This offensive of ours could be almost as deceptive as Rommel's desert victories, which took him to the gates of Cairo, and then back again into the sea. A small balance of force would have gained him Cairo or Alexandria."

But the end of the Falaise battle was also the time to take risks. To say that the enemy was off-balance and unable to counter-move would be a mild description of the plight of the German Army in France at that time and for three weeks afterwards. From approximately mid-August to the end of the first week in September a very great opportunity existed, greater even than a comparison of forces would suggest. The German Army of 1940 had not consisted largely of the legendary panzers. Germany's petrol shortage was chronic even then. The bulk of the German Army walked and the bulk of its supply vehicles were horse-drawn; railways played a great part in its concentrations.

Now, in 1944, the panzers had been decimated, the bulk of the railways destroyed, and the roads were scourged by

Allied air power. The Germans could move in numbers only by night and at walking pace, and much of their heavy equipment had been lost. The Allied armies on the other hand were more than half mechanised or motorised. That is to say, less than half the troops had to walk, although their supplies were entirely motorised. The opportunity existed, simply by taking away the supply trucks from approximately half the force, to send the other half motoring forward into Germany at 30 miles an hour, or ten times the speed at which the retreating German forces could react. This is certainly what the Germans would have done, had positions been reversed.

But the Germans had a unified command and the Allies had not. Field Marshal Sir Bernard Montgomery had controlled the land battle in Normandy, while the numbers of troops involved were approximately half-British, half-American. But this was only a temporary arrangement for the control of four armies—First Canadian Army, Second British Army, First U.S. Army, and Third U.S. Army. With the arrival of the Seventh U.S. Army, which had landed in the south of France and was now headed generally in the direction of Strasbourg, the majority of the troops would be American (although the vital navy and merchant shipping forces were still largely provided by Britain). By previous arrangement, Eisenhower was due to take over the actual control of the battle, which would now really be controlled by two subordinates—Montgomery, commanding the two armies that made up the British 21st Army Group, and General Omar Bradley, commanding the armies that made up the U.S. 12th Army Group. This was the unsettled and unsettling background for what would be one of the most critical decisions of the war.

On August 17, immediately after Falaise, Montgomery suggested to Bradley that both their army groups, consisting of 40 divisions, should drive north, the British for Antwerp, the Americans for Aachen. On August 23, Montgomery was able to suggest this to Eisenhower, stress that it meant halting many divisions, and point out that a decision based on halting either some British on the left or some American divisions on the right had to be made. Naturally, the commanders concerned were not going to like it, particularly not General George S. Patton, but exactly the same decision had had to be made by the Germans in 1940, when they withdrew support from Army Group B in the north in order to reinforce the decisive drive by Army Group A through the Ardennes to the Channel coast. Eisenhower simply agreed with everyone, and announced that he was taking over command on September 1.

Broadly, he had three alternatives—the Rhine, the Ruhr, or Antwerp and its estuary. The Rhine and the Ruhr were offensive concepts with an element of risk. A hold on the entire bank of the Rhine, or the capture of the Aachen–Ruhr area, would cripple Germany economically and might bring the war to an end by Christmas. The capture of Antwerp and the Scheldt estuary would be defensive, giving the necessary port capacities to replace the Normandy beaches and wage a long campaign throughout the winter and spring, deferring victory to 1945. But, although Eisenhower made up his mind on many occasions, and can be quoted as supporting all these objectives, his mind never firmly stayed made up; and so, in fits and starts, his armies tried for them all, more or less simultaneously, and succeeded nowhere. Worse, he had his army and army group commanders snarling at him and at each other.

Meanwhile, the German High Command was beginning to recover from the shock of the apparently fatal catastrophe in Normandy, although some had anticipated it and realised that the war was lost. On September 3, Hitler ordered Field Marshal Walter Model to build up an armoured force to counter-attack Patton's drive; on September 4 Field Marshal von Rundstedt was made commander-in-chief in the west; and on the same day Reichsmarschal Göring pulled 20,000 trained parachute troops more or less "out of the hat" and offered also to supply 10,000 Luftwaffe men for infantry training. And Hitler was scouring the depots and garrisons of both the Army and the Navy, and even the police and the paramilitary labour force of the Todt organisation, to form new divisions to replace those lost in Normandy. And, because of the immense distances they had advanced, the Allied spearheads had lost some of their impetus.

Nevertheless, all this frantic reorganisation took time to effect and the onward rush of the Allied armoured columns seemed irresistible. It was 1940 all over again, but with wild scenes of liberation on the one side and the bitter fury of the defeated on the other.

CHAPTER SEVEN

DOLLE DINSDAG

Blitzkrieg: September

In Holland, Tuesday, September 5, 1944, was *Dolle Dinsdag*—"Mad Tuesday." Maurits van Dongeren was now twelve and a half years old and living with his parents in Haagdoornstraat, Arnhem, just south of the road bridge, so he had a good view of the Germans coming back from defeat in France. They looked like refugees, in ramshackle convoys of old cars and carts or walking and pushing their gear in baby carriages. The occupation had become oppressive by now, with constant curfews and round-ups of able-bodied young men for work. But the neighbours no longer laughed when the van Dongeren family jumped at loud noises, such as the banging of a door. In 1943 the United States Air Force had bombed Nijmegen in daylight (in mistake, it was rumoured, for Cleve in Germany—not merely the wrong town, but the wrong country), and some bombs had also fallen into Arnhem.

Maurits saw the bombs over Nijmegen as little specks shining black and white in the sunlight, like strips of tinfoil, and thought that was what they were. Then a bomb arrived five houses away and a neighbour, running out into the street, tripped and fell over the body of a little girl. She was headless, armless, and legless. Only the remains of her skirt could identify her. After that, no one laughed about bombing. But Arnhem was still a backwater of the war. About a week or so after *Dolle Dinsdag*, the Germans even moved troops out of the town, although they had bunkers near the road bridge and a flak battery in the Betuwe.

Philip van Heerde, who had been fourteen years of age when he saw the first German troops enter Nijmegen, was now old enough to be picked up by the Germans for work in a labour camp, so he had gone "underwater", as the saying went, and was now living on a farm near Zutphen.

Mr. Brugmans, the civil servant from Rotterdam, had left

the city and taken up a similar appointment in a small country town in the province of Limburg, where he had been born, in order to get more to eat and also to avoid "railroading" to Germany. His position was doubly awkward in that he was a Protestant in a strongly Catholic province and a civil servant who had to serve the Germans, too. Normally, a military occupation is hedged with formal rules for both occupier and occupied, but even so, the situation is extremely difficult for the local government authorities, as I was later to realise myself when, as a minor representative of the occupying power, I had dealings with German civil servants who had to carry out orders that were extremely unpleasant for their own countrymen. But when an occupying power is on the verge of defeat, the situation can become ugly indeed.

Mr. Brugmans was in Nijmegen that first week of September, on a visit, and he did not like it in the least.

"I found a restaurant with chairs on the street and asked for a drink. They had gin. How was that possible, after four years? It was expensive, but good. Then I watched the show. Germans driving like crazy, speeding it up. They were scared. 'Look at them,' said the inn-keeper, 'they're going home.' There was a girl running around amongst the German soldiers with a big orange bouquet, the Dutch Royal colour. She was asking to be arrested and raped. Or was she an undercover girl—an agent of the Germans? I didn't like Nijmegen at that moment, it was spookey. Thought I'd better leave. After a couple of hours, I got a tram to Mook (the railways weren't running). Inside, it was full of farmers, people who have a true feeling for changes in the weather. 'Look at the Germans,' they said. 'The English, all they have to do is tie a piece of string to the last German truck, and they'll be towed into Cologne.' But the English and the Americans waited too long, and the Germans got time to regroup their forces. As far as we could see, the Germans could have been defeated in that first week of September."

But the Allies were still pouring into Belgium, the road convoys stretching back 250 miles and more to the Normandy beaches. And fighting was still going on along most of that 250 miles, large parts of which were "Indian country," and contained many more German than Allied troops. The hardest going was nearest the sea, on the axis of advance of the First Canadian Army. They were over-running the "Rocket Coast," where the V-weapons that were bombarding England were sited; and every port had a strong German garrison that did not retreat but hung on with orders to fight to the proverbial "last round." Every port, from Le Havre to Dunkirk, had to be either taken by set-piece assault or cordoned off by siege lines. This separate battle of the ports went on throughout September (Dunkirk held out to the end of the war) and absorbed the resources of most of the First Canadian Army, so that only the British Second Army was available for the "blitzkrieg" role.

The "Rocket Coast" had been the most heavily fortified part of Hitler's West Wall, the place where the invasion had been expected all along, even after the Normandy landings; and the landward defences acted as a brake on the entire left flank of the Allied advance. These garrisons, positioned on the flank of the breakthrough, were too strong to be ignored; and anyway, the harbours themselves were necessary to a continuation of the advance, apart from the requirement to knock out quickly the maze of V-weapon sites in the surrounding countryside. London was then undergoing a much heavier bombardment than in the "blitz" of 1940, merely from V1s, and it was not known what V2 and V3 would do.

But where these special conditions did not apply, the British and Canadians ignored even large bodies of Germans left far behind the tank spearheads, and in what was to become famous as the "Brussels Swan," there was no such animal as a front line. A part of German Army Group B, struggling to get back to Germany, found itself occupying a "pocket" about 100 miles long, stretching from south of Compiègne to north of Cambrai, while the spearheads of the Second Army were driving for Brussels and Antwerp.

Even so, this was merely an area containing more confused German troops than confused British troops; and while the British were riding, the Germans were hiding or walking. Similarly, the main axes of advance represented slowly moving traffic jams, in which most of the vehicles were British, although some were Canadian, American, and German. The confusion was made worse by the fact that the maps ran out somewhere north of Beauvais and a school atlas was a valuable capture.

We ran off our map somewhere in the Compiègne pocket. When I saw "we," I mean about eight NCOs and men in one three-ton truck, which had been detached previously from the First Canadian Army to the Second British Army for a special job near Bayeux and then ordered to rejoin the First Canadian in the middle of the Brussels Swan. We were simply given a sheet number and map reference and told to go there. As it happened, the map reference was all right, but the sheet number was wrong. This meant that by going to the map reference on the wrong sheet, we left the area of the 21st Army Group and entered the area of Army Group B. It wasn't very dramatic, just odd.

We left Bayeux early in the morning of September 3 and some distance the other side of Caen, just short of Lisieux, ran into the area of recent liberation. It was all flags and friendship from then on. At the very top of a hill, where you could see for miles along the road of the advance, an old French lady had laid a cloth-covered table by the verge of the road and was offering tea in a jug to the occupants of passing trucks. Just behind us, the driver of a giant tank-transporter stopped to accept the invitation. Behind him was at least a mile of more tank-transporters, all carrying tanks, and they perforce, had to stop too; and behind them every other following vehicle for as far as eye could see. It was a really massive traffic jam.

Somewhere short of the Seine, on a lonely road holding only wrecked vehicles, we pulled off into a field for the night and slept either in or under the truck. Next day, September 4, we were into the traffic jam again, with some vehicles passing back, including 20 truck loads of German prisoners, silent and contemptuous of the jeering, spitting French. One German jabbed his finger to his forehead, to indicate they were crazy, and grinned; this raised a storm of yells, cries of "*Les Boches, les Boches!*" and a multitude of even ruder gestures. On the other side of the Seine, when we halted at a café for water (but hoping for coffee) we got the coffee, and as they would not take money from us, we handed over

NIJMEGEN ROAD BRIDGE—1940
The central span lying in the Waal after being "blown" by the Dutch Army half an hour before the Germans entered Nijmegen on 10 May.
Photo: Nijmegen archives.

ARNHEM ROAD BRIDGE—1940
The Dutch Army demolition has not been very effective. Although the bridge is impassable to vehicles, assault troops could still cross. Compare to aerial photograph of the German Army demolition of this bridge in 1945.
Photo: M. van Dijk.

THE CANADIAN ARMY CROSSES THE RHINE —March, 1945
Approach section of a floating Bailey bridge being pushed into position by a bulldozer on the east bank of the lower Rhine at Emmerich.
Photo: W. L. Lugrin.

DORDRECHT BRIDGE—before the war.

BLITZKRIEG—May, 1940
Parachutists rush the bridge from both ends simultaneously, taking the defenders by surprise. A German war artist's impression.

BLITZKRIEG—May, 1940
First stage — air attack on aerodrome and bridge defences, by medium bombers and stukas. Here a Ju 87 dive-bomber plunges on a pin-pointed target.

instead a tin of Spam and a tin of sardines. The result was electrifyingly unexpected. Kisses all round from madame, who was about thirty-five, and two even prettier girls. We all reddened like sunsets with surprise and gratification, even our young driver who had tried to evade them but was caught.

Some distance beyond the Seine, in the Île de France department, we drove into a hill town where there were no flags flying from the windows, no cheering crowds, no vehicles, and indeed no people; just one sullen individual on a street corner, although there were unsmiling faces at windows. Odd, we thought, are they pro-German around here? We were into the third village on, and almost at the map reference, theoretically, when we passed a military headquarters. The sign, black lettering on a yellow board, read: *Feld Kommandantur.* Out of date, of course. Funny they hadn't pulled it down, though. A few minutes later, we arrived at a wide expanse of empty fields where the headquarters of the First Canadian Army should have been, according to the map reference. No sign of it. And no one working in the fields, either. Odd, this was harvest time and up to then we had always seen peasants hard at work. Grey-blue smoke drifted across the deserted landscape and we found it came not from rubbish heaps but from barns and haystacks that could have been fired only within the last half-hour or so.

Then the first intact, moving vehicle we had seen for some time drove up; this looked better, it was a jeep driven by a Canadian Signals officer. We were about to ask him, but he asked first: "Where's HQ First Canadian Army?" Eventually, he went one way, and we went the other, and God and the Germans alone know what happened to him. We did not find our HQ, which was near the coast in the Dieppe area, and not north of Paris in the Compiègne area, until the evening of Tuesday, September 5, after a three-day zig-zag journey of nearly 350 miles during which we seemed to have passed across the lines of communication of four armies—one of them German. Not only did we have a *Dolle Dinsdag*, we had a mad Sunday and Monday to start with.

I have not told this story because it was exceptional, but because it was typical of those last few days when the Germans really were on the run and, apparently, the sky was the limit. As a result, I was to coin what may well become the classic definition of a blitzkrieg: "a confused mess all mixed up with an even more confused mess, and all moving in the same direction." Although somewhat lacking in grace, it is a good deal more accurate than the "planned down to the last button" type of military explanation.

In fact, the blitzkrieg momentarily created a series of ripples that ran through northern France, Belgium, and on into Holland in three days—those particular three days: Sunday, September 3; Monday, September 4; and Tuesday, September 5. They were all mad. This is reasonable, because it is the object of a blitzkrieg to defeat by disorganising, rather than fighting; although there was fighting, sometimes by rearguards, more often by over-run units as important to the command system as army headquarters.

The ripple that was to reach Holland on Tuesday, September 5, started at Douai in the very early hours of Sunday, September 3. General Sir Brian Horrocks, the commander of XXX Corps, had ordered his two armoured divisions—Sir Alan Adair's Guards Armoured and Major-General G. P. B. (Pip) Roberts' 11 Armoured—to over-run Belgium in one bound, and by night. Tanks are vulnerable at night, at least they are when they are static, and it is difficult to see very much out of them even in daylight. Such a night run by a mass of armour was unprecedented and would certainly not be expected by the Germans. But all normal rules were to be disregarded and Guards Armoured was ordered to take Brussels, the Belgian capital, while 11 Armoured was directed to seize Antwerp and its docks, deeper still into Belgium.

The Guards, with the shortest distance to go—93 miles—and by no means all of them unopposed miles, had its leading brigade on the outskirts of Brussels just before dark on September 3, having taken 15 hours to cover the distance. As darkness fell, the tanks drove into the city and at first there was no uproar, no reaction. In wartime, there is nothing abnormal about convoys of tanks, armoured cars, and other military vehicles. One of the first German vehicles to be encountered was a staff car carrying an officer in full-dress uniform with red stripes, obviously on his way to some social function. I was later told by a Belgian that his first sight was of two tanks crossing a street intersection and it took him a moment or two before he realised that they were like no German tank he had ever seen before.

When the Belgians realised what was happening, Brussels went mad. Surging crowds, the women offering kisses and the men champagne, swarmed onto the main thoroughfares and swamped the street fighting. At times, advancing columns of British vehicles were occupying the same street double-banked with columns of retreating German vehicles, and neither able to shoot the other. One furious Guards officer, secure in the priority of importance rightly according to the headquarters of 5 Brigade, had only just begun to reprimand the leading vehicle of a column that was obstructing his path when one of the occupants replied with a resonant *Achtung!* and a fusilade of shots followed. Harsher arguments ensued before that particular traffic jam was cleared.

Some British soldiers completely disappeared, literally swallowed up by the city. One was lost until the morning of September 4, when he reported for duty in a pitiable state and minus all formation and unit signs, as well as badges of rank. He said he had taken refuge in a civilian hospital where the nurses had given him comfort and a bed for the rest of the night and had cut off all his badges as souvenirs while he slept. He stuck to this very good story.

On that day, September 4, 11 Armoured Division rolled into Antwerp. The first Germans they saw were sitting at tables in the outdoor cafés, not even bothering to look up at the sound of passing tracks. The docks of the great inland port on the Scheldt were taken intact, with all the cranes and other machinery in working order; enough dock space to solve virtually all the Allies' supply problems. But the Germans still held the estuary that led down from Antwerp to the sea. Roberts did not realise at the time how vital this was, nor, had he realised it, had he anything like sufficient force to clear the estuary on the Dutch side.

It is fairly easy to see now, with benefit of hindsight, that whatever main objective was allotted to Eisenhower's forces, the capture of the Scheldt estuary should have been a priority for a subsidiary advance at least. But, of course, only 48 hours before, even Antwerp must have seemed a near impossible prize. At least, an Antwerp with the docks intact; for the Germans had made a sorry mess of Cherbourg earlier, making its capture by the Americans nearly meaningless. But now, even so, anything seemed possible—provided the German rout continued.

On September 4, Guards Armoured were in "a very dangerous state of elation," as Brigadier J. O. E. Vandeleur was to write. He was then a lieutenant colonel commanding the newly formed Irish Guards battle group, with his cousin, Giles Vandeleur, as deputy. On September 2, he had devoted a single word to describing the situation of the enemy opposing them. That word was "chaos." But now, the men were stupid with exhaustion and lack of sleep, plus the effects of the astounding welcome in Brussels, plus the optimism resulting from the obvious disorganisation of the enemy.

Colonel "Joe's" officers mess party in Brussels the previous evening had been interrupted briefly while host and guests, aided by a Honey tank, had sallied forth to take Luftwaffe headquarters, which someone had discovered was housed in a building just down the road from the house they had occupied for the night. Next morning, a nest of 88s and mortars sited at Brussels airport, which had been intermittently throwing explosives into the city, was chosen as a training exercise for No. 1 Company, which had a high proportion of new recruits. Supported by tanks and field guns, and watched by many spectators, the airfield was taken by the recruits, who suffered no casualties and gained valuable experience.

Then, on the afternoon of September 4, a Belgian came to Lieutenant Colonel "Joe" Vandeleur in Brussels and told him that a party of men from the *Armée Blanche* (the Belgian Resistance movement) were surrounded at Waterloo, 26 miles south-west of Brussels. They were holding out in a farm called Hougomont against seven German tanks and 200 infantry. This would have been a compelling lure for any British soldier, but for Colonel "Joe" it was irresistible. Hougomont's previous claim to fame was its successful defence by a German garrison stiffened by two companies of the Grenadier Guards against repeated assaults by

Napoleon's Grand Army on June 18, 1815. Later that day, the final charge of the British light cavalry against the shaken French had been led by Sir John Vandeleur, an ancestor of Colonel Joe's.

Colonel Joe in a scout car rendezvoused at Quatre Bras with three tanks carrying 10 Guardsmen on the outside as passengers, and set off for Waterloo. Nevertheless, he had a feeling that something unpleasant was going to happen and ordered the Guardsmen off the leading tank. Almost immediately, it was brewed up by a Panther and the colonel's scout car was knocked out also. The Belgian had bolted. It looked like an ambush, and although one German tank was knocked out, this time the Guards lost the Battle of Waterloo.

Next day, Mad Tuesday, September 5, Brussels went mad again. Hysterically cheering crowds were shouting "Peace! Peace! Antwerp has fallen! The Germans have surrendered!" The mayor, wearing full regalia, officially thanked God and the Irish Guards for liberty and the end of the war. The Guards looked at each other doubtfully; there were many young soldiers among them but none so young as to believe that one.

Sure enough, that evening new orders came through: advance and seize a bridgehead over the Albert Canal, anywhere you like on a front of 20 miles, but get it. On September 6, the division moved off. By dark the same day they had a bridgehead at Beeringen. But it was not until September 10 that the 30th U.S. Infantry Division occupied Fort Eben Emael, on the wrong side of the canal, which had been abandoned that day by the Germans because the firing embrasures were still blocked with the wrecked guns that had been put out of action by General Student's glider-borne engineers on May 10, 1940. Oddly, the commander of the German troops holding Eben Emael and the Albert Canal was General Student, with a newly created formation. A fresh battle for the strategic waterways of Belgium and Holland had begun.

CHAPTER EIGHT

THE ALBERT AND THE ESCAUT

The Bridges of Belgium: September 6–10

The 1944 assault differed in two main ways from that of 1940. Firstly, the axis of advance was roughly north instead of approximately west—a difference of 90 degrees. Instead of advancing along the line of the Waal and the Neder Rijn, the attacking forces would have to cross them. Otherwise, there was not a great deal of difference. The Maas would certainly have to be crossed, preferably at Grave, where the Germans had tried and failed in 1940; and also the nearby Maas–Waal Canal.

In addition, there were two other major canals in Holland—the Wilhelmina and the Willems; and two in Belgium before that—the Albert and the Escaut. The smaller rivers in the path of the advance were too numerous to mention. On the other hand, the Hollandsch Diep at Moerdijk had been much wider than any of these, and the problems set in 1940 by the Old Maas at Dordrecht and the New Maas at Rotterdam, not to mention the Maas at Gennep, had certainly not been less.

The differences lay not so much with difficulties in general but with an alteration in geographical emphasis. The blowing of the great road and rail bridges at Nijmegen and Arnhem had, in the context of a westward advance, denied the Germans nothing of importance in 1940. But to a rapid northward advance, they were essential. The emphasis is on "rapid," because the bridging of even major rivers is a routine requirement for the engineers of any army. But this takes time. And it also requires the forward movement of large quantities of heavy material.

This brings us directly to the second major difference between 1940 and 1944, and by a long way the more important of the two. The German assault had been launched directly from the German frontier, close to the Ruhr, and with only about 100 miles to go. The Allied assault of 1944 had to be launched from northern Belgium, also with about 100 miles to go. The difference was that in order to get to northern Belgium the Allies had already advanced over 300 miles, most of it within a week, from improvised bases back in Normandy. Their real bases were of course in England and America.

Even the shortest main supply lines started in the London docks, headed south-east towards Margate, doubled back westward past Dunkirk, Calais, Boulogne, Dieppe, and Le Havre to the beaches of Normandy, where all the men and material had to be landed, and then these bumped off by road over an endless succession of Bailey bridges, passing on the way Le Havre, Dieppe, Boulogne, Calais, and Dunkirk, all of them useless except for Dieppe, which was opened on September 8. The direct sea route was London docks—Antwerp docks, and Antwerp alone had the necessary port capacity. But the German 15th Army still held the coast and the estuaries from just north of Bruges right into Holland.

The effect of all this was apparent in the plans to get a bridgehead over the Albert Canal north-east of Brussels. The purpose of the bridgehead was to concentrate between the Escaut in the north and the Albert in the south all the resources required by XXX Corps for its part in the great attempt to breach the main river-lines of Holland. The CRE (Commander, Royal Engineers) of Guards Armoured Division was Brigadier C. P. Jones (now General Sir Charles Jones, chief royal engineer of the British Army).

His principal difficulty was that he did not have, and could not get immediately over the strained supply lines, anything like sufficient bridging material to span the Albert Canal at any point. The only possibility would be a partially demolished bridge capable of being repaired with the sparse amount of material he actually had. In order to improve the chances of getting such a repairable bridge, Brigadier Jones asked General Adair if he would spread out the reconnaissance troops of the 2nd Household Cavalry Regiment along the whole 20-mile front and to allow the Royal Engineer reconnaissance parties to go forward with each armoured car squadron.

This was agreed, and the armoured cars drove forward into what was obviously "a deteriorating situation." This was caused by the arrival of the German 719 Infantry Division, which had left The Hague for Brussels on September 2 and, failing to reach the capital before the Guards, had now been given the task of firmly holding the Albert Canal.

"As we approached the canal [wrote Brigadier Jones], reports of bridges being blown began to come in and the situation began to look pretty bleak. However, at about 1300 hours, I got a R.T. message from my reconnaissance party on the right to the effect that it was within sight of Beeringen bridge, which was blown but apparently not completely demolished; that the gap appeared to be 30 feet, but that no close reconnaissance could be made as the far bank was strongly held and covered by fire. But this was too good a chance to miss, so I asked the Divisional Commander to chance his arm and go for Beeringen."

32 Guards Brigade Group was ordered up to carry out the assault crossing, with the Royal Engineer squadrons and all available bridging material of the division close behind them. The attack went in at 1430 hours on September 6 and secured a foothold, about 200 yards in radius, on the far bank of the Albert Canal. By 1730 Brigadier Jones was on the blown bridge with his officers, and glad that he had ordered up all the bridging material. There was one 30-foot gap, but there was also a 110-foot gap. Of the supporting piers, one was destroyed, another damaged.

The weather had broken and the rain poured down from a black and moonless sky; there were also German mortar bombs, shells, and bullets, from very close range, as the engineers worked on throughout the night. Part of their fire was drawn, however, by the actions of some Belgian bargees, who had begun to moor their barges nearby as the basis of a floating footbridge. Brigadier Jones noticed this, thankfully, and sent engineers to help. The decoy worked, and by 0415 hours the next morning, September 7, a class-40 bridge spanned the Albert Canal at Beeringen.

In the cold light of dawn, that bridge looked "shaky in the extreme," as Brigadier Jones wrote later. However, by shoring up certain points to reduce vibration, the engineers made the structure strong enough not merely to take the Guards Armoured Division but the whole of the British Second Army besides, plus General Corlett's XIX U.S. Corps. Indeed, the affair is still considered as a classic assault river-crossing by an armoured division. The large and complicated bridge had taken 12 hours to repair, mostly in the dark and under fire, and every minute of those hours had been precious.

It was still the morning of September 7, with the two Guards brigades already across and fanning out and the 8th Armoured Brigade across in support, when the first heavy German counter-attack came in, getting to within 300 yards of the bridge before being stopped. The British noted with surprise that the Germans were actually attempting to advance, something they had not done since Normandy.

The reason was that not merely had the 719th Division come up from Holland, but General Student's newly-formed and very formidable 1 Fallschmirm Armee had been brought up to the Albert Canal and the equivalent of two divisions had been thrown in to attack the British bridgehead at Beeringen. *Dolle Dinsdag*, September 5, had been almost the last day on which there was no German front, merely a stream of disorganised, retreating units shambling back to Germany on foot or in any form of transport they could commandeer.

By Thursday, September 7, the Germans had a screen along the canal line and were steadily reinforcing it. Many of the units had been hurriedly formed or re-formed in Germany; others came from General Gustav von Zangen's 15th Army, which had been holding the coastal defences in Belgium and Holland. Had the decision been taken to send strong Allied forces round Antwerp along the Scheldt estuary to the sea, these divisions would have been trapped. As it was, they were able to escape across the Scheldt, hold the north bank, and still supply reinforcements to hold the Belgian canal lines. Nevertheless, the British put 11 Armoured Division across the Albert and began to push the Germans back to the next canal, the Escaut.

Even so, the only really speedy advances were those made by the B.B.C. and the newspapers, of which the Sunday editions were by far the most formidable. Bourg Leopold, a

Belgian garrison town, fell to the B.B.C. on the one o'clock news on September 9, at a time when the Germans in Bourg Leopold were actually attacking the Coldstream Guards, and with some success. Indeed, this had been the pattern in Normandy from the beginning and although notorious among the troops was unsuspected at home or by the world at large; however, the people of the occupied countries were well aware of a marked tendency to "over-advertise."

Whether this string of premature victories represented government policy as put over by the British Ministry of Truth, or merely keen competition among newsmen to obtain undeniable "scoops" is uncertain. It certainly did have the effect of totally discrediting all newspaper and radio stories from then on, as far as the troops were concerned, much to the fury of pressmen and politicians later, when they discovered that even the truth, when coming from such sources, was disbelieved.

Therefore, the situation was that while the advance on the ground was slowing against increasing enemy pressure, the respective publics of Britain and the United States were still rollicking forward in a kind of continuous "Mad Tuesday." One major decision at least was to be publicly excused by Eisenhower, on the grounds of the influence of the public opinion so formed.

On September 10 the Irish Guards battle group were probing forward behind the armoured cars of the Household Cavalry, whose task was to reconnoitre routes. Always important for an armoured division, this task was vital when, as now, the Guards had run well off their maps and had only a rudimentary idea of what was in front of them, although they knew they had left a good many Germans behind and on both sides of them.

What happened that evening was not planned. Even the axis of advance was not that which had been ordered, because the rudimentary local motor maps now being used were quite inadequate to indicate where the ground was suitable for tanks and where it was not. Up ahead, the Household Cavalry wirelessed back that they had found a new German-built road, not shown on any map, which ran parallel to the Escaut Canal for a short distance before turning to cross it at a bridge over De Groote Barrier. The bridge was also German-built —a heavy timber trestle affair constructed to replace a bridge blown by the Belgian Army in 1940. It was intact, but strongly held, and eight miles away.

The Irish Guards approached the bridge from the side road parallel to the canal, and stopped to reconnoitre short of the crossroads about 400 yards south of the bridge. The crossroads should have been held but was not, and it looked as if the bridge garrison, with three 88-millimeter guns covered by Spandaus, was on the north bank, and, further, that a slight jink in the approach road to the south would prevent their guns coming into action until an attacking force was close. The Irish had got too far ahead of their own guns to call up artillery support, and the only engineer officer with them, Captain R. D. Hutton, had lost contact during the day with the troops he was supposed to command.

Colonel "Joe" summoned him and said: "I am going to charge the bridge with a troop of tanks. I want you to go with them and make sure the thing's safe." Hutton replied that he had no engineers with him, and no knowledge of the bridge either, "Whereupon four weary guardsmen were called for from the side of the road, and that was that!" wrote Hutton afterwards. "None of them had the slightest idea about demolition technique—especially of the German variety."

The idea was to give the Germans so little time that they would not be able to blow the bridge until the Guards infantry were across. They would be covered by the fire of the tanks until just before charging the bridge, and two more tanks were to be ready to race across after them. As the tanks opened up with covering fire, they flushed an 88-millimeter gun and its tractor, which made a dash to escape over the bridge and was knocked out while crossing it. Its ammunition truck caught fire, lighting up the scene.

Up went a green Véry light, a signal from the infantry that they had reached the jink in the road 100 yards south of the bridge and that the tanks should lift their fire onto the bridge itself. For several minutes the tanks poured fire onto the bridge; then up went a red Véry. The infantry were at the bridge and the two assault tanks could now race across.

As they crashed through the burning wreckage around the disabled 88, the infantry dashed across the bridge after them under a hail of Spandau fire, and flung themselves into the ditches. One of the first Germans to surrender clapped a Guards officer on the back and shouted, "Well done, Tommy, well done!"

The attack had succeeded because it had come out of the side road so suddenly, and the Germans were expecting German tanks to cross. Now it was up to Captain Hutton and his ersatz engineers to "delouse" the bridge before someone had second thoughts and blew it under them. Captain Hutton reported:

"I discovered that the sides of the road were covered by a confusion of wires, fuses, etc., of every description, easily visible from the light of the burning ammunition truck and the sporadic shellbursts. Having shot through everything I could find with my revolver, the wire-cutters by now having fallen into the canal, I ran back. A towpath ran under the near side of the bridge, and on this I found my three men still cutting a tangled mass of detonating fuse. Also on the towpath were two Germans, one quite dead and the second suffering considerable pain from a severed right leg. Were these part of the firing party?—we never found out, for the second German, who was beyond coherent speech, died the next day."

The news of the capture, when wirelessed back to Division, was not believed, and confirmation by independent witnesses was demanded. But once convinced, Division authorised 5 Guards Brigade to cross. For some odd reason, XXX Corps counter-manded this order, and the Irish were heavily counter-attacked during the day, but continued to hold onto what was now known as "Joe's Bridge." Tactfully, it was never decided whether this referred to Captain Hutton's unit, known as "Joe's Troop," or to the Irish Guards group commanded by Lieutenant Colonel J. O. E. Vandeleur.

Next day, the corps commander, General Horrocks, arrived in person to tell them that their capture of the bridge had enabled him to bring forward the date of the next great advance. They would have the honour of leading it. "This last remark took the gilt off the gingerbread," the historian of the Irish Guards was to comment later. There was an extraordinary idea, prevalent among both generals and patriotic journalists, both British and American, but especially the latter, that there was nothing the soldiers liked so much as a chance of being shot in a good cause.

CHAPTER NINE

"MARKET GARDEN"—SIX PLANS FOR SIX BATTLES

September 10, the day the Guards got a bridgehead over the Escaut, the day the U.S. 120th Infantry Regiment occupied Fort Eben Emael on the wrong side of the Albert Canal, was also the day on which one plan for an airborne assault on Arnhem was cancelled and a much more ambitious airborne plan proposed. Further, it was the day on which Montgomery failed to convince Eisenhower that the First Canadian Army and the 3rd U.S. Army should both be halted, in order that their transport could be diverted to supply one great decisive push by the bulk of the two armies—Second British and 1st U.S.—to break through the Dutch water-lines, outflank the Siegfried Line, and attack the Ruhr.

In retrospect, it can be seen that this decision doomed the operation from the start. Eisenhower did not forbid the attack, he let it go forward, but with insufficient resources, in the hope that the Germans could be kept on the run everywhere, so that all five Allied armies could simultaneously arrive on the Rhine in 1944.

Montgomery accepted the scaling down of support for his plan, but immediately began to press for the date of the attack to be brought forward from the last week of September to an earlier date, because with every day that passed the Germans grew stronger and the attack had correspondingly less chance of success. Eventually, he got a date of September 17, which allowed detailed planning to begin on September 13—a very short period for any airborne operation, let alone the greatest airborne operation of all time.

What made this situation more critical than it would normally have been, was that the controlling organisation was effectively only about a month old. The First Allied Airborne Army was born officially on August 8, 1944, but was not really functioning as an entity until some weeks later, and at the time the operation was to be carried out in co-operation with the British Second Army, there was not even a direct telephone line between General Lewis H. Brereton's headquarters and the HQ of the tactical air force supporting Second Army.

The First Allied Airborne Army differed not merely in size from the tiny, picked force the Germans had used in 1940. It was compartmented by different nationalities and services. The soldiers of three armies were represented. Major General Matthew B. Ridgway commanded the U.S. XVIII Airborne Corps, consisting of the 17th, 82nd, and 101st Airborne Divisions. Lieutenant General F. A. M. Browning commanded the I British Airborne Corps, consisting of the 1 Airborne Division, plus special troops, the 1st Polish Independent Parachute Brigade, and the 52 (Lowland) Infantry Division, which had been trained for mountain warfare and was air-transportable, like the German 22 Airlanding Division in 1940.

The airmen of two air forces were represented. These included the IX U.S. Troop Carrier Command, and two groups of R.A.F. transports and tug aircraft, numbers 38 and 46. This army of soldiers and airmen was commanded by an air general, Brereton, with a good record in the Pacific.

To put it mildly, the single-service command structure, which had served the Germans well in 1940, was missing. Then, the bombers, the fighters, the transport aircraft, and the parachute troops had all been members of one service, the Luftwaffe. There was no built-in split between the aviation general and the airborne troops, as there was with the First Allied Airborne Army. The air force commanded while the force was in the air, and the soldiers took over when they had been landed on the ground. Nobody had to see it through from start to finish or take entire responsibility for everything. And there had been no time to modify existing attitudes.

Nevertheless, the use of this force in some way or other at the decisive moment was logical; it was the only reserve the Allies had. Now, if ever, was the time to use it. Further, General George C. Marshall, the U.S. chief of staff, and General Henry "Hap" Arnold, commanding the U.S. Army

Air Forces, were pressing for an experiment with large-scale airborne attack deep in enemy territory. Experiment, it would necessarily have to be. The only true comparison was with the exceedingly bold German use of airborne forces, first in the Low Countries and then in Crete.

The Allies had used larger airborne forces in Normandy, but these were intended to be dropped close behind the beaches by night. In fact, they had mostly been scattered all over the place in a chaotic series of drops. One of the few bright spots had been the taking of the Orne bridges by glider-borne troops of the British 6 Airborne Division, landing accurately less than 100 yards away, so that the defenders were overwhelmed before they knew what was happening. Generally, however, the operation had not gone according to plan and the fault lay, one way or the other, with the crews of the transport aircraft. The weather had been gusty and cloudy, making accurate navigation and flying exceedingly difficult—airborne assault is essentially a fair-weather form of attack.

The other factor always present is the flak. Transport aircraft are slow, unarmed, and unarmoured, and in order to drop accurately, the pilots must fly a steady straight-and-level course at dangerously low heights. If the flak is heavy, this requires considerable courage and means heavy losses. It will be recalled that 90 percent of the first-wave Junkers in 1940 had failed to return. The flak had been heavy and the courage of the pilots high. But in June, 1944, a significant proportion of the transport pilots seemed to have flinched, resulting in chaotic drops. At any rate, this was the deduction that must have been made by the planners, although not the sort of thing to be publicised even in peacetime, let alone wartime, when our boys are all brave and the enemy are all brutes.

Very much hush-hush at the time and for long afterwards, but present in many minds, was the fate of a high proportion of the British 1 Airborne Division in Sicily, when at the first sign of flak ahead, the American transport pilots had dropped the British troops, including their general, into the Mediterranean. Although kept out of the press, this story had taken only about five minutes to go round the whole British Army, both overseas and at home; and, most unfairly, this was taken to be a typically American performance. That is, talk big and bolt. For their part, the Americans tended to regard their British allies as rather stolid and unenterprising and this, too, was not without its grain of truth.

But the situation for the forthcoming operation was to stand all preconceptions on their head. In popular mythology, the Americans were supposed both by the British and the Germans to be cowardly; the British were supposed both by the Americans and the Germans to be slow, rigid, and unimaginative; while the Germans were supposed both by the British and the Americans to be plan-happy and essentially incapable of rapid or effective improvisation.

First Allied Airborne Army held a preliminary planning conference on the new operation during the evening of September 10. It was actually two operations, "Market" and "Garden," the first code-name referring to the airborne scheme, the second code-name referring to the plan of the ground forces that were to link up with the airborne troops.

It was similar in conception to the German operation of 1940, but its aims were much wider. The ultimate objective was the Ruhr. But the immediate objectives were to advance to the Zuyder Zee, so cutting off all German troops still in Holland and simultaneously establishing an armoured division on the high ground around Apeldoorn as a springboard for the attack on the Ruhr. In brief, it was a typical "left hook," designed to swing right round the flank of the Siegfried Line and Rhine defences guarding the Ruhr against direct assault.

The first stage of Market Garden was a three-division airborne assault on the key waterways: The canal and river bridges near Eindhoven were to be taken by the 101st U.S. Airborne Division; the Maas bridge at Grave, the Waal bridges at Nijmegen, one at least of the Maas–Waal Canal bridges, plus the high ground around Beek, Berg en Dal, Wyler, and Groesbeek were to be taken by the 82nd U.S. Airborne Division; while the road and rail bridges at Arnhem, plus the ferry, were to be taken by 1 British Airborne Division. When Deelen airfield, just north of Arnhem, had been taken, 52 (Lowland) Infantry Division would be flown in.

The link-up mission was given to the British Second Army, of which XXX Corps would be the spearhead.

This all sounded very impressive, but it was much weaker than it looked. Indeed, it could succeed only if the intelligence estimate was right—that the screen rapidly being built up by the Germans during the last few days, and in the week still to come, was only a thin crust with very little behind it except chaos and disorganisation. In short, the situation as it had existed on *Dolle Dinsdag*, September 5.

There were two main weaknesses—Market had one, Garden had the other. The airborne weakness lay in the shortage of transport aircraft; there were not enough to bring in all three divisions simultaneously. There would have to be two or even three "lifts" in some cases, all of them liable to delay by the weather.

The weakness of the ground forces lay in the shortage of road transport. Already, in order to keep Horrocks' XXX Corps going, many British divisions had been left behind in France, "grounded" for lack of transport. Even with the help of some American trucks, they could hardly keep up with a further swift advance of the leading corps, which, having lines of communication 400 miles long, was now about to extend them deep into enemy territory for another 100 miles. The shaft of the spear was going to be very long and very thin, whereas Montgomery's original idea had been for an advance by two armies, one British, one American, supported by all the transport resources of two further armies, one Canadian, one American. The fact that the American army that was to be halted must necessarily be Patton's, played a part in scaling down the power to be put behind the "left hook."

Patton claimed that he could go clean through the Siegfried Line, cross the Rhine in one bound, and enter Germany; and in the prevailing optimism of the time, even cautious men thought he was exaggerating only slightly. In fact, the Germans had already taken the necessary measures to stop him well before the Rhine. The Siegfried Line was being manned and reserves of armour moved up. This was not known at the time, but it was an obvious counter-move, and it was deliberate.

Equally unknown, but quite fortuitous, was a German

order of September 3, issued by Field Marshal Model. The mauled 5 Panzer Army, then retreating from France, would need to be refitted. The 9th and the 10th S.S. Panzer divisions, which together formed II S.S. Panzer Corps, would do their re-fitting in the area of Arnhem. The remnants of these two once formidable divisions, veterans of both Russia and Normandy, therefore directed their retirement towards Nijmegen and Arnhem.

But hardly had they settled in their new quarters, when on September 9 Model issued fresh orders. 10 S.S. Panzer Division was to move off into Germany for re-fitting. 9 S.S. Panzer Division was to transfer its heavy equipment to its sister division. Later, the skeleton of this division would also move to Germany, as the basis on which a new 9 S.S. Panzer Division would be built. These moves took place only at a snail's pace, because of the state of the Dutch and German railways at the time.

The very disorganisation of the Germans made the task of Allied intelligence extremely difficult. There were many reports, but it was hard to know what credence to give to each item of information. But already, by September 10, the day on which Market Garden was approved and the first airborne planning conference took place, Second Army had noted: "Dutch Resistance sources report that battered panzer formations have been sent to Holland to re-fit, and mention Eindhoven and Nijmegen as the reception areas."

In the weekly intelligence summary for the week ending September 16, issued by SHAEF, General Eisenhower's headquarters, one of these divisions was definitely identified as 9 S.S. Panzer Division, the other as probably 10 S.S. Panzer Division. It was presumed they were to be re-equipped with tanks from a depot at Cleve, the nearest sizeable town in Germany opposite Nijmegen. Lieutenant General Walter B. Smith, Eisenhower's chief of staff, testified after the war that he brought this information to Montgomery's attention, but it was "ridiculed."

It may be that Montgomery, having fought so hard for his plan, and being eventually granted it in weakened form, would not have it altered any further; perhaps the in-fighting with Eisenhower, Bradley, and Patton in order to get any sort of plan going at all, had exhausted him. In any event, there is an oddly uncharacteristic lack of thoroughness about Market Garden, over-laying a time-table that allowed nothing for unexpected delays or for anything to go wrong.

Undoubtedly, Montgomery well knew that time was running out for the entire operation; that it should have been launched earlier; but that if it did succeed and Germany surrendered in 1944, not only would many lives be saved but the Russians could probably be kept out of Europe and the future of the entire continent would be determined for the better. It was only a small chance, because the active opposition to Hitler inside Germany had been thoroughly crushed after the abortive revolt of July 20, 1944, and the Allied "unconditional surrender" policy was well calculated to stimulate German resistance even in a desperate and apparently hopeless situation. But the stakes were great indeed.

If the crowning stroke of the campaign appeared to be a knock-out blow mounted too late with too little, the airborne reserves that were to carry it out had been thought by some to have been offering too much too often. In the space of about four weeks, the First Allied Airborne Army had produced eighteen abortive plans, three of which, although cancelled, had very nearly come off. General Omar Bradley, commanding the U.S. 12th Army Group, was to complain that "Almost from the day of its creation, this Allied Airborne Army showed an astonishing faculty for devising missions that were never needed." And in the official U.S. Army history, Charles B. MacDonald was to write: "The paratroopers and glidermen resting and training in England became, in effect, coins burning holes in SHAEF's pocket."

Bradley had good cause for his complaint. During the great exploitation opportunity in late August and early September, his army group experienced a critical shortage of fuel and relied on the services of the transport aircraft to alleviate it. But the aircraft were taken away from him to support an airborne operation instead, so that not only was Patton, his "star" general, slowed, but the American advance into Belgium side-by-side with the British Second Army was slowed also, to a point where it was lagging badly behind the British. And Bradley, although he favoured a two-pronged attack, did realise the importance of the British drive through Belgium as a part of it.

The infuriating point was that the target of the airborne troops was Tournai and the date set was September 3. Bradley told Eisenhower that the operation was pointless, his ground forces would have captured Tournai by then. Indeed, they were in Tournai the previous evening and on September 3 Montgomery was complaining about their presence there, as the American columns were obstructing his path to Brussels.

Heavily armed ground forces are generally superior to lightly armed airborne forces, and yet in this instance, because Eisenhower was being pressurised both by Washington and by the Airborne Army, he approved the airborne plan in spite of Bradley's protests, and to implement it took away from him the transport aircraft bringing in fuel. Bradley lost six days' supply, at an average of 823 tons per day, for a gain of precisely nothing. The alternatives could have been put crudely and brutally: Which would you rather have—two riflemen or a tank?

This vacillation by Eisenhower in turn affected another vacillation. Bradley was continually being pressurised by Patton for the resources that Eisenhower had agreed should go into the northern thrust, and Bradley half-agreed with Patton. He thought there was sufficient force to support both a northern thrust through Holland on one side of the Ruhr and another thrust by Patton's Third Army "to seize the crossing of the Rhine river from Mannheim to Koblenz," although this involved breaking through the Siegfried Line, at its strongest and deepest point, where it was farthest from the Rhine and the mountain range of the Hunsrück barred the way to the river.

The loss of tonnage over Tournai convinced Bradley that this was now impossible, but nevertheless Patton continued to divert resources to himself, while Bradley looked the other way, apparently because a success in the north would mean headlines for Montgomery instead of headlines for Patton. In this inauspicious situation, the preparations for Market Garden began.

Market Garden was not a plan for a single battle. It consisted of six plans for six battles, all intended to dovetail into each other, and all to take place simultaneously. There were the three airborne battles of Eindhoven, Nijmegen, and Arnhem to be carried out by Lieutenant-General F. A. M. Browning's I Airborne Corps. There was the battle of the "corridor" linking all those towns to the Dutch border at Valkenswaard, to be carried out by General Horrocks' XXX Corps. And there were the flanking battles to be carried out on either side of the "corridor" by VIII Corps and XII Corps, also part of the British Second Army, but as these had very little transport they would move only at walking pace.

Essentially, the four main battles consisted of the movement of many vehicles having varying speeds and operating in restricted spaces.

On the first day, Sunday, September 17, three separate streams of heavy aircraft would fly from England to Holland. To Eindhoven would go 424 American C-47 transport planes carrying paratroops and 70 Waco gliders towed by British bombers. To Nijmegen would go 480 American C-47 transport planes carrying paratroops and 50 Waco gliders towed by British bombers. To Arnhem would go 145 American C-47 transport planes carrying paratroops, plus 4 Waco gliders, 341 Horsa gliders, and 13 of the huge Hamilcar gliders, towed by British bombers. Approximately 1,880 transports, bomber-tugs, and gliders were involved.

Routes had to be planned so as to avoid any of the three streams passing over heavy flak concentrations, while paying due consideration to the airfields from which the machines would start, the targets on which they would arrive, and the wide turning circles of the transports and bombers for the return trip. For instance, the 480 transports flying from the Grantham area to Nijmegen were 35 minutes long; that is, it took 35 minutes for the stream to pass a given point. They were to fly a tight formation, whereas the streams of glider-towing bombers would necessarily take up much more air space.

These, however, were merely the passenger-carrying machines—the airborne buses. To allow them free passage, it was necessary to knock out many German airfields and flak sites and also to provide continuous escorts along the streams. For these purposes, the U.S. Eighth and Ninth air forces plus the Royal Air Force supplied from England a force of 1,113 bombers and 1,240 fighters on September 17. This brought the total up to more than 4,200 aircraft of all types, the operations of which were so tightly integrated that the British 2nd Tactical Air Force, based on the Continent, were forbidden to go within 20 miles of the operational areas for some hours before and after the delivery of the airborne troops. Only three years before, heads had been shaken in America at the daring proposal to fly three transport aircraft together and simultaneously drop parachute troops from them, although of course the Germans had already done a good deal more than that.

At the same moment as these streams began to pass over Holland, XXX Corps was to break through the German "crust" on the border of Holland and Belgium, supported by No. 83 Group of the 2nd Tactical Air Force, and start racing for Eindhoven, Nijmegen, and Arnhem, as a prelude to a further bound from Arnhem towards the Zuyder Zee. XXX Corps consisted of Guards Armoured Division, 50th and 43rd Infantry divisions, 8 Armoured Brigade, and the Royal Netherlands Brigade. What this amounted to was a force of 20,000 vehicles—armoured cars, tanks, trucks, transporters, guns, command post caravans, and so on. And because of the low-lying, marshy land to be traversed, for much of the way they would have only one road along which to move, and that road never designed for densities and weights such as these.

Supplies of virtually everything except fuel were cut to a minimum, particularly ammunition. There was sufficient fuel in each vehicle to take it 250 miles beyond its ultimate destination. Ammunition for the artillery was severely rationed, as was the ammunition for the tanks, on the principle that if a speedy advance is possible, there will necessarily be little fighting. This was not realised by either the British or the American public; they assumed the opposite, that the force that advances the fastest has done the most fighting, whereas fighting slows everything down.

But one item could not possibly be excluded, and this was a heavy drain on transport resources right back to Normandy. It was perfectly possible that, although the airborne troops took their objectives, the Germans would still blow the bridges in their faces. Therefore a plan had to be made for the most pessimistic forecast—all bridges blown.

Over 1,300 vehicles were engaged in bringing bridging equipment from dumps in Normandy, along the long line of communications, and from the newly opened port of Dieppe. These moved the loads to a major dump at Bourg Leopold, beyond Brussels, where other transport columns were ready to go forward as and when required. To avoid unnecessary use of the roads, the spearhead of XXX Corps, Guards Armoured Division, carried with it only an absolute minimum of bridging equipment.

But should the airborne troops fail to capture the bridges, although succeeding in holding both river banks, four main columns were organised to go forward from Bourg Leopold when called. These consisted of the River Maas Group—878 vehicles; the Maas–Waal Canal group—483 vehicles; the River Waal group—380 vehicles; and the River Neder Rijn group—536 vehicles. In the optimistic case of all bridges being captured, 766 of these vehicles were earmarked for the bridging of the River Ijssel, beyond Arnhem.

Further provision was made for yet another set of alternatives—possible assault crossings of the Maas, Waal, and Neder Rijn, which would require special units and boats.

And all this had to be improvised from Normandy (where some of the Seine bridges had been dismantled to provide sufficient bridging material), along cratered roads, with only a brief pause, and without the use of intact railways such as would normally handle such loads.

General Bradley was to criticise Montgomery afterwards for demanding too much in the way of American transport resources for Market Garden, and clearly forgot, for he does not mention it, the very distinct possibility of the bridges being blown and the necessity for doing something about it in advance. As his problem was the Siegfried Line and the Hunsrück, this is perhaps understandable; plus the fact that most of the main bridges, although not all, were in fact captured more or less intact.

Montgomery's bridging columns were entirely British, either Royal Engineers or RASC units (Royal Army Service Corps) and vehicles; but had more transport been available, the two flanking corps could have advanced much faster and so prevented the "Battle of the Corridor," or "Hell's Highway," as the American official historian calls it, which helped place a brake on the rapid advance to the relief of the paratroops at Arnhem.

A much more imponderable factor, difficult to measure, was the relative efficiency of the formations involved, British, American, and German. Yet it was an extremely important factor, possibly the most important of all. Assessment is complicated, not merely by national bias, but by formation and unit bias, and, of course, the vast canvas to be considered. However, it is now 25 years since these events took place, and the formerly strong loyalties have relaxed sufficiently for many of those who took part to come up with surprising verdicts that would have been violently contested at the time. Battle builds binding loyalties, but objective assessments provide lessons and may save lives in the future.

The advantage of battle experience was with the Germans; their field formations had been fighting continuously for five years, their doctrines had been proved, their organisation tested, and their conscript civilians had become professional soldiers. But the fortress divisions that had escaped from the coast had poor-quality personnel, considered as fighting soldiers, that is. They included men of low medical category, including those suffering from stomach ailments who were gathered for administrative convenience in special units, the middle-aged, and the elderly. They were good enough to hold concrete forts, but at a disadvantage in any violent activity, such as carrying heavy loads for long distances or living like an animal in a hole in the ground day and night in cold and rain or icy mud.

All these are the real essentials of a fighting soldier's trade, which is for fit young men only, because you can only fight if you can first live, sleep, and eat like a pig, without catching pneumonia, dysentery, or just dying of exposure and exhaustion. Suburban man does not take kindly to this life without acclimatisation.

Probably the most furious prisoner taken during this period was an infantryman hauled out of a ditch on September 9 by the Irish Guards (after they had sprayed it for ten minutes with high-explosive shells and machine-gun bullets). By trade, he was a deep-sea diver; he had been given a rifle and told that he was a trained soldier, and was still complaining about it. His capture caused the British intelligence staff to report that the Germans had now literally "plumbed the depths" in their search for reinforcements. On the other hand, prisoners taken by the same unit the previous day had been "hefty S.S. men who looked first-class soldiers, and were determined to give no information."

American authors tend to describe British units as "veteran" and U.S. units as "green," largely because Britain had been in the war longer. In fact, most of the British Army spent most of the war in England, without opportunity to learn at first hand. Only two of Montgomery's 14 divisions had battle experience prior to Normandy, and it was the wrong sort of experience, gained in the desert. The infantry had suffered very heavy losses in Normandy and the reinforcement position was critical—that is, there were no more reinforcements and one infantry division had already been broken up in order to bring other divisions up to strength.

Battle experience generally amounted to no more than two to three months. German experience generally would be an equal number of years. The organisation of the armoured divisions had proved clumsy in battle conditions and, as we shall see, the lessons had to be quickly learned and a more flexible mixture of tanks and infantry had just been introduced. The artillery was extremely good, but would be of little use in a lightning thrust along one road.

Airborne divisions normally have little battle experience. One moment they are living in safety and at peace, the enemy no more than a newspaper headline; the next, they are in the middle of an actual enemy, surrounded on all sides, and without hope of immediate relief; and, finally, after a few days or a week or so, they are usually withdrawn from battle. The initial test, without possibility of gradually getting to know the enemy, his strengths, weaknesses, and methods, is severe. But the ordeal is brief and in no way compares to that undergone by the ordinary infantryman, whose chances of survival in the long term are exceedingly small.

The U.S. 82nd Airborne Division was unusual, as parts

of it had collected nine months' experience of continuous fighting in various ground campaigns, mostly in Italy, including Anzio. It was probably the best of the three airborne divisions.

The British 1st Airborne Division was part-experienced, but many of the best leaders had been posted elsewhere, some of the units had no experience at all, and while some were very well trained and led, the general performance was likely to be uneven. Later, the Germans were to comment on it. It was also a lucky division, many of its units having been dumped into the sea off Sicily earlier. What experience it did have, led to the formulation of a doctrine with which no other airborne division agreed: that it was better to choose a favourable dropping zone some distance from the target than to land disorganised on or alongside the target. Its commander was an infantry soldier of experience, recently appointed, who was in no position to contradict his own "experts." It was this division that was to be given the most difficult and dangerous task allotted to any formation during Market Garden, and there was a good deal of foreboding in many quarters.

These facts are no argument against Market Garden as a whole, however. They do not favour the alternative—Patton's drive to the Rhine—because Patton's infantry were poor; even the bakery company of 9th S.S. Panzer Division had fought them off. One of Patton's biographers, Ladlislas Farago, was to write:

"Many of Patton's spectacular forward plunges occurred in the face of very light or no resistance. While Crerar's Canadians had to hack their harrowing path down the Falaise road through crack units of the German Panzer Army, XV U.S. Corps raced to Alençon encumbered by only the feeble opposition of German units the corps history described as 'badly hurt' and as 'remnants of divisions in the process of wholesale reconstitution.' On the other hand, whenever resistance developed and could not be bypassed, the Third Army drive slowed."

Patton's skill lay in finding "breaks" for his inexperienced troops to exploit, and it may be that all the boastful sound and fury was mainly for their benefit. However, it was to support Patton's drive that Montgomery's original conception had been scaled down; and now, in the third week of September, there were no "breaks" any more, for anyone.

CHAPTER TEN

"RING ZON 244"

Escaut to Eindhoven: September 17–18

The objective of XXX Corps was Nunspeet on the Ijsselmeer. The corps was to get here within six days at the most and hold the area Arnhem to the Zuyder Zee. Arnhem was to be reached in two days. The task of the airborne corps was to seize the river-crossings and nodal points along the axis of advance and thus ensure uninterrupted passage for the tanks and motorised infantry. VIII Corps and XII Corps were to protect the right and left flanks.

The enemy strength immediately in front of XXX Corps was estimated as six infantry battalions supported by 20 tanks and self-propelled guns. As usual with British intelligence, this proved sadly optimistic. The position at Arnhem was not known.

The planning emphasis was on speed. There must be no delay. Nevertheless, among the 20,000 vehicles that were to race forward into Holland were two large and awkward groups—the bridging column of about 5,000 vehicles and the administrative tail of the airborne forces with about 2,000 vehicles. These might have to be called for suddenly and quickly. They were an inescapable result of the problems set by the water barriers of the Rhine delta.

The procession was to be led by Guards Armoured Division, starting from "Joe's Bridge" on the Escaut Canal. The distance to Arnhem, to be covered in two days, was 70 miles; and the Zuyder Zee lay 30 miles beyond. If this area was gained, the German Fifteenth Army in Holland would be trapped. Undoubtedly, they would try to break out, and the whole of XXX Corps might well be cut off. But the country around Apeldoorn lent itself to defence and, supplied by air, XXX Corps might well hold its ground until the rest of the British Second Army came up. They would be reinforced early by 52 (Lowland) Infantry Division, which would be flown in to the airfield north of Arnhem as soon as it was captured. Nevertheless, it was an extremely daring plan, with a very tight time-table, and was only justified by the tremendous gain at stake—the last chance for an early end to the war.

The first 70 miles, from the Escaut to Arnhem, was much the most difficult from the typographical point of view. For most of the way there was only one practicable road, flanked by marshy ground, so that the attack would have to go straight up the road and hit enemy resistance head on. The chances of the tanks by-passing enemy strongpoints were few and far between, from the beginning. Theoretically, it was an impossible proposition; but most such propositions become practicable when thought is given to them and the necessary resources are available.

Two days before the attack, Lieutenant A. R. J. Buchanan-Jardine had taken two scout cars of the Household Cavalry straight down that single road to Valkenswaard and back again, in a move so swift and bold that the surprised Germans were in every case just too late in opening fire. His report, together with what he had been told by Dutch civilians, showed that the five miles or so to Valkenswaard was held in depth by tanks, self-propelled guns, and bazooka-armed infantry.

Normally, in such a situation, an infantry division would attack in order to try to break open a hole through which the armour could pour; but this does not always succeed, because an infantry attack is necessarily slow and allows the enemy time to reinforce and build up defences further back, particularly when the ground favours the defender, as it did here.

The decision was taken to "blow" the tanks forward by combining a heavy artillery barrage with pin-point attacks by cannon-and-rocket-armed Typhoons, 11 squadrons of them. They were the equivalent of the German Stukas of 1940, but because of their high speed and flat angle of dive, precise target identification was difficult. Trains and road convoys were one thing, but concealed infantry and camouflaged, well-hidden tanks and self-propelled guns were another. Further, soldiers and airmen tend to think differently and do not even talk each other's language.

A further decision was made that the airmen would know

the ground plan in detail and that R.A.F. officers would control the air attack from the ground, their wireless vehicle being placed beside that of the ground commander. Although both the corps commander, General Horrocks, and the divisional commander, General Adair, had come up to watch this critical operation, it was actually to be carried out by the Irish Guards group led by Colonel J. O. E. Vandeleur. It was fortunate for him that the necessity of liaison with the R.A.F. kept his headquarters out of its normal position, immediately behind the leading squadron of tanks.

Two other unusual measures were taken. A bulldozer on a tank-transporter was well up, in case the Germans had destroyed the bridge just outside Valkenswaard, and a "contact man" from the U.S. 101 Airborne Division was in attendance with a 10-mile-range radio set.

The time set for the attack, early afternoon, was late in the day for such a break-in, break-through, and break-out battle; but this was decided by the airborne timings, which were not exact and depended on the weather, and also on the fact that the Typhoons were from 83 Group of the Second Tactical Air Force, and they were not allowed into the air until all the aircraft of the First Allied Airborne Army had both come and gone and got well clear of the area.

At 1900 hours on September 16, the weather forecasts being favourable, General Brereton made the decision for the airborne operation to begin at 1300 hours next day, Sunday, September 17. R.A.F. Bomber Command struck first, during the night, dropping 890 tons of bombs on German fighter airfields, and by one particularly effective raid making sure that none of the new Messerschmitt 262 jet fighters could take off.

On the morning of September 17, 100 more British bombers escorted by Spitfires attacked three coastal defence batteries in Holland; and later, 816 Flying Fortresses of the U.S. Eighth Air Force, escorted by P-51s, attacked 117 flak positions. September is an awkward month for flying weather, but by 0900 hours the autumn mist and haze had cleared from the airfields in England. At 1025 the 18 transports carrying the pathfinder teams began to take off; these units were to be dropped 20 minutes before the main forces began to arrive.

Back in the Pas de Calais the night had been lit by the

flashes of gunfire and the golden glow of flares where three more battles were being fought for Calais, Boulogne, and Dunkirk, as the bomber force for Market Garden droned in.

At 1230 hours on September 17, General Horrocks received the signal for which he was waiting—the airborne force was on its way. At 1245 their fighter escort appeared, attacking flak positions; and shortly afterwards the southern stream of transports carrying 101 U.S. Airborne Division to Eindhoven, flying very low and slowly, seemingly without end. At 1345 the leading squadron of tanks moved across Joe's Bridge to the start line.

At 1400 the preparatory and counter-battery part of the 300-gun artillery programme began; at 1430 the heavy mortars of the two divisions opened up; and at 1432 the 240 field guns began their rapid barrage fire. That was the signal for the leading tanks to move up to the positions held by the infantry of 50 (Tees and Tyne) Infantry Division. At 1435, the commander of the leading tank, Lieutenant K. Heathcote, ordered: "Driver, advance!" and the armoured rush was on.

The barrage moved on at 200 yards a minute, and the tanks roared on behind it, towards the frontier of Holland just ahead. The first stretch of ground beside the road was marshy; the next stretch was thickly wooded—good for infantry, bad for tanks. Infantry and armour of 50 Division were to do what they could on either side of the road, while the Irish Guards advanced down the ruler-straight embanked road in the centre. In the smoke and dust of the howling barrage, the leading tanks several times ran into their own shellfire and this saved them.

No. 3 Squadron, supported by the infantry of No. 1 Company, reported: "Advance going well." But behind them, just as they crossed the frontier, the German gunners they had bypassed came to life. Amazingly unshaken by the fire of 300 guns, they opened up with deadly accuracy on the following squadrons. In two minutes, nine tanks went up in flames—half a mile of roadway was littered with their burning hulks. As the survivors leapt from the turrets they were cut down by small-arms fire.

The following tanks edged into what cover they could find, while the infantry riding on them were off in an instant and into the ditches. There was no telling where the fire was coming from until Lance Sergeant Cowan's tank spotted and knocked out a self-propelled gun and took the crew prisoner. Having seen so many of their friends killed only minutes before, they were in a bad temper and the German prisoners talked, pointing out the positions of the various guns. Now was the time for the Typhoons, circling above in their "cab rank" and waiting for orders. In the next hour, they flew 230 sorties in support of the Guards. The historian of the Household Cavalry was to write:

"To those of us who were, as yet, onlookers, the sudden dive, followed seconds later by a terrifying hiss ending in the dull roar of an explosion, was shattering enough. To the enemy, sheltering in their trenches or behind their gun shields, the effect must have been appalling."

Two hundred yards behind the exploding rockets came the Guards, in a savage mood. "I have never seen Guardsmen so angry, nor officers. The Krauts got rough treatment that day," wrote an officer witness. Typhoons and bad temper took the attacking infantrymen on, while the armour worked past the smoking red-hot hulls of nine Shermans. The medium guns were down to their last rounds of ammunition—the remainder being still on the wrong side of the Seine, hundreds of miles away. But at 1730 the Guards had the bridge just outside Valkenswaard, and they were into the burning town just after dark.

The streets were filled with Dutch civilians shouting themselves hoarse, Germans still fighting, Germans trying to get back to Germany, and Germans coming in to help the garrison, including two men on bicycles who had been sent to get news of the American parachutists near Eindhoven. Shortly afterwards, the German commander at Eindhoven telephoned a message to the commander at Valkenswaard, telling him to hold on, and this message was duly delivered by the mayor's clerk to Guards' HQ.

The Guards then opened up contact with Eindhoven via the Dutch telephone operators, but all that could be learned was that the Germans still held it and there was no sign of American parachutists. On the other hand, the Guards had definitely identified their immediate opponents as I and III battalions of Fallschirmjäger Regiment 6, plus two battalions of 9 S.S. Panzer Division, the latter being quite unexpected. The historian of the Irish Guards wrote:

"Intelligence spent the day in a state of indignant surprise: one German regiment after another appeared which had no right to be there."

Horrocks had hoped to reach Eindhoven, six miles north of Valkenswaard, on the first day; but the airborne timings had made his first day only 10 hours long instead of 24 hours, the opposition was much stronger than had been expected, and the path that had been cut through it was little more than one road wide. On either side of the road, as darkness fell, what the weakened Irish Guards wryly called the "bazooka boys" were still active. An advance through the night, when tanks that were almost blind became increasingly vulnerable, particularly if the crews were drugged with weariness, lack of food, and sleep, would have been hazardous.

What had been possible on several occasions during the Normandy break-out was no longer so, and this was only partly due to unfavourable terrain. The main reasons stemmed from the basic drawbacks to the blitzkrieg technique—while ever-lengthening lines of communication tend to attenuate the attacker's striking power, the defender is simultaneously being driven nearer and nearer his base depots, dumps, and reinforcements, and taking desperate measures to improvise fresh units. In the case of Market Garden, the attackers were driving into a narrow salient between Germany itself on the right hand and the 250,000 German fortress troops in coastal Holland on the left hand. Speed was vital, but both terrain and the enemy were likely to impose delays.

News of the results of the airborne landings was important to the ground forces, but at 2100 hours on September 17 Guards Armoured Division was still relying mainly on intercepted enemy broadcasts, which implied successful drops. The air force reported that all bridges on the main axis of advance were still intact and unblown at 1500 hours, but anything could have happened after that. Late in the evening it was reported that 101 U.S. Division had taken its objectives between Eindhoven and Grave, and that 82 U.S. Division had captured the great Maas bridge at Grave, as well as bridges over the Maas–Waal Canal, but had failed to reach the Waal bridges at Nijmegen. 1 British Airborne Division was close to the Neder Rijn bridges at Arnhem and holding one end of the road bridge. It was not clear whether or not the Waal and Neder Rijn bridges had been blown.

The mounting of such an airborne operation in daylight had been considered very risky, and the soldiers had had first to win a battle with their own air arms in order to get a daylight operation at all. Up to and including Normandy, the Allies had used the cover of night for all large-scale airborne operations. This was the first time that they were to attempt anything comparable to the German invasion of the Low Countries in 1940, and the planners had steeled themselves to accept losses of transports and gliders of up to 30 percent. If this occurred, far fewer aircraft would be available for the second and third "lifts" and the supply runs; and reinforcement and supply of the airborne troops would be slowed. If losses were higher than estimated, then some of the reinforcements would never even leave their airfields; like the Germans in 1940, there would be no aircraft remaining with which to fly them into the battles.

But the results were astounding. Losses of transports and gliders en route were only 2·8 percent of the force employed on the first lift. Similarly low were the losses of bombers and fighters. The American official historian calculated the total number of aircraft sent off as 4,676 transports, gliders, bombers, and fighters, and states that only 75 failed to get through to their targets. From the air point of view, the operation had been a brilliant success, as well as the largest of its kind ever carried out up to that time or afterwards.

From the soldier's point of view, the accuracy achieved in the drops was astounding; without exception, the best ever of any operation or exercise. The U.S. 101 Division reported a "parade ground jump"; the U.S. 82 Division reported "without exception" the best landings they had experienced; and the landings of 1 British Airborne Division were almost 100 percent. More than 20,000 parachute and glider-borne troops had been landed behind the enemy lines in less than an hour and a half.

But in what really counted—the capture of the Rhine bridges—the seeds of disaster were already sown. Only the Mass bridge at Grave was securely in Allied hands. This was the nearest of the three major bridges. But resistance at Nijmegen had proved too strong for the Americans, and the town itself, both river banks, and both Waal bridges were firmly held by the Germans. The airborne plan has been criticised as being partly responsible. At Arnhem, certainly because of a defective divisional plan and not because of initial strong resistance by the Germans, the rail bridge over the Neder Rijn had already been blown, but only after a long delay had the paratroopers managed to reach the north end of the road bridge. That delay was to be critical, because the Germans managed to rush reinforcements across it to Nijmegen before the British paratroops cut the road at the north end. So one end of this bridge was now British, the other end German.

After Normandy, Guards Armoured Division had reorganised in a less musclebound way, so that it now consisted of four battle groups controlled by two brigade headquarters. Under 5 Brigade were the Grenadier Group and the Coldstream Group, usually known as "Group Hot" and "Group Cold", and under 32 Brigade were the Irish Group and the Welsh Group. Each battle group consisted of one armoured battalion and one infantry battalion of the same regiment, which always worked in cooperation.

The term "regiment" is used here in the British sense; that is, a method of recruiting from specific localities in order to give some colour and tradition to battalions, the number of battalions being limited only by the man-power potential of the area. Most English regiments were raised on a county basis, but the Guards, being the Household troops, were special in many ways. In peacetime, they provided the "fuss and feathers" so loved by the English for so long (and the despair of tank enthusiasts between the wars); and their social stratification was extreme, almost a parody of the English class system, in that there was virtually no "middle" to connect the other ranks with the officers, who were drawn mostly from the aristocracy, old and new.

There are many ways of producing effective fighting units, and this appears to be one of them. In any event, the Irish Group that had broken through the best part of four good German battalions on the road to Valkenswaard had consisted only of two under-strength battalions of Irish Guards—the 1st and the 2nd, being infantry and armour respectively.

The new organisation of the division was sufficiently flexible to make full use of the blitzkrieg technique when the terrain allowed. By far the fastest method of advance is on a number of parallel routes and not on a single road, which tends to become one large, non-fighting traffic jam, although it is easier to control. Once beyond the marshes and woods of Valkenswaard, there appeared to be opportunities for an advance along more than one road, and on Monday, September 18, as soon as the mist cleared, the armoured cars of the Household Cavalry were sent out far ahead to reconnoitre routes for the tanks, which were given two main axes of advance—north to Eindhoven and east towards Leende, Geldrop, and Helmond.

There were no real motorways in the area, most roads were country roads spanned by country bridges, the capacity of which was not known. Nor were the opposing German units known, let alone their dispositions, except for reports by Dutchmen that proved far more reliable than information previously obtained from Frenchmen and Belgians, who almost invariably multiplied the Germans by 10. The Guards had got into the habit of automatically dividing such "statistics" by five, and so were not used to the coldly detailed accuracy of some Dutch civilian reports. But the Dutch could report only what was already in the area; they could not know of fresh German units about to enter the battle.

The Allies had been doubly unfortunate to begin with, in the choice of their main opponents. Most of the German forces came under Army Group B, commanded by Field Marshal Model, and one of his senior commanders was General Student. Finding 20,000 airborne troops dropped on one's lines of communications on a Sunday morning might have shaken an ordinary general, and the resulting orders might well have been confused. But Model had the nickname of "the Führer's Fireman," gained on the Russian front, where he had a reputation for dealing coldly and effectively with apparently disastrous situations. And Student was the pioneer of airborne forces, the original expert on their strengths and weaknesses. Even so, German reaction might not have been so rapid and effective had not these two outstanding commanders been convinced, literally from the first minute, of the seriousness and extent of the Allied attacks.

Model's headquarters were in a country hotel just outside Arnhem, beside the dropping zones of 1 British Airborne Division, and he escaped from the hotel only just in time, his servants leaving a trail of burst suitcases behind them as they fled. Very shortly afterwards, the field commandant of Arnhem, Major General Kussin, was shot dead. Student's headquarters were at Vught, just south of 's Hertogenbosch, giving an unrivalled view of both streams of transports passing south and north. It was clear that this was no feint, indeed Student's main sensation at the sight was envy—what could he have done with resources like that?

Two hours later, the operation order for Market Garden was lying on his desk—taken from the body of an American officer in a wrecked Waco glider that had crashed nearby. Student was not too surprised at this carelessness; it had happened to him in 1940, when, against all orders, a German officer had carried his own operations order into battle and it had fallen into Dutch hands.

The German appreciation was that XXX Corps was the main enemy; if that corps could be slowed, stopped, or cut off, the lightly armed airborne troops would become merely a minor nuisance. This was based on their own experience of such operations and was undoubtedly correct. Therefore, on the first day they reinforced Nijmegen and began to take measures to bring pressure to bear all along the flanks of the Allied operation, as far south as the Escaut Canal bridgehead.

On September 18, 50 British Infantry Division held off the bridgehead attacks, but farther north around Veghel German probing attacks began to come in, light at first, and nervously conducted, because the Germans did not know the enemy situation either and were afraid of being caught and crushed by the British armour while dealing with the lightly armed Americans. Later, when their own armour arrived, they became much more confident; the heaviest fighting took place some days later.

This then was the situation when the Household Cavalry moved out of Valkenswaard on September 18. The countryside being wooded and the morning misty, they tended to bump opposition at close range; this varied from a case of one Panther and two self-propelled guns to many cases of bazookas fired by determined infantry from the hedges. The tactics were for the surviving cars of the squadron to "loop," with one troop going west and one troop going east in search of an easier passage that ended, often as not, in a bridge too light to bear even the weight of an armoured car. Nevertheless, by continually dodging down sideroads, one or two troops of the regiment were almost bound to get through. Two did in fact manage it at widely separated points.

Lieutenant Palmer's troop included a scout car carrying an American sergeant with a wireless set. At first they were baffled by fragile wooden bridges; then they met scattered but surprised enemy and burst through them; and eventually linked up with 101 U.S. Airborne Division at Woensel, north of Eindhoven, where they met the division's second-in-command, Brigadier Gerald J. Higgins.

His news was not good. The northern approaches to Eindhoven were still in enemy hands and the important road bridge across the Wilhelmina Canal at Zon had been blown when two separate American units had managed to get within 50 yards of it. There had been some confusion about objectives here, and it was possible that the bridge could have been taken. However, the Americans now had both banks of the canal, the assault on the enemy-held bank having been carried out by a swimming force consisting entirely of Major James L. LaPrade (a battalion commander of the 506th U.S. Parachute Infantry Regiment), a lieutenant, and a sergeant.

Their initiative had been followed up by a waterborne assault force that had found a rowing boat and requisitioned it to carry reinforcements across. The opposition consisted of some Germans in a house on the south bank. Shortly afterwards, the airborne engineers constructed a footbridge and then began preparatory measures for re-bridging. Of course, they knew exactly the size of the bridging problem it presented and, via the Household Cavalry, were now in wireless contact with Guards Armoured Division. A number of messages were passed.

First, the fundamental fact: "Stable boys have contacted our Feathered Friends"—"Stable Boys" being the most polite description normally used by the Foot Guards to designate the Household Cavalry.

Next, technical bridging details from the parachute engineers, including the primary fact: The gap to be bridged was approximately 100 feet.

This message went straight to Brigadier C. P. Jones, the CRE, who passed the query: "Will 110 feet of class-40 Bailey fill the bill?" In a surprisingly short time the American reply was received: "Yes."

This enabled Brigadier Jones to call forward to Valkenswaard, along the traffic-jammed roads from the Escaut, the exact number of cumbersome vehicles required for this particular task.

At 1400 hours came the wireless message: "For your information, U.S. Airborne telephone number is Zon 244." This was service indeed, and on ringing Zon 244, Guards Armoured Division found that they had got a doctor on the line. After welcoming them to Holland, the Dutchman brought an American officer to the telephone, and the Guards put an officer of the Royal Engineers on the other end; between them they finalized the bridging operation in theory.

All that had got through so far was a troop of armoured cars. The advance was going at no more than walking pace, because the roads were bordered by terrain similar to that between the Escaut and Valkenswaard, where a handful of well-sited 88s, self-propelled guns, and tanks could hold up much superior numbers. The Irish Guards asked for air support and the reply came: "No Typhoons available yet today." This may have been because of the weather, which was holding up the next lifts due to fly over from England, and the possibility of the 2nd Tactical Air Force's inadvertently getting in the way. Yet it was vital to the entire operation to get on quickly.

Therefore the Grenadier Guards battle group was sent to

try the western route discovered by Lieutenant Taylor's troop, cross the same bridge over the de Run River, and get on to Eindhoven at top speed. The first troop of tanks to reach it was commanded by Lieutenant P. G. A. Prescott (now lieutenant-colonel, commanding the 2nd Grenadier Guards in Germany).

"My troop led the Squadron down a narrow road across some very open flat country [he recalled]. I came to a dyke some 20 feet across with banks about 6 feet deep with what appeared plenty of water in it. The bridge, of wooden construction, looked very weak, so I stopped my tank short of it, got out and had a look. The bridge did not appear likely to take the weight of my tank. I remounted and reported this to the Squadron Leader. He was of course some way back, not at the site, and also a most forceful and brilliant leader. I was told fairly abruptly that the cavalry had reported it suitable for tanks, and so would I please get on with it! I therefore told my driver to take the bridge as fast as he could in order to get to the other side. This could have been a mistake, for if we had crept over it we might have set up less vibration. As we reached the centre, I felt the bridge subside a bit, but we got over without it collapsing. However, as I looked back I saw a gap at each end about a foot wide and also that the bridge was sagging badly in the middle. My troop sergeant was following some 50 yards back, and I told him over the radio not to attempt it. But by then he was just about on it. On reaching the centre, the bridge finally broke and his tank subsided into the water, on its side and half submerged. Luckily, all the crew escaped."

That Sherman, lying on its side in the water among the ruins of a wooden bridge, when taken together with the lack of air support along the better roads, adequately sums up the reasons for delay; and also makes clear, from the "press on regardless" tone of Prescott's orders, that a lack of a sense of urgency among the ground troops cannot be numbered among the delaying factors.

Prescott was now alone on the wrong side of one bridge and Lieutenant Palmer's troop was blocked both ways, because of the blowing of Zon bridge. The U.S. 101 Airborne Division had landed in compact groups north of Eindhoven and south of Nijmegen and their primary responsibility was 15 miles of road, which they were later to call "Hell's Highway." They had captured most of this on September 17, and on September 18, while advancing south to Eindhoven, were principally worried about events on the western flank. General Student's headquarters at Vught were only a short distance away to the north-west, and he was sending units into the fight as they became available. Consequently, Palmer's troops were sent to support some hard-pressed Americans, fought alongside them until dusk, and then evacuated the paratroops on the armoured cars.

A similar fight—it may even have been the same fight—was witnessed by Pastor Willi Schiffer, then serving with a Fallschirmjäger battalion that Student had ordered into action on the afternoon of the previous day. On September 18 they came down the railway track from Schijndel towards the station at Eerde, south-west of Veghel.

"The heavy-weapons companies were held back, while the light infantry companies walked straight into the machine-gun fire of the Americans who were hiding in the station [he recalled]. In a bitter man-to-man fight, the Americans were driven away and we went on along the railway track. Supported by flak guns brought up from 's Hertogenbosch, we finally collected enough troops to attack the railway bridge in front of Veghel, which we took in the afternoon. Shortly afterwards, to our complete consternation, we received orders to withdraw! What had happened? The Battalion HQ and HQ Company, which had remained in Schijndel, had been attacked by armoured cars, operating singly, from the direction of St. Oedenrode, and they were afraid that an attack would now follow into our flank. Their fears were groundless, as it was several days before larger units could be brought forward by both sides, and the real battle began. But the very next day a Regiment of our 59th Infantry Division had to retrace the path we had already taken, and were wiped out."

As Lieutenant Palmer's route had proved useless for tanks, the major effort by the Guards was being made on the main road to Eindhoven. The opposition broke at about 1800 hours on September 18, and Brigadier Jones radioed for the bridging equipment. The Americans by then had cleared most of Eindhoven, and the Guards drove straight through without stopping until they reached Zon and the blown bridge. Although their formal objective for September 17 had been merely Valkenswaard, they had hoped to reach Eindhoven on the first day and link up there with the Americans. But no one had got to Eindhoven on the first day, and the link-up had not occurred until the evening of September 18, approximately one day behind time.

The American failure to capture the bridge at Zon now caused further delay, but this was mitigated by the speed with which the canal was bridged. Brigadier Jones reached Zon before the bridging convoy, which arrived at 1930, and promised the divisional commander that the first vehicle could cross at 0600 hours next morning. The estimate was not quite accurate. The first armoured car rolled over the new bridge at 0615 hours on September 19, followed by 5 Guards Brigade.

With most of the key points along the road held by Americans, Nijmegen was now only a few hours' drive away. But probably because the area of 101 U.S. Airborne Division was comparatively secure, General Brereton was to divert to it resources actually intended for 82 U.S. Division, which needed them far more. Possibly correct from the aviation point of view, this further emphasised the inherent imbalance of the air plan. The more exposed the division, the less it got in the way of air transport, reinforcement, and supply. 1 British Airborne Division at Arnhem, 70 miles from the Escaut, was given so little that it was flown-in in dribs and drabs, a procedure that has been described as like feeding Oxo-cubes to a lion one by one. Now 82 U.S. Airborne Division at Nijmegen was to be cut down in favour of 101 U.S. Airborne Division, which, at Eindhoven, was a mere dozen or so miles from the Escaut bridgehead.

To make matters worse, the weather clamped down and nearly half the reinforcements either returned to England or were lost. This was particularly serious, because it was mostly artillery units that were affected; of 66 guns despatched to help the paratroops repel heavy attacks, only 36 guns arrived, and these were all the lighter pieces up to 75 millimeters. The Luftwaffe, however, was less affected by the weather and put up 125 fighters, so that the advancing columns had clear evidence that things were going wrong. This was to make the subsequent battle for Nijmegen extremely bitter.

It would not be true to say that battle has been forgotten. It never took place, because while it was being fought, the bulk of the war correspondents were still back in Brussels. On their way to Nijmegen, the Guards passed close to a truly forgotten battlefield—Boxtel, south of Vught, through which Student was funnelling part of his forces towards the "corridor." That also had been a September battle, in the year 1794, when the British had been trying to hold back the armies of Revolutionary France.

A defeat had been avoided by the steadiness and discipline of the 33rd Regiment of Foot, commanded by Colonel Arthur Wellesley, fighting his first action. Afterwards, while speaking to the wounded, he came across the right-hand man of the Grenadier Company, Private Thomas Atkins, a soldier of 20 years' service, dying of bayonet and bullet wounds. "It's all right, sir," Atkins had gasped. "It's all in the day's work." Fifty years later, as the Duke of Wellington and commander-in-chief of the British Army, he was asked to approve a new pay form on which a name typical of the common soldier was to be entered as a model. To the surprise of the staff officer who had brought the form, Wellington remained some time in thought. His last battle, that of Waterloo, was now history, but his mind went back to a canal and a line of windmills by Boxtel. "Private Thomas Atkins" was the name he chose.

CHAPTER ELEVEN

NIJMEGEN—THE 1944 SOLUTION

82 U.S. Division: September 17–18

The war correspondents (newspaper and radio) were rationed at the rate of two per airborne division. The 101st U.S. were allotted two Americans; the 1st British, two British; while the 82nd U.S. had one American and one British, because Lt.-General F. A. M. Browning and advance elements of the Airborne Corps HQ were to jump with Major General James M. Gavin and his men. The pair with the 82nd were William F. ("Bill") Boni, now executive sports editor of the *St. Paul Dispatch and Pioneer Press*, St. Paul, Minnesota, and Cyril Ray, then representing the B.B.C., later of the *Spectator* and *Sunday Times*, and now of the *Observer*. Both were to come in by glider with the first lift on Sunday, September 17. Their reactions to the news were very different.

Bill Boni had had two previous briefings, both with the 101st, both "scrubbed"; one had been a drop outside Paris, the other on canal crossings at the Franco-Belgian border. Now he was to go with the 82nd instead, and to Holland. On the briefing maps were familiar names—Grave, Groesbeek, Berg en Dal, Beek, Wyler. . . . "I remember the captain was tracing his pencil over the area where we were to land, and I thought to myself, 'Good Lord, that's where my grandmother used to take me for excursions when I was a little boy.' I was born in Holland, and she lived in Nijmegen. . . ."

Cyril Ray was a seasoned correspondent (Bill Boni calls him "a fearless little bastard"). He was with the Navy at first, serving with Lord Louis Mountbatten's trouble-prone destroyers and later at the North African landings. He had covered the Eighth Army up Italy, taking in the vicious battle of Ortona in a participant role as well as that of correspondent, and had been mentioned in dispatches for leading a platoon of Canadians that had lost all its officers and NCOs. This could hardly have happened in the British Army, but he points out that the Canadians were more individualistic than the British, and would "have a go."

He had spent Christmas, 1943, in a house with German parachutists living next door, a knife-edge situation, for so vicious was the street fighting in Ortona that no one fought in the streets any more—they blew their way forward from house to house, "mouseholing," and every house entered had to be taken room by room. He had not forgotten Ortona, nor the Ardennes, which he covered later, but found the battle, south-east of Nijmegen hard to remember.

"I was sour on it. For me, the whole of Market Garden was a dead flop. I had been due to go to Arnhem, but was taken out of that and sent with the Americans. I was the only Englishman there, except for Corps HQ. I felt sure that the British had had it, and before I was switched to Nijmegen, felt that my goose was cooked. Then came this anti-climax, with the Americans. I felt this was a much safer option, and meanwhile all the chaps at Arnhem were dead ducks. Lots of people knew Arnhem was wrong, at the time. Browning told me that he said to Montgomery that it was "one bridge too far," when Monty had first explained the operation. It was uncharacteristic of Monty; he was starved in favour of Patton, and resented it, I think. Horrocks also seemed to act out of character, the 'beau sabreur' apparently dawdling his way up to Arnhem. Urquhart was very sarcastic about that in his book.

"As for the battle around Wyler and Groesbeek, I don't remember it clearly. The 82nd was a good division, extremely professional, but approached the battle like blood-thirsty boy scouts, armed to the teeth. Grenades hanging all over them. Our gliders landed in the centre of a circle held by paratroops who'd dropped previously. The American soldiers stormed out of the gliders, armed to the teeth, and met two cows and a Dutch farmer. Then they started to dig in, a peaceful landscape and warlike soldiers. But a most un-Dutch landscape of hills and woods. I went and found a pretty country hotel, and when the proprietor and his daughter came out of the cellars I bagged the honeymoon suite. I could then go and tell Bill Boni we were fixed up."

"The landing I can recall as having been made in what had been a turnip field," said Bill Boni. "Much of it was ploughed soil, and that was the part where our glider landed, with relatively little incident. The lieutenant in charge of a recon platoon offered to take us along, since he was going out to look for stray Germans." The offer was declined, because both correspondents needed to find someone with a wireless set who could transmit a news flash for them. At General Browning's HQ, a British major let them scribble two brief messages and, tucking them in his blouse, promised to have them transmitted. Boni continued:

"I believe that we landed in the Groesbeek area, but it was on a sand road through the woods, north of there and running from the Mook-Nijmegen highway towards Berg en Dal, that we found this little hotel. There we re-encountered the recon lieutenant, with quite a cluster of POWs. On the day we landed there was, actually, very little gunfire we were aware of. Later, we busied ourselves digging foxholes when it became clear (or should I say audible) that there would be some shelling by 88s. Not that I had any particularly stirring experiences myself. But I can remember sitting on the basement steps of the little hotel while a soldier named Freddy told us how he'd brought back a baby from a patrol they had made into the nearest little German settlement at Wyler, simply because it was alone, abandoned, and crying. I believe he turned it over to a Dutchwoman for care. It was certainly on the second day the artillery, reinforcements and supplies came in, and I can recall with reasonable vividness standing in the shelter of the woods watching the formations of Dakotas [C-47s, to us] coming over in unbroken Vs in the face of considerable anti-aircraft fire from the direction chiefly of the Reichswald."

Cyril Ray, an experienced and unbiased witness, thought it unlikely that the British public would "appreciate that the best-trained and most professional airborne unit engaged in the operation of which Arnhem was a part was the United States 82nd Division which landed at Nijmegen." And he points out that 1 British Airborne Division was both "insufficiently trained in street-fighting and under a commander it didn't know."

As the direct result of a bad plan, it got itself involved in street-fighting and the resulting delays allowed the Germans to send reinforcements south over the road bridge on the first day, which were to intervene with decisive effect against the 82nd on the Sunday evening; and the subsequent disintegration of the entire division was to allow the Germans to send further reinforcements south over the road bridge to hold up XXX Corps. As Ray remarks, "We tart up our reverses so heroically that it takes an effort to grasp that Arnhem was not merely a British defeat, but a German victory."

The 82nd had some advantages over the 1st British. They got a much larger share of the available lift, and the bulk of the division, less one regiment and the bulk of the artillery, came in to Nijmegen together; however, had they been heavily counter-attacked by tanks, the diversion of the bulk of their second lift to the already secure positions of the 101st might have had awkward results.

Although they did not have such heavy anti-tank guns as the British, there being no American gliders large enough to carry them, the 82nd had a great advantage in communications—their radio sets worked. But the real American superiority lay in the smooth working that comes only from long experience under the same leaders, a principle that applies to every kind of organisation, warlike or peaceful, from banks to parachute brigades. Orders were generally verbal and the minimum necessary, which is bad from the historian's point of view afterwards, but at the time is a priceless asset.

There was one other major difference that was profoundly to affect the fate of both divisions. This lay in the intelligence estimates of the enemy forces available for counter-attack near the drop zones. Both were wrong, of course, but wrong in profoundly different ways. Although SHAEF had heard reports of two S.S. Panzer divisions being stationed near Arnhem, this information was quite definitely not available at the level of the division concerned; the British did not expect to meet armour in any quantity.

On the other hand, unsubstantiated reports of a massive build-up of German armour in the Reichswald Forest, bordering the American drop zones south-east of Nijmegen, had come from Dutch sources. There was one mention of 1,000 tanks. And even if the tried and tested method of dividing by 10 was employed, this still gave 100 tanks; and against parachutists minus most of their artillery such a force could be formidable.

According to the American official history, this information became "a major and pressing element in the predrop picture of German forces." Therefore, in considering the operational decisions, it must be borne in mind that the British planned in the belief that they would not meet armoured forces, while the Americans planned on the basis that they might encounter substantial numbers of tanks.

It must further be remembered that this was 1944, not 1940. The Dutch had had no tanks, no self-propelled guns, and only a handful of armoured cars. Indeed, the self-propelled gun was a war-time development, largely improvised by putting a large-calibre gun on the chassis of a tank designed to take a much smaller gun in a revolving turret. The gun of an S.P. would not traverse 360 degrees, so it was not a tank; it was merely an efficient method of getting a large gun to go cross-country and into action without the tiresome travail of stopping everything, unlimbering the gun, turning it round, and generally offering an inviting and cumbersome target to all and sundry.

The Dutch artillery had been slow in getting into action against the German parachutists, precisely because of this difficulty. That the self-propelled gun was a very different proposition was soon to be convincingly demonstrated. In 1944, the artillery component of armoured divisions normally consisted of such mobile tracked and armoured guns.

In one respect only were the British and American plans similar. The object of the whole operation was to gain control of the road from Nijmegen to Arnhem by capturing the Waal bridges at Nijmegen and the Neder Rijn bridges at Arnhem; but no attempt was made by either division to seize these bridges instantly by *coup de main*. It will be recalled that the Germans had tried (and failed) to take these identical objectives in 1940 by variations of the "Trojan Horse" theme; and that those bridges that were really vital were taken by simultaneous attack from both ends, as at Moerdijk, or by seaplanes actually landing in the river, as at Rotterdam. This was the original book of airborne warfare, as written by General Student. Why were these lessons disregarded?

As far as the 82nd were concerned, General Gavin was a firm believer in the principle of landing on both sides of a bridge, as close to it as possible, even if this meant heavy losses; because landing far away and then walking up to the target was bound to mean even heavier losses, and probable failure. For this reason both he and other commanders in the 82nd had doubts, to put it mildly, about the chances of British success at Arnhem. Cyril Ray was not the only person to feel that that operation was doomed.

But as far as the 82nd was concerned, the real threat was believed to lie in the Reichswald, and not on the "Island" between Nijmegen and Arnhem. Gavin thought so himself, and Browning agreed. An armoured attack out of the Reichswald would take the entire Market Garden operation in flank; not merely Gavin's division, but XXX Corps as well. This was the underlying appreciation.

Equally important was the fact that, as the Germans had found in 1940, the Nijmegen area was awkward to attack, in that a concentration of force would achieve little except the blowing of the bridges by the enemy, and that the solution, if there was one, was to scatter the attack force in terms of space so as to attack as many different objectives as possible at the same time. This was Gavin's solution, too, although his means were different; and, like the Germans in 1940, he had insufficient resources to attack simultaneously at all points and was therefore compelled to draw up a priority list, on which the Waal bridges came bottom.

In 1940, the Germans had wanted the high ground south-east of Nijmegen, at least one bridge over the Maas–Waal Canal, the bridge over the Maas at Grave, and, if possible, the road bridge over the Waal. They had taken the high ground easily, and simultaneously three bridges over the Maas–Waal Canal at Heumen, Malden, and Hatert (but losing Malden to counter-attack), had failed to take the vital Grave bridge, and failed at the Waal bridges also, although these were not vital.

Gavin saw the situation in almost exactly the same light and these were his objectives also. He got the high ground, the bridge at Heumen (which he calls Molenhook), and the bridge at Grave on the first day, doing much better than the German 254 Infantry Division in 1940, because Grave bridge over the 800-foot-wide Maas was much more important than any of the bridges over the 200-foot-wide Maas–Waal Canal. Although he had the advantage of airborne troops, whereas the Germans could call only on a handful of ersatz "Fifth Columnists" from Special Battalion 100, Gavin was not operating next door to the borders of the United States, his division was 60 miles or so inside enemy territory with lines of communication that were exclusively airborne. This meant that for re-supply and reinforcement, he had to have an air-head.

His solution was to site this on the high ground between Nijmegen and the Reichswald, which he regarded as the key to the whole area. The 300-foot elevations here dominated both the Waal and the Maas–Waal Canal, and also blocked off any attack from over the German border, either from the Reichswald itself or along the Kleve–Kranenburg road that fringes Holland at Wyler and runs at the foot of the high ground through the border at Beek directly to the road bridge at Nijmegen. This was to be the eastern flank of his division.

The western flank lay around the bridge at Grave, and the Maas–Waal Canal ran almost north-south and almost through the centre of the divisional area, so that at least one bridge there had to be taken to ensure the internal communications of the division. Compared to these objectives, Gavin judged the Waal bridges less vital.

Although he considered several plans for taking the road bridge from the area of the airhead, if conditions allowed, no forces were available to drop on either side of the road bridge, or even merely on the Lent side of the river, where the ground favoured defence and was difficult for tanks. The objection was that if the bridge was taken but the high ground lost, the bridge was useless because it was dominated by the high ground. Remembering the possible threat from the Reichswald, plus the difficult country to be traversed by XXX Corps, the 82nd had to be prepared to fight a heavy battle alone for possibly three or four days.

Although the area of the Market Garden operation was

generally unfavourable for armoured warfare, it was "pre-eminently suitable" for airborne forces, in Gavin's opinion. "Parachutists can land in pretty rough terrain. Their greatest obstacles are tall timber and deep marshes and flooded areas." This gave considerable flexibility to the attack and to the selection of the airhead, which should theoretically be sited actually on the main target so that reinforcements and supplies go directly to where they are wanted within an area that has to be defended anyway for tactical reasons.

Gavin's choice was in accordance with this principle, whereas the British 1 Airborne Division plan breached it entirely, their drop zones being far from the target and of no tactical importance, so that they had to fight two battles instead of one over a much larger area than necessary, with far fewer forces than Gavin had. It is hardly surprising that re-supply to their airhead failed, because the delivery of this vital tonnage by air is always difficult. The enemy may be taken by surprise by the initial landings, but expects the follow-up; and in this case, as German units were still holding out in the Pas de Calais, they would receive early and accurate warning of all the succeeding lifts as they crossed the coast.

On the night of September 16, 82nd Division held a question-and-answer conference of the regimental and battalion commanders, in which each officer outlined his own plan and was then questioned by the others as to what he would do to contact them, what he would do if his unit was landed in the wrong place, and what he thought the most important points were. In this way, each commander gained a thorough knowledge of what everyone else intended to do, so that he could do it himself if necessary and there would be proper coordination whatever happened. As Gavin wrote, "airborne units are beyond correction and control for some time; everything must be right the first time." As far as the soldiers were concerned, wrote Gavin, the veterans were "calm, businesslike and quiet." Although their "apprehension and concern was no less than that of the recruits, they seemed to show it less. The young troopers seemed to talk more, they jitterbugged, they yelled and shouted and generally displayed more levity than they usually did. Perhaps it was a subconscious yet ostentatious manifestation of courage; perhaps it was camouflage for a deep-seated concern and worry over the outcome of the impending battle. The veterans thought the latter. . . ."

The first lift consisted of 482 transport aircraft carrying the 504th, 505th, and 508th Parachute Infantry regiments as well as HQ units, plus 50 gliders carrying mainly HQ units plus the 80th Antitank Battalion for defence of the landing zones. The total of personnel was 7,477. Next day, the second lift, consisting of 450 gliders carrying mainly artillery, were to land inside the airhead on the hillslopes from Wyler to Mook —that is, within the tactical perimeter already encircling the top-priority target of the division. The two regiments that landed there on September 17 were to undertake two additional tasks—the capture of bridges over the Maas–Waal Canal and a quick dash to the Nijmegen road bridge, if it could be managed.

Colonel Reuben H. Tucker's 504th Regiment had the task of dropping to the west of the Maas–Waal Canal and taking the big Maas bridge at Grave. Of his unit at that time, he wrote:

"The 504th Regimental combat team that jumped in Holland were all veterans of Sicily and approximately 9 months fighting in Italy to include Anzio from D Day, 22 January, 1944 to 23 March—no breaks. It might be well to point out that many of us commanders felt that General Urquhart's troops stood a good chance of much trouble since they were jumping so far from their target, the bridges at Arnhem. Open space or not, we always planned to jump right on the target. The Div. Comdr.—General Gavin—told me he didn't care how I did it, but to get the bridge at Grave. I ordered E Company to jump on the south end of the bridge and the rest of the battalion on the north end. We had no clear DZs but landed on houses, churches, roads, ditches and wherever we came down—but no open fields. As a result of this direct action the 504th had control of its targets by 1800 hours, 17 September—four hours from the time we jumped from our planes."

This was a really big prize, the bridge at Grave that the Germans had failed to get in 1940, thus forcing a time-wasting diversion of 9 Panzer Division in its drive to link up with the corridor of airborne troops holding the key bridges from Moerdijk to Rotterdam. But the 504th had other subsidiary targets—the bridges over the Maas–Waal Canal at Heumen, Malden, Hatert, and Neerbosch (which the American histories call Honinghutje).

Hatert was attacked by elements of both the 504th and the 508th, as were the Neerbosch bridges the following day. But the Germans blew both these bridges, although demolition was not complete at the northernmost and Neerbosch would be repairable. To the south, Malden bridge blew up in the faces of the attackers, but once again, as in 1940, the complicated lock-bridge at Heumen, the most southerly of all, fell to the assault. In 1940, it had fallen to a detachment of Special Battalion 100 consisting of four men dressed as Dutch gendarmes plus about 30 men posing as German deserters being escorted over by the gendarmes.

In 1944, the attacking force was in uniform and much larger, consisting of a company from the 504th under Captain Thomas B. Heldeson. They used the standard tactics of keeping the bridge swept by fire while creeping in on it. The buildings controlling the locks were on an island in midstream, and heavy return fire from Germans here held up the Americans until darkness allowed them to move in closer, get onto the bridge, and cut all wires they could find. This was the only bridge over the canal to be captured intact and was subsequently used by XXX Corps, although it involved a diversion from Grave over minor roads.

At the airhead there was almost no opposition as yet, merely cautious German reconnaissance followed up on the second day by attacks from units put together in a couple of hours from soldiers on leave, convalescents, Home Guards, etc., who had been told that the Americans had no artillery—indeed, the normal first reaction to an airborne landing. The Americans were probably better informed than the Germans, because they had a Dutch captain with them who immediately after landing found a civilian telephone and started to make a number of calls asking for information. Someone suggested by-passing all these Dutch civilians and putting through a personal call to the Führer himself, who would surely know best of all. After dark on September 17, General Gavin was startled to hear the loud wail of a locomotive whistle, as a train drove through his airhead less than 100 yards away and carried on merrily into Germany, without a shot fired. The next one was not so lucky.

Also on the evening of the first day, the first attempt was made on the road bridge at Nijmegen by a platoon from the 1st Battalion of Colonel Roy E. Linquist's 508th Regiment. The Dutch had reported that it was guarded by only 18 men. Because their radio failed, they simply vanished as far as Gavin was concerned. Later in the evening, Gavin ordered the complete 1st Battalion to try for the bridge. Members of the "Underground" promised to lead them there and said also that they knew the location of the building in Nijmegen that housed the apparatus for setting off the demolition charges. Companies A and B led off after dark, with Company C in reserve; B got lost, but A got as far as the main roundabout in the city centre, Keizer Karel Plein, before coming under fire.

The "Underground" vanished, as they so often did on these occasions, and General Gavin thinks that his men may have been betrayed to the Germans. However, it is just as likely that the "Resistance fighters" were boastful riffraff with a liking for self-importance, capable of little more than spitting on a German soldier's grave. There were many of these in the occupied countries, as well as better men.

As Company A were forming up to attack, a German motor convoy drove up through the streets on the opposite side of the roundabout, stopped, and with a clattering of boots and clank of equipment, the soldiers in the vehicles began to dismount. These may have been the armoured cars and armoured half-tracks of the reconnaissance unit of 9 S.S. Panzer Division, which Oberst Walter Harzer, commanding the remnants of this division, had sent across Arnhem bridge before the British were able to reach it and temporarily stop traffic. They were to reinforce S.S. Battalion "Euling," already in Nijmegen, which had just previously been transferred from the 9 S.S. to the 10 S.S. Panzer Division. It will be recalled that the latter was to be brought up to strength as soon as possible, while 9 S.S. was to be reduced to a skeleton and then transferred to Germany for complete re-building.

On September 17, it was no longer a division and was referred to merely as the "Battle Group Harzer." However, it was able to play a decisive—indeed the decisive—part in blocking Market Garden because Harzer was an energetic and canny officer who in true army style was holding a larger amount of effective armoured fighting vehicles than he was showing on his returns. Every quartermaster is familiar with this trick, but Harzer was no quartermaster, and the result was that the German armoured forces sited near Arnhem and Nijmegen on September 17 were larger and more effective than even the German High Command was aware.

Gavin was probably running his own version of this trick by holding ample forces in the 'airhead' just in case the threat from the Reichswald did materialise. The evidence available to him after landing was conflicting—and he chose to act on the basis of the more pessimistic reports, for which he can hardly be blamed. Had there been another Harzer on the Kleve–Kranenburg road, the 82nd would have been in trouble, and Gavin would have had to answer for the results. Indeed, one of the more amusing aspects of the pre-Market Garden arguments is Bradley's bitter complaint about Montgomery's asking for more American help and transport than he really needed, as if he had never in his life heard of the old Army rule: If you want 50 pens, ink, you indent for 100 pens, ink, and expect to get 25 pens, ink. The tragedy now beginning to evolve lay in the fact that the full number indented for really were required.

The 82nd did have a long, lightly held, sensitive front in the area of the airhead. The slopes and meadows nearest to the German border were fairly open, giving good fields of fire; but to the west of them were woods that could hide an army. If the Germans once got in there, it would be impossible for the troops available to get them out. It was a maze of trees and forest.

On September 18 the Germans launched their first dangerous counter-attack, over-running a company of the 508th holding the drop zone of Wyler where, a few hours later, the 450 gliders of the second lift were due to land, followed within minutes by the supply drop. It would take about one-third of the force to collect those supplies. The Americans regrouped to counter-attack only just in time, but although they drove the Germans off the landing zones, these were still under German small-arms fire.

Indeed, this was to be the front line during the winter of war still to come. So intricate, undulating, and wooded was it that when I visited it as a mere tourist in March, 1945, not merely the gliders and broken equipment were still there, but many of the dead also, still lying in and around the farm houses or up in the woods, with the odd live German still about to keep things moving. By then, it was a very horrible place. Everything, from slit trenches to corpses, appeared to be mined or booby-trapped.

It was on the morning of September 18 that the first genuine news came out of Arnhem, and by a peculiar route. Most of the British messages were not getting through because of defective wireless sets. This was a telephone message from the public utilities service of Arnhem, disguised as a technical report on power stations and waterworks, and made to a Dutch intelligence unit in the area of the 505th Regiment. The Americans noted it was: "Dutch Report Germans Winning over British at Arnhem."

But it was not before the morning of September 19, a day later, that the leading units of XXX Corps linked up with Colonel Tucker's Regiment at Grave. Both Bill Boni and Cyril Ray were there to see it. For Boni, it was a moment of disappointment, for he met the English major to whom he had entrusted the "hot" news that the 82nd had landed in Holland. "The major saw us coming and, even before we could ask, said (and I assure you this is not the typical American seeking to quote the typical Englishman): 'Oh, by jove, you chaps, I entirely forgot to send your signals.' "

What Ray principally remembered was the boy scout band from the village marching out to meet the tanks of Guards Armoured. Because scouting was forbidden by the Germans, they had hidden their uniforms since 1940; but they were bigger boys now, although the uniforms had not grown in the interval. Simply bursting out of their clothes, drums banging and fifes squealing, they went out to meet tanks garlanded with flowers and girls. Possibly it was the Royal Netherlands Brigade, who were usually given jobs of this sort for obvious reasons. Then, said Ray, "There was a great, jolly gathering of the CO and former COs of the 1st Grenadiers —Browning, Adair, and the current one."

Oddly, although Second Army appear to have been poorly informed on the state of affairs in Arnhem, an accurate estimate was available at HQ First Canadian Army, far back in the Pas de Calais, still fighting the battle for the ports. As early as September 20 I noted in my diary: "We learn from well-informed circles that the papers (as usual) had been laying on the bilge rather heavily in respect of the airborne invasion of Holland (the affair is going badly, whereas the papers say different)." It was then a fact that no war correspondent could tell the whole truth about any battle, or anything like it. Nevertheless, a great many people's historical judgements are still based on what they vaguely recall of what the censor let through 25 to 30 years ago, which was then embroidered by London journalists as the mood moved them.

In 1941, for instance, it was fashionable in London to "plug" the superiority of the German airborne forces. There were shrill demands that the British Army get with it and, like the Germans, employ world-class heavyweight boxers as paratroop officers. This particular item, which I still treasure, was based on lies told by German journalists that fooled even Göring. Years after, when I met the famous boxer in Hamburg (on a film set) I still believed he had been a hero of Crete and was surprised when he seemed uncomfortable at the mention of the place. The facts were that he had not been a company commander but merely a "number" on a mortar, and had spent the battle almost totally incapacitated for that most unromantic of reasons, dysentery.

Having experienced the full rigours of this in Normandy, I did not consider it in the least funny; although for a military historian it was an invaluable experience, particularly when considering campaigns such as Agincourt, for instance, as you knew exactly what the poor bastards were suffering and that it had nothing in common with anything experienced in civilian life. You also knew that it had nothing to do with lack of hygiene, a careless assumption all too easy to make regarding mediaeval armies.

Arnhem, even more than Dunkirk, was to get the full "build-up" treatment from the British press at the time and ever after. It is as if French naval historians claimed the Battle of Trafalgar as a French victory, largely because some of the beaten French ships fought with the utmost gallantry, which they did. Similar distortions of what really happened at Arnhem, when many survivors and contemporaries are still living, tend nowadays to produce a quiet rage among airborne people, particularly those who took part in successful actions with better divisions. Therefore, it must be said from the outset that the second Battle of Arnhem was a crushing defeat for the British and an unmitigated disaster for the Dutch.

CHAPTER TWELVE

"CHARING X" to "WATERLOO"

1 British Airborne Division: September 1–17

One feels the utmost sympathy with Major-General R. E. Urquhart, commander of 1 British Airborne Division. The division simply came apart in his hands as though it had been badly stuck together with glue. It was appalling and some aspects were quite unexpected.

A commander depends initially on the accuracy of the information he has about the enemy, and the information available to Urquhart was a farrago of nonsense that, insofar as it had any definite meaning at all, was untrue. A commander depends in the field on his communications, without which, quite literally, he cannot command; and Urquhart found himself 70 miles behind the enemy lines with wireless sets that, inexplicably, did not work. He could not control his division, nor could he radio his plight back to Second Army.

He then made what certainly appeared to be a correct decision—to try to control at least the brigade that had the top-priority task, the capture of the bridges—and as a result, like any sergeant, found himself cut off and hiding in a house with Germans outside the door. Nor could he rely on that supposedly "steady British infantry," which according to so many patriotic historians has so often in the past saved the day even for incompetent commanders, which Urquhart certainly was not. Almost immediately the advance into the town began, the outbreaks of indiscriminate firing showed the poor training of his troops; and he was to witness a frightful panic led by an officer flying from a non-existent enemy. He was to assign tasks to units that they should certainly have been able to carry out, and was to see them dissolve helplessly, generally not producing the least effect on the Germans, from bad leadership or poor training or, more usually, both combined.

Some of his battalions were so bad that afterwards the Germans declared that they felt sorry for them, as one would naturally for any group of hopeless, bungling incompetents. And yet for the German commander, Harzer, the main source of his pride in the victory he had won had lain in the means he had had to carry it out, for a large proportion of his infantry were not soldiers at all—they were railwaymen, labour corps workers, Luftwaffe aircrews and ground staff, men theoretically incapable of taking on trained infantry at street-fighting.

At the same time, this remarkably uneven, and usually unlucky, division had managed to produce in some battalions, leaders and soldiers who really did deserve all the acclaim, and more, that has been indiscriminately showered on the formation as a whole. The one really outstanding feat of the whole sorry mess was the capture of the north end of the main road bridge, in spite of a plan so bad that everyone else expected it to fail, in spite of the loss of the jeeps in which they should have got there; and then the holding of that position, not for the two days required by Montgomery but for twice that time—four days; and not against female clerks of the Luftwaffe and other line-of-communications troops, but against heavy tanks and self-propelled guns manned by crack soldiers who really knew their business. Holding a position "to the last round" is in the main a happy figure of speech for public morale and the newspapers; here, literally, it was very nearly true. They held out, literally, to the last magazines of Bren and Sten ammunition, when the enemy was using tanks, and they had no means whatever of combating armour.

Those four days by the bridge were both bitterly contested and also the only part of the battle that counted. By date-reckoning the division as a whole held out for nine days, but it would be truer to say, not that they held out, but that they remained in position. The Germans judged correctly that the main threat came from XXX Corps, and therefore took blocking measures both at Nijmegen and mid-way across the "Island" at Elst, which was in fact to be the front line until April, 1945—six months later.

While they were building up their barrier against XXX

Corps, they merely corralled off 1 Airborne Division; when the southern barrier was completed, they then turned on the airborne with all the advantage of heavy equipment and blew it to pieces at their leisure. The sole exception was at the road bridge, which they needed in order to get reinforcements quickly onto the "Island," and which was therefore subject to all-out attack from first to last. This therefore makes the four-day defence even more remarkable than it appeared at the time.

Perhaps even more remarkable is the fact that some who took part in that defence criticise it, not from the aspect of determination, naturally, but of technique. They believe, on thinking it over, that the defence could have been more offensive, on the lines of the "mouseholing" method developed by the Canadians at Ortona, and that it was a mistake simply to wait to be burned out—in fact, that it is a mistake ever to sit still and wait to be attacked.

This was indeed the German appreciation of the British at all levels throughout the war, and of both the senior commanders at Arnhem. Urquhart quotes General Wilhelm Bittrich, commander of II S.S. Panzer Corps, as saying: "We must remember that the British soldier will not act on his own initiative when he is fighting in the town and it becomes more difficult for officers to exercise control. He will be incredible in defence, but we need not be afraid of his offensive capabilities."

Oberst Harzer, in a letter to me, expressed the same opinion of the higher leadership, that the British would first make sure of great superiority of numbers and then come at the objective by the shortest and most obvious route. By the time of Arnhem, he thought, they had learned a bit, but not much. "With the battles for Arnhem and Nijmegen I could detect, perhaps with a little more caution, the same tactics."

Bittrich's appreciation of what would happen is corroborated by Urquhart's report on what did happen. In attack, the airborne did tend to bunch, to do nothing unless told to do it, were well behind the Germans in infiltration tactics, tended to over-estimate the effect of German weapons and to under-estimate the effect of their own, to indulge in nervous, indiscriminate shooting for the first 48 hours, and generally show all the signs of poor training in the attack. The only exception to this rule was at night, where the Germans appeared to be poorly trained and the British had the advantage. In defence, the British gained confidence after a while and were more effective.

This being the state of training and discipline in the division generally, it was unlikely that any defects in planning would be made good by superlative performance at the level of the individual soldier. And the plans were defective. Almost without exception, a second-class solution was accepted for what seemed at the time to be adequate reasons, but were not; and a series of second-class solutions led unerringly to a first-class defeat.

In the first month of its existence, the First Allied Airborne Army had produced eighteen separate plans for possible operations and had carried out none of them. The 1 British Airborne Division had been required to produce sixteen plans for operations that never came off; and in many cases, these were cancelled at the last moment, only after the planning had been completed, the units moved to their airfields, "sealed," and briefed.

The effect of this on the planning staff is difficult to imagine, unless one has had similar experience of cancelled operations. The enthusiasm that comes from belief begins to wear off, some of the urgency is blunted, the meticulous attention to detail lost. This is particularly the case where the operation involves a high element of personal risk for the planners, who will be dropping themselves into enemy territory. The subconscious excitement cannot be sustained for too long, and in the absence of this, the keen edge of urgency is blunted. In place of mental images of how the plans may work out, comes the feeling, "Oh, well, it won't really come off anyway."

If it did, almost anything might happen. The last detailed and accurate picture of enemy dispositions, received mainly from Dutch sources, had been prior to the Normandy invasion in June. Since then, the Arnhem area had been in turmoil with no clear pattern apparent. The only known fact was that the Arnhem training area had a barracks capacity for 10,000 troops. There was a report of 10,000 troops concentrated at Zwolle, well north of Arnhem, which, if correct, might represent the evacuation of the Arnhem barracks, or alternatively, one or two battle-scarred panzer divisions reforming. Zwolle was 35 miles from Arnhem. But of recent, direct evidence of German troops in the Arnhem area, there was nothing, just a blank.

As far as the strength of the British force was concerned, that depended not on the size of the division, but on the size of the lift. There was a shortage of transport aircraft, most of which were American and had to be borrowed. There were 157 transports available for the first lift, compared to 482 for the 82nd and 436 for the 101st U.S. divisions. The number of gliders was much larger, 320 as against 50 and 70 for the two U.S. divisions respectively, but these took up far more airspace than did the transports and therefore could not achieve anything like the same concentration.

The most effective comparison, however, lies in the number of infantry battalions in the first lift. Both American divisions landed almost complete in front-line infantry, with three regiments each, of three battalions per regiment. The British division had in the first lift only two brigades, of three battalions each. The second lift was to bring in another British brigade, while the third lift was to bring in the Polish brigade.

To put it another way, 1 Airborne Division was to land in the following proportion: one-half on the first day, one-quarter on the second day, and one-quarter on the third day. This is what contemporary airborne people call feeding Oxo-cubes to the lion, one by one. The division would never strike as a division, even if the weather was favourable throughout, which, in September, was most unlikely.

Worst still, the divisional plan arranged to split the two brigades involved in the first lift. The targets of the whole operation—the bridges—were to be attacked only by the three battalions of the 1 Parachute Brigade. The gliderborne infantry of the 1 Airlanding Brigade were to hold the non-tactical drop zone eight miles away for the following lifts, and so would contribute nothing whatever to the success of the first day's operations. In sum: The attacking force on

BLITZKRIEG—May, 1940

:ond stage—parachute troops dropped at low level right on top of, or very near to, the target. , alternatively, an attack by Trojan Horse units—soldiers disguised as civilians or in Dutch iform, previously infiltrated up to the target, usually a bridge. Here the aircraft is a Ju 52, the rkhorse of the Luftwaffe, used both for parachutists and air-landing troops, as well as supply missions.

GRAVE BRIDGE—20 September, 1944

:onvoy of urgently-required ammunition and supplies being attacked on the bridge by a Focke-ılf 190, after having fought its way through from Eindhoven. The sketch was made by Corporal ade-King, of the Household Cavalry Regiment, who is one of those depicted at the bottom of the embankment.

DORDRECHT BRIDGE—
10 May, 1940
German parachu
ists holding th
bridge again
Dutch counte
attacks. They a
setting up the
own heavy machin
gun, replacing th
knocked-out Dutc
machine-gun on th
right.

NIJMEGEN ROAD BRIDGE—1944
British Army transport crossing over the Waal after the capture of the bridge by Guards Armoured Division and 82 U.S. Airborne Division.
Photo: Archivist, Nijmegen.

NIJMEGEN RA
BRIDGE—194
29 September,
Although the br
was captured in
by a comb
British and An
can force, Ger
frogmen blew
pier on 29 Sep
ber and bro
down the ce
span into the W

September 17 was not 1 Airborne Division but merely 1 Parachute Brigade.

This extraordinary situation arose through the muddled command set-up, the division between the soldiers and the airmen, further addled by most incompetent intelligence work and photographic interpretation.

The obvious place to land was on target—by the riverside and on both sides of the bridges if possible. But this was vetoed by the airmen on two grounds: heavy flak on the "Island" plus routing difficulties. If the transport stream turned south after the drop, they would be likely to run into the stream coming back from Nijmegen, and if they turned north they would be flying over the Luftwaffe airfield of Deelen where flak was also believed to be strong. If correct, the flak argument was a reasonable one, for heavy flak meant heavy losses of transport aircraft, which in turn meant reduced strength available for the following lift.

These flak reports were in fact pessimistic. But even if they had been correct, the obvious counter was air attack, particularly by Typhoons, the flying artillery of the time. The Second Tactical Air Force, who already knew the area well, could certainly have dealt with the flak but were not allowed to operate because of a veto from HQ First Allied Airborne Army, in case they got in the way of their operations. This is, of course, ridiculous, but such was the position at the time. It was later altered.

Just possibly the argument with the airmen might have been taken further, but for the analysis of the suitability of the "Island" in providing dropping zones for the parachutists and landing zones for the hundreds of gliders. It was reported as unsuitable. As regards parachutists, this was unspeakable nonsense, particularly at the south end of the road bridge. Further, a fair number of gliders could have been landed there, or even landed on the water in the shallows of the south bank of the Neder Rijn. There was nothing whatever to prevent a reasonable force, either of parachutists or glider-borne troops or both, from actually landing on target.

The north side of the road bridge presented a slightly more difficult problem, but hardly insuperable, because the road continued off the bridge onto a long straight ramp, an ideal landing strip, and it was surrounded by reasonably open spaces. It will be recalled that the German pilots of the Junkers 52s had of their own volition made emergency landings on main roads when the airfields were blocked, and a three-motored transport aircraft is a much more awkward landing proposition than a glider, as it has a much longer run and even a slight accident may cause it to catch fire.

S. J. D. Moorwood, who was a captain in the Glider Pilot Regiment at the time, but had to force-land 10 miles from Arnhem because of damage to the tug aircraft, has commented:

"I do not think that the brass-hats ever appreciated the skill of the glider pilots, particularly with the Horsa glider. It was possible to land, reasonably safely, almost literally on the objective, or, if necessary, we could have landed in the river. You will remember that on D-Day five out of six Horsas detailed to land on the bridge over the River Orne actually landed *in the dark* within 100 yards of the objective."

Landing in daylight, it should have been possible for the gliders to put down, not only close to the bridges, but along the main road from Nijmegen to Arnhem. Here, as Guards Armoured were subsequently to find to their cost, the country favoured the infantryman rather than the tank; and, indeed, the defence generally. None of the effective German counter-moves that were in fact made would have been possible had this been done. The link between Nijmegen and Arnhem would have been severed in the first half-hour, and by occupying a position that was of tactical value to Market Garden as a whole.

However, convinced that they were lucky even to obtain a daylight drop from the airmen, who up to now had always insisted on the cover of night, Urquhart accepted the second-best solution and chose dropping and landing zones on the heathland west of Arnhem, which were near perfect for their purpose. The drawback was that they were between seven and eight miles from the targets—the bridges. The initial landings might achieve surprise but the subsequent attack on the bridges was almost bound to be expected and opposed.

To cut down this delay to the minimum, it was planned

to send Airborne Reconnaissance Squadron racing to the bridges in their armoured jeeps, followed by 1 Parachute Brigade and a strong force of engineers, mostly on foot, and towing the heavier loads behind them on small hand trucks. This was a risky procedure, but more serious was the splitting of the first two brigades to land.

The dropping and landing zones had to be protected for the following lifts on D plus 1 and D plus 2, September 18 and 19. Only an optimist could consider that the defensive role was tactical, although the divisional plan envisaged 1 Airlanding Brigade on the drop zones forming the left flank of a box, with the 4 Parachute Brigade, when it arrived on September 18, forming the north line of the box on the high ground behind Arnhem, and the Polish Parachute Brigade, when it arrived on September 19, forming a line south of the bridges on the "Island."

Arnhem was, after all, an important German training area capable of holding a minimum of 10,000 troops; and it was to be attacked on the first day by only some 3,000 lightly armed men. Airborne troops were not the surprise weapon they had been back on May 10, 1940, with an unknown potential. The Germans had not merely carried out the pioneer work, they had studied the answers, too. It really does seem that someone should have cried "Halt!" and either produced a better plan or scrubbed the entire operation.

General Urquhart was not really in a position to do this, because he had never before taken part in an airborne operation. His experience had been in the desert and in Italy as an infantry brigadier, and he had not taken over the division until January, 1944. His predecessor, General Eric Down, was a most experienced airborne soldier whom the War Office had sent to India to raise a new airborne division there.

By September, Urquhart had realised that there was "a certain naïveté in upper level planning," when for Operation "Comet" 1 Airborne Division alone were to take the crossings of the Maas, the Waal, and the Neder Rijn.

Two of his juniors, Brigadier Shan Hackett and the Polish General Stanislaw Sosabowski objected, the latter violently, interrupting Urquhart's explanation of the plan with, "But the Germans, General, the Germans!" Comet was to become

Market Garden, using three airborne divisions instead of the single one originally proposed, in itself an apt comment on planning at the level of HQ First Airborne Army.

At lower level, the trouble was age. Tony Hibbert, the brigade major of 1 Parachute Brigade, was then twenty-three and feels, regretfully, that he could do very much better now. He was then too young to stand up to older, senior officers if he felt that a plan was unsatisfactory, as this one was. The bridge problem should have been re-thought, instead of merely taking the word of R.A.F. bomber pilots about the flak, and tamely going elsewhere. If necessary, the brigade should have been dropped on the houses by the riverside. Anything, rather than land seven to eight miles away, because this posed a most awkward problem to the brigade.

This formation, which was to fight the real battle of Arnhem, was both well trained and experienced; it had captured the Bône airfields in North Africa and the bridge over the Simeto in Sicily. But what it was being asked to do was to walk through a built-up area for many miles before reaching its target, in the middle of a town containing barracks for 10,000 men. The brigade itself was about 2,000 strong, and without heavy weapons or vehicles.

There were two alternatives: to advance the battalions into the town one after the other, on the same road, a method that gives concentration and control, enabling the brigade to fight as a brigade, but is necessarily slow; or to advance the three battalions in line, on three separate roads, which means faster progress when unopposed but is basically weaker, because in a built-up area, as opposed to open country, the battalions are unable to help each other. On the other hand, although one or even two battalions may very well be stopped, one is almost bound to get through to the objective. This was the plan adopted, and this was what happened. The brigade fulfilled its task, but the force that reached the objective and occupied it consisted of a single battalion; the others were held up, for good, in the built-up area.

In sum: It was not 1 British Airborne Division that attacked the bridges at Arnhem; it was not even 1 Parachute Brigade; but merely the 2nd Parachute Battalion, and not all of that actually reached the bridge. Instead of a complete division, the striking force consisted of only about 600 men. This was the inevitable result of decisions taken higher up.

Major Hibbert kept a log, which is instructive. On August 31, he wrote the operations order for "Linnet" and at 2300 hours on September 3 learned that it was cancelled, because the Americans had reached Maastricht. Next day, September 4, planning began for Operation Comet. Next day, Tuesday, September 5, which was *Dolle Dinsdag* in Holland, he noted a "faint odour of mortality" about Comet, in which the division was to take Eindhoven, Nijmegen, and Arnhem on its own. On September 6, there was an "orders group," on the 7th a postponement for 24 hours, on the 8th a postponement for 24 hours, on the 9th at 1000 hours a postponement for 48 hours, and on the same day at 1800 hours the whole thing was cancelled. Next day, September 10, he flew to a planning conference and learned that this plan (No. 15) had been cancelled also, stifled at birth almost, and was "just in time to hear details of Plan 16, which from our point of view differed little from COMET. New name MARKET."

On September 13, he wrote the brigade operation order. There were two targets—the main road bridge (code "WATERLOO" bridge) and the German pontoon bridge just to the west ("PUTNEY" bridge). The brigade was not concerned with the less important railway bridge ("CHARING X") still farther to the west. The targets were to be seized by 1 Airlanding Reconnaissance Squadron in their armoured jeeps, which would cover the seven or eight miles at high speed. The three marching battalions would follow after them, 2nd Battalion on the right, nearest the Neder Rijn, 3rd Battalion in the centre, 1st Battalion on the left, nearest the hills to the north.

The 2nd Battalion (under Lieutenant-Colonel J. D. Frost) was to form an L-shaped defensive position, the lower stroke being on the south bank of the river covering the approaches to both bridges; it was to be accompanied by a detachment of Royal Engineers with three flame-throwers. The 3rd Battalion (Lieutenant-Colonel J. A. C. Fitch) was to assist in the capture of the main bridge ("WATERLOO"), and then face east. The 1st Battalion (Lieutenant-Colonel D. T. Dobie) was to occupy the high ground north of Arnhem, thus denying the enemy direct observation over the town and also out across the "Island" towards Elst and Nijmegen. The effect would be to form a kind of brigade "box" around the town, very thinly held.

On the second day, they were to be reinforced, particularly to the north, by 4 Parachute Brigade; and probably on the third day the Polish Parachute Brigade would land south of the bridges, move over them, and take up positions to the east. 1 Airlanding Brigade had the task of holding the airhead out on the heathland to the west of Arnhem from D-Day on. XXX Corps was to arrive within two days, if possible, and 52 (Lowland) Division was ready to be flown into Deelen airfield, some seven miles north of Arnhem, when that was captured, to assist in the drive to the Zuyder Zee. A great deal depended on the weather, and on Saturday, September 16, Major Hibbert noted: "Weather report good, hopes for op very high."

Those carrying out the planning were under considerable mental strain, because so many factors had to be taken into account and jig-sawed together, plus the administrative work involved in concentrating the division at its airfields. Those with fewer responsibilities had their worries, too, but of a more personal sort.

For instance, the Reverend C. A. Cardale, who was then a private working in the telephone exchange, was suddenly told at 1630 hours on September 16 that he was to drop with the 2nd Battalion. A corporal who had been on leave had not come back, and Cardale was to take his place instead. That gave him from 1800 to 2015 hours to get ready. His job at the telephone exchange had kept him "in the picture" as to how many cancelled operations there had been already, and he did not expect they would really go this time. However, he made his preparations.

His principal preoccupation was pipes. Operations play the devil with pipe-smokers, because of the danger of breakage. Cardale bought himself a new pipe, as a reserve, and had a satisfactory smoke with it. He then considered his personal kit in the light of the probable duration of the operation, and selected his red beret, tobacco pouch, two pipes, two lighters, 14 ounces of tobacco, sweets, chocolates, cigarettes, and two 24-hour ration boxes holding biscuits, dehydrated meat, pressed oats, and teacubes.

At breakfast on Sunday, September 17, the missing corporal had still not come back.

"I wished he had," [wrote Cardale in a contemporary narrative]. "No one wanted much breakfast and we were soon in the trucks moving to the airfield. There we had two sandwiches and one cup of tea. Threw sandwiches away and took an airsickness pill. Emplaned at 10.00, I at No. 4. At the last moment, we had a view of the Don R waving to us. He could not go because of a motor bike accident. Over England for some time, a lovely view. At last the sea, slightly hazy, then land again. Am sure I would have recognised Holland in any case. Lakes and rivers and flat land. Saw a few crashed gliders and my heart alternately sank and came up into my mouth. Wasn't airsick at all and smoked cigarettes through nervousness. I still hoped for a recall! Then the Red light was on. It was perfect outside and no Ack Ack as far as I remember. At last the Green light and someone shouted, "Go!" Our platoon officer pushed his bicycle out first and followed it, a matter of seconds before I went also. Soon we were all in the air. It never dawned on me it was dangerous and I enjoyed every second of the flight down after my chute had opened. I was loaded with gear plus a rifle on a cord 20 feet long which lightened your final descent by landing first. Weather was perfect. Landed and dazedly got up."

Cardale found himself facing a sergeant operating a movie camera. Although Cardale did not get back, the film did, and friends who recognised the soldier on the screen told his mother, who knew only that he had been reported missing. At the first re-grouping, an hour after moving off the drop zone, Cardale decided to take the opportunity for a smoke, took out his new pipe—and found that it was now in two pieces.

"At last we had to move forward. After about 50 yards came across a carload of dead Germans. The first dead I had ever looked upon. Fascinated me for a while and then the whole sickening feeling was over. I was there and had to make the best of it."

The pathfinders of the 21st Independent Company had already landed, ahead of the main stream, to "home in" the main force and mark the drop zones. The first arrivals after them were not paratroops, however, but a horde of Dutchmen on bicycles who delightedly began collecting the discarded silk parachutes, as Private John Wilson observed. The first casualty was an NCO busy collecting rifles from a wrecked glider; he dropped one, and it shot him through the head.

At first many people in Arnhem did not realize that an airborne attack was beginning. Certainly, there was the noise of planes and of flak, but these were commonplaces of wartime. Certainly, the night had been a disturbed one, with searchlights sweeping the sky for raiders, but many nights were like that. Certainly, a great bomber formation had passed over in the morning—and headed on into Germany. True, in the morning fighters and fighter-bombers had strafed targets in and around Arnhem, but certainly not on an unusual scale. Keeping the preliminary air attacks to a normal level of intensity had helped achieve the surprise. And besides, the paratroops and gliders did not land in Arnhem, but well outside to the west.

Maurits van Dongeren, who was now nearly thirteen years old and who had really seen very little of the German paratroop attacks on Rotterdam before his family fled and took him eventually to Arnhem, saw nothing of the British airborne landings. They were taking place too far away, and he lived by the bridge. His family had thought Arnhem a place of safety and could not know that the great span a few hundred yards north of their house was now code-named "WATERLOO," and that on Major Hibbert's map the lower strokes of the "W" almost touched their new home. The only hint of any crisis had been the "press-ganging" of Dutch youths in the last few weeks to help build defences that were not yet complete.

One of the first Germans to realise the magnitude of what was taking place was Herbert Kessler, a nineteen-year-old instructor-NCO from Siegen, then serving with a training regiment of Fallschmirmjäger—Panzer Division "Hermann Göring" at Katwijk-an-Zee. Most of the recruits had been schoolboys when General Graf Sponeck's airlanding units had come down at Katwijk on May 10, 1940, nearly four and a half years previously. The majority had only been called up in April, 1944, and even the standard of training was not as good as it had been.

"They were extremely youthful soldiers, round about the age of 18, who knew neither death nor wounds" [he wrote]. "That September was blessed with many sunny autumn days and the soldiers were enjoying their stay on the coast, never remotely suspecting the possibility of going into action. Then, on a beautiful Sunday, the air was suddenly full of engine noises and flak blazing away. When the soldiers saw that the planes were towing behind them transport gliders, they looked at each other in complete consternation. But the resulting rush and tear were proof of the seriousness of the situation. None of the companies had any means of transport, except bicycles; and because to march by day was unthinkable, the danger of attack from low-flying aircraft being so great, my unit did not leave until it got dark. To avoid being seen by enemy aircraft, we assembled in a wood, and the leader of the battalion gave us an inflammatory speech, beginning: 'Comrades, at long last the hour has come!' continuing in the same strain, and closing with the words: 'I demand unconditional effort until we have achieved complete success. I know that I can depend upon every one of you,' etc., etc., etc. Naturally, promotions which were due were speedily made, and this drove the waves of enthusiasm even higher. Then, after we had been warned of possible resistance by the local Dutch Underground, we moved off at dusk towards Arnhem."

CHAPTER THIRTEEN

A MATTER OF TIMING

The March to Waterloo: September 17

What had woken the Dutch on the morning of May 10, 1940 was the sound of aircraft engines, while above them the German paratroops riding to Rotterdam had seen the Arnhem bridges vanish in brilliant flashes of light, followed by rolling clouds of black smoke pouring upwards. On September 17, 1944 the roar of approaching aircraft formations was commonplace, and this time also they were merely passing over, but from west to east, towards the German frontier. J. McMahon was bomb-aimer in one of them, a Halifax bound for Gelsenkirchen in the Ruhr. If the hazy conditions made Gelsenkirchen hard to find, that great bridge down there would be an excellent secondary target, he thought, and passed the word to the navigator to plot its position, for he did not know then that the town was Arnhem. The main target was indeed obscured, and the great bomber turned slowly and set course for the bridge. Then occurred a freak change in cloud conditions. The ground below cleared and there—on track, lit by bright sunlight, and without sign of German opposition—lay another Ruhr town, Oberhausen. McMahon changed his mind about the bridge.

"My aim was good," he wrote. "Mine were the only bombs dropped on Oberhausen that day and my picture was the main R.A.F. press release. There is no doubt in my mind that had Oberhausen not come into view then, I would later have demolished the bridge at Arnhem even while British forces were dropping. It was not until next morning that the story of the Arnhem drop was released, and I paled at the thought."

It was a natural enough reaction, but as events were to show, the destruction of Arnhem bridge as the paratroops began to drop, would have been the best possible solution to the impossible task they had been given.

At Arnhem, the timings were important and deadly. In

the nature of things, they were not exact. Nor were the flight paths. Officially, there were two main airstreams, one to the south of Antwerp and one to the south of Rotterdam. General Gavin, headed for Nijmegen, found himself a spectator of the 101st's drop on Eindhoven before the pilot corrected for drift.

The 82nd's airstream was nearly one-and-a-half hours long. The northerly stream carrying 1 British Airborne Division was much longer, because of the glider element; and also much slower, because of the glider element. Transports carrying paratroops can fly a tight formation, whereas gliders are towed some distance behind tug aircraft struggling along at just above stalling speed. On May 10, 1940, the Germans had attacked with 11 gliders, carrying only seven or eight men each; 1 Airborne Division's first lift included 358 gliders, some of them enormous and capable of carrying the largest anti-tank guns.

Consequently, it could not be said that the division landed at any particular time, but merely that the pathfinders of the Independent Company started to jump from 12 aircraft at about 1200 hours; and that the main stream began to arrive at about 1300 hours, divided into a parachute contingent and a glider contingent. The latter, being slower, had started first, its rear elements being rapidly overtaken by the leading elements of the paratroop aircraft.

The Germans had already reacted when some parts of the division were still crossing the Channel. The route over the sea was marked by ditched aircraft and burning flak ships, the first casualties on both sides having been incurred hundreds of miles from Arnhem. The route over the land was outlined by flak, but not very much of it, and by the activities of the fighters as they dived on the flak positions.

And while the tail of the formation was still over the Channel, the head was already turning round and coming back, to give the effect of two immense streams of aircraft passing each other, conveying the impression of overwhelming force and power.

No less impressive was the scene on the drop zones, for both aircraft in formation and paratroops coming down always give a visual impression that roughly doubles their real numbers. As the German war correspondent Erwin Kirchhof wrote: "In those first few minutes it looked as if the descending masses would suffocate every single life on the ground."

It seems likely that it was not the main landing, but the arrival of the pathfinders in 12 Stirlings somewhere about noon that interrupted Field Marshal Model's lunch at the Tafelberg Hotel in Oosterbeek. This was the forward headquarters of Army Group B, securely situated behind three main river-lines—Mass, Waal, and Neder Rijn.

Model seems to have been under the impression that it was an attempt to capture him and that he only just managed to escape "through the eye of a needle." He packed one suitcase and dashed for his car. Within a few minutes it was pulling up outside the Feldkommandantur in Arnhem. Here, Model informed the area commandant, General Kussin, that airborne landings had begun two or three miles west of Oosterbeek and that the news should be radioed to Hitler at the Führer HQ in East Prussia. Model then drove on to Doetinchem, east of Arnhem, where General Bittrich, commander of II S.S. Panzer Corps, had his headquarters.

At 1340 General Bittrich began to issue orders: 9 S.S. Panzer Division was to send its armoured reconnaissance unit to Nijmegen via Arnhem. The bulk of the infantry, formed into "alarm units," were to carry on westward through Arnhem to oppose the airborne landings directly. There were only a handful of armoured vehicles with them, and 9 S.S. was no longer an armoured division in any sense of the word, but merely Battle Group Harzer. It numbered only 3,500 men scattered widely in billets as far away as Zutphen and Apeldoorn, some 15 miles north-east of Arnhem.

The 10 S.S. was stronger and sited in the border area between Germany and Holland. This division was ordered to concentrate, then move on Nijmegen via Arnhem. Its task was to occupy the road and rail bridges over the Waal and hold a bridgehead south of Nijmegen, taking under command all German troops already in the area. The nearest unit was Major Euling's II Battalion of S.S. Panzergrenadier Regiment 21, which crossed the Neder Rijn at Pannerden and linked up early with the 750 German troops then in Nijmegen.

In short, Model and Bittrich had decided within the first hour or so that Nijmegen, and not Arnhem, was the point that required urgent and powerful reinforcement.

The historian of 9 S.S. Panzer Division, who fought at Arnhem, states that after Model's "mad drive" from Oosterbeek to the Feldkommandantur, he "scraped together" for the Battle of Arnhem "a very poor defensive force."

The only unit in position to act quickly was Sturmbannführer Sepp Krafft's S.S. Panzer Grenadier Depot and Reserve Battalion 16, at Oosterbeek. It was a battalion in name only, and numbered 12 officers, 65 NCOs, and 229 soldiers, and as its commander reported, "was mainly composed of half-trained 17–19-year-old personnel, forty percent of them graded as unfit for action." But, he added, "We knew from experience that the only way to draw the teeth of an airborne landing with an inferior force, is to drive right into it. From a tactical point of view, it would have been wrong to play a purely defensive role and let the enemy gather his forces unmolested."

At 1345 Krafft ordered the 2nd Company to make a probing attack while the remainder concentrated or reconnoitred in the Wolfhezen area, close to the drop zones and between two possible routes of advance into Arnhem. Neither of these routes was near the river.

Initially, these 300 men, most only partially trained and many marked for light duties only, represented the Germans' largest and finest force immediately available for the defence of Arnhem. The rest were the scraping of the defeat in Normandy. In the first 24 hours or so, 48 prisoners were interrogated by the British. They proved to have come from 27 different units, some unarmed. Twenty-four hours later, the number of different units totalled 42, including coast artillery and the German Navy. Among the first prisoners were one Japanese civilian, one female auxiliary in uniform, and one "gentleman of the road" (i.e. a tramp). To describe this sort of opposition as "poor," smacks of understatement. It seemed as if the most optimistic rumours of German weakness were correct. Further, the two brigades were arriving at the drop zones with a perfection never before achieved and virtually without interference from the enemy. Indeed, it might have been an exercise, except for the smoke still rising to the north from Deelen airfield, lately bombed.

Even so, it took some time for units to assemble and it was 1530 before 2 Parachute Battalion moved off on foot towards the bridge some seven miles away. At 1630, 1 Parachute Battalion started on its walk towards the high ground north of the town, and at 1700 the 3rd Battalion, advancing into the centre of the town, between the two other battalions, first met opposition.

General Urquhart, finding that the armoured jeeps of the *coup-de-main* party that was to race for the bridge were missing, and that his wireless sets were not working, got into a jeep and drove after Frost's 2nd Battalion in order to tell him personally that he would have to take the bridge on his own, and to hurry. But as the 2nd Battalion proved to be somewhat spread out and trying to infiltrate past an armoured car, he merely left a message for Frost and drove off again to look for Brigadier G. W. Lathbury, commanding 1 Parachute Brigade, who was with the 3rd Battalion.

While Urquhart was racing about, far from his HQ, trying to find out what was happening and to influence local events personally, his opposite number, General Kussin, the commandant of Arnhem, was doing exactly the same thing. At 1715 he drove into Wolfhezen and conferred with Sepp Krafft. Kussin told Krafft that he had just visited one of his battalion's sentry posts farther west; that it was "manned by the sick, convalescent and odd details of the battalion," and that "all was well." Krafft urged Kussin to return to Arnhem by a detour to the north, but Kussin was in a hurry and continued along the Wageningen–Arnhem road. A few minutes afterwards, Krafft heard a burst of machine-gun fire.

Kussin had run into a skirmish between B Company of 3 Parachute Battalion and a German force consisting of infantry and two armoured cars. The cars had easily knocked out the company's 6-pdr anti-tank gun, because it was being towed and so could not be got into action swiftly, and as the leading platoon had no Piats, they were now without an effective counter-weapon.

Minutes later, Urquhart himself ran into this skirmish and the first thing that caught his eye was a camouflaged

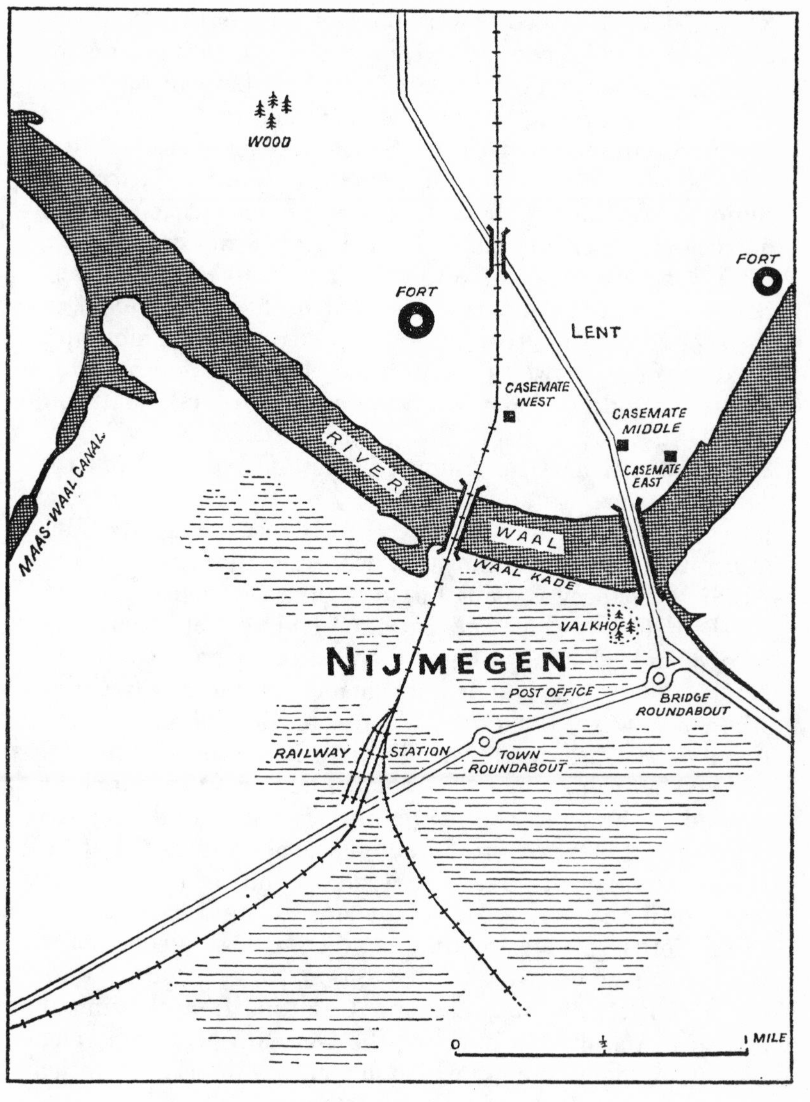

WOOD
FORT
FORT
LENT
CASEMATE WEST
CASEMATE MIDDLE
CASEMATE EAST
MAAS-WAAL CANAL
RIVER
WAAL
WAAL KADE
VALKHOF
NIJMEGEN
POST OFFICE
BRIDGE ROUNDABOUT
RAILWAY STATION
TOWN ROUNDABOUT
0
½
1 MILE

Citroën staff car containing four dead men. The officer hanging out of the door on the right-hand side was Major-General Kussin. The other bodies were those of his interpreter, driver, and orderly. The car had driven, brakes squealing, into the leading platoon, and both Kussin and his batman had tried to make a run for it, but had been riddled by bursts of wild and undisciplined firing from both sides of the road.

The general's death made very little difference, except to Major Ernst Schleifenbaum, from Siegen, who was his chief operations officer, for Field Marshal Model rang up and told him: "You are responsible that we hold Arnhem." Schleifenbaum wrote a few months later that he had "felt giddy" at the thought, as the situation was "a pretty thorough mess-up." Next morning, however, he felt that the situation was under control, as indeed it was, as a result of measures taking during the night.

At 1800 hours, the armoured cars and half-tracks of the reconnaissance battalion of 9 S.S., nearly complete, raced into Arnhem and tore across the great road bridge, heading south for Nijmegen and the decisive intervention there. Although firing was going on, and some German units blew up their stores, Frost's 2nd Battalion had not yet reached the bridge. Indeed, at 1930 hours there was only one man on the bridge. He was a Dutch policeman, Constable van Kuijk, whose post was at the northern end. The German guard, some two dozen elderly men manning light flak guns, had fled.

At about 2030 hours, German infantry from Nijmegen arrived at the south end of the bridge, and minutes later, A Company of 2 Parachute Battalion reached the houses at the northern end of the great steel span, to find German vehicles still crossing it. Half-a-dozen parachutists could have had the bridge for the asking any time between noon and 2000 hours. It was not even prepared for demolition. Now no one had it for the span itself was no-man's-land. Counting from the time of arrival of the first pathfinders, the Germans had been given more than eight hours in which to react. In their disorganised state, even this had not been quite enough.

Neither the British nor the Germans arrived at their opposite ends of the bridge in a bunch, but straggled out; and there was a brief burst of firing across the span that wounded the commander of the S.S. detachment coming from the south end. Like so many Dutch bridges, it was much larger than, say, its equivalent over the Thames. In order to clear the low-lying ground on the approaches, which flood in winter, the roadway at both ends was carried up on a massive ramp for a considerable distance before meeting the great upflung arc of steel that actually spanned the width of the river in its normal state. The open girderwork gave very little cover for infantry, and to take one end of the bridge by sending men across from the other end was a short form of suicide. This fact dictated the pattern of the ensuing battle.

At 2045 hours a platoon from A Company led by Lieutenant J. H. Grayburn tried to dash across, but lost eight men in the first few seconds after covering only 50 yards. The fire came mainly from an armoured car and also light flak guns in a pillbox actually on the bridge. The survivors ran back to cover, followed by Grayburn, who had been wounded in the shoulder. This ended the first attempt by the leading elements of the 2nd Battalion.

Meanwhile, numbers of assorted troops were moving towards "Waterloo" bridge. These included Frost with his Battalion HQ and Lathbury's Brigade HQ without Lathbury, parties of Engineers and Royal Army Service Corps amounting to about 100 men, medical personnel, motor transport, some 40 German prisoners, and a bevy of Dutch guides.

The latter halted for some time, arguing among themselves as to which was the better of two roads, and as neither of these roads was shown on the British military maps, the discussion was wearing for the British, particularly as the sound of fairly general firing was coming from the north, where Krafft's men, supported by a few armoured vehicles, were contesting the advances of the 1st and 3rd battalions. This left flank of the 2nd Battalion's advance was vulnerable and open during the march to "Waterloo," and some platoons were in fact swallowed up by it, so that even to this day it is not known what happened to them.

On the right flank, which lay on the river to the south, there was intermittent firing from the direction of "Charing X," the railway bridge. The northern end was held by a small detachment of Germans manning three flak guns, the south by a demolition team of under a dozen men. It was the objective of a platoon of engineers from 9 Field Company, but C Company of 2nd Battalion attempted to take it on their way into Arnhem. At 1830 hours there was a loud explosion, and one section of the bridge collapsed into the Neder Rijn. One route to the south bank had been closed. When B Company arrived at "Putney," the pontoon bridge, they found that the centre part was missing. A second route to the south bank was closed.

Darkness came soon after 1930, and C Company took a wrong turning into the town and disappeared, being cut off there for good. It was impossible to creep forward stealthily and infiltrate towards the bridge, because, as Major Hibbert wrote, "although we were taking every precaution to be silent, every few yards Dutch civilians would come rushing out of their houses shouting their welcome at the tops of their voices."

Nevertheless, Brigade HQ had got to within 500 yards of the northern end of "Waterloo" by 2045, the time of Lieutenant Grayburn's first unsuccessful attempt to seize it. Hibbert knew by now that they were not going to get any immediate help from the remainder of the brigade. He had got through by radio to Lathbury at 1930, and had been told that the 1st Battalion was trying to by-pass trouble near Wolfhezen, while the 3rd Battalion had run into considerable opposition and would have to halt for the night.

Captain D. J. Simpson, with 10 engineers, was bringing up the rear of Brigade HQ. When he arrived,

"The position at the north end of the bridge was that an assault had just been made and had failed. The battalion was re-forming for another attack, this time with the assistance of two sappers with a flame-thrower. The attack went in and was a great success. The pill-box, which was the mainstay of the defence, blew up with a great roar. The whole area was as light as day and the remaining Germans came running from the bridge silhouetted against the flames from the pill-box. The north end of the bridge was ours."

Two attempts were made to secure the south end by crossing the river. A patrol was sent to B Company with orders to cross by barge, but could not find B Company; and there appeared to be no barges. The brigade defence platoon was told to cross by boat, but could find no boat. Then, quite unexpectedly, Major Lewis' C Company of the 3rd Battalion joined Frost's men from the north, having got into the town along the railway line. This welcome accession of strength to a force of around 400 men, of whom less than 300 were infantry, proved to be largely an illusion. While Major Lewis was giving orders, one complete platoon vanished. Another platoon was ordered to occupy a house just north of the bridge, and they were never seen again. The third platoon suffered severe casualties while moving into another building. Clearly, they were no match for these particular German troops at house-fighting by night.

At Brigade HQ, all wireless contact had gone completely, even though they had the sets in an attic with aerials sticking out of the roof. There was not even a whisper on the large 76 set, although the small 22 set was receiving 2nd Battalion loud and clear. As their HQ was only 30 yards away, the unassisted human larynx would have done just as well. The set owned by the engineers in a building farther away could pick up Brigade only intermittently, and the only transmissions they could receive with fair regularity were those of the B.B.C. Home Service, with London telling the world about the battle of Arnhem.

During the night, the defenders holding positions in the houses immediately to the north of the bridge were to be cut off from the rest of the division by more than a wireless failure. The Germans, having virtually no wireless sets left after the debacle in Normandy, relied on the civilian telephone network to gather the nearest units for an immediate counter-stroke. Their moves, therefore, were based on much better information and were much better coordinated than those of the British. And the whole of II S.S. Panzer Corps had undergone thorough training in anti-parachute work prior to the Normandy landings.

Very rapid switches of command were smoothly executed. The reconnaissance unit of 9th S.S., which had gone to Nijmegen, was transferred to 10th S.S.; and the reconnaissance unit of the 10th was sent to help the 9th. This was commanded by Major Brinkman and was given the task of closely encircling and attacking the 2nd Parachute Battalion's small perimeter in the houses north of the bridge.

As we have seen, they were more skilled at this sort of work than were the British, who simply sat in their houses and waited to be attacked, and almost certainly they were much less weary and thirsty than the paratroopers, who had been without rest since the early morning and had had nothing to drink for eight hours or more. The houses were close together, and they simply moved forward in the darkness across the gardens, covered by bushes, until they could fire through the windows, in some cases by resting their machine-guns on the windowsills. In short, they made silent advances right up to their enemy before opening fire.

While this close encirclement was going on around the northern end of the bridge, the remainder of Harzer's force, under Major Spindler, formed a blocking-line right through Arnhem to the river west of the road bridge. They faced west, to oppose any further advance of British units into the town towards the bridge.

So, while Brinkman's force faced into Frost's perimeter around the bridge, Spindler's force had their backs to the bridge and faced outwards towards the bulk of the British troops trying to get into Arnhem—that is, the remainder of 1 Parachute Brigade. The blocking-line was weak at first, and by no means continuous, but reinforcements had already been summoned by telephone and it became continually stronger.

Mr H. B. van Horst, who had returned to Arnhem after a spell in Canada before the war, remembered the glow of fires down by the river, silhouetting the tall chimneys of the power station, and of how restless his children were, asking for their bedroom doors to be left open. It was quiet now in the street outside, after the confusion of the afternoon when the Germans had blown up some of their dumps and a fair number of soldiers had evacuated the town. He thought the paratroops would certainly arrive in the morning.

In the middle of the night he heard cautious movement in the street, and peering through the aperture of the letterbox in his front door, he could make out some dim figures creeping past. Who were they? British or German? A few minutes later, the rhythmic clatter of boots on the roadway signalled the open approach of marching troops. The light was too bad to make out their uniforms or equipment. Then a sharp command rang out: "*Drei! Vier!*"—and the soldiers burst out singing, to a well-known march melody:

> "*O du schöner Westerwald*
> *über deine Höhen pfeift de Wind so kalt*
> *Doch auch der kleinste Sonnenschein*
> *Dringt tief ins Herz hinein.*"

CHAPTER FOURTEEN

TO THE LAST MAGAZINE

Battle of Arnhem Bridge: September 18–20

Harzer, a big, burly officer, had been storming round, whipping up reinforcements and putting them into the positions where they would do most good. The little armour he had consisted mainly of half-tracked infantry carriers, but at midnight on Sunday he received news of actual tank reinforcements. Hauptmann Knaust, commander of the Bocholt training and depot battalion for armoured infantry, the panzer grenadiers, reported that his unit would reach Arnhem early on Monday, September 18, bringing with them 10 training tanks, vintage roughly 1940. Harzer directed them to join Brinkman's group at the road bridge as soon as they arrived, because it was imperative to reopen the bridge to traffic. It was the natural main axis of II S.S. Panzer Corps for the Battle of Nijmegen.

Field Marshal Model had expressly ordered that neither the road bridge at Arnhem nor the road bridge at Nijmegen were to be blown up, as both were vital to the operations of his corps. Until Arnhem bridge had been well cleared of the British, reinforcements and supplies for the 10th S.S. would have to cross the Neder Rijn on the ferry at Pannerden and then use minor roads to reach Nijmegen. It was a poor route, not really capable of handling masses of heavy material. Therefore, as long as Frost's men hung on to the bridge, they were directly affecting the Battle of Nijmegen in favour first of Gavin's 82nd U.S. Division and later of XXX Corps as well.

At dawn, two platoons from B Company broke through the German ring near the pontoon bridge and reached Frost, a welcome reinforcement. At about the same time an artillery officer, Captain Harrison, succeeded in making a lone journey in the opposite direction. His object was to bring the guns of 3 Battery forward to Oosterbeek, from where they had the range to fire on the area around the bridge. This was important in the early stages, because Harzer's artillery initially amounted to only four 2-centimeter and two 8·8-centimeter flak guns, although a mortar battery was on its way.

At 0800 the Germans made a rush for the bridge from the south end, firing all guns. Once the span was crossed, the ramp was covered and overlooked by the houses alongside it, in which Frost's men and Brigade headquarters had established themselves. In addition to Piats, a short-range, spring-loaded, one-man gun firing an anti-tank projectile, they had just completed the siting of four six-pounder anti-tank guns, high-velocity weapons. The Germans had to run a real gauntlet, in what were basically vulnerable vehicles—armoured cars, open half-tracks, and unarmoured trucks.

Major Hibbert wrote in his diary:

"There were already four or five lorries burning fiercely on the north end of the bridge, which had been knocked out the night before, but this did not deter them. A daisy chain of Hawkins grenades had been laid in pairs on the road in front of Brigade HQ. A certain amount of mortar and flak fire was first put down to cover the breakthrough. Then two half-track vehicles made a dash for it. The first one went slap over the mine belt without damage and raced up the road. Hardly a shot was fired, everybody was so surprised, and the Germans in the back had the cheek to wave to us. The next half-track also got over the mine belt, though a mine went off under the track. This did not seem to damage the vehicle, but one German sitting on the back was catapulted into the air and landed in the road. When he hit the road he clanged, he was so full of lead. By this time the Piats and 6-pounders had got the drill and in quick succession two armoured cars, eight or ten half-track vehicles and five or six lorries were knocked out and set on fire. Most of these vehicles were fairly full of Germans who provided very good target practice for the Brigade HQ personnel who were in the attic. The highest individual scorer was reported to be Lieutenant Harvey Tod who claimed 8 with his American carbine."

The Royal Engineers were in the Van Limburg Stirum-school on the opposite side of the road to the Brigade HQ building and a little farther north, but still overlooking the ramp leading down from the bridge into Arnhem. They could do nothing about the armoured cars, but the open half-tracks were targets for everything, including grenades; and when one was brought to a standstill, the passengers were shot down as they tried to get out. Seeing what was happening, the commander of one half-track turned off the ramp and took a path leading directly under the walls of the school. Captain E. M. Mackay, in charge of the Royal Engineers party, heard the clanking of its tracks below his window, and stuck his head out to look. Five feet away, the half-track was passing, with the German commander looking at him. The German grinned and got off three shots with his Luger, smashing Mackay's binoculars, before the engineers shot him down and the half-track, out of control, crashed into the wall of the school.

The ramp was now partially blocked by a disordered zigzag column of stranded or blazing vehicles. The attempt to break through had taken about an hour, and its failure was marked by increased mortar fire and shellfire from the German positions on the south bank of the river around the bridge, and by British shellfire in reply. The van Dongeren family, in their new home on the south side, had seen nothing of the airborne landings the previous day, but now found themselves trapped in the house. Like the airborne troops opposite, they were soon short of food and Mr. van Dongeren ventured out once to collect potato peelings from their dustbin. They had come to Arnhem only for the sake of Mrs. van Dongeren's nerves; now they were caught in the middle of a battle, and the noise was due to get very much worse, as the Germans moved up artillery and tank reinforcements to this site.

In the northern part of the town the situation was quite different. Very early in the morning Mr. van der Horst had found four Dutchmen in German Army uniform resting on his doorstep, trying to read an Allied surrender leaflet, written in German and English only. They got him to translate it for them, and talked of paratroopers with blackened faces hiding in all the houses. "Can't do much against them with our rifles, but just wait till our Tiger tanks got here.

Then we'll chase them out of the houses. We got the tanks, they haven't. We'll beat the bastards!"

At about 1000 hours that morning, a group of children began to shout, "There's a Tommy coming up the road!" This was the first paratrooper they had seen. He was dressed in a brown uniform with a maroon beret, and had his hands above his head. Behind him marched a German soldier with a rifle. An hour later, there were more excited shouts. This time it was a group of about 20 paratroopers and three Dutch civilians, all under armed guard. Mr. van der Horst assumed that the latter had been caught helping the British and that they would be shot. Then a convoy of German trucks began passing into Arnhem, followed soon after by tanks carrying infantry on them.

During the afternoon, there was the tremendous excitement of watching the second lift come in, with very heavy losses this time. Even so, the Dutch were enthusiastic. A few hours later, their optimism was damped by watching yet another group of British prisoners marched along the road to Apeldoorn, about 50 of them this time. An hour later came an even larger batch, of about 100. And with them the first jeep they had ever seen, being proudly shown off by its new owner, a German officer.

As early as 0730, General Urquhart had been officially reported at Division as "missing," although in fact he was merely with Brigadier Lathbury and out of wireless contact. But during the day, the report became literally true. Both Urquhart, the divisional commander, and Lathbury, his appointed successor, were cut off in a house with a German self-propelled gun outside the door. No one now commanded the division, and there was an argument between the two remaining brigadiers, Shan Hackett and Pip Hicks, as to who should take over.

This was the day when the Dutch message reached the 82nd U.S. Division at Nijmegen: "Germans winning over British at Arnhem," and it was true and could not be remedied. German reinforcements were coming in faster than British reinforcements, the available troops were too few for their tasks of holding the bridge, holding the dropping zones, holding the areas for the supply drops, and attacking north of Arnhem. This day the landing of reinforcements was delayed from the morning to the afternoon, because of bad weather over the airfields, and the supply dropping zones were mostly held now by the Germans. Eventually, the decision was taken to send two more battalions to try to reach Frost at the bridge, but they could not get through.

Both in Arnhem and in Nijmegen, contemporary Dutch narratives published during or just after the war express nearly speechless indignation at the barbaric horror of the Germans, in that they deliberately set fire to houses in both towns for purposes of illumination at night. We should of course all be incoherent with fury if it was our house that was being burned down wantonly by foreign troops. In fact, it was not wanton at all, and it was done by both sides. Major Hibbert, who logged the battle at the bridge from first to last, and whose diary I am following in all cases where contradiction and confusion become apparent, noted at 1700 hours on Monday, September 18:

"As it got dark it was decided to set light to several wooden huts round the bridge in order to keep the area illuminated and so prevent German movement and infiltration over the bridge. This was highly successful and kept the whole area as light as day. The Germans too seemed to have the same idea and proceeded to set fire to most of the houses outside the perimeter. In the process they set fire to the house next door to Brigade HQ and only by the action of very energetic fire-fighting squads on each floor was Brigade HQ saved."

Tuesday, September 19, was the day the Germans, having cordoned off the bulk of 1 Airborne Division in a harmless perimeter to the west, really began to get a grip on the positions held by Frost's men around the bridge, which was as vital to them as it was to the British. This was the heart of the Battle of Arnhem. The casualties here were mainly killed and wounded, not unwounded prisoners; and the defenders took more prisoners than did the attackers, although as the perimeter contracted, they could not hold them.

On this day, some Germans who wanted to surrender to the Royal Engineers in the school were told that it was impossible and that they must fight on to the end, which they did, none surviving. Elsewhere, there was one parachutist who had spent all the war in England and was taken prisoner four hours after landing. That is, in five years of war, he did four hours' fighting. It made him a "hero of Arnhem" automatically, largely due to the brilliant reporting of Stanley Maxted and Alan Wood.

In another unit, a number of men including an officer got into slit trenches and would not get out for any consideration whatever; they remained there, cowering, throughout the battle. And these too were automatically "heroes of Arnhem."

Such degradation of the meaning of words makes it necessary to critically examine all claims and revert to the reactionary standards hitherto accepted: that no man should surrender unwounded, and that even then his wound should be of a nature that totally incapacitates him; that no unit should surrender unless it is unable to resist further, from lack of ammunition or other sufficient cause; and that men taken prisoner should in all circumstances attempt to escape, regardless of whether or not the chances of success are hopeless, because this forces the enemy to use up manpower wastefully in guarding prisoners. That is the ideal, and few of us (certainly not this author) could live up to it; nevertheless, it is the standard by which individual and unit performances must be judged.

On Monday, the Germans had first tried to rush the bridge and when that failed began to press in on the perimeter from the east, in order to drive the paratroops to the west, away from the bridge road. That is, they were attacking roughly from the area of the power station near the waterfront, on the Nieuwekade, in the general direction of the Rijnkade and the church of St. Eusebius, as this would open the road for heavy reinforcements to pour south across the bridge for the Battle of Nijmegen, which was raging simultaneously.

On Tuesday, instead of attempting to rush the bridge from the south, they brought up guns and a few tanks to bombard the paratroops on the north bank of the Neder Rijn; they continued to drive from the east with infantry, more tanks arriving during the day; and they adopted the policy of methodically burning the defenders out of their houses, one by one. The attack began at about 0700 and meanwhile the German guns on the south bank opened fire. Methodically and systematically, they began to shell all the churches in Arnhem.

This was a great relief to the paratroops who, up to that moment, had supposed that the church steeples were occupied by German artillery observers. But it meant an inferno of noise for the van Dongeren family, for the German guns were sited near them and one large tank or self-propelled gun was sitting outside their front door, putting shell after shell into the tower of the Groot Kerk, the most prominent church in Arnhem.

"Soon there was only one wall of it left standing" [recalled Maurits van Dongeren]. "The street was full of yellow flame. When this gun was shooting, we couldn't go out the front, but we could get out at the back into our garden. The neighbour whose back garden fronted ours said, 'If that thing fires, come into my house.' So we did and got into one of his front rooms. When we looked down the street, we couldn't see the bridge, because of the houses further down the street, we could only see the big church the gun was firing at. We only heard the fighting at the bridge and the sound of shells falling in our area. Perhaps they were aimed at the tank? The house was shaking all the time and there was no glass left in the windows. We all slept together in a back room, on the floor or on a sofa or table. We could only nap for 15 minutes at a time and then we would be woken by explosions, except for my little sister who didn't realise what was happening. At night, we could see flames alongside the window, as everything had been blown down. We had no food and this was when Dad got potato peelings from the dustbin just outside. We could hear the cows bellowing to be milked."

Maurits was now twelve and his sister Dieuwke was six years old. It was for the sake of these young children that his mother had abandoned their house in Rotterdam and come to Arnhem in the first place, and she was still highly nervous, shaking whenever there was an unexpected loud noise, such as a door banging. Now the noises were really loud, and really deadly, much more ominous than those of the German airborne attack on Rotterdam. Only this can explain what was to happen next day.

During the morning and again during the afternoon, the Brigade HQ sets picked up XXX corps (although they could not get Division). First, there was a Canadian voice, apparently transmitting less than 20 miles away. Eventually Hibbert got a message through that they were holding the north end of the bridge and how soon could help reach them? The answer was: We are putting in an attack on Nijmegen bridge at 1200 hours, and hope to be with you soon. The last message was at 1700 hours, it was still "soon," but it sounded as if the bridge attack had failed (which was the case).

During daylight, the Germans made two attempts to get artillery close up to the British positions around the bridge, and both failed. They ran out a 2-centimeter flak gun, with crew. The crew were killed by snipers almost instantly. A second crew ran out to man it, and were all shot down. After that, the gun was deserted.

Next, two old Mark III or Mark IV tanks came round the corner and began firing. Under cover of this a large 15-centimeter gun was unlimbered and laid directly on Brigade HQ. The first three shots thoroughly ventilated the attic, which was rapidly evacuated, and Captain "Slapsy" Miller was sent to ask for mortar fire. When it was next possible to look out, there was no 15-centimeter gun, merely a large crater in the road where it had been. Apparently one of the mortar bombs had detonated its ammunition.

Other Mark IIIs were roaming about the area, pumping shells into the houses at will, out of range of the Piats, and usually beyond effective rifle range. Tanks are not really effective for fighting in built-up areas, because they can only operate in penny packets and being blind when closed down, the commander has to have his head out of the turret. The attack is slow, cautious, and can have only one end—the defenders will be burnt or blown out of the houses they hold.

At noon, with "tanks coming up in relays from the waterfront," the engineers listening in the school to the B.B.C. news broadcasts heard that "everything was going according to plan and that relief was imminent," according to Captain

Mackay's contemporary narrative. Later, "I turned on the six o'clock news and learnt with amazement that we had been relieved," he wrote.

Help was in fact at hand—for the obsolete Mark III training tanks from the Bocholt depot. At 1930 hours the first of a number of Tiger tanks, weighing over 60 tons, rolling down to the ramp from the north. They were armed with 88-millimeter anti-aircraft guns, a long-range, high-velocity weapon of extreme accuracy and penetrative power. They were probably from 506 Heavy Tank Battalion, recently formed in Germany, which had been promised to Harzer the previous day.

With their enormously long gun in a hand-operated turret, seven-inch-thick frontal armour, and poor mechanical reliability, they were far more formidable in defence than in attack. Two or three Tigers, in the right sort of country, could hold up any Allied armoured division. For short-range work in a built-up area, they were less effective than the American Shermans or the British Churchills, and their crews handled them gingerly. Nevertheless, that 88 was a nasty gun.

Captain D. J. Simpson was with the Royal Engineers in the school building, one of the first targets.

"The Tiger rolled slowly up the ramp until it was opposite the north-west corner of the school at about 25 yards range. Its massive 88-mm gun turned steadily until it aimed at our northern room. It seemed to spit a shell at us and a six-foot hole appeared in the west wall. Again it fired, this time at the southern leg, and another piece of wall disappeared. Contrary to our expectations the Tiger turned its gun south and backed down the ramp. Apparently it was a little nervous of staying in one spot too long and that was the last we saw of it that night. We now had no shortage of loop-holes and the men took up their positions with all available ammunition and explosives. We thought that they must surely attack in strength and try to finish us. The only sound now was the crackling of the fires, the occasional crack of a rifle and the noise of heavy guns miles to the south of us. We had so few men now (4 killed and 27 wounded out of 50) that we all needed to be awake. Our boots made so much noise in the quiet night that we raided the remains of the linen cupboard and bound our boots with blankets, sheets, and even with ladies stockings. Our nerves began to show the tremendous strain. The men's faces, in the flickering light of the fires, looked terrible—their eyes red from want of sleep, three days growth of beard, blackened by fire fighting and whitened again with thick plaster gave them the grimmest of appearances."

Once a house had been burnt, the ruins were too hot to enter for between 12 and 24 hours, so there was no chance of counter-attacking. In any event, there was virtually no food —two boiled sweets represented a major meal—and lack of sleep plus Benzedrene was making men see double. Although Major Hibbert was still logging events, many men's memories were confused and hazy. Private Cardale, for instance, was with A Company, holding three of the four houses nearest the north end of the bridge, the most important position and the most heavily attacked. Tanks coming along the waterfront methodically tried to set the houses on fire, and a heavy gun on the south bank of the river shelled those on the west side of the bridge; possibly this was the one that drove the van Dongerens out of their home.

On Tuesday, September 19 they were still acting offensively. Tanks and armoured cars were stalked with Piats and damaged or knocked out. A house was lost, and then retaken. But the houses that were burned over their heads were unapproachable, and slowly they were driven north, away from the bridge, except for a party including Cardale that got under the bridge and fought on from there. Probably, he was with Lieutenant Grayburn's platoon, for he describes a flexible fighting defence under a "*very* brave officer" who was so badly wounded in his last attack to keep the Germans off the bridge that he had to be carried back.

Cardale recalls being burnt out or blown out of a number of buildings, including an ironmonger's shop. In this, he lost his pack with the 14 ounces of tobacco and his 48-hour ration, although the tea they were brewing at the time was saved. In another, he was collecting Bren magazines in one room for a Bren gunner in another room, only a thin partition wall separating them, when two shells thunderclapped into the other room and Cardale was blown the full length of his room.

Captain A. P. Wood, then a platoon commander in the 2nd Battalion, described what it really looked like:

"Row upon row of houses aflame, Jerry tanks everywhere, roaming at will, and being attacked by us with Piats, Sticky-bombs and 36 grenades. It had now been 72 hours of ceaseless fighting—no sleep, a day without any kind of food, and some ten hours since the last water had gone. Every house was defended or taken hand to hand, each floor told its story—shrapnel pock-marks, bullet marks, blood-spattered stairs, floors and walls, our own dead and those of the enemy everywhere, some still locked together as they died."

Yet at one moment, there was a brief truce. Two Royal Army Medical Corps men put out a white flag from the cellar of the advanced dressing station, and the attackers agreed to make a brief pause in the battle.

"The Jerries came along to dress and evacuate their own wounded, but they also carefully and tenderly dressed our wounded, before taking them off to a P.O.W. Hospital. How strange—kill at one moment. The next, a tender exchange, a fixed smile, the offer of a cigarette and help. And when all was over, the ferocious fighting started again. By now, the 2nd Battalion had virtually ceased to exist as a fighting unit, although there was fight left in everyone still alive, even the wounded."

The truce may have been the one organised by Major Hibbert on the last full day of fighting, Wednesday, September 20. In the morning, Brigade had at last contacted Division on a 22 set, and Urquhart and Frost were able to talk. The division commander, who had escaped from his temporary imprisonment, congratulated Frost and his men and asked them to hold for the arrival of XXX Corps, without help from the rest of the division, which was stuck in the Oosterbeek area.

Frost said his own position was "satisfactory" for the time being, but that he needed food and ammunition at once, also a surgical team. Urquhart suggested that he might ask the

DUTCH DEFENCES—1940

A typical 1918-style trench system behind a waterline of marsh and river.

GERMAN ATTACK—1940

But the German soldiers fall from the skies, miles behind the waterlines—on the Dutch capital itself. Here a formation of Ju 52s is dropping a parachute unit on the outskirts of The Hague, with orders to capture the Queen of the Netherlands and her Government.

ARNHEM IN GERMAN HANDS—6 September, 1944

An R.A.F. reconnaissance photograph taken eleven days before 1 Airborne Division dropped seven miles away, with orders to take the road bridge (*background*). In foreground, a German Army pontoon bridge.

THE NEDER RIJN AT OOSTERBEEK

Photograph taken by the author during a motorboat tour of the Dutch waterways in 1952. The photo was taken in mid-stream at the point where the escaping men of the Airborne Division had to cross, in boats or by swimming.

local civilian population to bring in food, ammunition, and stores from the supply containers, which had fallen in the wrong place the previous day. Frost replied that the battalion was in the middle of a devastated area, with no one else living there except a large number of aggressive Germans who had them completely surrounded, and that it was impractical for civilians to wander to and fro carrying supplies for the British.

Brigade then passed back their estimate of casualties inflicted on the enemy by a force that probably never numbered more than 500 men and considerably fewer now: 8 half-tracks and armoured cars destroyed, 6 Mark IV tanks destroyed, 20 to 30 lorries destroyed or damaged, 1 Tiger tank damaged, 300 to 400 killed or wounded, 120 prisoners. The number of prisoners was known to be correct, but as the first 80 of them had been sent to the civilian prison on Sunday night, they must have been freed soon after.

Frost was badly wounded early in the afternoon and shortly afterwards General Urquhart came on the air again from Division. His message was that the bulk of the division was being attacked from both sides, east and west, and that far from Division's being able to come to the help of the 2nd Battalion at the bridge. Division would probably have to call for support from the 2nd Battalion. Major Gough replied for Frost that 2nd Battalion were in "great spirits" and could easily hold out for another 24 hours. Hibbert noted that this was indeed the general feeling, but that the facts hardly supported it: A and B companies driven back almost to Brigade HQ, 50 percent casualties, six pounders under short-range rifle fire, no more Piat ammunition left, and very little small-arms ammunition.

Soon after mid-day, Cardale's party retired from the bridge back towards the Brigade HQ building, which, although it had great holes blown in its walls from 88- and 105-millimeter guns, was still holding out because it had not caught fire. Most of the other houses, however, were now in flames or already burnt out. The German tactic was to smash down the walls with heavy shellfire, then throw in phosphorus grenades to ignite wooden and other inflammable wreckage, and, finally, to keep the flames under heavy fire so as to prevent the defenders from putting out the blaze.

About 30 of Cardale's party got over a broken wall before the retreat was spotted; after that the Germans systematically shot every man who attempted it. Then, while going through a passage between houses, Cardale came on a dying paratrooper, a man he did not recognise, although the man apparently knew him. In his pencilled narrative, scribbled soon after the event, Cardale wrote: "I never knew him but he knew me & he was very near death, but he looked up as I looked down to him and said, 'Are the medics on their way, Tony?' I lied, and said, 'not far behind,' or something pretty akin to that." In writing to me of his experiences, Cardale admitted: "I had this incident on my conscience for years after and used to dream about him. I can *still* picture his face setting into death. Yet if I'd stayed with him where would I be now—with him, I suppose."

Eventually, they got into a house opposite HQ, but when the first man tried to cross the road he was shot down. Then small-arms fire came in at all the windows, and a German soldier stuck a light machine-gun into the room, in broken English ordering them to surrender.

"We were totally worn out, most had no ammo, and some gave in. We flung away rifles and equipment and filed out down to the river bank. We were lined up between two small tanks, their guns turned on us, and searched. Then they marched us through the town. We flung away our helmets and put on our Red Berets—our last act of holding our heads high."

Shortly after dark, the Brigade HQ building was set on fire. This was very serious, because there were 250 wounded men, British and German, in the cellars. An attempt was made to move them to another building, but this was fired also before much could be done. Further, many of the wounded required much more than first aid. Consequently, a truce was arranged; and in the confusion, when no one could fire at anyone else, the defence more or less dissolved.

Shortly before midnight, Major Hibbert saw the Germans march off a large party of British walking wounded, followed by about 30 unwounded paratroopers being marched north under guard. This was probably Cardale's party, which numbered 28 when they surrendered. The remaining defenders in the HQ area had already been regrouped for further fighting and consisted now of two platoons each of five sections commanded by an officer.

Hibbert called on them to report their arms and ammunition state. Almost all were armed, and most had automatics. The ammunition supplies, on the other hand, when averaged out, showed one full magazine for each Bren or Sten. Or about three seconds' uninterrupted firing. Used sparingly, this might have enabled them to hold for four or five hours the next morning, but as there was no sign of XXX Corps approaching, and they had been driven away from the bridge, it seemed better to attempt a break-out by sections during the cover of darkness. Accordingly, they did so; but the German cordon was close and continuous.

The Royal Engineers in the south cellar of the blazing school building numbered 50 men. Five of them were dead, 31 of them wounded, and only 14 were in any way fit to fight. Simpson led their break-out, Mackay bringing up the rear, with the wounded in front of him. In a matter of minutes, their effective strength was halved. Simpson and six men were wounded, and one man was killed.

That left Mackay with six unwounded men, the remnants of the original 50. All carried automatic weapons, and they doubled back, trying to get through the ring of tanks and S.S. men. Instead they ran into about 50 Germans standing beside two yellow-painted Mark III tanks. The Germans were the more surprised, and the six engineers all emptied their magazines in three seconds, losing one man killed and one man wounded. Mackay got away with the other four.

The 50 had now been reduced to five, and those magazines had been the last ones. They were now completely unarmed. So they split up and Mackay hid in a garden, pretending to be dead when a German patrol marched through. He was still "dead" when an NCO kicked him in the ribs, but became "alive" when a soldier ran a bayonet into him.

Major Hibbert, like most of them, failed to break through, so tried to hide in the hope of getting away later. Most of the ruined houses were still much too hot to hide in, and so he chose a coalbin, with a door only 18 inches square, which he shared with Anthony Cotterill. Next morning, several

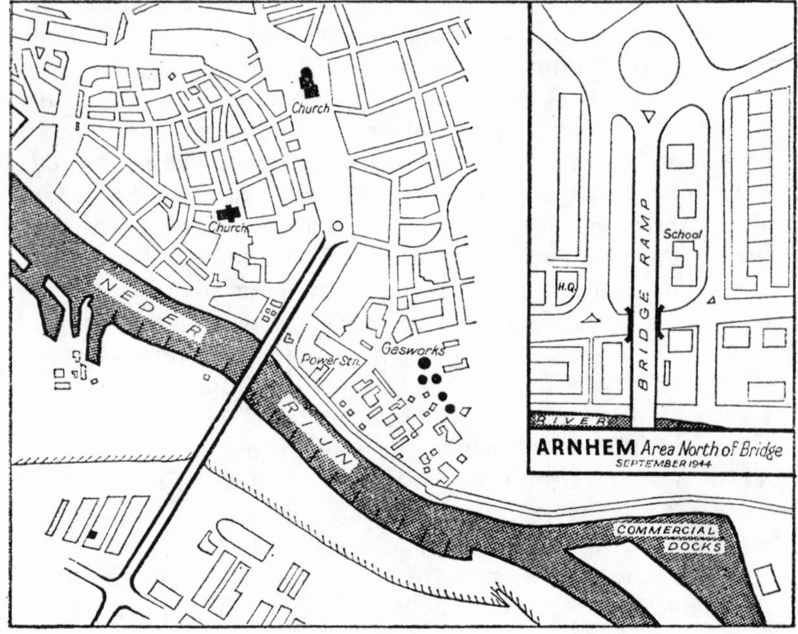

Germans chose the coalbin to lean on, and one fired a bullet into it. Not until about 0900 did a conscientious section of Germans pass, and they discovered the two evaders.

"We were marched off to the square in front of the cathedral, where a very depressing sight met our eyes. About twenty officers and 200 O.Rs., which represented nearly all the unwounded survivors of the bridge, were drawn up. We now had the opportunity to have a closer look at the people we had been fighting with. They were from the S.S. Division Hohenstaufen, which had recently come from Russia, and more recently had been badly battered in the battle of France. The first thing that struck one was the youth of the junior NCOs and men; the majority seemed to be not more than 16 or 17, although the least any of them would admit to was 18. All were thoroughly pleased with themselves at having put us in the bag, and large numbers of them came to look us over. Talking to some of them they said that, though they'd fought on both the Western and the Eastern fronts, they'd never had such a hard fight. The salvage was dealt with very systematically. All the clothing, equipment, arms, and ammunition, that had been captured from us, was carefully sorted and stacked in heaps against the cathedral walls. Although it was very depressing to see the amount of arms and equipment they had won from us, it was most satisfying to see how small was the amunition pile—half a dozen rounds of 6 pdr ammunition (belonging to a gun which had been knocked out) and a very small pile of ·303. It at least made one feel less guilty about being taken prisoner, and made one realise that even if we had sold our lives, it wouldn't have been dearly."

1 Parachute Brigade had been ordered to take Arnhem road bridge and hold it for two days. They had taken it and held it for four days. Their casualties almost equalled those of the entire 82nd U.S. Airborne Division at Nijmegen, parts of which had been engaged in very bitter fighting. Even more indicative was what happened afterwards, remembering that the captured men were dazed with exhaustion and lack of sleep and food, and some were wounded. The Germans had Hibbert only until Saturday, September 23, in the evening, when he jumped from a truck and bolted in a hail of bullets. That was the start of a long stay in occupied Holland and an eventual safe crossing of the Neder Rijn with about 120 other escaped airborne men.

Mackay and Simpson, both wounded, had got away the previous day from a camp near Emmerich in Germany, by sawing through iron bars. On Saturday, they stole a boat and rode it down the Rhine current to Nijmegen, with Arnhem, still burning, on their right hand, where the remainder of 1 Airborne Division were fighting to the last. Many of the escapees outdid the exploits of James Bond, and it is as well to remember that the iron bars were real bars and that the bullets were fired from real machine-pistols by real Germans.

At about the same time as Cardale and his companions, the last defenders of the bridge, were being marched off into captivity on the north side of the Neder Rijn, the van Dongerens were coming out of their house on the south side of the river, almost opposite, for all firing near the bridge had ceased. Indeed, the bridge was not to be the scene of battle again for another six months, in April, 1945. But the dying down of the battle had the opposite effect on the van Dongerens and their neighbours from what one might expect. —All except for Mr. van Dongeren, that is, who remembering Rotterdam, argued vehemently that they should stay, that it was better to be in a house and have some protection around you than to flee into the open fields. And doubtless he remembered, too, that their flight from the Battle of Rotterdam had led them merely to the battle of Arnhem.

But the houses were still vibrating from gunfire farther away, and Maurits recalled that there was "something like a panic." There was a terrible feeling of, "We must get out, we must get out!"

"Inside a house," [he explained], "you feel all the time that the walls are going to fall on you. You want to be in the open, where you are free. In the house, when there was shelling, it was a life of panic, standing in the doorways to be safer. All the time you want to do something, but you can't, so tension builds up. Then, when you hear no more firing, you rush outside."

They all ran for the fields at about 4:30 P.M., as far as he could recall, which is the same time as Cardale recalled that his party had surrendered and flung down their equipment. Maurits remembered the sight of dead cows lying in the fields—dead because they had not been milked. The fields were bordered by shallow ditches about two or three feet deep, most of them narrow enough to jump over. At dusk, about 7:00 P.M., there were about 25 people gathered in the fields near the houses. They saw the fires in Arnhem south and heard battle noises there, so they decided not to return to the houses for the night.

This was about the time of the truce for the transfer of wounded, followed by the last flare-up around Brigade HQ. Not knowing that this was the last flicker of organised resistance, they set off across the fields in the flame-lit dark and within minutes were machine-gunned by three or four fighter planes of unknown nationality. Probably these were German fighters attacking British positions north of the bridge, a gambit the Luftwaffe had tried without much success for the last two days, and perhaps a few stray bullets or empty cartridge cases struck near the refugees, who were in such a state of panic that judicious assessment was beyond them, quite apart from the fact that they really had no experience to go by.

They immediately fled away over a wider-than-usual ditch, which had less than two feet of water in it, on top of a lot of mud. Little Dieuwke lost her shoes in the mud, sucked off her feet, and could not find them again. A man wearing a hat and carrying his belongings in a white pillow case put both pillow case and hat down on the near side of the ditch, and then jumped over it. Having cleared it, he then recollected that he had left his belongings behind, and went back to get them, picked up his hat (which Maurits said had now a bullet-hole in it), put it on his head, and jumped over the ditch for the third time, still minus the pillow case.

They then all made their way across the fields to the southern part of the village of Elden, which is north of Elst on the main road between Arnhem and Nijmegen, and found shelter for the night in a farmer's cowshed.

By this time, I must confess, as Mr. van Dongeren proceeded with his narrative, my hair was standing on end. Mrs. van Dongeren was showing an unerring instinct for the site of the next battle that would have been of incalculable service to a veteran war correspondent. They were nicely placed, next day, to watch the drop of the Polish Parachute Brigade near Driel and Elst. These were the last airborne reinforcements, arriving later than planned, and many of them in the wrong place—just throwing Polish money away after British.

"From Elden you can see very easily to Oosterbeek" [recollected Maurits]. "I heard the planes and then saw the red, white, blue and orange parachutes in the air. The planes were very low, but the Germans fired only when the parachutes came out. I saw some parachutes collapse, and the men fall fast. Then German soldiers came round the farm, looking for parachutists, and came into our cowshed. They were very young soldiers, very nervous."

The very same scene was being watched from south of Elst by the occupants of the leading cars of the Household

Cavalry and of the first 50 tanks of the Irish Guards. The flak firing at the parachutists was rising from German positions half a mile ahead of the leading elements of XXX Corps. Nijmegen bridge had fallen to the final assault of the Guards and the Americans at dusk the previous day, Wednesday, September 20, about two hours after Arnhem bridge had fallen to Major Brinkman's group of Battle Group Harzer. The two bridges had changed hands almost at the same time, both intact, because Field Marshal Model had ordered that they should not be blown.

In retrospect, his decision was correct for Arnhem bridge, wrong for Nijmegen bridge. But if Frost's battalion had not held on for so long at Arnhem bridge, Model might have been right about Nijmegen also, for then he would have been able to reinforce quickly with heavy units. As it was, Euling's battalion, plus the original garrison, had held out there in defence of the town and the bridges from the evening of the 17th to after nightfall on the 20th. For exactly the same length of time as Frost, that is, and at the same time. And these two battles had decisively affected each other.

Now that the real battles for Arnhem and for Nijmegen were over, the "Island" was to become the next battlefield; and nothing seems more inevitable than that the van Dongerens should move to another deceptively safe and quiet place of refuge.

CHAPTER FIFTEEN

THE BATTLE OF NIJMEGEN

D plus 2: September 19

Operation Market began at approximately 1300 hours on September 17 with the opening of three simultaneous battles at Eindhoven, Nijmegen, and Arnhem. Operation Garden began at approximately 1430 hours with the advance of the Irish Guards on Valkenswaard. The first day was therefore in reality less than half a day by the clock, and in terms of actual daylight only some six hours long, sunset on that day being at 1847, last light at 1941 hours.

If 1 British Airborne Division was to be relieved within 48 hours, XXX Corps would have to reach Arnhem bridge by late morning or early afternoon of September 19. There were hopes that it might be possible for the Coldstream Guards to reach the Zuyder Zee by the evening of the 19th, and thus complete the first part of the whole operation.

In the considered view of Colonel A. N. Breitmeyer, who was at the time intelligence officer of the 2nd Grenadier Guards, this was "an ambitious plan depending on all links falling into place according to schedule, but had we got the high ground in the Apeldoorn area nothing could have stopped us." The Grenadier Guards Group were to be in the van of that advance, taking over from the Irish Guards who were to break through the thin "crust" of German resistance in the initial stages. But no real break-through took place, partly because the German "crust" was thicker and tougher than expected, partly because the going was bad and favoured the defence, partly because the attempt to go round the enemy opposing the advance up the main centre line failed when it was found that the bridges would not support the weight of a tank, and partly because support from the 2nd Tactical Air Force was not available on the second day.

Between Zon and Grave, however, a distance of some 25 miles, American paratroopers held all the bridges. The leading troop of the Household Cavalry left Zon at 0615 on September 19 and reached Grave two hours later, just after 0800, easily outdistancing the tanks. The armoured cars pressed on to within two miles of Nijmegen and found that the road bridge over the Maas–Waal Canal at Neerbosch was too badly damaged for immediate use. With the help of the Americans, they reconnoitred a diversionary route to the intact bridge at Heumen. The 2nd Grenadier Guards reached Grave bridge at about 1000 hours and halted short of it. Breitmeyer, as intelligence officer, went forward with his CO to meet General Browning; and then they were all sent on to General Gavin's HQ in the woods south of Nijmegen, where a combined plan was drawn up.

By now, the Grenadier Guards should have been nearing Arnhem bridge, but were in fact some eight miles short of Nijmegen bridge; and Arnhem bridge lay about 10 miles beyond that by road, although the direct line distance was shorter. And, although Arnhem bridge was still held on the north side by the remnants of 2 Parachute Battalion, Nijmegen bridge was held on both sides by Euling's S.S. Battalion. Three attacks in two days, carried out by the Americans at strengths not exceeding that of two companies, had failed to get anywhere near the bridge.

Both Browning and Gavin considered that it was more important to hold the high ground securely than to risk losing it by attacking the bridge in strength. No serious German attack from the Reichswald had yet materialised, and all the reported German "tanks" had proved to be 2-centimeter flak-guns mounted on armoured half-tracks. The first dangerous attack was not to occur until September 20, but at the time no one could know that.

An important element in the planning on this day was the bad weather over England and the Channel. The fly-in of a glider infantry regiment to reinforce the 82nd was cancelled and so too was the planned drop of the Polish Parachute Brigade at Arnhem. The 82nd did receive a supply drop, but the aircraft flew high and the loads were scattered, making the task of collection more lengthy than unusual. As this normally involved a third of the men already landed, it was a more than usually serious dilution of strength at a critical time.

By early afternoon the Guards were closed up behind the Americans in the southern outskirts of Nijmegen, the armoured cars of the Household Cavalry had got as far to the east as Beek, where from an American position on the high ground they could observe the road bridge, which was still intact. Indeed, it was far more heavily defended than it had been in 1940, when the casemates, pillboxes, and trenches had not been backed by artillery.

88-millimeter guns cited 400 yards north of the Waal were firing on the Americans, who were unable to reply. Two Daimler armoured cars elevated their two-pounder guns, to extreme range and drove the crews of the 88s out of their emplacements. Then a single 88, farther away, opened up; but this was quelled by calling up the divisional artillery and giving them the map reference. They hit with the first salvo, aided by the excellent defence overlay maps that pin-pointed all known enemy positions most accurately. The Germans then moved up four 105-millimeter guns and opened fire. To this there could be no reply, because ammunition was "desperately short" and the little left was wanted to support an attack now being planned.

Meanwhile, the armoured cars engaged the casemates sited north of the bridge, which were within their range, before withdrawing at about 1600. Captain Cooper remained with the Americans to relay information, while they were being steadily shelled.

"Decided to get into trench with the Americans and stayed there one and a half hours, by which time completely deaf and covered with dust." [he wrote]. "This sort of shelling is perfectly bloody and gives you a splitting headache and seems to jar the whole system. Every now and again the Spandaus opened up from the other side of the river and bullets whistled over our heads. These American troops are splendid types—extremely brave, very cheerful and indifferent to the worst. The bridge, an enormous girdered affair, has been wired for blowing, which the 'Underground' have twice cut, and is covered by every conceivable German weapon."

The Dutch "Underground" played an important part in the decisions made that day, through the Dutch liaison officer with the 82nd, Captain Arie D. Bestbreurtje. The historian of the Irish Guards wrote:

"The Dutch Resistance gave rather confused information, but they were emphatic about two things: That the German demolition control centre was in the Post Office, and that the road bridge could not be blown anywhere because a youth called Van something had cut the leads from the Post Office to the bridge, or alternatively, that the 'Underground' had removed all the explosive charges from the bridge. This story was rather doubtful. Why should the Germans blow the bridges from the wrong side, and did they never inspect or test their preparations? But however doubtful, the story could not be ignored."

Therefore, the decision was made to make a quick dash with combined forces for three objectives—the road bridge to the east, the railway bridge to the west, and the post office in the centre of the town and almost midway between the southern approaches to both bridges. Each task force was to be composed of mixed British and American units, led by guides from the Netherlands Interior Forces.

The eastern force, which was to take both the post office and the road bridge whose demolitions it was supposed to control, consisted of the tanks of 3 Squadron, 2 Grenadier Guards, and the infantry of 2 Company, 1 Grenadier Guards, plus Companies E and F of the 2nd Battalion, 505 Parachute Infantry.

The western force, which was to take the railway bridge, had five tanks from 3 Squadron of the 2nd Grenadiers, led by Captain J. W. Neville, a platoon of infantry from the 1st Grenadiers travelling in three carriers, plus Company D of the 2nd Battalion, 505 Parachute Infantry, commanded by First Lieutenant Oliver B. Carr, Jr.

The eastern column moved off at about 1600 hours for yet another attack on the road bridge, the fourth in three days. All went well until the leading tank, commanded by Lieutenant J. Moller, came in sight of the traffic roundabout 300 yards south of the bridge. Then it was immediately knocked out by an 88, and Moller was killed. Other Shermans tried to ease past the blazing hulk and were in their turn either knocked out or damaged. The American paratroopers under First Lieutenant James J. Smith got to within a hundred yards of the roundabout, then had to withdraw.

For the rest of the afternoon, they left the streets and tried to get forward by moving along the rooftops and blasting a way through houses, but were unable to reach the roundabout. Indeed, they made absolutely no impression on the German defences, which consisted of loopholed houses and slit trenches dominated by the Valkhof.

This site had originally been chosen by the Romans as the key to Nijmegen and had been fortified by the Second Legion; then by Charlemagne; then by Frederick Barbarossa; and now the remains of Barbarossa's fortress afforded cover to anti tank guns and infantry of the Waffen S.S. amply equipped with automatic weapons. The bridge roundabout, the Keizer Traianus Plein, gave radial fields of fire down all the approach roads at its south-eastern corner.

However, in the centre of the town, the post office was captured. "There was nothing in it but civilians in the cellars and dead Germans behind the counters," wrote the Irish Guards historian. There was no sign of any demolition mechanism connected with the bridge, but as the building was excellently placed, it was chosen as headquarters for the remainder of the battle of Nijmegen, which was to be controlled from there.

The railway bridge party under Captain J. W. Neville assembled in the lane outside the town, and he particularly recalled that

"the Americans were in an extremely lighthearted mood, quite undaunted by the prospects, indeed they remained in high spirits throughout. There was only one war correspondent present, who took some photographs which subsequently appeared in the *Daily Telegraph.* I asked him which paper he represented and learned that he came from a women's magazine. Heaven knows how he got there; for a certainty, the usual gang of war correspondents, who we got to know quite well in the campaign, were still playing poker in Brussels."

This was the reason why the Battle of Nijmegen was to be so inadequately reported, in contrast to Arnhem, and why it could later be suggested that the men who fought at Nijmegen had "let down" the men who fought at Arnhem.

"Our party had been given a guide, a Dutchman who spoke very little English," [wrote Neville]. "Nevertheless, by following his instructions we were able to reach our goal, which otherwise would have proved extremely difficult. The paratroops rode on the backs of the tanks and we set off with the infantry carriers disposed between the tanks, keeping about 40–50 yards between each vehicle. I myself rode in the middle, giving instructions concerning the route on the wireless. This went well out to the west, with the result that the railway bridge was approached from its western side. To begin with, the advance was comparatively uneventful, with occasional shots from buildings. In at least two cases, civilians opened fire. The principal trouble came from a house in which there were several Spandaus, and these were knocked out with the 75-mm gun from the leading tank. At this stage we expected the opposition to increase, but it would appear that they were in isolated houses, for the last 400 or 500 yards before we reached the railway line were comparatively uneventful. No doubt the Dutch guide had some part to play in this result."

The column halted at a crossroads while the leading tank reconnoitred. Looking back along the route they had come, Neville saw a Panther tank cross the road at the nearest intersection, headed for the scene of the shooting, with the crew apparently so intent on the place where the column had last been in action that they were in fact looking the wrong way.

About 200 yards from the southern end of the bridge, Neville called a halt and went forward with the American officer. The railway line was carried up to the bridge on a long embankment, not negotiable by tanks, but there was one point where the road beside the Waal passed under the embankment. As they subsequently discovered, on the other side of the embankment was a ramp that led up to the railway line and the bridge. On the side facing them, however, were many dug-in positions for heavy machine-guns and anti-tank guns, firing over an open space about 100 yards across.

"As the light was beginning to fade, we decided upon an immediate attack. The plan was simple, if unimaginative.

Three tanks were to charge the opening in the embankment while the other two gave covering fire. At the same time the Americans, aided by the infantry carriers, were to gain the embankment to the south and drive out the machine-gunners from the flank. Alas, the plan did not work. As soon as the leading tanks moved forward across the open space, they came under heavy artillery fire from a battery on the north bank of the Waal. Clearly, these guns had been calibrated in advance. The leading tank was hit and destroyed immediately, and the next was hit immediately afterwards. All but one of the crew in the leading tank were killed and my own driver, contrary to orders and with misplaced bravery, jumped out of my tank and went to the rescue of those trapped. As a result, two crews were rescued but my driver sustained serious burns. Our attack had lost its impetus and the lot of the Americans was no better. They came under exceedingly heavy machine-gun fire, not only from the embankment in front, but also from Germans who were by then on all sides. The Germans also had the support of two self-propelled guns, which appeared through the tunnel in the embankment and were engaged by our tanks. By this time it was dark, and since we had failed to make any impression on the defences, I decided to call off the attack during the night.

We withdrew about 100 yards and commandeered several houses to form a temporary headquarters. There were about six seriously wounded men who probably would not have survived without medical treatment, whom I decided to send back in a carrier. The Americans, despite the reverse and a few casualties, were still quite unmoved. We placed our three remaining tanks in strategic places and everyone else took cover in the adjoining houses. The American commander, who was otherwise a most co-operative man, refused at this stage to have anything to do with sentries, on the grounds that his men needed 'a good night's sleep.' Despite some forceful words from me, he remained adamant. To protect themselves against surprise attack, their so-called 'sentries' slept behind the doors, so that any intruder would have to wake them up before getting in. My own expectation was, that we would be rushed during the night; and at frequent intervals we could hear the Germans moving around us.

Looking back on it in the light of what happened next morning, it is obvious that the Germans, far from making a plan to attack us, were withdrawing."

As at Arnhem, so too at Nijmegen the Germans selected a small proportion of houses and public buildings for burning, so that the streets would be brightly illuminated for their anti tank guns and automatic weapons. Darkness was dangerous, as under its cover infantry might be able to creep forward and rush them from close range. The same principle applied to Captain Neville's tanks, similarly blinded by night; and indeed his small force, having simply driven past a number of German-occupied buildings on their way to the railway embankment, had in fact lodged itself among the German defenders. He was understandably anxious at having Germans behind him, and the Germans were equally concerned at having been apparently cut off from their main force and, in particular, the escape route over the Waal offered by the railway bridge, upon which a so-called "hare track" had been constructed.

The people of Nijmegen did not see the fires as a "compelling military necessity," but as an outrage; a "senseless destruction," a last outburst of fury showing "the immeasurable brutality and bestiality of the pagan national-socialists." That evening, wrote one Dutch witness,

"the centre of the town is like a hell. A rustling sound like that of a waterfall, uncanny and terrifying, fills the air and, seized with panic, thousands and thousands fly from this doomed Nijmegen. Those who live on the outskirts, stare in terror at the whirling sea of fire from which huge columns of smoke emerge to write a fierce indictment on the night firmament. While the fire is doing its destructive work, an incessant rain of shells come screeching and whistling over the burning town. There are no words to describe this holocaust."

A burning city is indeed an appalling, spectacular, and beautiful sight; and it is true that the flames do hiss and roar, the sparks showering upwards like golden butterflies. It is also true that the situation always seems much more serious than it really is, the end of the world, until sufficient comparative experience has been gained with which to make a cooler judgement. The citizens of Nijmegen were fortunate to be denied this comparative experience, although they were later to become connoisseurs of shellfire.

Nevertheless, the emotional incoherence, the groping for the right word or phrase, is an accurate expression of how many people felt that night, at that particular place and time. Even the incoherence is echoed in the narrative of a German soldier, fighting that same night and at that same time, but in a different place—along the canal road from Helmond to Eindhoven.

"If only I could describe it properly, the close-combat in the Dutch woods!" [he burst out]. "I wish I had the chance to go back to this country, Holland, and tell what happened there. Point out every tree and bush and piece of ground where the Allied parachute-containers burst open as they came crashing down into our lines. It was the 19th of September, at the hydrochloric-acid factory by the canal road—a fight against the parachute troops on the ground and snipers in the tree-tops. That night, the former General der Flieger Student himself took part in the German counter-attack. We came up against hard, bitter opposition and our desperate attempt at attack was brought to a halt. It was raining and many of our men slipped and slithered down the wet slope into the canal, where they drowned. Then the Americans let the hydro-chloric-acid into the trenches, which were partly filled with water. This acid caused terrible injuries on the bodies of the soldiers; few survived this ordeal."

The soldier, Karl Max Wietzorek, had fought with a para-chute regiment in Normandy, the remains of which were now part of the Battle Group Tuchstein. The counter-attack in which they took part involved other German formations, in-cluding the 59th Infantry Division on the western side of the "corridor" and the 107th Panzer Brigade on the eastern side, all trying to cut what was soon to become known as "Hell's Highway."

That night, the pocket panzer division, which had hur-riedly been rerouted from Aachen, got to within sight of the

Bailey bridge spanning the Wilhelmina Canal at Zon and was firing on the command post of the 101st U.S. Airborne Division until Major-General Maxwell Taylor himself brought up reinforcements and drove them back. This attack caused some chaos among the drivers of the supply-column vehicles, one of which was burning brightly on top of the Bailey bridge.

Worse was to come farther south at Eindhoven, where a cluster of parachute flares bursting out over the town signalled an attack by about 100 twin-engined bombers, which dropped their loads systematically and accurately, some of them diving to within 300 feet of the columns of vehicles slowly passing through the town. In 10 minutes it was all over, and 18 Royal Army Service Corps trucks had been destroyed.

But the chaos created was out of all proportion. The first half-dozen trucks to sustain direct hits held artillery ammunition, which began to burn and explode. The next line of vehicles to go up held fuel, and from them the flames spread to trucks loaded with small-arms ammunition. To the whistle and thunder of exploding bombs was added the sharper crack of shells blowing up and the stutter of cartridges. The road was strewn and blocked by wreckage. An officer of the Household Cavalry, Captain Profumo, rapidly mustered all available Dutchmen to help clear the debris; and the column got on the move again. But the loss of so much ammunition, at a time when there was a severe shortage in Nijmegen, could not be made good immediately.

CHAPTER SIXTEEN

THE WAAL AND THE VALKHOF

D plus 3: September 20

At dawn on Wednesday, September 20, the supply column that had been moving up through Eindhoven under the protection of the armoured cars of A and D squadrons of the Household Cavalry, had reached Grave bridge. It had started from Bourg Leopold in Belgium the previous afternoon and included 800 vehicles as well as a number of anti-aircraft guns, bridging equipment, and engineer units. Two troops of roadbound armoured cars provided only illusory protection from flank attacks to such an unwieldy convoy, and the commander of a part of it decided to halt for the night rather than risk the Panthers still roaming about. Major Ward, the armoured car escort commander, fell out with him over this, and carried on through the night with the remainder of the column.

In the darkness, aided by a divisional sign that was pointing the wrong way, he took a side road leading to Heesch, where the Germans were reported to be in force, and had the column turned round rather than risk so many vulnerable and valuable vehicles. It was with bent wings, dented radiators, and drivers falling asleep at the wheel that the head of the column reached Grave bridge, where three Focke-Wulf 190s attacked it.

"We were machine-gunned whilst stationary, with no chance of going forwards or backwards or getting off the road" [recalled Major Roden Orde of the Household Cavalry]. "I never thought human beings could move so fast into ditches. When we recovered after the attack I saw Corporal Eric Meade-King quietly puffing at his revolting pipe as he sat by a canal cutting with a half-finished drawing of Grave bridge."

Meade-King, who had studied at Westminster School of Art, always rode in a three-ton lorry with a sketch book under his seat, ready for opportunities like this. He found that his art training stood him in good stead in the army, as he was often excused duller duties in order to paint officers' coats of arms on the turrets of their armoured cars, or the names of dead men on white crosses, or divisional signs, and, once, a foxhunting mural on the walls of a German barracks (then the officers' mess). Fortunately, his sketches survived the war, although the three-tonner was burnt-out before the end.

The sudden reappearance of the Luftwaffe, even in small numbers, seemed an omen of change; and was due to the peculiar Allied command system that achieved a general denial of tactical air support to the whole operation, while managing at the same time to give the Luftwaffe local air superiority, although the German planes could be numbered only in hundreds, while the Allies counted by thousands. Adverse weather also played a part, but only a small part, in this surprising reversal of conditions in Normandy. Consequently, the ground troops had to rely largely on their own efforts and had nothing like the close air support given by the Germans in 1940 to both their airborne troops and the ground forces moving along the corridor from Gennep to Moerdijk and Rotterdam. The almost complete absence of help from "flying artillery" was a major factor both for the landed airborne divisions and the troops and supplies moving up along the corridor to their aid.

During the night of September 19–20, a number of plans had been devised by various people, with many blank spaces to be filled in at the last moment, agreements secured, arrangements made, and so on. No doubt the urgent necessity of crossing the Waal and relieving the visibly wilting Arnhem bridgehead helped these negotiations to go smoothly. Considering that the plans entailed the dovetailing of British tanks, infantry, engineers, and artillery with American paratroops, engineers, and artillery, plus the Netherlands Interior Forces, in a complicated four-pronged attack of the utmost danger and difficulty, this was truly remarkable.

The previous precedent—that of May 10, 1940—indicated

that the bridges would be blown. All through September 20, 1944, it was expected that the bridges would go up at any moment; and the nearer the attackers got to the bridges, the greater became the likelihood that they would detonate in two thunderous columns of smoke.

Consequently, one-half of the plan was an assault crossing of the Waal west of both bridges by Colonel R. H. Tucker's 504th Parachute Infantry Regiment. This in face of fire from the artillery component of the 9th S.S. Panzer Division, now under command of the 10th S.S., which Oberst Harzer described as possessing "tremendous fire-power, from almost entirely armoured vehicles, handled in the most clever and flexible manner, which until Battalion Euling cleared out of Nijmegen prevented the Americans from gaining a bridge-head."

To oppose it, a hundred British and American guns were to be brought up, plus the tank guns of the Irish Guards, and these were to literally "shoot" the American parachutists across the Waal. Consequently, Brigadier C. P. Jones, Commander, Royal Engineers of Guards Armoured, received a telephone call early on the 20th: "Have you got any assault boats?" To which he replied: "Yes—32 serviceable."

Having set the wheels in train, he drove over to Gavin's HQ. "I found that they proposed to carry out an assault crossing of the Waal, in the power station area, with the idea of taking the bridge defences in the rear, in conjunction with an attack by the Grenadier Group from the south on to the near end of the bridge, a formidable project," he noted soon after. He offered them rafts and Royal Engineers to ferry their anti-tank guns across, and this was accepted. Then he hurried off to make sure that all this equipment would actually be there by early afternoon, although the exact site for the crossing had not then even been selected.

Colonel Tucker had been told what he was in for the previous day at 2100 hours by his divisional operations officer, and that he was to contact General Horrocks next morning and "iron out as smooth an operation as could possibly be done." Consequently, while Brigadier Jones was ironing out the assault boat problem at the American HQ, Tucker was at the British HQ, from where he went forward with Colonel Giles

Vandeleur (commanding the Irish Guards tanks because Colonel "Joe" was ill) in his reconnaissance car as

"neither of us was sure as to where the crossing should be made. I had warned my battalion commanders the night before what to expect, but basically I wanted my 2nd Battalion to form a base of fire along the river bank. The 3rd Battalion was to lead the assault, followed closely by the 1st Battalion. The 3rd Battalion was to fan out to the east, getting about 1,000 yards north of the Nijmegen highway bridge. The 1st Battalion was to fan out to the west, maintaining contact with the 3rd Battalion and form[ing] with them an arc around the northern exits of the bridge. A short order, but you must remember these battalion commanders had been with me in combat for more than a year. They understood me and I them, and all their officers and men. With the advice of my combat engineer company commander, I picked the crossing site when we had reached the river bank and could see the tiny beach available for launching our boats. They were British engineer assault craft which carried 16 men, propelled by paddlers; they did not arrive until 30 minutes before we were to jump off, and our troops had never seen them before, but they would be steered by our engineers.

"About one hour before the crossing, General Horrocks walked around my troops with me, and he could not get over it as he said: 'Look, some of 'em are sleeping, others are joking with each other, others are dreaming of home, no doubt. Don't they realise they are to make a daylight river crossing in the face of a determined enemy and many will be dead or wounded in a couple of hours [?] I wonder if they can make it?' I told him we all wondered, but we'd do our best and these were all veterans. By this time, the Irish Guards tanks had been positioned behind the factory which ran along the edge of the river. They could fire, then roll back behind the buildings to reload or change their positions."

The attack was timed for 1500 hours and the current was expected then to be running at not less than three knots, which is a fast walking pace. The boats would go downstream at this rate during their passage to the far bank, and it was this factor of drift that decided the American engineer to pick an exposed launching place for the boats upstream rather than the canal entrance downstream. I have driven a motorboat in that river, and not only is it impressively wide when seen from a boat in midstream, but the water is a fast-moving roadway sweeping one down towards the sea.

At the same time as Tucker had been told what was expected of his regiment on the 20th, the Grenadier Guards of "Group Hot" had been notified that their task for that day would be the clearing of Nijmegen, without reinforcements, because the 325th U.S. Glider Infantry Regiment had been unable to land, owing to bad weather. The two Grenadier COs, together with the CO of the 2nd Battalion, 505th Parachute Infantry, had worked out a combined plan by 0400 on the 20th.

Instead of putting in their main attack along the southeast road to the bridge via the "bridge roundabout," where they had been held before and where the Germans were well prepared to meet them, they would instead attack from the west towards the Valkhof. This meant methodically clearing the town to procure enough space for the final assault on the Valkhof and the bridge it guarded, and also protecting the western flank.

Captain Neville's force, still surrounded by Germans near the railway embankment, was ordered by wireless to clear the town near the railway bridge. Pressure was to be maintained towards the "bridge roundabout" and Hunner Park, but this was not the main assault. The culmination of these concentric attacks was to be the rushing of the road bridge, or an attempt to do so, and the bridge approaches were to be kept under continuous fire from 25-pounder field guns, using the ammunition just brought up by the Eindhoven convoy.

The attack began at 0830 from the big "town roundabout," the Keizer Karel Plein, from which the roads radiated northeast towards the fire-swept open ground at the southern end of the road bridge, which, reading from left to right, consisted of the Valkhof, Hunner Park, and the "bridge roundabout," all heavily fortified and entrenched.

This was not a job for an armoured division, and not all the tanks were, or could be, employed. Basically, in street-fighting only the two leading tanks in any one street are of any use, as they alone can fire; apart from which, they are vulnerable both to short-range bazookas fired from houses on their flanks and to anti-tank guns firing down the street in front, and if snipers can keep the tank commanders' heads down, the vehicles are almost blind. Consequently, the battle was fought mainly by the infantry of the 1st Grenadiers, supported by the tanks of 2 Squadron, 2nd Grenadiers.

At first, the attack went well, each section of the town being cleared methodically by one party of infantry, another party waiting behind them to leapfrog through to the next section, under cover of their fire and that of the tanks, towards the Valkhof and Hunner Park, while the 2nd Battalion of Colonel Vandervoort's 505th Parachute Infantry, also supported by Guards' tanks, pressed forward from the south-east towards the right-hand objective, the "bridge roundabout."

Lieutenant-Colonel P. G. A. Prescott, M.C., who now commands the 2nd Battalion of the Grenadier Guards, was then a troop leader of 2 Squadron. After their abortive attempt to cross the river near Eindhoven, which had put their troop sergeant's tank into it, they had been in reserve, and accepted this gratefully.

"Initially I was placed under command of 4 Company of the 1st Battalion"[he wrote], "and our task was to clear the main street from the 'ring road' up to the Valkhof Gardens overlooking the road bridge. I married up with the infantry company south of the ring road and we soon set off across this road. I recall seeing the American parachutists dug in along the road in the gardens between the two carriageways. One could not but gain the impression that they were very tired. We made reasonably good progress down the street with the infantry clearing the houses, while the tank troops, of necessity on a one-tank front, gave fire support up at the windows. I recall coming under small arms fire at one time and having to close down, and shortly afterwards having mortar fire directed onto my tank and closing down once more. My troop corporal was shot through the arm while in the cupola of his tank, but was able to continue in command. We reached the open square in front of the Valkhof Gardens and stopped to take stock. The Company Commander informed me that enemy machine-gun fire was sweeping the square from each flank and that the garden itself was occupied by dug-in enemy infantry. We made a plan to clear the houses on the east side of the square and then to press on down the street to the right towards the bridge roundabout some 200 yards away, and itself only some 200 yards from the bridge.

"I had lost my troop sergeant at the bridge the day before, and now had only three tanks, so my troop sergeant was now a lance sergeant. I ordered him to move his tank forward into the north-east corner of the square and to engage the enemy in the gardens at close quarters. I myself advanced right-handed down to the street to the right while the infantry cleared the houses beside us. Almost immediately, my troop sergeant's tank was knocked out by a bazooka, he himself was killed instantly and all but one of the crew killed by machine-gun fire as they bailed out. The remaining crew member was very severely wounded in the abdomen and took cover beside the tank. I had only just entered the street to the right when I saw a German lean out of the window above me, aim a bazooka at my tank, and fire. He hit us on the engine deck, but we did not catch fire.

"I could clearly see the bridge roundabout ahead of me and was just about to move forward again, when I saw an S.P. gun move out of some shrubbery there. We fired at each other almost simultaneously. But his shot was armour-piercing, ours H.E., as we were primarily giving close support to infantry against infantry. My tank was knocked out, and we bailed out, running for cover into the houses alongside. The house we entered had no back door and therefore we ran along the square to regain cover, followed by pretty inaccurate machine-gun fire. I took command of my troop corporal's tank, the only one now left in my troop.

"I met a U.S. medical corporal who volunteered to go forward under a red cross to tend the wounded man beside my troop sergeant's tank. He was shot at all the way across the square. But he reached the tank, gave first aid, and under cover of smoke grenades which we threw returned to us again under enemy fire. He told me that the Guardsman was dying and that there was nothing he could do. Shortly after, unknown to me, the operator from my knocked-out tank,

Guardsman W. Meadows, made two attempts to reach this wounded man. Both were frustrated by enemy fire. He was subsequently awarded the D.C.M. I mention these incidents, not because they are history, but because they perhaps indicate the intensity with which the Germans resisted our advance."

The citation for the D.C.M. gained by Guardsman Meadows shows it even more clearly. While one Spandau swept the knocked-out tank belonging to the troop sergeant, two more Spandaus opened up on the infantry section that was protecting its flanks, and three of them were seriously wounded.

"Summing up the situation, this Guardsman dismounted from his tank, and under this intense enemy fire, ran across the street and carried back one of the wounded men. Then, although he himself was wounded in the hand, he again crossed the street and rescued a second wounded man from the middle of the road, which was still under a hail of enemy bullets. Once again, in spite of being wounded a second time, he crossed the road, forced a German Spandau man to surrender by jumping down on top of him in his trench, and carried back a third wounded comrade who lay near the knocked-out tank. He was for the third time wounded, this time in the neck, and it was with the greatest difficulty he was persuaded not to attempt to rescue a fourth wounded comrade, as the condition of his own wounds was becoming serious."

It was this battle that the British war correspondent and military historian, Chester Wilmot, was to dismiss in one line as "mopping up," in the course of his thesis that XXX Corps did not do its utmost to relieve the airborne troops at Arnhem. In fact it was a very vicious, even battle between, on the one hand, an S.S. battalion well equipped with anti-tank guns and bazookas and closely supported by their divisional artillery, and, on the other, a British battalion supported by a squadron of tanks and the divisional artillery with ammunition rationed.

There was in addition one U.S. battalion attacking from the south-east, but this gave the attackers some numerical superiority only in the first and last stages of the fight. The reason for this was that two new battles began at about 1100 hours.

Some two and a half hours after the combined British and American attack had begun in the centre of Nijmegen, General Eugen Meindl's II Fallschirm Corps put in a seven-battalion attack at two points on the long perimeter held by five battalions of the 82nd U.S. Airborne Division. At Mook and Riethorst in the south, dangerously close to the vital intact bridge at Heumen, the German parachutists came in under a hail of 88-millimeter shells and Nebelwerfer bombs against the American parachutists, and drove them back. Gavin called on the Coldstream Guards for tank support, and got it.

But the more immediately dangerous attack was that south-east of Nijmegen, which re-took Wyler and Beek and drove the American parachutists back up the hill to Berg en Dal. From here, one can walk into Nijmegen, and the Germans very nearly did. The American commander, Colonel Lou Mendez, by shifting his platoons about quickly, managed to conceal the fact that there was a gap a few hundred yards away through which the Germans could have strolled into Nijmegen along a route leading to the "bridge roundabout."

General Gavin only heard the details of his own attack to get the bridge at second-hand, the next day, and explained to me:

"On the afternoon of the assault crossing of the river, the 82nd Airborne Division became deeply involved with a German attack coming from two directions. One German force over-ran the town of Mook and another over-ran the town of Beek. From mid-afternoon until long after dark, I was almost totally preoccupied with shifting reserves, visiting unit commanders, and seeking to stabilise that side of the Division area."

The attack of Colonel Tucker's 504th Parachute Infantry across the Waal west of both bridges was timed for 1500 hours, covered by a smokescreen to be put down previously by the 25-pounders of the Leicestershire Yeomanry. This was vital, because the launching beach was in full view of the Germans on the Lent side of the Waal, and the Americans had never seen the boats before and would have to be taught how to use them before they could embark.

The opposition was not a matter of small-arms fire, but of the mobile artillery of 9 S.S. Panzer Division plus flak emplacements. How accurate these guns were was shown when one of the Royal Engineer trucks carrying six out of the 32 assault boats promised by Brigadier Jones to the Americans tried to get to the site by moving out onto the road parallel to the river. In an instant there were only 26 boats instead of 32, and the number of trucks had been reduced by one.

At 1430 the tanks of 2 and 3 squadrons of the Irish Guards moved slowly into position, the former having good fields of fire but being as exposed as the Americans to deadly accurate shellfire, the latter having less good fields of fire but being protected by rubble. At 1455 the British and American guns put down smoke on the far bank, before lifting to fire high explosives on the German positions farther back. The Americans carried their assault boats down to the river and then gathered round Major Thomas of the Royal Engineers for a brief lesson in boatmanship. Then they launched them and scrambled in, packed so tightly that they could hardly move. Under the weight, some of the boats grounded again in the shallows at the water's edge, and some men had to get out, push, then scramble in again.

Colonel Tucker was now at the top of the power station with his radio man and Colonel Giles Vandeleur, who was to control the fire of his tanks. General "Boy" Browning was there as well.

"The entire crossing area was spread out below us" [recalled Colonel Tucker]. "The first wave of the 3rd Battalion (Major Julian A. Cook) raced through a hail of lead across the beach area, loaded into the assault boats, and set out for the other side, roughly 400 yards away. There was direct fire from Germans 88s, flak wagons, 20 mm canon [*sic*], MGs and rifle fire kicking up splashes in the water beside the boats. Some men were hit direct, others blown into the water, but those still able to used their helmets and even their hands to paddle furiously towards the shore. Of the 26 boats that made up the initial wave, only 11 were in condition to return."

The Irish Guards historian wrote: "Each boat took twenty-five minutes to cross and return. No praise is too high for their courage, especially that of the second and third waves, who stood on the bank watching the fate of the first." The smokescreen was blown away by a fitful wind and the packed, burdened infantry jammed in their frail canvas craft were exposed nakedly to the enemy guns.

Most of the 88s and 20-millimeters were flak guns and could not depress their muzzles sufficiently to engage the boats as they neared the Lent bank, and instead took the exposed Irish Guards tanks as targets; but nevertheless, the rippling spurts of water as bullets hit the river or bursting shells sent their fragments to the surface looked to one American just like "a school of mackerel on the feed." One boat capsized 20 yards from the Lent bank and the heavily loaded men went to the bottom. One of them, Private Joseph Jedlicka, finding only a few feet of water over his head when he stood upright, held his breath and walked into shallower water, reaching the shore fully equipped and still holding his automatic rifle.

Colonel Taylor recollected:

"I cannot ever forget General Browning's remark when the first wave of the 3rd Battalion charged up the sides of the dike in the face of homicidal fire and, using bayonets and grenades against the enemy behind the dike, established a very small bridgehead which grew bigger as time went by. He said, 'Look at 'em, unbelievably wonderful men and certainly great soldiers.' I also could and did ask Colonel Vandeleur to direct tank smoke or explosive fire against particular Kraut guns. They and their fire were invaluable. Then I came down and jumped into one of the boats with my G-3 and went across the river to arrive just as grenades and fire were brought down on Fort Lent. What happened there was grenades and mortar fire into the fort area, then a running drive right into the Fort. The bridge into the fort was kept clear by riflemen who fired at anything that moved. I went into the fort behind the initial troops."

This old moated building was Fortress West, in 1940 used

by the Dutch merely as a barracks; and it was on the very same dyke, under its walls, that Sergeant van Dijk had assembled the crew of his casemate and marshalled the troops into some sort of order for the retreat to the west on the evening of May 10, 1940. The Germans had now installed 20-millimeter flak guns and machine-guns on top of the building, but from the Irish Guards it was now getting "particular attention—even armour piercing shot to keep the defenders' heads down," wrote their historian.

"Colonel Tucker had told the tanks to shoot anywhere, any time at anything. His troops, he said, would fire amber Véry lights if the fire was coming too close to them. No Véry lights ever went up, not necessarily because the Irish Guards' shooting was so good—though, of course, it was—but because all the Véry cartridges had got wet in the crossing."

The American units had got totally scrambled in the crossing, and at first no units existed, merely bunches of men, many of them strangers to each other, determined to get forward. The Irish Guards were running out of ammunition, and some of the Browning machine-guns were actually "running away"—that is, having become so hot from almost continuous firing, they would not stop until the last cartridge had been fed in. It was hard to make out where the Americans were, particularly as Colonel Tucker had gone over to lead from up front.

"At four o'clock Major Tyler saw figures moving on the railway bridge and reported that he could distinguish American uniforms or, maybe, German" [wrote the historian of the Irish Guards]. "Being over-excited, he said a different thing every minute, and so did every other tank commander. In fact, no one could possibly tell at that distance, through the smoke and girders. But at five o'clock the American Command Post said that their troops controlled the northern end of both bridges."

This piece of information confused a good many people in Guards Armoured at the time, has been accepted by most historians, British and American, ever since, and as it could not possibly be made to fit other information in my possession, was a source of puzzlement to me, too. The favourite version, British in origin but copied by American historians also, is that an American flag flying in fact from the railway bridge and put there by Colonel Tucker's men, was mistaken for an American flag flying from the road bridge, which report caused the Guards tanks to charge the road bridge.

The basic fact appears to be that Captain Neville's party got the road bridge early on the 20th, but being cut off physically and their wireless sets suffering from the same sort of trouble as was being experienced at Arnhem, were unable to tell anyone. As Neville's force consisted of both American and British infantry, as well as British tanks, it may well have been that an American flag went up on the railway bridge as an alternative means of signalling. Captain Neville's recollection is:

"By the middle of the morning our infantry were over the railway bridge but I can no longer recall the exact timing in relation to the main attack by the 504th Parachute Regiment over the river in assault boats. At all events the two parties made contact during the afternoon. The difficulty was that, having captured the bridge, we were unable to make any contact on the wireless, either with the Squadron Leader or Battalion Headquarters. Communications had been bad all the time and we could not raise a reply on any of the sets. The result was that we were unable to profit by the capture of the railway bridge and the attack on the road bridge continued unabated. In fact the Commanding Officer, who was no doubt concerned to discover what was going on, sent his driver in a scout car with a staff sergeant; they drove straight into the enemy and were killed. By the time that messages by Bren carrier had been sent back, it was already too late to switch the advance and the battle for the road bridge was in its final stages. Viewed from our side, one had the impression that we had inflicted very little damage during the fighting; however, when one looked at the scene afterwards, this was far from the case. Besides the number of dead there were machine-guns, half-tracks, a self-propelled gun and two anti-tank guns."

According to American records, there were 267 dead Germans on the railway bridge.

CHAPTER SEVENTEEN

"ONE MAD RUSH"

Nijmegen Bridge: Evening, September 20

From mid-afternoon of September 20, the Battle of Nijmegen is best considered as a triangle north of Nijmegen. Its base was the south bank of the Waal, running from east to west from the "bridge roundabout" through Hunner Park, the Valkhof, along the Valkade to the railway bridge, and past the railway bridge to the power station on the west by the Maas–Waal Canal.

The left-hand, or western side of the triangle was the line of advance of Colonel Tucker's 3rd Battalion, which was striking right-handed to the north-east across the "Island" towards the third bridge—the bridge that, north of Lent, carried the railway line to Arnhem over the main road to Arnhem.

The right-hand, or eastern side of the triangle was that same Nijmegen–Arnhem road that began at the "bridge roundabout" and was carried over the river by the largest single-span bridge in Europe.

At that point the river was 550 metres wide, and the bridge, supported by four piers, had a centre span 244 metres long over the deep water in the middle of the Waal. As the road at both ends of the bridge was embanked, in effect that road was carried almost in a straight line and high above the level of the surrounding countryside for a distance of 1,300 metres—or something like three-quarters of a mile. I have taken these figures from a Dutch military map, because the soldiers' estimates of distance, like many of their timings, were only approximately accurate. But what impressed them was the sheer size of the road bridge; it was a giant, dominating with its great central arch the entire countryside around Nijmegen.

The critical time was around 1800 hours, three-quarters of an hour before sunset. Having begun to cross the Waal at 1500 hours, Colonel Tucker's 3rd Battalion had not turned due east and made directly for the northern ends of the rail and road bridges; instead, they had driven inland to the north-east, gaining a deep bridgehead.

"Three hours after the crossing had been initiated, the 3rd Battalion was fighting 1,000 yards north of the road bridge while the 1st Battalion was maintaining contact with the 3rd Battalion and had fanned out to the west" [recalled Colonel Tucker]. "Prisoners were streaming back by the hundreds, other hundreds had been killed. One item of interest to you—the 504th was busy carrying out a combat mission. We didn't believe in sitting on our duffs at the bridge. I knew we had to get well out, then clean up the areas in back of us."

The Germans defending the road bridge were about to be caught in a trap that would snap shut as soon as the Americans had cut the Nijmegen–Arnhem road at the apex of the triangle, the bridge beyond Lent, 1,500 yards north of the Waal.

Meanwhile, the battle around the southern end of the road bridge was reaching its climax. Fixed to the wooden railing around the Valkhof was a plaque that read: *Hic stetit, hic frendens aquilas, hic lumine torvo Claudius Civilis* ultrice*

* Civilis was a leader of the Batavians, whose stronghold was on the 'Island' between Nijmegen and Arnhem. In A.D. 69 he led a revolt against Vespasian, which resulted in naval battles on the Maas and Rhine, and an assault by the 2nd Legion on his position at Nijmegen. Fighting for Civilis were the eight Batavian cohorts who had distinguished themselves as river crossing experts during Vespasian's British campaign in A.D. 43. For fordable rivers, the technique involved the use of horsemen to break the force of the current upstream and to rescue stragglers downstream, but for major rivers such as the Rhine the methods of the First Century A.D. were much the same as for the Twentieth Century—first, horsemen swimming across to gain a bridgehead, then a pontoon bridge, and finally a semi-permanent wooden bridge built on piles. The assault on a hill fort such as the Valkhof—or Maiden Castle in Dorset, which has been better excavated—began in the same way as for an opposed river crossing, with the setting up of a fire base. The defenders were harassed and then overwhelmed with artillery fire of all kinds and calibres, from stone-projectors firing 100-lb balls to catapaults or spring guns firing iron bolts and incendiaries, with arrows and slingshot the equivalent of small arms fire. When the defenders had been suitably decimated and shocked by this incessant rain of missiles, the armoured infantry assaulted.

vidit adesse manus, in English, roughly: "Here Claudius Civilis stood gnashing his teeth, from here he watched doggedly the eagles of the avenging host approach."

The fall of the Valkhof in A.D. 1944 showed no great change of broad principle in 2,000 years. Field guns and mortars had been hammering the dug-in defenders all day; in the later stages these were backed up by tank guns. The final assault began at 1530 hours, with very little time for planning; but the Germans had not expected an attack from the south as well, and two platoons of the Grenadiers crawled up the embankment at one point, cut the wire on top, and got into the Valkhof.

After costly hand-to-hand fighting, the Grenadiers established themselves on the eastern edge of the fort and were then able to fire on the bridge and on the Germans dug in around the bridge embankment to the south. In the centre, with more heavy losses, the Grenadiers managed to work their way through the blazing streets until they could fire on Hunner Park, backed up by the tanks, while simultaneously the Americans were beginning to wear down the defenders of the "bridge roundabout." As the historian of the Grenadiers wrote: "At this point all serious German resistance seemed to crack. They were overwhelmed by fire."

Guards Armoured consisted of the Grenadiers, Coldstream, Irish, and Welsh Guards. They were the blade of a narrow-pointed spear with a very thin, long shaft behind them stretching back to Eindhoven, a corridor in many cases little more than one road wide. The Welsh Guards were back at Grave, guarding that vital bridge that was in effect the base of the spear-blade. The Coldstream were acting as armoured reserve to the long perimeter held by Gavin's 82nd, and were in action at a number of points on the 20th where the attacking Germans of Meindl's corps had either driven back the Americans or were threatening to do so. The Irish Guards were using their firepower to cover Colonel Tucker's regiment attacking over the Waal. The battle inside Nijmegen was being fought by the Grenadiers alone, aided by one American battalion. The battle that day, of attack and counter-attack, ran in a great half-circle round Nijmegen, and by now the British forces, even more than the American, were well under-strength, having had no replacements for their casualties for a longer time.

The armoured reserve in Nijmegen consisted of No. 1 Squadron of the 2nd Grenadiers, commanded by Major J. Trotter, with Captain Lord Peter Carrington as second-in-Command. Late that afternoon Major Trotter called an "orders" group in the doorway of a Nijmegen hotel. We know what those orders were, because Sergeant P. T. Robinson had to make a statement a day or so later, which was written down by a sergeant-major.

"His orders had been to take the bridge at all costs to enable us to link up with the American paratroops who had previously crossed the Waal approximately one mile west, and were believed to be clearing north of the bridge. No. 1 Troop was selected to lead the Company over the bridge in one mad rush in the hopes of contacting this force to form a bridgehead."

Robinson was the commander of No. 1 Troop. He recalled afterwards that Major Trotter then shook hands with him and said, "Don't worry, I'll let your wife know, if you don't come back."

They all knew what had happened to Lieutenant Prescott's troop an hour or so before, and to Lieutenant Moller's troop the previous evening. It was very likely that Sergeant Robinson's troop would not be coming back. Robinson was a regular soldier of considerable experience, having joined the Grenadier Guards in 1934 and become a troop commander at the time of the Battle of Caen. He was exceptional, not only in his experience, but in the fact that he was a sergeant and had no title. His family were Essex fishermen, a trade that breeds steady, wise, and determined men who normally are not very talkative. Questioned nearly 25 years after the event, he would go so far as to admit that the task had appeared a nasty one, but pointed out that it was also just a job. Not all soldiers grow old. They lack the opportunity.

Lord Carrington, who was then a captain and is now the Minister of Defence, was less inhibited in his recollection of how he had viewed the prospect of the operation at the time: "We thought that someone must be round the bend, to order an assault on the bridges. They were certain to be mined, and would probably be blown up under us as we crossed."

There were four tanks in Robinson's troop, all with 75-millimeter guns except for Robinson's, which had the deadly 17-pounder. As second-in-command of the squadron, Lord Carrington would cross immediately after Robinson's troop and try to control the operation as a whole. There would also be one light reconnaissance car carrying Lieutenant A. G. C. Jones, then leader of 1 Troop, 14 Field Squadron, Royal Engineers, whose job was to "delouse" the bridge after it had been captured. He is now a brigadier at Aldershot.

Jones had heard the Dutch tale that the post office "contained a special cable leading to the bridge by which it could be blown up." In a contemporary narrative, he wrote:

"At about 1630 hours I got into a house on the river bank, and saw the huge bridge, with someone from our side shooting straight down the line of it. I tried, with binoculars, to see if there were any demolition charges, but there were none visible. I left the house and went up behind the forward company to see how close they had got to the bridge. They had just lost their company commander in addition to a lot of men and were in no condition to push on much further, so I decided to go back. When I got back to my car at about 1800 hours, I found an urgent order from OC 14 Fd Sqn to report to the roundabout near the bridge at once. I arrived at the roundabout at 1820 hours and found a troop of 2 Gren Gds tanks lined up ready to rush the bridge. The OC told me that the Americans were reported to be on the far side of the road bridge and that I would be going with the troop of tanks. . . . It transpired subsequently that the American signal to indicate that they had reached the north end of the railway bridge was misinterpreted to mean that they had reached the north end of the road bridge. This mysterious mistake had the fortunate effect of speeding up the operation!"

In recollection 25 years afterwards, he was adamant that someone, either the CO or possibly the brigade major, "were under the impression that the Americans had got there first, and that is why they ordered Peter Carrington to go." The

Grenadiers deny this, saying that the attempt to rush the bridge was the planned climax to a methodical day's work in clearing the town up to the bridge approaches. As the Irish Guards historian noted, there were many inaccurate reports, guesses rather, as to what was happening on the far bank, and some of these may still have been afloat. Apart from that, the Americans *were* north of the bridge—about 1,500 yards to the north—so that an accurate statement of affairs could well be misinterpreted.

However, it is a fact that Colonel Tucker's men had not then cleared back as far as the road bridge, or anything like it, although they had patrols criss-crossing the area; there was no American flag flying from the north end of the road bridge—and no one at the south end thought there was. Indeed, the Grenadiers very well knew who then held the north end of the bridge.

According to Sergeant Robinson's contemporary statement, zero hour was 1813. He then led his troop slowly forward onto the bridge. They could hear very little inside the machines, because of the noise of the engines and tracks. Immediately behind him was Lance Sergeant Billingham's tank, whose gunner, Guardsman Leslie Johnson, shortly afterwards wrote of the action in a letter to his father, describing it as apparently "suicidal." "It was not quite dark, as we went over," recollected Lord Carrington. "What struck me was the absence of anyone, either at our side of the bridge or on the other side. This I found intimidating. There was tension behind the emptiness of it. We knew there had been fighting for this place for a couple of days, and that this assault was the culmination."

As Robinson's Sherman nosed its way onto the bridge and came into view of the far bank, Johnson in the tank behind saw an 88-millimeter shot strike the road in front of the "point tank," not hitting it directly, but damaging it and putting the wireless out of action. As Robinson threw out smoke and reversed, the 88 changed target to Billingham's tank, and this time Johnson saw the flash of the gun firing. The gun itself he could not see because it was positioned in front of a burning house that was pouring out smoke to the west of the north end of the bridge. Johnson got off four rounds in that direction, but it was probably Sergeant C. Pacey's tank that hit. Anyway, the 88 stopped firing.

All four tanks reversed off the bridge, and because the wireless of his own tank was out of action, Sergeant Robinson dispossessed Billingham and took over his tank, so that Johnson now had Robinson as his tank commander. Robinson had heard very little of the firing as long as he was in his tank, but as he ran from one to the other he was aware of tracer bullets going past him in the fading light, and yet another 88 opened up. Over the radio, the CO was ordering the attack to go in at all costs.

Sergeant Pacey's tank moved forward again, followed by Robinson, into a hail of fire only half-perceived inside the tanks. Three anti-tank guns were firing on them from the east and a further two from the west side of the bridge.

"We had barely travelled 50 yards" [stated Robinson], "when a Panzer-Faust struck a nearby girder. It seemed that projectiles were coming from every angle, yet strangely we remained intact. Not only was the bridge defended from both flank and front, but we suffered repeated attacks from the air in the form of men hanging from the girders and dropping grenades, while snipers endeavoured to keep us running blind."

Both Pacey's and Robinson's tanks opened fire with their Brownings, raking the bridge girders around and above them. Enemy dead and wounded began to fall out of the girders onto the roadway "like ninepins," and the anti-tank shot was coming in so fast that it seemed like small-arms fire, hitting everything except the tanks. "I swear to this day that Jesus Christ rode on the front of our tank," declared Johnson.

At the far end was a road-block that could be negotiated only by turning the tanks broadside on; and it was covered by an anti-tank gun. Pacey stopped his tank, and was passed by Robinson, going flat out. As they came out from behind the road-block, Johnson saw the gun at the side of the road, about 50 yards away, about to open fire; he opened fire first and destroyed it with three shots, the Sherman charging the gun and going over the bodies of the crew. Still flat out, tracks splattered with blood, flesh, and bits of uniform, they careered down the ramp from the bridge, Robinson bellowing into his microphone for the rest of the troop to keep up. "He has a voice like a bull," wrote Johnson, "and that, I think, annoyed me more than anything. It was coming through my earphones like claps of thunder." In fact, only Pacey was left. The other two tanks had been hit.

Then, as they came to a wide tree-lined avenue where the road curved, Robinson spotted a self-propelled gun. It fired one shot, and missed. Robinson never gave it time to fire another. The tank slowed, Johnson swung onto the target, and then began pumping in high explosive as fast as the loader could run the shells into the breech.

Directly opposite was a church, with German infantry swarming in and out. Johnson opened fire with the turret Browning, until Robinson told him to stop and use the 75-millimeter gun instead. Shot after shot went in, until the church burst into flames, lighting up the avenue like day and showing more infantry beating up the line of trees. Again, the tank switched target, before moving on again. "If you see anything move, shoot it!" was Robinson's motto, and when after travelling about three-quarters of a mile they saw a railway bridge loom up ahead, they went under it slowly, tensed for anything. Nothing happened, until the avenue took a wide sweep to the right.

"We went round about 15 m.p.h., machine-gunning as we went" [wrote Johnson]. "Suddenly there were two terrific explosions right on the front of the tank. The blast from them came down the periscope and into my eyes and I thought for a minute that I had been blinded."

Robinson had seen a number of men jump into a ditch, and this was what he was firing at. In return, they had thrown two grenades at the tank, causing

"so much smoke and dust that I was compelled to halt until it subsided. Suddenly, I saw one American paratrooper who I beckoned over, and then from nowhere there suddenly appeared a further thirty of his comrades, who gave me a most royal welcome, climbing all over my tank. It was the first time

I had ever seen a tank kissed, whilst frankly I too felt like kissing them."

Johnson wrote that their officer was a captain who said "we were the sweetest guys he had seen in years. They had run out of ammunition, food and everything else; they hadn't even got a cigarette between them."

It was now completely dark, and although British tanks had crossed the bridge, it was not in British hands. The crews of the tanks that had been hit had bailed out and were taken prisoner except for Lance Sergeant Knight, who lay down and shammed dead, not a very difficult thing to do in the circumstances. A hit on a tank by an explosive projectile that does not penetrate can cause the crew to black-out momentarily. Anyway, Knight lay in a ditch by the north end of the bridge while what felt like half the German Army walked over him. One gave him a deliberate kick, and grunted, "Todt," satisfied that he was dead. When they had gone, Knight found that one of the two knocked-out tanks was still a "runner" and brought it up to Robinson's support afterwards, crewless.

Lord Carrington had followed Robinson's troops across, passing a burnt-out tank on the way, and reached the far end, where the road led down from the bridge on a long ramp. There were still Germans milling around, one of whom fired a bazooka at him, so he stayed there and for a short while, which seemed terribly long, his tank was the British garrison of the bridge.

What were needed were not tanks but infantry. It is necessary to get inside a tank to appreciate how blind the occupants are, even in daylight. In darkness, a tank is simply a sitting target for infantry, who can work close with impunity to fire bazookas or drop grenades down the turret hatch, if this has been kept open for the commander to look out. For this reason, tanks usually withdraw at night, or if they have to stay forward, are closely guarded by infantry. But the infantry of the Grenadiers were still scattered in their firing positions amid the blazing ruins of Nijmegen, and there was "an ugly period of half an hour when we didn't know what was happening," said Colonel Breitmeyer. Robinson's troop had simply disappeared over the Waal into the night, and only

Lord Carrington's tank was in contact. Two companies of Irish Guardsmen were sent to join him, but it was 45 minutes before they could get there.

Lord Carrington was now released from his position and could try to join Robinson. Up to now, he had no idea why he had not been hit. "I can only imagine the whole thing was luck. There was no real reason why it should have succeeded." Travelling fast to avoid the bazooka shots fired at him, he "zoomed" down the road to join Robinson, where the situation was very tense.

The tanks could not go on because of the darkness, and they could not go back because they had to hold the road at all costs. The Germans were all around them, and the Americans were low on ammunition. Already, one American officer had considered the position hopeless and had thought it would be necessary to surrender. Robinson had replied that although two of his tanks had been knocked out, the remaining two were still runners, and so he could not surrender. He let the American use his wireless to contact Guards Armoured.

Then, Johnson wrote,

"We were joined by Lord Carrington, making a total of three tanks, and like that we stayed all night with never a wink and our nerves like razor blades. Our idea was, for the Yankees to take up ground positions a few yards from the tanks and give us some sort of protection during the night. Tanks are useless in the dark. But the Yanks had other ideas and took up positions the other side of the railway. That was no earthly use to us at all, so we got the Brownings out of the tanks and put one at each corner of our little square. The enemy was so near at times, we heard him talking. Anything that moved had had it. We just waited for him to come and finish us off, but the fool never came. He never realised there were only three tanks holding that road to the bridge."

Colonel Tucker mentioned this tactical argument, too, but naturally from the infantryman's point of view.

"I had a temporary Command Post beside the road and saw only three tanks. Lord Carrington all night long kept calling for more security. I asked him what it was he feared since there was a whole American battalion 1,000 yards to his front. He said he wanted people dug in around his tanks—that we didn't have. I knew we had to get well out, then clean up the areas in back of us."

Meanwhile, back at the road bridge, Lieutenant Jones was completing the "delousing" process in the dark, now aided by the whole of his troop. While doing it, they took 81 prisoners hiding behind girders or in the large compartments built inside the tops of the concrete bridge piers, "all of whom were in a very bad way indeed." But Jones had followed immediately behind Sergeant Robinson's troop in his reconnaissance car, and as the last tank slewed through the gap in the road-block he stopped the car near the northern end of the bridge, for this was where the wires leading from the charges to the control point should be, logically, and in fact proved to be.

"The first thing I saw was about half a dozen wires on the footway at the side of the bridge. These I cut. I walked up to the roadblock and saw about ten Tellermine 35 in a slit trench near it. These were obviously designed to close the block. I removed the igniters and threw them in the river."

Jones then walked back along the bridge towards Nijmegen, and found a set of charges lying on the footpath just north of the second pier.

"These had been designed to cut the concrete roadway, but had never been placed in position and were quite safe. I went to the west side to see if there were any charges underneath the bridge corresponding to those on the deck."

But there were only what Jones took to be three dead Germans, who were in fact wounded, one very badly, and immediately surrendered. He put the badly wounded soldier in his car, and continued to walk beside it in the direction of Nijmegen. As he approached the central span, four more Germans came from behind a girder and surrendered.

"I handed the seven men over to the CO and reported that, in my opinion, the bridge was safe and all that was now necessary was a detailed search."

This was carried out by the entire troop, aided by a German prisoner who volunteered to show Jones where the charges were.

"He then led us to the next pier, where we found the charges on the girders of the bridge directly under the place where the charges were found on the road, just to the north of the pier. There was an elaborate system of staging and the charges were made of TNT packed in green painted boxes, each charge with a serial number corresponding to a serial number painted on the girder. The charges were to be fired electrically, and the detonators were in and connected to one of the wires which I had previously cut on the deck. We removed these and decided to check the rest of the bridge, though our prisoner had said there were no more charges."

This proved to be so; all the charges were placed to blow the concrete roadway north of the central span.

"When we got back to the roadway again, it was quite dark and there was about a platoon of Americans on the bridge. They had just killed an SS officer who had been shooting at them from the arch."

Three men from two different companies of the 3rd Battalion had reached the bridge soon after Robinson's troop crossed, according to the American official history. Colonel Tucker thought they might have been from one of Major Julian Cook's patrols, who got there before he did.

"I went out on the highway bridge that night" [he wrote], "and even took a couple of shots at where Krauts were in the girders. I don't know now, nor have I ever known, why the tanks didn't belt across that night. Nothing bigger or more disastrous in their way than sharpshooters or ineffectual grenades. That was just my thinking at the time, but remember, I wandered a good way across the bridge that night and crawled up girders, but other than rifle fire from defenceless riflemen, the tanks could have streamed across."

That was the infantryman's view, discounting the bazookas and the vulnerability of tanks in the dark, riding blind and noisily through the night. Both Lord Carrington and Sergeant

Robinson had previously and specifically raised the same question with me in their interviews. Without prompting, Robinson had said, "We could have got to Arnhem that day, but we would have been knocked out next morning. There was no cover for tanks on the Island." Lord Carrington had said the same thing. "No tank could possibly have got across the Island to Arnhem. Infantry were required, and we were way in front of the infantry." He meant, of course, not merely infantry specially trained to understand the weak points of tanks and to work with them against other infantry; but an infantry division with its full complement of guns. Such a division, the 43rd Wessex, was on its way but had not reached Nijmegen yet.

The only person to whom I put the question specifically, including that of the chances of the 43rd Wessex, was Oberst Harzer, the German commander at Arnhem, who replied: "As far as the ground was concerned, there was very little they could do to launch an attack, because it was possible to move only on top of the dykes." And in fact the way was blocked by units of 10 S.S. Panzer Division, established at Ressen, only three miles north of Nijmegen. Had the tanks gone on, that is as far as they would have got.

In coming to a judgement, it must be remembered that it was Guards Armoured Division that had made the wild night drive through the German rear areas to Brussels only a few weeks before. If it had been possible to repeat this feat on the "Island," they would have done it; but it was not possible. It is also as well to remember the Germans. Judging that except for those at the road bridge, the British parachutists at Arnhem were not worth bothering about, they had concentrated on reinforcing Nijmegen with units of 10 S.S. Panzer Division as fast as they could be ferried across the Neder Rijn at Pannerden.

In the marshy terrain of the Betuwe between Arnhem and Nijmegen, infantry and guns were more important than tanks, and it was with these principally that they had already formed a screen at Ressen, south of Elst, facing towards the Waal. This was to have been merely the preliminary to an attack to clear the British and Americans out of Nijmegen. But few pontoons were available and ferrying was a slow business.

The consequent delay was a direct result of Colonel Frost's hold on the northern end of Arnhem road bridge, which for more than three days had closed to the Germans the only good route to Nijmegen. The British defence of Arnhem bridge had collapsed only an hour or so before the first two British tanks raced across Nijmegen bridge, and the way was open to the Germans to reinforce rapidly in the Betuwe. But with the capture of the bridge intact, their last chance to re-take Nijmegen had gone. And the bridge was intact, largely because Field Marshal Model had wished to use it for his own attack.

General Bittrich stated:

"After reconnoitring the bridgehead I suggested to Field Marshal Model that the Nijmegen bridge, which had already had a demolition charge in position, should be blown up. Field Marshall Model rejected this suggestion . . . arguing that the bridgehead might be the point of departure for future attacks towards the south."

Arnhem road bridge had not been prepared for demolition, and at the end some of Frost's men gave their lives uselessly in trying to prevent what they thought was a last-minute attempt by the Germans to blow it up, actually the last thing the Germans wanted.

The capture of Arnhem bridge intact was Harzer's primary objective. Even Nijmegen bridge was prepared only for part-demolition. There was no intention of dropping the entire structure into the water, as the Dutch had done in 1940, but merely to blow a large gap in the roadway north of the great centre span, so that if the bridge was recovered it would be repairable. The man who saved Nijmegen bridge for the Allies was therefore Field Marshal Model.

However, as Colonel Breitmeyer pointed out, in strict military logic the bridge should have been blown, regardless of Model's order, as soon as the Grenadiers had taken the Valkhof and so commanded its approaches. The confusion of the Germans, and the number of different units by then well mixed up, probably prevented this. "It seemed to me," said Breitmeyer, "that there was no one person on the spot, on their side who was capable of taking a decision. Its capture, in the event, meant very little, if anything. The bridge was not much used after, and so all that hard fighting was for nothing." This is a bitter pill to swallow, particularly for soldiers like Sergeant Robinson, who had been told that the capture of the bridge might shorten the war by six months.

It was a bitter irony also for the Dutch Underground, one of whom, a young man called Jan van Hoof, had schemed for weeks beforehand to try to save the bridge if the Allied advance should reach Nijmegen. On Monday, September 18, the day after Gavin's men landed, he carried out some scheme he thought would render the demolition charges ineffective; but the details of what he actually did are quite unknown, for he was killed the next day while acting as a guide to one of the Allied columns attempting to take the bridges and the post office.

A year or two after the war, Jones, then a captain, received enquiries from Holland about the demolitions.

"I stated that at no time had I seen any evidence that the wires had been cut. I believe, on afterthought, that the bridge needed about five minutes work to make it finally ready for demolition. All the wires and circuits, as far as I could see, were intact, and all charges were in position (except the tellermines which would have been used to close the road block). I had to write to the Dutch and say that I had seen no evidence to support the story about Jan van Hoof. I am not sure how the matter turned out, but as he, poor lad, was dead, and we were very much alive, I believe that it was as well that the whole thing was allowed to drop."

A quarter of a century after, it is possible only to speculate that either the Germans made good any damage he did, or that he cut the wrong wires. The latter is the strongest possibility, as the Dutch Underground were mistaken in their theory that the post office was, against all logic, the demolition control centre. This would not make his action any the less brave, but would instead allow it to symbolise the whole of Operation Market Garden, a gallant attempt to cut short the war that failed by a wide margin and was now visibly falling into ruin.

CHAPTER EIGHTEEN

BATTLE IN THE BETUWE

September 21

September 21 was the day on which Market Garden was irretrievably finished. This was not apparent at the time, certainly not immediately, because communications were so poor that the commanders had insufficient information, particularly as to the situation in Arnhem. On that day, a number of separate movements were taking place that were to prove immediately decisive.

The most important movement, we can see now, was that of the Wossowski Battalion of recruits and NCO instructors from the Hermann Göring Division, which had started their cycle-ride from Katwijk-an-Zee to Arnhem on Sunday, September 17. On September 20, they had been combing through a woodland area by the Ede-Arnhem road where paratroops were supposed to be, and had found only dead men—a sobering sight for the recruits. At dawn on the 21st they took their place in the western cordon formed by a rag-bag of units provisionally known as "Tettau's Division," (after its commander) which was not a division at all, lacking all organisation and equipment, including even field kitchens. Many of the "battalions" in the "division" were not battalions either, but merely collections of refugee soldiers from the debacle in Belgium and Holland who had been stopped by the field police and sent to a collecting centre. One such "battalion" consisted of men from 28 different units.

In such a "division" the young recruits of Wossowski's command ranked as "elite troops," and no doubt this was why they were directed down a country road from Wolfhezen towards the 100-foot-high hill of Westerbouwing, overlooking the Neder Rijn ferry, and also overlooking the long, sausage-like perimeter now held by the airborne troops west of Arnhem.

After riding down the road from Wolfhezen towards

Oosterbeek, they turned off onto a narrow forest track and stopped, still sitting on their bicycles, in no recognisable military formation, and "quite unworried," according to one of the NCOs, Herbert Kessler.

"There was no trace of the enemy anywhere, when suddenly, from the flank, we were attacked by murderous machine-gun fire. Some were hit before they had time even to throw themselves to the ground, let alone take cover. On the left of the path was a hedge and low trees, and at their edge the Inn Westerbouwing with an observation tower in which the enemy had obviously sited a defensive position. From there, the English must have watched our unit approach, brought machine-guns into position, and opened fire. When we had got over the first shock, the order came through: 'Company attack—attack!' The heavy train had already set up their M.G.s and were busily returning the fire. The soldiers snapped out of their surprise and started to go forward into the brush and open fire, so that we could now hear our own weapons in action. In this way, single groups penetrated the low wood, moved towards the hotel, and occupied the building in which the enemy still was. The first prisoners were taken in the observation tower and sent to the rear. Superficially, the first sight of the enemy soldiers confirmed that these were indeed elite troops, fellows tall as trees, well fed, and excellently equipped."

Regrouping around the hotel, the Luftwaffe soldiers then carried the attack forward towards Oosterbeek itself, and the heights of Westerbouwing were securely in German hands.

The hill overlooked the low-lying polderland on both sides of the Neder Rijn, at Oosterbeek and far over the Betuwe, so that the roads leading to the ferry site from both banks of the river were clearly commanded. This ferry site was the objective of British and Canadian Engineer units that had just moved up from Bourg Leopold to Nijmegen. The original orders were to build class-40 rafts on the Betuwe side of the river in order to ferry tanks across to the north bank. One of the units was 20 Field Company, Royal Canadian Engineers, in which Lieutenant W. W. Gemmell was a platoon commander.

While Herbert Kessler's battalion had started from Katwijk in a blaze of patriotic exhortations and judicious promotions, Gemmell's unit had moved off from St. Omer in northern France after "a rash of Church Parades, confessions for the R.C.s etc., and a grapevine rumour that we were going on a 'hot' operation somewhere."

When they moved off, the sight of Gemmell's armoured scout car caused a riot all the way to Holland, but particularly when passing through Brussels. The reason was that while building "Monty's Bridge" over the Orne at Caen, the company had been dug into the grounds of the Institute Botanique, boarded up against looters, but insecure where the driver of Gemmell's scout car was concerned.

"Somehow he managed to get in and give the place the once over," [wrote Gemmell], "and to cut it short he purloined, of all things, a gorilla's skull. He asked me if he could mount it on the front of the car just ahead of the windscreen, and I told him O.K. The results were wonderful."

The skull had been drilled, mounted, and adorned with horse's tail hair and a German helmet.

"With the proper application of the hair for Hitler's moustache, and the lock across the forehead, the damn thing *did* look like the good old Fuhrer. With the addition of the helmet, the effects on the civvy population were devastating. You see, the helmet was so fixed that the visor was just over the eye-sockets, but they had tied a cord through a hole in the back rim of the helmet and the cord passed down through the windscreen to the inside of the car. A tug on the cord, and the helmet tipped up. It sure was a good Hitler and made the natives laugh out of all proportion. I never saw a crowd of people laugh so hard at the fool thing as the citizens of Brussels."

Eventually, the car rolled across Grave bridge, halting momentarily while a bunch of Spitfires jumped a formation of German fighters that had dived to attack the bridging convoy, and instead of proceeding immediately to the ferry opposite Westerbouwing went into a staging area on the outskirts of Nijmegen. In front, Arnhem was still unattainable; and behind, the road had been cut.

The two flanking corps had barely reached Eindhoven, so a 30-mile stretch of highway was wide open to any sort of attack. A concerted assault from both sides of the corridor was being planned by the Germans for the following day, but many of the attacks were almost accidental, and the 101st Airborne were too thin on the ground to do more than mount a mobile defence.

Major T. Garnett, quartermaster of the Grenadier Guards, recollected the supply columns moving up in two lines, the vehicles jammed nose to tail, the traffic movement being interrupted from time to time by German traffic movements taking place at right-angles to the British line of advance, as German units escaping from Belgium and Holland collided with it and were forced to fight their way home.

"The main reason for the cutting of our L. of C. was these German units, trying to get away and forced to attack in order to do so. One of my vivid memories was witnessing American troops passing along the long lines of transport in very good formation to attack these marauding Germans who were causing the trouble."

On the morning of September 21, the battle was still going on inside Nijmegen. Although the bridges had been taken, only a part of the town had been captured. At dawn, the armoured cars of the Household Cavalry moved off for the small bridgehead in the Betuwe, in order to assist the Irish Guards on the main Arnhem road and also to probe for weak spots on the flanks. "A gulped breakfast of cold baked beans and a mug of chlorinated tea is not the best send-off at half-past four in the morning," wrote their historian, Major Roden Orde.

"It lay heavy and regurgitating on the stomachs as the men climbed into their chilly turrets. Sounds of street fighting echoed between the houses as the cars circled the eastern part of the town. Towards the river bank could be heard the harsh crack of shells bursting on the cobble-stones. The Squadron wheeled past the roundabout and its knocked-out guns. Poor Nijmegen—suburban and rather genteel before the war, one suspected—now looking indescribably forlorn. Broken glass and discarded equipment lay strewn about the place and a damp mist shrouded the roofless houses. In the half-light the mass of the bridge loomed up, gigantic and seemingly out of focus. There was a smell of cordite in the air, and pallid waxen corpses sprawled grotesquely across the pavements, bearing testimony to the severity of the previous day's fighting. Many Germans had also been killed on the bridge itself, and lay crumpled beneath the spot where they had been shot down from the girders. A slumped figure was still strapped aloft, shot dead as he had tried to snipe at passing traffic. One could not but admire the courage of such men, and again one felt the label 'fanatic' to be a rather cheap jibe. However, warnings that others were still very much alive made every car commander peer upwards intently, ready to spray the steel framework with bullets at the slightest sign of movement."

But the armoured cars failed to find a way through the defences the Germans had established in the Betuwe, and so there was nothing for it but a head-on attack by the tanks directly down the road to Ressen, Elst, and Arnhem, where the armoured vehicles on the raised road had to advance on a one-tank front, perched up like coconuts to be knocked off by the anti-tank guns already placed there in readiness.

The hasty nature of the operation, due to its urgency, played a major part in taking away what little chance there was of success. The situation (we now know, but it was far from clear to those concerned at the time) was not unlike that at Valkenswaard. The single good road. A determined enemy with anti-tank guns and infantry, plus tanks, sited in orchards on either side of the road. And again the Irish Guards attacking with the support of Typhoons, plus infantry from another division, backed by artillery.

But this was not a set-piece attack, it was improvised at the end of a long line of communications. The losses sustained by the Irish Guards at Valkenswaard and after had not been made good; they were seriously under-strength. The arrangements for Typhoon support to blast the enemy guns and armour were haphazard, particularly the wireless link, which failed; and there was no air support (except for the Germans). Artillery support was not immediately available and when it did become available later, was pathetically weak. The additional infantry were not British, but American airborne, who were not allowed to take part in the armoured advance; and there were some misunderstandings between them, because British tanks and American paratroopers had not been trained to work together.

The 10th S.S. Panzer Division "Frundsberg" held an east-west aligned blocking position, facing south to Nijmegen, astride both the main road and the secondary roads (which were unsuitable for tanks). Later in the day, so that Frundsberg could give undivided attention to the spearheads of XXX Corps, Harzer formed a north-south–aligned blocking position to the west, facing west, with the miscellaneous units that were now part of the 9th S.S. Panzer Division "Hohenstauffen." These consisted of Schorken's Battalion, M.G. Battalion 47, Kauer's Battalion (Luftwaffe ground staff), Köhnen's Battalion (Marine Kampfgruppe 642), and a Dutch Landsturm battalion.

The German defences were then L-shaped, with the upper stroke of the "L" on the Nijmegen–Arnhem railway embankment, the lower stroke consisting of S.S. troops blocking the main approach and with their screens out as far as the Waal in the south-east corner of the "Island." When the leading Irish Guards tanks drove over the bridge at 0300 on September 21, there was virtually no information to be had from the Americans as to what lay ahead, and even adequate maps were lacking. In a properly prepared attack, defence overproof sheets were issued, showing the enemy positions in detail, down to individual machine-gun sites. But this takes time, and there was no time.

There has been much criticism of the lack of urgency in XXX Corps, made mainly at the time by 1 Airborne Division, who thought then that they were taking on the bulk of the German forces and could not understand why the spearheads were not simply driving down the road; and did not realise that the main German effort was being made, not at Arnhem, but to the south at Nijmegen. The airborne were not fighting two panzer divisions; the only panzer division worthy of the name was the 10th S.S., and they were mainly concerned to stop the spearheads of XXX Corps. This criticism was based on incomplete information and is not now normally made in airborne circles. However, neither the Irish Guards nor the American airborne were entirely happy with their own efforts to get forward that day, and their criticisms—of themselves and of each other—are more interesting, being closer to the facts. Even so, there were misunderstandings.

Major-General Tucker has already described how his men were carrying out their "combat mission" by scouring the area with fighting patrols during the night, which the Grenadier Guards tanks considered insufficient protection (and, it is fair to add, any tank commander would agree with them). But Tucker was also critical of the Irish Guards who took over during the night.

"Just an added point, which I have never understood," [he wrote]. "The next day the tanks moved across to continue the drive to Arnhem but they stopped where (and I had warned them of this) two Kraut 88's opened up on their lead tank and stopped the advance. Then they tried one avenue at a time with two other approaches while I had suggested going up all three at the same time. I even asked our own division to turn me loose and let us accompany them but they told me 'no.' Basically I have always claimed there was not enough driving experience present. I still feel Arnhem should have been reached by a smashing drive."

The leading squadron of the Irish Guards was commanded by Captain (now Colonel) R. S. Langton, M.C., M.V.O., and it was a squadron in name only; it was down to six tanks.

"The other squadrons were not much stronger," [he wrote]. "The artillery could not even get into Nijmegen, let alone over the bridge, but because of the urgent need to get to Arnhem we decided to go without Field support but hoping for some Medium support initially, from the other side of the river (this in fact never materialised). I am a great admirer of General Tucker but I would make a criticism in my turn. I took my 'Squadron' over the bridge at 0300 ready for the advance. I personally spent the final hours going round the American positions trying to get information. But there were no positions (or at least not where they were said to be); there were patrols wandering around without apparent aim and at first light there appeared to be no proper bridgehead and, apart from the warning about the two 88s, there was very little helpful information about routes, etc.

"I was given my orders at 1040. H Hour was 1100. My tanks had taken up positions up the road and I therefore only had time to give out my orders over the radio. These were quite simple—the situation at Arnhem is desperate, every intelligence is non-existent (except for the two 88-mm guns mentioned by Tucker), our task is to go hell for leather up the road and get to Arnhem bridge. I was later fairly criticised by the leading tank commander, who survived but was badly shot up. He said that, once the advance started, all he could hear on the radio was my shouting: 'Faster! Faster!' This is quite correct, and was all I could say, or feel, under the circumstances. We went past the sites where we had been told the 88s were and drew a sigh of relief, but round the next bend my three leading tanks were shot off the road one after the other (leaving three!). The 88s had withdrawn to a strip of wood and *together* with a troop's worth of tanks (including a Tiger) could pick us off at will. Tucker therefore is wrong in inferring that we were stopped only by two 88s. In addition there were tanks and a great deal of infantry in the orchards, left of the road (as I learnt to my cost). He is also wrong in saying that the lead tank only was knocked out; in fact, I lost 'half' my 'Squadron.'*

"But he (rightly, in my view) says that we should have advanced on three routes. However, the Irish Group were not strong enough to do this adequately on their own; the time factor was all important, and it would have delayed the advance; and there were no maps which adequately showed the roads. I think my thoughts were entirely on the tanks—they provided our mobility and that was what we needed to

* For many hours, Stephen Langton's tank *was* the "spearhead" of Second Army.

get to Arnhem. I neglected to tie up properly with the infantry commander (because of lack of time), so that when mobility failed us and we failed to get round those fatal bends, there was no immediate Infantry/Armour plan to put into action. But how could there be, when the 'Squadron' consisted of three tanks and the 'Company' one platoon plus! Had it been possible to bring up the rest of 5th Guards Brigade, it might have worked. But the Coldstream were in operations south of Nijmegen, the Grenadiers were fairly decimated from the night before, *and* there was confusion further back, on the centre line."

In Langton's view, the vital missing factor was the lack of just that closely integrated Typhoon support that had blasted the tanks forward against just such opposition as this at Valkenswaard.

"But after Valkenswaard there was no sign of them—only of the German air force, including two jets, the first we'd seen. I feel we could have got to Arnhem, as we were and as we tried, had we had even limited air support.

"But I don't see how Tucker's 'smashing drive' could have been achieved. Personally, I am convinced that the advance had outstripped the support (logistic and operational) that it required, and this surely goes back to the overall strategy of a broad front advance (Eisenhower) or a rapier thrust (Montgomery). The Arnhem rapier thrust fell between the two stools, it was too successful to start with and no one was ready to support the final event; the steam had gone out of the Commanders and Staffs. I will freely admit that I have never been entirely happy that the Irish Group did everything we could to get on. We might indeed have battled up the centre road, but the initial knock was a serious one in terms of men and tanks, as was the immediate attempt to get round on the right. Again, with air support—yes, we could have made it. *But*, had we made it, what then? There would have been less support from behind—the centre line was cut next day—and I believe that not only would we have been in the bag with the Airborne, but the Germans would have held the 'Island' and almost certainly retaken Nijmegen. I do not know why the U.S. Airborne were not permitted to help the advance, because certainly it would have been a great bonus, and with their help we might have made it—but with the same doubt as to what would have happened had we done so!"

Field Marshal Model was in fact planning a counter-offensive to re-take Nijmegen with 10 S.S. Panzer, so his appreciation of the situation was similar. However, Tucker, basing his opinion partly on what he was told at the time by a British officer, takes the view that, "There was not enough driving experience present. We had the drive bred from knowhow and experience. Some of the tankers had it, but without desiring to get in a world skirmish, I say your foot elements dragged their feet."

His information was wrong. The only available infantry division—the 43rd Wessex—was with its 5,000 vehicles then stretched out all the way from Nijmegen to Eindhoven in the confusion of the fighting along the centre line. It may perhaps seem unfair to give the "casting vote" to the Germans, but Oberst Harzer, a panzer leader of great experience, was on this same day confronted with a similar problem—the unsuitability of the Betuwe for tanks; and on the following night, what happened to his Tigers at the hands of the 43rd Infantry Division spelled out in capitals the valid reason why the Irish Guards had waited for daylight before attacking.

They were still attacking, under a pathetic artillery barrage, when the final airborne reinforcements for Arnhem arrived—the 1st Polish Parachute Brigade—little more than 700 strong, the last Oxo-cube for the lion. Half the transport aircraft had lost their way in bad weather conditions, or been shot down, before this forlorn little band arrived.

"The first Dakota transport planes were sighted at quarter past four and the Germans greeted them with a heavy barrage of flak which swept up to meet them from positions half a mile ahead of the leading Irish Guards tanks and 'D' Squadron cars" [wrote Major Orde]. "The pilots, undeterred by the bursting shells, deviated neither right nor left, but flew straight on with extreme gallantry. Many planes could be seen to have been hit and crashed before attaining their objective. The others, enveloped in bursting shells and appearing to the ground onlookers to be extremely cumbersome and slow, carried on."

The air forces were now paying in full for having refused to risk flak losses on the first day when this would have been justified by the immediate capture of the bridges; or rather, the aircrews were paying for a decision taken much higher up. And the Luftwaffe were making them pay with fighters as well as flak, for in spite of concentrated attacks on the German aircraft industry in 1944 by both the British and American air forces, German aircraft production had reached its highest peak of the war. In this month, September, 1944, the Luftwaffe received 3,013 single-engined fighter aircraft, newly built or repaired.

"All at once the air seemed filled with hundreds of parachutes like so many swinging mushrooms floating slowly down to earth. One failed to open and plummeted to the ground. The rest disappeared behind the horizon and the village of Elst" [wrote Major Orde]. "The ground battle, which had appeared to halt momentarily to gaze skywards at the arriving Poles, was quickly jerked back to its own sphere of action by a thud, followed by the crackle of exploding bullets, as yet another Irish Guards tank was hit and burst into flames. Traffic piled up behind the stricken Sherman and although several other tanks tried every trick they knew to get off the road and continue cross-country, they only succeeded in getting themselves hopelessly bogged down. Infantry was the one hope of forcing a way up the road to Elst, and they could only achieve their object if supported by an adequate artillery barrage."

The feeble shelling that day was due to an ammunition shortage caused by the cutting of the "corridor" from time to time, and this was due to become absolute the next day.

The Poles should have landed at Driel, not at Elst, so that they could cross the Neder Rijn by the ferry into the airborne perimeter at Oosterbeek, under the hill of Westerbouwing. But the hill, held only by a platoon of the Border Regiment, had been captured that morning by Herbert Kessler's company of the Wossowski Battalion. The Poles had been dropped half a day too late, and in the wrong place. And by landing successfully near Elst, nor far from the main Nijmegen–Arnhem road, they had proved wrong the experts who had declared that the terrain on the Betuwe was unsuitable for parachutists.

But, at the same time, they had not proved right the experts who had declared that the flak defences on the Betuwe were too heavy. Most of the guns had only just come into position, rushed there from the Ruhr; and, while the landings on September 17 came as a complete surprise, not to say shock, to the Germans, on the 21st they were receiving advance warning by radio from their coastal fortresses in France and Holland of the incoming fleets of vulnerable transport planes.

It was not surprising that some of the Polish officers were beside themselves with rage at what they had felt from the beginning would be a bungled operation. Poland was already being torn apart by one barbaric enemy, the Soviet Union, and now they were to be beaten by the Germans because the British had made a bad plan.

But the Germans were alarmed by the Polish landing, by accident so near to the main Arnhem–Nijmegen road; Model and Bittrich did not realise it was an error, they thought it was an attempt to cut the road and to move into the rear of 10 S.S. Panzer Division, which was holding a blocking position against the advance of XXX Corps.

Harzer was given the task of stopping the expected eastward attack of the Poles, and he encountered exactly the same problem already met by the Irish Guards at Ressen. "Unfortunately, the terrain round Driel did not permit the use of tanks, otherwise we would have managed to scatter or destroy this Polish parachute bridge before nightfall," he was to comment.

The solution was infantry, and it was mainly with infantry, German and Dutch, that he set up on this day the "Barrier Unit Harzer," which took over a north-south defensive line along the Arnhem–Elst railway embankment. The result was to relieve the immediate pressure on the airborne perimeter around Oosterbeek, and to provide a start-line for an attack across the Betuwe towards Driel. These were the troops who had rooted out the van Dongeren family from their bolt-hole near Elden while searching for Polish parachutists, and put them on the move once more in search of safety.

After taking Westerbouwing early in the morning, Herbert Kessler's company had carried on the attack, and by noon was "completely shattered," according to notes he made at the time.

"Fighting amongst the trees made it particularly difficult to recognise the enemy. Snipers up in the trees caused considerable losses, enemy automatic weapons changed their positions frequently and it was therefore very difficult to silence them and there were more losses."

Half the company of some 300 men were dead or wounded by nightfall, and thinking back, Kessler saw another factor, the inexperience of the recruits, whose first action this was. Some of the British battalions had suffered in the same way for the same reason, but now, after only a few days' experience, the survivors had become cunning and also gained a confidence in their weapons that at first many of them had lacked. Kessler's company went into reserve, and that evening

"the English supply planes arrived and disgorged their loads. There was no clear front line and this caused a large percentage of the parachutes to come down in the German positions. The soldiers became their own suppliers and were not dependent on the unit kitchen any longer. The best and finest tinned foods, things of which one dared only to dream, complemented by cigarettes and chocolate, rained down on us. We even found a folding bicycle and, to make things complete, a copy of the London *Times*. We were flabbergasted!"

Re-supply of the Germans by the British and American air forces had become routine, almost from the first, because the airhead was much too large to be held for long. And because the Allied air commanders had refused to take merely theoretical heavy losses in order to establish a realistic perimeter around the bridges, they now took actual losses that were even heavier in a cause that was lost, and in doing so helped the enemy more than their own troops.

The most tragic of these occurrences took place on September 19, when Flight Lieutenant D. S. A. Lord of 271 Squadron, Transport Command, was awarded a posthumous V.C. for dropping supplies, most probably to the enemy.

There were many witnesses because the starboard engine of his machine was already burning as he approached Arnhem at 1,500 feet, and the obvious thing to do was to bail out or turn away from the stream and force land. Captain A. P. Wood recalled,

"One Dakota dipped low and was seen to be ablaze in the area of the wing. However, blazing like a torch, it came on and on and made the first container drop; veered away, circled and came in extremely low, at I would say 500 feet, blazing furiously but dead on course; I saw no parachutes, but the burning wing fell away and the Dak crashed to earth."

Major Perkins of the Royal Engineers was closer to the drop site, and could see that in fact one man bailed out before the aircraft broke up and that the containers were falling to the north of the positions now held by the airborne, who had insufficient transport to go out and collect them. "I fancy the Germans did quite well on our rations!" he commented, but "the R.A.F. and U.S.A.F. were certainly doing their stuff right nobly."

The man who parachuted was a sergeant observer who landed near a troop of 17-pounder anti-tank guns commanded by Lieutenant G. A. Paull. An open-air man from Dorset, the spectacle of the re-supply operation reminded him forcibly of "grouse being driven towards the shooting butts," a very apt simile, because the Germans had in fact set up the equivalent in light and heavy flak by now. The observer had lost his shoes during the parachute descent, so Paull gave him a spare pair of boots.

"Out of 163 aircraft that brought supplies during that terrible ten minutes," wrote Paull, "13 were lost completely and 97 others damaged by flak." The overall gallantry of the aircrews made a great impression on all those on the ground at the time, and strongly contrasted with previous poor or uneven performances in Sicily and Normandy. The improvement was enormous and notably contributed to the successes at Eindhoven and Nijmegen. But at Arnhem, nothing now could retrieve even a crumb of success from a bad initial plan.

Paull's unit, 2 Airlanding Anti-Tank Battery, R.A., had arrived in gliders on September 18, with the second lift. It consisted of four troops of 6-pounders and two troops of 17-pounders, the latter carried in the giant Hamilcar gliders towed by four-engined Halifax bombers. Paull's "X" troop was attached to 156 Battalion of 4 Parachute Brigade, which by September 21 "had received a terrific hammering." In their retreat from Wolfhezen, two of Paull's guns were reported lost on the north of the railway embankment, the crews having been killed. "They've bloody well had it," were the actual terms in which the message was conveyed. "But I'm an awkward cuss," said Paull. "I crawled up over the embankment unobserved, got to the guns, and hooked the first one onto the towing vehicle. I drove that first gun over the embankment, then went back for the other."

Paull had fought in North Africa, Sicily, and Italy, but many of the men in the airlanding brigade were inexperienced, and on arriving at Arnhem, he had been astonished to find himself in an apparently deserted wood. Where had everyone gone to? The answer was they were all taking cover unnecessarily, with their heads down, instead of firing.

Next morning, it was the turn of the Germans to be astonished. They had brought up some armour during the night, and dawn revealed it sited openly within the range of the big 17-pounders; a number were put out of action before the rest made for cover. But now the Germans were pressing in and harassing the shrinking perimeter with fire.

"There was very little time to think about anything except the job in hand" [wrote Paull]. "The continuous noise of guns and mortar fire was at times almost deafening, seeming to come from every direction, and communications were practically nil. The arrival of Major-General Stanislaw Sosabowski's 1st Polish Independent Parachute Brigade Group gave morale a boost, but the general tone of enquiries was, "What has happened to XXX Corps?" The position was almost desperate, we were heavily outnumbered, short of food, sleep and ammunition, with little prospect of being able to recoup."

Back in Nijmegen, while the leading battalions of 43 (Wessex) Infantry Division struggled through the traffic and the rejoicing inhabitants towards the bridges that led to the Betuwe, the Grenadier Guards units that had captured the bridges were withdrawn into the town to meet the generals and the war correspondents. Sergeant Robinson was introduced to Montgomery and Horrocks, then filmed, interviewed, and recorded by all the correspondents who had missed the battle. Captain Lord Carrington recalled that

"The Duke of Rutland and I had found the German Army wine store in Brussels and had taken some of the contents with us in our tanks. Champagne is not improved by being alternately baked and frozen, but even so, I remember bitterly that Chester Wilmot drank my last bottle of champagne on that occasion."

CHAPTER NINETEEN

DASH TO DRIEL

September 22

"Without meaning any offence to General Urquhart, I feel that he stuck too stubbornly to his orders. German paratroopers would have occupied the entire town of Arnhem on the first day. That would have made the attempted counter-attacks less simple. In the event, he played into our hands by staying at Oosterbeek." So Oberst Harzer wrote in answer to various queries I put to him. This mistake, he explained, gave him time to collect his units around Arnhem in an orderly manner, reinforce Nijmegen, and then turn against the airborne perimeter at last and give

"the troops of Urquhart real hell. And apart from that, I had moved a 'Barrier Unit Harzer' into the marsh between Nijmegen and Arnhem, so that the attack to the north was indeed not a pleasant walk for the 43rd British Division. There was very little they could do to launch an attack, because it was possible to move only on top of the dykes."

This is the position as it really was, on the German side. But it was not apparently the picture as seen by Second Army intelligence at the time. That, as ever, was incredibly over-optimistic. In his history of the Household Cavalry, Major Orde quotes the narrative of his CO, Colonel Abel Smith:

"Late in the evening of the 21st the following orders were received by 2 H.C.R.: *'Intelligence believes that the enemy will withdraw during the night. 43 Infantry Division will relieve the Guards Armoured Division during the night, and continue the advance next day. One Squadron of 2 H.C.R. will advance to Arnhem, covering 43 Division at first light.'* On receipt of these orders I immediately drove off to 43rd Division Headquarters as the Intelligence appreciation of the enemy intentions seemed extraordinary. The enemy had fought most tenaciously all day, and if they could hold us a little longer, the airborne troops would be doomed. The G.1 was soon found. He was not yet in the picture, having only just arrived to take over. The Divisional Commander had gone to bed, giving orders that he was not to be disturbed."

Colonel Abel Smith therefore passed on the order, with an amendment that showed his own doubt in the belief that the enemy would withdraw. His narrative continues:

"It was appreciated that the enemy could hold all the direct routes to Arnhem; therefore patrols would in the first place move east and west along the north bank of the Waal in the hope that the enemy would not expect us in that direction. Should either patrol get through, after two or three kilometres, it would move north to the Neder Rijn."

The Household Cavalry had tried precisely the same gambit on September 21, and failed. There was really no reason why they should succeed on the following day. But on the 22nd, luck was on their side. September is a month for mist, haze, and fog, and at dawn the north bank of the Waal was shrouded in a thick mist—impossible for aircraft but perfect operating conditions for probing patrols of armoured cars.

Even so, the troop that tried to infiltrate to the east was soon held up by an anti-tank gun screen near Bemmel. Captain Wrottesley's troop, which moved west along the north bank of the Waal in visibility of about 50 feet, passed through the defenders' screen without incident, although they could hear the Germans talking.

"But we reckoned that they were as blind as we were, certainly could not see enough to man their weapons, and if they heard us, probably thought that we were friendly vehicles—anyhow that was what we hoped to be the case, and the desperate situation of the Airborne warranted corresponding risks on our side."

Only one German was actually seen in the fog, and because it was important to keep silent, he was not fired at. At

THE ASSAULT ON HOCHELTEN—
31 March, 1945
A rough notebook sketch made by the author the same day, of the scene as it appeared from the west bank of the Rhine.

ARNHEM—
17 September, 1944
Complete surprise achieved—the German Commandant of Arnhem, Major-General Kussin, shot dead in his staff car on the way back to his headquarters.
Photo: Major Hibbert's collection.

ARNHEM BRIDGE—1944
A German Mark IV tank knocked out just east of the bridge by the paratroops.
Photo: Major Hibbert's collection.

THE "ROMANTIC RHIN

The twin castles know the "Hostile Broth perched hundreds of above the river. An ass across the Rhine would be very costly unlikely to succeed

REMAGEN BRIDGE

Photo taken by the au in 1950, showing the t towers on the west and a pier (*left*).

REMAGEN—1950

On right, the twin-to on the west bank appr to the bridge (demolish On left, the twin-to on the east bank, u the bluff of the Erp Ley on which German guns were emplaced

about 0800 hours, the armoured cars had linked up with the Poles south of the Neder Rijn near Driel. There they remained, to act as wireless link and to help the Poles hold off Harzer's men, who from their defensive blocking position along the north-south railway line were now sending out patrols preparatory to an attack. "The Polish general was charming but quite fanatical, and if he had thought it the least possible would have asked us to fly our armoured cars into battle!" commented Lieutenant A. V. Young.

Major Peter Herbert, commanding C Squadron, had decided to reinforce Wrottesley with Lieutenant Young's troop before the fog lifted. They took the same route, going about six miles to the west along the banks of the Waal, then turning north and on coming to the Neder Rijn turning east towards Driel.

"Things were exceptionally quiet at this time," wrote Young. "We passed several Mark IVs which we liked to presume at the time had been knocked out, but these we discovered later from Peter Herbert proved to be very much alive!" The Germans did know that these armoured cars were British, but the fog was still thick and the vehicles were out of sight before a gun could be swung on to them.

Having reached Driel, Young then went off with one other car to reconnoitre possible crossing-points of the Neder Rijn, fought a German patrol, picked up three parachutists, and captured a map belonging to the river engineer at Driel. His wirelessed reports, together with those of Captain Wrottesley, were the first definite and detailed news to be received of the British position in Arnhem since Market Garden had begun.

And then the fog began to lift.

As it did so, C Squadron HQ and Lieutenant Hopkinson's troop were passing through the leading elements of 43 Division, which had come into the bridgehead during the night, their carriers and trucks parked beside the road. The route ahead, said Lieutenant Young, consisted of "very, very narrow country roads, in the main sided with ditches, which you will appreciate is very difficult operating country for armoured fighting vehicles." Young's troop had made it. The remainder got no farther than the village of Osterhout, for as they emerged from the forward positions of the infantry, the mist began to clear and within a few minutes normal daylight conditions obtained.

"As the leading scout car of Hopkinson's troop became level with the village (the height of the road above ground level gave this effect to the eye)," [wrote Captain Clyde], "there was an unpleasant crack, a puff of smoke, and that was the scout car. I saw a figure jump clear and roll down the embankment. It was Corporal Bland. Trooper Harold Read, the driver, was killed on the spot. Then the chaos started."

Unfortunately, the optimistic intelligence appreciation, apparently borne out by reports of the ease with which two troops of armoured cars had got through to Arnhem, misled Major-General Thomas, the commander of 43 Division. It seemed as though immediate and vigorous action might secure a break-through, while a delay could be fatal. He therefore cancelled his fire-plan, which would have required time to execute. But the intelligence estimate was false, and the success of the armoured cars a result of good fortune. Further, the division had not yet been able to deploy as a division because of the traffic jams in the "corridor," and even if all of it had been in Nijmegen, the bridgehead over the Waal was still far too small.

The attack on Osterhout was therefore made by a single company of 7 Somerset Light Infantry, part of 214 Brigade, commanded by Brigadier H. Essame, whose jeep had been driven off the dyke road by the same burst of fire that had burnt out the leading armoured car. His brigade was coming into the bridgehead over the railway bridge, while 129 Brigade was to enter the Betuwe over the road bridge to support the direct road approach to Arnhem via Ressen and Elst. This brigade was still strung out along the road to Nijmegen and even 214 Brigade in the lead had not yet had time or space in which to deploy. The battalion following the Somersets was 5 Duke of Cornwall's Light Infantry, and they spent the morning waiting their turn in the streets of Nijmegen.

As this was the action that forms the principal basis of the charge by Chester Wilmot that XXX Corps showed marked lack of urgency in moving to the relief of the airborne, it needs to be examined. Presumably Wilmot was expressing not merely his own opinion but that of others as well, because the American commander, Colonel Tucker, seems to have heard the same tale: "One remark made by a British officer sticks with me. Said he, 'If only we could have had a hard driving infantry division with our lead tanks rather than a mediocre outfit, the story would have been different.'" Harzer does not agree.

However, the story is best told in a contemporary narrative written by Lieutenant-Colonel George Taylor, who commanded the Duke of Cornwall's Light Infantry that day, and whose job was to pass through the Somersets after they had taken Osterhout. He therefore bore no responsibility for the first phase of the battle, but he did write his account in 1945, long before Chester Wilmot had published his criticisms. Perhaps it should be stressed that this is not a scholarly argument. What Wilmot is really saying is that more of the Somersets should have been more willing to get killed than they really were.

It is one thing for Lieutenant Paull to criticise the airborne for taking cover unnecessarily in slit trenches instead of manning their weapons, because this is an outright foolish thing to do; it concedes the fire initiative to the enemy without costing him anything and actually reduces the defenders' own chances of survival. An attack in the open, without artillery support, is a very different matter; and even with artillery support, the casualty figures both for 1914–18 and in Normandy in 1944 show how great an advantage rapid long-range fire gives to the defence. In fact, fire *is* the attack.

And this is merely the technical aspect. It does not raise the wider question: Who wants to die for Winston Churchill, democracy, and the Four Freedoms? Except in direct defence of one's family, friends, or country, most of us would carefully calculate the risks and desire some chance at least of survival.

The full plight of the airborne was not realised until fairly late that day, when the wirelessed reports sent back by the cars of the Household Cavalry had been received, digested, and passed on in the form of direct orders to units. Even so, a rash attack would simply be throwing good money after bad. The situation in Arnhem had gone beyond the possibility of repair, and the airborne perimeter was so small and overlooked that it no longer had a military meaning. Had that early morning mist been forcast, then an infiltration attack might have been mounted, and might have been successful; but it could not be foreseen, and the attack had to be made under blue skies.

"One of the difficulties that had to be faced up to at this period was the limited amount of artillery ammunition available," [wrote Colonel Taylor in his narrative]. "For this reason the 7th SLI had to spend a great deal of time finding out exactly where enemy strongposts were located before the precious artillery ammunition could be used. The methods left to do this quickly are generally limited to attempting to draw fire by feint attacks or the use of fighting patrols. There is, of course, always the hope that the fighting patrols will suffice to dispose of the enemy. This, however, is seldom realised in practice. Once an enemy is finally 'dug in' then to attack him without firm support is a form of suicide. At Osterhout the enemy resisted tenaciously, and Major Sidney Young, the best company commander in the unit, was killed. It became obvious to the CO of 7 SLI, Lieutenant Colonel Borrodaile, that a battalion attack with full scale artillery support would be necessary. This attack by the Somersets was fixed for 1600 hours. In the early afternoon, the 5th DCLI moved over the railway bridge into an assembly area behind the big embankment. At about this time, a Staff Officer of XXX Corps came forward and told me that news had been received that the 1st British Airborne Division were in a desperate position and that the DCLI must link up with them that night. Two Dukws carrying ammunition and medical supplies were given to the battalion to be delivered to the airborne troops. The great risk of the operation was obvious to all. However, it was made clear to all concerned that the stakes were so great that nothing was to be allowed to stop the 5th DCLI and the tanks of 4/7 Dragoon Guards."

The plan devised by Brigadier H. Essame was designed to open the way "brutally and effectively," with a 40-minute barrage from the divisional artillery, a medium regiment, a heavy battery, and the brigade mortars. This was the time to spend what little there was in the way of ammunition. Then the 7 SLI were to break through Osterhout, the DCLI were to pass through them, and while part of this battalion held the flanks, and while the Germans were still off balance, the remainder were to mount on the tanks, carriers, and other vehicles for a headlong dash to Driel.

"Under the cover of a heavy artillery barrage, the 7th Somersets swept over the embankment to the attack," [wrote Colonel Taylor]. "Soon, news reached us of their success and I gave the command, 'Advance.' Prisoners, many of them wounded and a pitiful sight, were being brought in by the Somersets as our 'B' Company felt its way forward through the shattered village. Rumours of enemy tanks caused them to move off the main road and go through a tangle of gardens and orchards, which caused a slight delay. . . . But no sign of the enemy, so I told them on the wireless, 'Push on, change of plan, seize "D" Company's objective,' as this would save time. Then through the village came the head of the main body of the battalion and it began to form up on the road north-east of Osterhout. Before it lay a fleeting chance. Would it be possible to make it before the enemy recovered his balance? Disturbing news was received that two enemy tanks could be seen about 1,000 yards away. The plan was reshaped and I ordered, 'Ignore them, mount your tanks and carriers.' Speed was more than ever essential, for the enemy would move his reserves to close the gap. Also, night was fast approaching and in the dark it would not be possible to move more than a mile or so. The vital minutes were flying. I threw off my equipment and ran to the slow, plodding platoon, galvanising them into action, as they came forward from the village. Soon they were all mounted on tank, carrier, or towed anti-tank gun."

The four infantry companies were split up between two distinct groups of vehicles, the leading column consisting mainly of armoured vehicles and anti-tank guns, the rear column being made up mainly of "soft-skinned" vehicles and anti-tank guns.

"Off the battalion moved, trucks clanking, motors roaring—dashing headlong," [wrote Colonel Taylor]. "Ignoring the danger of ambush and mines, they were soon in the streets of Valburg. The Dutch inhabitants, somewhat astonished at this eruption of armour and men, went wild with joy, shouting and cheering till their lungs almost burst, as the column moved quickly on. The light was fading rapidly as the head of it reached Driel, the leading tank being blown up on a mine at the entrance leading to the village. The journey of about 10 miles had been completed in under thirty minutes."

What they had done, after 7 SLI had torn a hole in the southern blocking position held by 10 S.S. Panzer Division, was to ride right across the front of "Barrier Unit Harzer," with their eastern flank open to attack, which was not long in coming.

"The sound of battle could now be heard behind the armoured column, and very shortly afterwards a D.R. came up to the command carrier and reported to me that enemy tanks were attacking the soft vehicle column. He had been standing at the cross-roads between Valburg and Elst to direct traffic and, seeing some tanks approach, had signalled them on. A few seconds later, to his horror, he saw the dark German crosses on the tanks. Fortunately, his motor-cycle was just round the corner, facing the right direction, and running to it, he moved up to Driel with all speed to report. I realised that, in the darkness, the troops of the soft vehicle column would have a very good chance of holding off the tank attack, and I turned my attention to the problems of linking up with the Airborne troops and delivering the two Dukw-loads of supplies."

A first-hand account of conditions in Arnhem was received from two staff officers of 1 Airborne Division, Lieutenant-Colonels Charles Mackenzie and E. C. W. Meyers, who had just rowed across the Neder Rijn in a reconnaissance boat and were on their way to contact XXX Corps. They had had no news of Frost's battalion at the bridge for 24 hours and assumed correctly that he had been overwhelmed.

Colonel Taylor's first thought was to re-take the road bridge, but further discussion convinced him that it would be impossible, and he decided to concentrate on getting men and supplies across the river, while firmly holding the south bank. In the event, only about 60 Poles got across. The transport consisted of six reconnaissance boats and one R.A.F. dinghy, soon reduced by two reconnaissance boats. The airborne engineers had intended to pull them back and forwards across the river on signal cable, on the same principle as a ferry, but the current was too strong and the cable broke. The two Dukws never reached the water. They were big, awkward vehicles—in effect, amphibious, open-topped trucks—and although they handled quite nicely in the water, the mist, the darkness, the mud, and the constricted roads defeated their drivers. They ended up in the ditch, short of the river, hopelessly bogged, defeated by the flood plain of the Rhine.

In giving all his attention to helping the airborne and allowing his column of "soft-skinned" vehicles with their accompanying infantry to repulse the German tank thrust on their own, Colonel Taylor was in effect contradicting in action the American Colonel Tucker, who saw no reason why tanks should fear infantry at night, if protected by their own infantry.

In fact, the German armoured column was moving very cautiously, with their own infantry right beside them in immediate contact, as Company Sergeant Major Philp of the Duke of Cornwall's Light Infantry discovered. His carrier was unable to keep up with Major Parker's jeep, the vehicle immediately ahead, and Philp saw it pass a tank that he presumed was British. "When I was within a hundred yards," he wrote, "I saw that there were a column of tanks and, more important, they were all marked with the black cross."

It was a traffic misunderstanding of the worst sort. The small carrier could not stop, but charged on; two of the German tanks politely pulled over to the side of the road; but the third did not get out of the way, and the carrier skidded to a standstill, head-on to the German tank and touching it. The tank commander leaned out of the tank and began to remove his goggles, whereupon Philp shot him. Both tank machine-gunners opened fire, but one gun was mounted too high and the other too low to hit the crew of the carrier, so they bailed out. As Philp stood up, in order to jump over the side of the carrier, he hit his head on the barrel of the

88-millimeter gun of the tank. Then he and his crew dived straight into a mud-filled ditch overgrown with reeds. "From this ditch I observed five Tiger tanks on the road above us, and about a dozen enemy infantry on the road about one hundred yards away." In the failing light, they escaped along the ditch and reported the position of the tanks to the oncoming "soft" column, which detoured round them and reached Driel safely, leaving an infantry company to hold the road.

Major Parker, assuming that the tanks would return to Elst for the night rather than remain in contact with infantry in the darkness, decided to set up an ambush for them at a convenient crossroads.

"I gave orders for complete silence," [he wrote], "and no small arms rounds to be fired unless attacked by infantry, because of the flash; Piats to be fired in a volley of three when given the order. No firing to take place until the leading tanks had hit the mines" [which they had laid across the road]. "We then heard the Tiger tanks shooting up 'B' Company, and as this was happening, a German motor-cycle combination came up the road from Elst, presumably to contact the tanks. He blew up, literally, on our '75' mines. Next, we heard the tanks returning, headed by a D.R. He also blew up. The leading tank was firing Véry lights every thirty seconds, to light the way. It was fairly obvious that they were 'windy.' There were five tanks. As the first tank reached the '75' mines, I gave orders for groups two and three to fire. There was a tremendous explosion and six Piat bombs hit the tank. This put him completely out of action. The next tank hit the mines, and received the same treatment. The third tank tried to back out, but hit a string of mines which had been pulled in behind it, came to a halt on the initial explosion, and, every time he tried to move, another mine went off. Private Brown went within a few yards before he fired his Piat; the tank was knocked out, but so was one of Brown's eyes. As he was put on the jeep and just before he lost consciousness, he said, 'I don't care—I knocked the so-and-so thing out.' It was his first action. The two remaining tanks completely panicked and tried to back out in a hurry. They both ditched themselves, the crews escaping into the wood. CSM Philp then made sure that every tank was incapable of further action, by dropping grenades down the turrets."

While doing so, Philp was wounded by British shellfire brought down by someone hearing the noise of tanks and seeing the fires. The link-up with the Poles had seen a similar accident, but a tragic one. Although both the Poles and the Household Cavalry armoured cars had shown recognition panels and fired yellow smoke cartridges, the leading tank of the relief force opened fire on the first armoured car it saw, killing Trooper Reginald Holmes. "The fiery Poles were beside themselves with rage, and it took all Lieutenant Young's powers of persuasion to stop them knocking out the first tanks to arrive."

When the Poles first arrived in the airborne perimeter, the same mistakes occurred, aided by the fact that their berets were grey, not red, and possibly a little trigger-happiness. Lieutenant Paull wrote,

"There were many cases of mistaken identity, resulting in exchanges of fire between friendly troops. A Polish officer came to me in an understandably agitated condition and in broken English said, 'Our men are shooting each other.' Some sense of sanity in this respect was fortunately restored before getting too serious."

Having been baulked in his attempt to get supplies over the river, Colonel Taylor laid on a fire-plan for September 23: "If we could not carry it across, we would throw it across." But not only were the airborne cut off, but the DCLI group also. Indeed, to Trooper J. W. Conway, of Lieutenant Young's troop, the situation then appeared bleak: "We had the choice of either being taken prisoners or fighting to the last man." General Sosabowski had already used Conway's wireless set to broadcast a message to XXX Corps: "All we can do now is trust in God. We have no food or ammunition. God bless you all."

Even more serious was the fact that Nijmegen had now been cut off by strong counter-attacks from both sides of the "corridor" near Uden and Veghel. Instead of being available for operations in the Betuwe, the Grenadier and Coldstream Guards had to be sent hurriedly in the opposite direction—back towards Eindhoven—to reopen the road. Fighting continued there for four days and during this period very little got through. XXX Corps also began to run short of food as well as ammunition. While the Germans in Arnhem were feasting on British rations, XXX Corps was in part subsisting on captured German rations. It was time, reluctantly, to decide to withdraw from Arnhem. And because of the wide, fast river with its muddy flood approaches, this would not be easy to carry out.

CHAPTER TWENTY

"A GHASTLY OPERATION"

Relief and Evacuation of Arnhem
September 23–26

Although the defenders of Arnhem captured most of the headlines, they were not the only beleaguered garrison. September 17–22 had seen also the Battle of Boulogne, and September 24–30 was to be that of the Battle of Calais; for while Second Army was fighting in Holland, the First Canadian Army was taking on large German forces in France, fronting the Straits of Dover, hundreds of miles away. Only at the end of September did the guns that had shelled Dover and the Channel convoys since the summer of 1940 at last fall silent. But these ports were thoroughly wrecked and of little immediate use for supplying Second Army, and German guns along the Scheldt still denied Montgomery the use of Antwerp as a port.

In these circumstances, the German base depot at Oss, midway between British-held Grave and German-held Hertogenbosch, became more than a knowing joke. There were in fact three German dumps at Oss, two of them issuing tinned food, bacon, meats, and carboys of Bols gin, while the third held sugar, cigars, apricot brandy, and so on. On September 20, armoured cars of the Household Cavalry had not merely engaged and sunk a tug towing a barge train in the River Waal, they had also discovered the wonderful world of Oss, which, wrote Major Orde, "was to remain for over a week a land of fabulous promise. It tempted the staidest into a sense of reckless plunder and adventure." Even the tank troop guarding divisional headquarters, "in a few carefree hours of freedom met the enemy head-on, fought a spirited action, and finally returned laden with drink and prisoners, the latter, we were informed, mostly bakers. . . ."

Later, "by tacit agreement, the British drew rations in the morning while the enemy helped himself to what he wanted in the afternoon." However, the Dutch caretaker very properly insisted on obtaining a signature for all issues. In fact, everyone was drawing from Oss. As Lieutenant Gemmell of 20 Field Company, Royal Canadian Engineers, wrote, "We were low on chow but did manage to locate a Jerry food dump. I know I had my fill of Limburger cheese."

On September 24, the Household Cavalry mounted a major raid on Oss. That day, wrote Major Orde,

"the Divisional Intelligence Summary was in excellent form. It stated that it was only 'remnants of the Panzer Division' which had cut the precious centre line. The morale of the German Army was to all intents and purposes 'non-existent,' and, in a final burst of wishful thinking, 'as for the left flank, nothing but elderly river guards were manning the defences'."

It was in this direction that the pillage party went. In Oss, two vehicles under Lieutenant Hughes and Winterbottom left the main party and went to one of the three dumps alone. It "was seething with Resistance men wearing orange armbands and carrying rifles." The storekeeper produced a ledger that "was already crammed with German signatures, interspersed between which were a few rather lonely-looking British names." Hughes had happily made his selection of goods and was having them wheeled out on a trolley when he noticed two significant facts: A party of well-armed Germans had just debussed from a truck—"in their tin hats they looked extremely sinister and businesslike"; and "of the Dutch Resistance there was now no sign—they had vanished into thin air."

The storekeeper, whose name was Alphons Hendrick Snoek, afterwards recalled, "We sneaked through the store and along the wall of the building. We hastened us to the surrounding wall on the other side. In normal times it is very difficult to jump over this wall, but now it went as quick as if we were greyhounds."

Hughes wrote, "so the three of us moved warily into a near-by house and from the first-floor window looked down into the warehouse yard. It was overflowing with Germans. One great brute was even doing the 'Lower Star Post crouch' under our very window." This latter manoeuvre, a peculiarly theatrical bending of the body, was used at Sandhurst as the only known answer to umpires who leapt out of hiding, crying, "You're under fire, what are you going to do about it?"

Hughes and his companions then retreated to a haystack, resigned to the loss of their vehicles and discussing the problems of correspondence from a prisoner-of-war camp. "In war," remarked Hughes, "nothing matters but the safety of one's kit. So long as I can keep my bedroll, all is well."

Some time later a troop of armoured cars arrived, under Captain Phillip Profumo, and it was the turn of the Germans to pile into their truck and evacuate at high speed. They had, however, thoughtfully loaded the British vehicles, which the Dutch Resistance were in their turn about to remove, being stopped only just in time.

"Next morning early," [wrote Major Orde], "a new Divisional Summary for the past twenty-four hours was circulated. There was only passing reference to activities on the left flank, but the relevant paragraph read as follows: 'south of the Maas enemy inf. approached OSS from the WEST this afternoon but were seen off by our armd. cars. They did NOT get near the important food dump at OSS which is reported as being very large indeed'."

The previous day Lieutenant Franklin's troop had, with the help of a very gallant Dutchman, reconnoitred a line of 88s that the Germans were using to support their armoured attacks on the "corridor," and were able to see both American paratroops and Coldstream Guards in action against them on the same day. The Americans were from a Dakota and a glider shot out of a formation flying in reinforcements. Despite the forced landing,

"fourteen paratroops in the most spotless order, their trousers beautifully creased, came over towards us. They had breakfasted in England, and on being asked how it was looking, one of them replied, 'As sweet as a green pea!' This was about their third attempt to get to Holland, they said, as they had had to turn back owing to weather being bad. I have never seen anything like their kit. They had jeeps, rifles, grenades hung all over them, chewing gum, and even brand new frying pans. 'Say, boys, which way is the battle?' demanded one of the Americans. We pointed in the direction of the 88-mms, and suggested that they should be careful; we ourselves had been ordered to await the arrival of tank and infantry reinforcements. 'Say, Buddy,' remarked a big fellow, 'we came here to fight and that's what we're going to do.' With which remark the entire party, complete with jeeps, motored off towards the enemy guns. We saw them disappear down a bend in the road. All at once there was a tremendous burst of firing and the sound of loud explosions and much shouting. After an interval the survivors came back."

Then a group of Coldstream Guards tanks and infantry appeared, and as everything was now quiet, Lieutenant Franklin's warnings were for the second time that day disregarded. The tanks rolled forward, and after the first three had blown up in quick succession, the advance was stopped and a proper attack, supported by mortars and infantry, was mounted. The German mortars replied, wounded Guards began to trickle back, and then an outburst of noise, "bangs, shouts and explosions," followed by silence. Most of the 88s had been knocked out, but seven Panther tanks had escaped.

"Three things I shall always remember," [said one Household Cavalry witness]. "The utter imperturbability of the Coldstream Guards as they went in to the attack; the sudden and extraordinary arrival right into the middle of the battle of their echelon lorries to disgorge hot food for the soldiers; and lastly, the sight of the commander of the group stalking about apparently unarmed and accompanied by a huge Guardsman, armed with a rifle with a telescopic sight, and whose other job appeared to be to feed his commanding officer on enormous bread and cheese sandwiches."

The optimism of Second Army seems not to have been shared in First Canadian Army. At least, my diary entry for September 1 contains the geographically accurate prophesy, "our troops might get stuck on the Siegfried Line," and that for September 23 ends " . . . with summer gone and the shadow of winter and a winter campaign upon us." The Siegfried Line ended in the Reichswald Forest, on the Rhine just east of Nijmegen, so that Arnhem outflanked it. Nijmegen did not.

On September 23 the situation in the Betuwe was still shaky, the reinforcement of Driel and the advance to Elst proving to be the unpleasant walk that Harzer had arranged. On this day, Brigadier Essame's brigade took Elst, not along the main Arnhem–Nijmegen road, but by driving from the west and penetrating Harzer's "barrier" of Dutch and German infantry backed by tanks. The job of 43 Division was to ferry the Poles across the river and put two of their own battalions across to enlarge the airborne bridgehead on the far bank. The task was far beyond the boating resources of the division; not more than a few hundred Poles got across, and they left the boats on the far side, where they were shelled to pieces in the morning.

The Germans held the high ground at Westerbouwing and north of Arnhem, with perfect coverage over both the bridgehead and the Betuwe; further, the approaches to the river were part of the soggy flood plain and were even more of an obstacle than the fast-flowing water; finally, the Germans were expecting them and had put out forward posts along the polder.

The 200 Poles who got across were more or less cancelled out by the 500 German Navy marines who joined Krafft's force opposite them on this day, although these men were without officers, almost without NCOs, and lacked both greatcoats and blankets. Stiffened with S.S., however, they were useful in defence, always the easiest form of warfare. Krafft's report declared that the Poles showed themselves to be "tough and skilful, if gruesome fighters," although the prisoners appeared to have "typically criminal natures"; and added that there was an "unconfirmed report" that they had shot a number of their prisoners.

Of the British prisoners, he wrote that the "NCOs seldom made statements and officers practically none"; the private soldiers did talk, but they "knew nothing or very little." British impressions of German prisoners were similar: "tractable, ignorant and fruitful sources of historic interest." Only one man, an S.S. soldier, gave information of value, after a "tactical squeeze." "Most agree that the war is lost." A high proportion of the prisoners were *Volksdeutsche* and Dutch, the former being Germans who had emigrated to Holland, taken Dutch nationality, and been called up after 1940.

Krafft noted, of the British prisoners, that "many showed great anxiety due to the erroneous idea that the Waffen S.S. shot all prisoners. A Flight Lieutenant Godman declared that while this was not officially advertised in England, it was generally understood." He also noted:

"The enemy treated our own prisoners quite well. Food supply was short, but so it was for the British as well—they were nearly starving. Valuables like rings, watches, etc. were always taken away, but papers were given back after examination. The Dutch S.S. volunteers were treated badly by the Dutch terrorists. They were abused, their uniforms torn and all the signs ripped off. The British did not take part in this but did not stop it. The British expect soldierly bearing and discipline even from prisoners. A Captain interrogating a German soldier, knocked the cigarette from his hand and demanded a correct deportment from him. Searching of the prisoners was superficial." [the British Intelligence report confirms this.] "The British troops were about 25 years of age on the average, and the best type, mentally and physically; and of good combat value. In spite of these being the cream of the British fighting forces, a number of cases occurred, particularly in the first few days, where certain individuals deserted to gain relief from battle fatigue. Towards the end of the fighting, many gave themselves up because of hunger and other privations, including breakdown of morale. The officers were the finest of the whole British Army. Very well schooled, personally hard, persevering and brave, they made an outstanding impression."

Krafft complained that the British "deceived Germans by shouting, in German, 'Don't shoot!' and then opening fire at the last moment." The British made the same complaint of "mock surrenders" by the Germans, and such tricks were undoubtedly used by both sides. Krafft noted that "in house fighting, the enemy was very skilled and had a great advantage over our troops, who, it must be remembered, were not all of the best type."

The British comment was that the fighting value of the German infantry was "poor," but that "the S.S. were very noticeably better than the Army." Of course, many of the German infantry were not infantry at all, they were field gunners without their guns, coastal gunners without their guns, Luftwaffe aircrew and ground staff without their aircraft, railway workers without their trains, concentration camp guards, and boys of the labour corps who had laid down their shovels for rifles.

Consequently, it was the S.S. and HG that, time after time, were called upon for the assaults. A particularly stubborn resistance was put up around the goods train depot by remnants of the forces that had tried unsuccessfully to reach Frost at the bridge. Herbert Kessler wrote:

"In the direction of the goods train depot, there were rows of houses in which the enemy still stubbornly hung on. An assault troop was formed with orders to storm these houses. We advanced by making use of every possible opportunity for cover. Just before the road had to be crossed, the enemy opened fire from the still-occupied houses with such intensity that the enterprise immediately collapsed. The assault leader, a sergeant, was killed, and there were many other casualties. The only thing to do was to retreat as quickly as possible. While the dead and wounded were brought in, once again respect for the Red Cross flag was clearly displayed by both sides. As soon as the stretcher bearers turned up, all firing ceased."

During the previous truce in a wooded area, Kessler had taken to his CO a British doctor who had come over under a Red Cross flag.

"He asked if we would let them get some First Aid material which was lying between the two fronts, because they had no more medical kit, not even bandages, and their losses had been heavy. I feel that the bad organisation of supply was partly the reason for the defeat of the British troops."

Lieutenant-Colonel M. S. Packe, service corps commander of the airborne, estimated afterwards that of the 1,431 tons of supplies dropped by the R.A.F., less than 200 tons were recovered by the British. The rest went to the Germans. This was a direct result of a perimeter too large to be held, particularly when reinforcements were delayed by bad weather. For this reason, the division had taken five days to arrive, instead of three days. Kessler confirms the fact, saying, "By my own observation, most of the supply containers which were dropped came down in our positions. We didn't need our own field kitchens, we were being completely supplied by England."

The condition of the wounded became very serious and a number of truces were arranged, contrasting strangely with the savage fighting before and after them. There was some accidental firing on the Red Cross, including that of a German S.P. gun that put two shots through a dressing station. "The surgeon on duty ran out with a Red Cross flag and protested in colourful language; the gun commander said, 'Oh! sorry' and went away."

The precise status of the wounded was sometimes a puzzle in these circumstances. One British officer went into this particular dressing station, now in enemy hands, had his wound seen to, then walked back to his unit, "brushing aside the German sentry's suggestion that he was now a PW."

John Wilson was with the remains of 21 Independent Parachute Company, the pathfinders, when

"The enemy sent over a Dutch civilian to arrange an armistice to evacuate the wounded. We agreed to this. The German CO told us he would hold fire till 12 noon on Monday, 25 September. Then he would come with 70 tanks and 'blow us to hell.' We refused to move and the threatened attack never came."

The threat was a bluff to obtain surrender; also a bluff was Major "Boy" Wilson's reply that he would destroy all the German tanks with his anti-tank guns. The result was a small action.

"We were later attacked by a few tanks, one of which was knocked out by the Company cook. However, during the truce it was a galling experience to see several of my friends who were 'walking wounded' being led away."

They were eventually taken to German hospitals, where

medical supplies were also short. However, the senior airborne doctor, Graeme Warrack, was later to comment on

"the stupendous efforts of the German doctors—they really put their backs into it and produced a good deal of stuff; considering that they had some 1500 of their own casualties, it was a good effort."

The position on September 24 was that the Germans had indeed received tank reinforcements—the first of 60 Tigers from Heavy Tank Battalion 506, which had arrived from Germany. But these great vehicles could not be used in masses in the narrow streets of Oosterbeek, and 45 of the 60 were given to 10 S.S. Panzer Division to thicken up the firepower of the defensive positions around Elst. Their guns completely out-ranged those of the British and American tanks.

As far as the airborne perimeter was concerned, the Germans decided to assault it with artillery and mortars, to save the lives of their infantry. They did, however, attempt to cut it off from the Neder Rijn by advancing along the river bank; and Herbert Kessler was one of those who manned a post out on the Rosande Polder south of Oosterbeek.

The British decision to withdraw from Arnhem appears to have been made on the morning of September 24 by General Horrocks, then at the headquarters of 43 Division. A possible factor in the decision to retreat may have been the fate of the class 40 rafts that were to ferry tanks over to the airborne. Lieutenant Gemmell's unit of Canadian engineers had now come onto the "Island," to reach Driel by the western route. But he heard that the pontoon platoon, "instead of turning left, as we did, carried right on into Elst, and the whole shebang was captured."

In any event, the first stage of withdrawal was to put a battalion from the Wessex Division—4 Dorsets—over the Neder Rijn to form a firm screen behind which the airborne could retire to the river and be ferried back across it. The assault-crossing of the Neder Rijn by 43 Division was definitely off. The code-word for the evacuation to take place would be "Berlin."

The attempt to pass 4 Dorsets over was an almost complete

failure. The plan looked all right, provided that the nature of the terrain was not taken into account, plus the fact that the Germans held the 100-foot-high hill of Westerbouwing. Only about 300 men got across, plus a few Poles. The latter were not cooperative and held on to the boats for some hours without making much use of them; possibly they felt that they were fighting soldiers, not mud-bound pack mules *cum* water-rats. The boats were then taken away by the Dorsets, whose own boats were in a bogged truck miles back towards Nijmegen.

Consequently, only two companies were able to make the attempt, and they had to wait three hours before struggling to get the boats and their own weapons and equipment by hand some 600 yards through orchards, over the flood dyke, down the steep, muddy face of the dyke, and over the flood plain to the river, which was now flowing at its fastest speed, to face a 50 percent loss of boats during the crossing.

Major W. M. C. Whittle, commanding B Company, wrote an account for the regimental history:

"The enemy opened up with counter-fire, and at least two of the ten boats in my company group were holed badly before reaching the bank. We were launching the first boat when they opened up with medium-M.G. fire from the opposite bank, the boat sank, and we had several casualties. We discovered that this fire was on fixed lines, and by moving a few yards the remainder of the boats were launched successfully. There was a strong current, and my two leading boats were swept rapidly towards the West where the factory, about 400 yards downstream, was ablaze, and we should have been beautifully silhouetted. By using spades as well as the quite inadequate paddles we eventually landed about 100 yards East of the factory and got ashore without much trouble, but only two further boatloads joined us. It was subsequently ascertained that of our ten boats three were holed before launching, one was swept downstream and landed below the burning factory, four crossed with us, and the other two were sunk during the crossing. On the spot the strength of B Company was 2 officers and less than 30 other ranks. Where the trees started there was a steep bank about 100 feet high, and the enemy were well dug in on the top of it. We started the assault and met very heavy opposition; it was only too easy for the Jerries on top to roll grenades down on us, and we eventually gained the top at the expense of 50 per cent of our strength, for when we occupied the trenches at the top we were reduced to about fifteen."

The other parties, similarly scattered, arrived if at all in small groups and were soon surrounded and forced to surrender. Major Whittle's party dug-in and waited for daylight, which brought sniping, machine-gun fire, a polite offer in perfect English to surrender, and an attack from "a well-meaning couple of Spitfires." A few Dukws had got across with supplies, but even these were swept wildly downstream by the force of the current.

There were 20 Dukws in all and the officer who brought them up to Driel was Lieutenant-Colonel E. C. W. Myers, Commander, Royal Engineers, of 1 Airborne Division, who had crossed the Neder Rijn on September 22 with Lt-Colonel Charles Mackenzie in order to contact XXX Corps, a desperate expedient made necessary by the wireless failures. Now, his intention was to get back into the perimeter with the Dukws and their supplies. He chose the ferry site at Heveadorp, under the hill at Westerbouwing, because here and here only did a road lead to the water's edge, carried across the flood plain by a ramp. The opposite bank was in enemy hands, but it was hoped that the Dorsets could clear it. He wrote:

"I was carrying a letter which had just arrived from General Browning, Commander 1 Airborne Corps. Its contents, which I had memorised, gave instructions to General Urquhart, the GOC 1 Airborne Division, to withdraw the survivors of 1 Airborne Division the following night if this night's attack did not succeed in relieving the situation. We got two Dukws safely into the river. I jumped on the third; it was the last to get across. We reached the North bank, only to discover that the infantry were held up by strong enemy fire right on the banks of the river. I decided that I must get on to my own

Divisional Headquarters in view of the importance of the message which I carried; for I knew, from what I had seen already, that the attack would not relieve the situation in the perimeter."

In order to reach the perimeter from the ferry site, Myers bent double and splashed eastward through the shallows of the river until he reached it.

Myers reached HQ at 0630 on September 25, and his deputy, Lieutenant-Colonel J. C. Winchester, records that Urquhart issued the plans for withdrawal about 1100. They were very simple. Two routes to the river bank were to be marked out with tape, so that the men could find their way in the dark. Winchester marked one route, which led in several places to within 40 yards of the enemy. The men would have to muffle their boots with cloth and make sure no equipment jingled.

The ferrying operation from the southern bank was to be controlled by the Commander Royal Engineers of 43 Division, Lieutenant-Colonel M. C. A. Henniker. His plan included a noisy, visual demonstration to the west by a brigade with pontoons and bridging lorries, in order to give the impression that an assault-crossing was intended at that point. Two ferry points were set up, one opposite Oosterbeek and the other downstream near Westerbouwing. Each point was manned by one British and one Canadian Field Company of Engineers, the British equipped with 16 light canvas assault boats, propelled by paddles, the Canadians equipped with 21 wooden storm boats powered by outboard motors.

The former were easier to man-handle towards the water but would not be able to cope with the current when it ran full; while the latter required about a dozen men to carry them, even when the going was fairly firm, but, although slow when heavily laden, had enough power to slant across the current without falling off downstream.*

The war diary of 5 Dorsets, who formed a reception area

* Storm boats (war surplus) are still in use and my own experience of them has been gained with a sub-aqua club operating in fast currents; I have also motor-boated along the Neder Rijn in peace-time; and have driven a Dukw.

opposite Oosterbeek, summed up the night of September 25–26: "The evacuation of the Airborne Forces was carried out according to plan. but torrential rain and shell and mortar fire made it a ghastly operation."

Of the two Canadian field companies, Major H. L. Tucker's 23rd was opposite Oosterbeek, while Major Jones's 20th was opposite Westerbouwing. Lieutenant Gemmell was with the latter unit.

"We waited in the orchard until dark and then in close behind the dyke. The storm boats and motors were ready to go. All we had to do was get them over the dyke and down to the river. I made the initial recce. You couldn't just walk across that dyke. Jerry had, I'd say, about six or seven M.G.s on the north bank; you had to spot the tracers and duck over when they went past. I couldn't see any signals from the paratroopers opposite our position but I did notice several flashes, presumably from flash lights, further up the river opposite the 23rd Field. Some 'nut' had ordered machine-gun tracer fire on our flanks to mark our position, but I am glad to say this was discontinued as it drew down a very heavy barrage of mortar fire and machine-gun fire, and the 88s started to open up, too. They must have been fairly close across the river. I got back across the dyke and told Major Jones that there was no apparent activity across from us."

He meant British activity, for there were clearly a lot of Germans there, and their fire was increasing. However, just so there should be no delay in case any paratroopers did appear, the Canadians decided to get the storm boats right to the water's edge. That meant crossing over the top of the dyke with the heavy boats, then struggling over some 500 feet of soggy floodland in driving rain to the Neder Rijn. The first boat to be launched was destroyed before the second one had even arrived. The Germans were throwing up flares to light the scene and Gemmell had previously told his sappers to "freeze" if this happened.

"But Jerry couldn't see us anyway, as there was a lot of mortar smoke around and as I recall, smoke from Arnhem, which we could see burning upstream. Also, it was raining hard. Then, through the gloom, I noticed a large dark, moving object coming downstream. I followed this apparent body of troops, then got over the dyke; and got about ten Sappers to line the dyke just where this 'thing' would approach, with M.G. fire still coming over. I ran the last 100 feet, challenged, and a weary voice replied, 'Friends.' It turned out to be a group of about 20 men of the Dorsets who had gone over the previous day. They were led by a Captain and had, believe it or not, swum the river."

The officer may have been Major Whittle, who had put his wounded and non-swimmers into a boat, then swum back at the head of about 15 men at 2300 hours. Gemmell concluded:

"I'll never forget those British paratroops. They had taken the hell of a kicking around for ten days but were still full of the old ginger. Lots of them came downstream to our area from the 23rd's, and got into some farmhouses; of course, out came the old tea, which brewed up into the best drink I ever had in my life, bar none."

Major Tucker, OC 23 Canadian Field Company, wrote in his report that he received his orders from Colonel Henniker at 1000 hours on September 25, giving time only for a brief reconnaissance of the area. It did not look inviting.

"The whole of this part of Holland is low-lying and the roads, which are built up well above the level of the surrounding terrain, are separated from the fields by wide, deep ditches. The roads are narrow, with soft shoulders, and totally unsuitable for heavy military traffic. Entrances to fields are also narrow and difficult to negotiate, even in the daytime when clear visibility may be had."

Eventually, he found a railway yard that offered hard standing space on which to concentrate his heavy vehicles. Two lieutenants reconnoitred the river bank for the best crossing-places and found two, but even so a bridge would have to be built on the approaches. In a few hours the convoy was brought up, the routes to the river taped, and 14 storm boats and 17 motors unloaded. Carrying them forward over the dykes was difficult.

"Two floodwalls blocked the path from the off-loading area to the launching sites. The first of these was about 20 feet high with banks sloping to about 45 degrees, the second was about half the height and the slope much less severe. These obstacles became most difficult to negotiate. The heavy rain softened the ground and the churning of men's feet as they struggled over with the storm boats soon created a slippery mess which lent no footing whatsoever. Hand ropes were fixed, but even with these the going was extremely difficult. The first boat was launched at 2130 hours, but it had been badly holed when the men carrying it slipped coming down the floodwall. It would have sunk before it could have completed a crossing. The next boat was launched at 2145 hours and set off with Lieutenant Martin in command. This boat did not return and neither Lieutenant Martin nor any of the crew has been seen or heard from since. Corporal McLachlan captained the third boat and returned bringing the first load of airborne troops; he completed 15 trips before he was relieved by a fresh crew. The fourth boat, in charge of Corporal Smith, made its way safely to the bridgehead, but swamped when a mortar fell close by on the return voyage. Smith and four of his passengers got back. The rain caused the motors to give endless trouble and was responsible for their failing altogether in many cases."

Colonel Henniker was with the assault boats of 260 Field Company of his own Division.

"The first assault boats, led by a sapper subaltern, pushed off into the stream at 2115. For a long time nothing happened. I paced the shore like a cat on hot bricks oppressed by the most gloomy forebodings. Had they upset the boats and all gone silently to the bottom, weighed down by steel helmets and rifles? Had they rowed straight into the waiting Hun on the far bank? Or had they merely been washed downstream to God knows where? It was a tense interval. But in battles the worst occurs as seldom as the best. Across the dark waters came the sound of dipping oars. Then I saw a boat. It held about a dozen men. I could see airborne pattern helmets. Never was there a more welcome sight. First one boat, then another, then another. About a hundred men came silently ashore with a few wounded. The boats stole back into the night. The bearing and demeanour of these men were first class. Whether reaction set in afterwards and these splendid soldiers later presented a less soldierlike appearance I do not know. Maybe, but they were all right on the night. More and more boats were launched and then I heard the motors of the Canadian storm boats start. No music could have seemed more sweet. Soon there was a steady stream of men filing back along the tapes. By the small hours of the morning the current had quickened and made the rowing of assault boats almost impossible. But the Canadian storm boats continued with unabated zest. If the assault boats got the first hauls, the storm boats certainly got the greater ones."

On the north bank, long queues of paratroopers formed along the tapes marking out the routes to the river, the noise of movement covered by heavy fire from the Wessex Division on the south bank. Major H. F. Brown, an engineer officer, wrote:

"We all shaved for the first time during the operation, muffled our boots, stopped all jingles, and started off in a silent swaying crocodile for the river. I led what remained of the 4th Parachute Brigade, 54 souls. We passed very silently within 10 yards of a German mortar position and eventually, guided by glider pilots at main turnings, we reached the river banks where orderly queues of men waited their turn for the boats."

Major Winchester acted as a beachmaster on the northern shore.

"The discipline on the river bank was excellent. There were very few ferry craft and most of the men had to wait a long time under heavy shell and mortar fire. Those who were strong swimmers took to the water, stripped except for their personal weapons, and made room in the boats for non-swimmers and the wounded, of which there were many."

Private John Wilson, of 21 Independent Company, recalled:

"There was a Bofors gun firing tracer across the river to mark the spot. At this point there was an orderly queue across the polder down to the river bank, and when the occasional mortar bomb burst near by, one noticed a unified bending of the knees by this queue. Apart from that, everybody remained more intent upon maintaining his place in the line."

Wilson was unlucky and was captured on the river bank "while waiting hopefully for some more boats."

Herbert Kessler was also out on the Rosande Polder that night.

"As soon as darkness fell, parts of two groups set off in order to reach a position beside the Neder Rijn opposite the place where on the other bank the enemy was waiting. We had hardly arrived in the place, and were still lying in the damp grass not daring to move, but watching in great suspense for any movement near us, when, a very short distance away, we saw the silhouettes of people in motion. As we knew that in this sector we were the only advanced posts, we concluded that these moving shadows were actually the enemy. To hesitate was pointless, and very soon wild shooting at short range began. There were losses on both sides. It seemed, however, that we had the stronger nerves, for the enemy retreated. Peace and quiet had hardly been re-established when a silhouette rose in front of our position and yelled, 'Don't shoot!' A closer inspection revealed an English Flight Lieutenant who had parachuted and was now lost. We breathed a sigh of relief when at last the sky began to turn light, for this was the sign to retreat to our rest positions."

Captain A. P. Wood, a survivor of 2 Parachute Battalion's fight at the bridge, recalled:

"We saw some Canadians with small boats. The sky was ablaze, Jerry was shelling the water and the river banks. Casualties were high, both on the banks and in the water. Some boats were overturned by swimmers trying to get aboard. I was with a Sergeant Glider Pilot and we decided to undress, apart from underpants and socks, and to take our weapons and swim. He had a Schmeisser and I a Thompson sub-machine-gun. We set out together, taking the fast tide and aiming for some 500 yards downstream. The Sergeant was the better swimmer and went ahead, but about the half way he just disappeared—I never saw him again. Exhausted, dirty and half-drowned, I recall I hit the muddy side of the river and was helped ashore by some Bod with the biggest pair of Don. R. gloves I've ever seen. I never saw his face—or knew his name. Looking back to the Arnhem side of the river, it was like hell—the odd shell and mortar bursts on our side seemed slight."

Major Tucker's report on his ferry site agrees.

"Many casualties were reported from the bridgehead, but on the river and on the south bank they were light. It was found impossible to keep complete records of the crossings made and the passengers carried. Paper turned to pulp in the driving rain. It was impossible to regulate the number of passengers carried in boats at times. Men panicked and stormed onto the boats, in some cases capsizing them. In many cases they had to be beaten off or threatened with shooting to avoid having the boats swamped. With the approach of dawn this condition became worse. They were so afraid that daylight would force us to cease our ferrying before they could be rescued. The maximum lifted at any one time was 36. All these men were packed into his boat by Lieutenant Kennedy on his last trip, the last trip made by anyone in this operation. The minimum lifted was 6, by a Corporal operating a boat which was leaking badly, who decided he could make one more trip and bring off a few men before his craft went down. It sank as it approached the south shore, but fortunately the water was shallow at this point. It is estimated that approximately 150 boatloads were brought back by the stormboats' crews and that approximately the average load carried was about 16 passengers. Thus, approximately 2400 to 2500 troops were brought off. CRE 43 Div ordered cessation of operations at 0545 hours, when it became evident that any further attempts to bring off men would be suicidal for the boat crews."

The combined total of those saved was under 3,000 out of the 10,095 men who had landed at Arnhem.

The German casualties seem to have been on the order of 3,000, or about half the British losses, although it is difficult for anyone to say because of the chaotic state of the hurriedly improvised units that were thrown into the battle. Harzer, looking back after more than 20 years, paid tribute to the "valour" with which the airborne defended themselves, but wrote:

"It is with personal pride that I regard this German victory, because it was achieved, not by regular units, but by railway workers, Arbeitsdienst and Luftwaffe personnel as well, who had never been trained for infantry work and were actually unsuitable for house-to-house fighting."

CHAPTER TWENTY-ONE

"THE BRIDGES ARE BLOWN!"

Model's Counter-offensive on the "Island": September–October

Up to September 25, the British had been attacking on the "Island," in difficult circumstances and with their supply lines cut south of Nijmegen. After only a very brief pause, the Germans went over to the offensive to drive the British out of the Betuwe. But first they had to clear the battlefield of Arnhem and round-up the remaining airborne troops, many of whom proved persistent evaders and escapers.

Lieutenant Paull escaped no less than three times. He was first taken prisoner while lying up in the woods and waiting for nightfall to cover his move towards the river. Ironically, while it was still daylight German patrols passed within a few feet of his hideout without seeing him, and then at dusk a corporal and six men came across him.

"The corporal handed me over to an S.S. officer who shook hands and said, 'Congratulations on a good fight—you were better yesterday, we were better today.' It rather reminded me of 'no side' after a pretty tough game of rugger. He gave me a corned beef sandwich and said I looked in need of a shave. The corporal searched me, pinched my watch and ring, but missed the small compass stitched under one of my shoulder pips."

Paull never could make up his mind whether the S.S. officer conveniently forgot about him, or whether he was genuinely overlooked in the eagerness to round-up more prisoners. In the darkness, Paull disappeared into a slit-trench, but there were German voices all round and he was soon a prisoner again.

"This time I was hauled out with a gun in my back by a very blonde young S.S. officer in a sort of camouflaged flowing imitation-leopardskin cloak who did not seem half as nice as my previous captor. He didn't speak, except for repeated orders to 'Hande Hoch!,' accompanied by jabs in the back with a gun. I was marched through the wood to a clearing by the roadside to join about thirty other Airborne troops, including a Glider Pilot, a Captain Muir, a Lieutenant Skinner of the REs, Sergeant McIver from Battery HQ and Cook Bombardier Monteith. We were formed up on the road in columns of three, with Muir, Skinner and myself at the head, and then marched down the road with the blonde S.S. officer in charge. After marching about a mile, we were told to halt, remaining in column by the side of the road. Suddenly, without warning, a German corporal got out of a slit trench and with a captured Sten, opened fire on us.

"Muir and Skinner, on either side of me, went down and complete surprise made me do the same. The shooting was terminated by the S.S. officer grabbing a guard's rifle and shooting the German corporal responsible.

"I got up, but saw that Muir and Skinner were riddled with bullets. Skinner was dead, but Muir was trying to attract my attention to his breast pocket. I tried to open it, but was prevented by a fat German officer who knocked my hand away, punched me in the face, and said, 'He is kaput.' There was an awful lot of shouting going on, all in German, so I knelt again by the side of Muir, who was trying to say something. I was again dragged away, and saw that Muir had died. There were a great many casualties as a result of this incident. I recall a C.M.P. Sergeant shot through the jaw and Bombardier Monteith with a bullet in his shoulder. The blonde S.S. officer tried to convey to me that the German corporal had panicked at the sight of our red berets, and told us to take them off in case it happened again. I almost lost my temper with him and through a Sergeant who spoke a little English said, 'The least you can do is arrange something about the wounded before marching us off.' They were a pretty arrogant lot, to say the least, but I had the satisfaction of seeing that the wounded were eventually attended to. To this day, I cannot make up my mind as to the real cause of this regrettable affair; I am inclined to think there was more to it than the red berets."

In fact, as the historian of 9 S.S. Panzer Division records, the paratroops were hated and also respected for one and the same reason—they were good fighters. Which meant heavy casualties for their opponents, and many friends killed. There was no hatred, only pity, for those British units that fought at Arnhem in an obviously incompetent manner, and were therefore not dangerous.

Anyway, as the only surviving officer in that column of prisoners, Paull was taken for interrogation to what was probably a divisional or battlegroup headquarters. Afterwards, he was given a meal in the officers' mess, of German sausage, dark bread, and coffee, and offered the loan of a shaving kit. When only one officer was left in the room, so that the two of them were alone, the German turned to Paull and said:

"Do you honestly think we've got a chance?"

"If you mean, of winning the war—not a hope."

The German looked round before he replied: "I do agree with you."

Then he asked Paull for his opinion of the Americans. Paull said, rather stiffly, "They are our Allies and we couldn't do without them."

"Yes, I know," said the German with a grin. "We have the Italians and you have the Americans."

Taking the German's shaving kit, Paull then went to a bathroom. When he came back, everyone seemed to have left the mess. There was no one to whom he could return the shaving kit. So, feeling rather mean, he stepped out of the back door of the building and made off into the night.

After a time he saw a house with a chink of light showing behind the blackout curtains. The Dutch owners took him in, but soon Germans could be heard marching about outside. Paull told the Dutch people that they would be shot if he was found with them. They replied that they were prepared to accept this risk. "But I couldn't accept it," said Paull. "So I left and tried to find my way to the river, but was picked up by a patrol."

On October 12, Lieutenant Paull's father received notification that his remaining son was "reported missing, believed to be a prisoner of war on the 26th September, 1944." This was the second such letter he had received. The earlier one,

HOHENZOLLERN BRIDGE, COLOGNE—1945

The Germans demolished the bridge as the Americans approached the cathedral (*background*). Many thousands of corpses still lay under the ruins of the almost completely destroyed city when this photo was taken by the author.

ARNHEM BRIDGE—1945

Author's perch in foreground, centre.

"LONDON BRIDGE" over the RHINE at REES
Sketch by Corporal Meade-King.

RHINE BRIDGING—EMMERICH, 1945
The completed east bank bridge approach sitting on a sliding bay, the first time this method had been used in Europe during operations.
Photo: W. L. Lugrin.

dated March 5, 1943, had reported Sergeant Robert William Paull, R.A.F., as "missing," his aircraft having failed to return on March 1, 1943. In June, 1948, Lieutenant Paull was sued by the father of a London evacuee child for £200 damages for allowing his dog, Bouncer, to bite the girl when she stroked it, at a time when he was in Offlag 79. As the local newspaper remarked, this set a nice legal conundrum: "Was a prisoner-of-war in Germany responsible for an action of his dog in Dorset?"

After the battle, more than 200 airborne men remained at large or escaped, hidden by the extremely efficient Dutch "Underground," which did not unnecessarily provoke the Germans, apart from attacks on railways, but kept all German units under observation. They were aided by both Dutch and German rumours that the "island" was to be used as a springboard by the Allies for another attack to outflank the Siegfried Line and drive for the Ruhr. As a result of this, the Germans began to evacuate the civilian population from Arnhem and the Ijssel Line and the consequent movements helped to conceal the fact that a number of the "refugees" were British soldiers in disguise.

Among them was Major Hibbert, who was still keeping a day-to-day diary, which he eventually left behind him, buried under a flagstone in the church of Otterloo, but recovered eight months later. He recorded the rumours, for instance, that Second Army had crossed the Rhine at Huissen on September 30, and noted that the "evaders," far from thinking at first of escape over the river, were rather concerned to organise and arm themselves in order to help with the assault-crossing when it came.

43 Reconnaissance Regiment was then holding the southern dyke of the Neder Rijn with observation and listening posts, as western flank guard to the British forces in the Betuwe.

"All sorts of extraordinary things happened at this time" [recalled Major A. C. Packer]. "At night a few survivors of the Airborne trickled across the river, one or two rowed across by Dutch Resistance men, and we acquired in this way three Dutchmen who attached themselves to us as unofficial members of our Intelligence Section, suitably uniformed. [This was to protect them in the event of capture, as the accepted laws of war proscribed death for anyone who, in civilian clothes, fired on uniformed soldiers.] We also had the company for a few weeks of a Dutch girl we called Kitty, who came over the river one night. She, too, donned battle dress, but what her precise function was I cannot now recall. However, I do remember being shown an article in the *Daily Mirror* headed 'Kitty of the Armoured Cars,' the writer of which, drawing heavily on his imagination, told how Kitty, like the angel of battle, and sitting on the leading armoured car, led us heroicly into forays against the enemy. A lovely thought, but it didn't really happen. . . . We did receive a nocturnal visit from the Mayor of Tiel to protest that his town (swarming with Germans) was being rather knocked about by our shelling. We did, too, arm and equip on orders from Division some 200 Dutch Resistance men. I hope they gave the enemy as much concern as they did us. It was their habit to return from night patrols into our outposts without previous warning, and I am afraid one or two got killed this way."

The odd thing about Market Garden and its aftermath, in contrast to 1940, was the lack of complaints about the "Fifth Column," in spite of the fact that, this time, there really was one. True, it lingered on in British suspicions of odd incidents—a signpost turned the wrong way, suspiciously accurate artillery fire, guides who lost their way and then disappeared when the firing started, a despatch rider who rode down a column yelling out, "Retreat—there's a pocket panzer division up the road!" (There was.)

But, on the German side, "Dutch terrorists" were normally invoked only as a convenient excuse for not doing what was impossible anyway. In Major Krafft's very detailed war diary, his failure to block the river road to Frost's battalion was explained by saying "The enemy would have got to Arnhem in the shortest possible time and would not only have occupied it, but strongly fortified it with the aid of Dutch terrorists."

Although some enthusiastic young men did turn up when the airborne first landed, they faded away with the first mortar bombs and Krafft's battalion was bothered only once, on the first day: "We did have trouble with Dutch terrorists about 2–300 metres from the Battalion's original defence position. They were suitably dealt with!"

Much the most effective action of the Dutch was the railway strike that began on September 17 and helped paralyse German transport, although a number of the strikers were executed. Much more use could have been made of what the Resistance really had to offer—rapid telephone communications and accurate information on the enemy and his movements, but apart from the railway strike, very little appears to have been coordinated by the Allies.

The traffic across the Neder Rijn on the night of September 25–26 had consisted of 3,000 British survivors of 1 Airborne Division, going south. The traffic on the following night, going the same way, consisted of a battalion of some 500 Germans with 20-millimeter guns who were not aware that 43 Recce Regiment had posts established as far west as Randwijk. These were driven in and the position was not restored until the 27th, by counter-attack from the tanks of 8 Armoured Brigade and a battalion of 214 Infantry Brigade, which wiped out the German bridgehead. In the early hours of September 29, the Germans attacked again, with novel means and in a vital place.

The main remaining bridges onto the Betuwe—Arnhem road bridge and Nijmegen road and rail bridges—were now of crucial importance, in view of the forthcoming German offensive against the large British and American forces being maintained there in what was, in effect, a salient thrust deep into German-held territory. How vulnerable it was is illustrated by the fact that the German positions on the "Island" came to within 500 yards of Nijmegen road bridge on its eastern side.

Both bridges were under constant shellfire and continual air attack, and on September 28 a particularly determined assault was made at dawn. German jets diving out of the sun near-missed both bridges, "dislodging one section of the frail railway bridge from its seating and causing slight damage to the more robust road bridge," according to Guards historians. There was no effective counter to the jets, because British jets did not arrive over Nijmegen until the spring of 1945 and these were in any case inferior to their German equivalents.

During this period there were two "Guardians of the Bridges" at Nijmegen: Colonel Henniker, Commander Royal Engineers of the Wessex Division, who was succeeded by Colonel "Joe" Vandeleur of the Irish Guards. As soon as the engineers had evacuated the airborne from Arnhem, they were detailed as bridge guards at Nijmegen. In addition, Colonel Henniker was given a machine-gun company, a troop of self-propelled anti-tank guns, and a troop of towed 17-pounder anti-tank guns. The latter were sited at the north end of the road bridge, while the mobile S.P.s were held in reserve on the south bank between the two bridges. Colonel Henniker wrote:

"From the bridge German tanks were visible. Much the likeliest hazard appeared to be an armoured attack. It would not have taken long to destroy it, because of its design. The bridge was a bowstring girder composed of a great steel arch on each side of the bridge, springing from masonry piers which stood in shallow water at either bank. The roadway was slung beneath the girder. Had German tanks been able to get onto the bridge, it might have been possible for their troops to throw a string of explosives over one of the steel arches and detonate it with a time switch. Quite a light charge placed in this manner would have demolished the bridge; and I made my dispositions accordingly. It did occur to me that saboteurs in a civilian vehicle might try to use the bridge and contrive to abandon a vehicle full of explosives on the roadway. Even though the bridge was often under fire, an extraordinary amount of civilian traffic flowed over it, and our sentries were kept busy checking it through. I asked for searchlights, because I saw also a possibility of the Germans slipping downstream with a boatload of explosives to attack the piers of the bridge. But the searchlights were refused by the nearest anti-aircraft artillery commander who pointed out that his responsibilities would be immeasurably increased if he had to illuminate the target he was supposed to defend."

Both the latter possibilities—Germans in civilian clothes in a civilian vehicle and an approach by boat or barge along the Waal—were of course typical ruses employed in 1940 by Special Battalion No. 100, whose task had then been the capture of the bridge, not its destruction, and they had indeed planned to approach by water. The battalion had now been enlarged to form the Brandenburg "Division" and by the neatest of ironical coincidences the reverse task—that of destroying the bridges—was given to them in 1944. But as it was 1944, they used the methods of 1944 and not those of 1940, although the principle was the same—the use of a handful of highly trained men at a key point.

They had employed the same methods against the Benouville bridge, near Caen in Normandy, in June of the same year; but through an embarrassing error, the operators blew the wrong bridge—the German-held one! Consequently, the gambit did not become known to the British Army and when used at Nijmegen a few months later, came as a stunning surprise.

It was Colonel Henniker's custom to visit the bridge guards both at last light and first light, the most likely times of an attack. On the morning of September 29 he had returned to his headquarters after "stand-to," when his adjutant came in and asked if the bridges were intact. "Having just been down there about ten minutes before, I was surprised by this question, but the Corps Commander had received a report from the Dutch that the bridges had been blown up." Then the telephone rang and the OC 553 Field Company was on the line to report: "The railway bridge has been blown up." Five minutes later the OC 204 Field Company, guarding the road bridge, wirelessed a message: "Bridge blown up."

"I went down to the bridges and found the men standing to. The railway bridge had a pier missing. The road bridge had a hole 70 feet long in the roadway, between the main bowstring chords of the centre span just where the arch enters the main South bank pier. The stringers, crossbracing and roadway were torn to bits and folded upwards. 'How did that happen?' I asked. Nobody knew."

Rumours that both bridges had been blown behind them spread rapidly among the troops now cut off on the "Island."

Sergeant-Major W. Critchley of C Squadron 43 Recce Regiment, helping to guard the western flank as far as the river, heard early, "The bridges are blown!" "What news," he commented, "with us on the wrong side. But is it news or rumour?" Shortly after, his squadron captured six Germans on the river bank, and B Squadron caught others.

"They were frogmen, dressed for the job, and telling us how they had done it. I sent a Don R. to check. It was true—the railway bridge completely demolished and the road bridge will take single-line traffic after repair. I decided to tell the chaps, and the only remark I got was, 'Now I suppose we get no N.A.A.F.I. rations,' fluently said in soldiers' vocabulary."

Major Packer recalled:

"I cannot now vouch for the numbers, but I can tell you that they were fine, powerful men—German Marines—who did a wonderful job. They were exhausted and came ashore in the darkness under the impression that they had reached German-held ground. Our chaps, seeing and hearing odd shapes flapping about in the mud, fired over their heads; and they, weary and armed only with knives, had no option but to surrender."

As the salient was very narrow and bisected by the Waal, what the Germans had done was to put a team of 12 frogmen into the water about five miles upstream of the bridges and let them ride the fast current down to the target. The explosives consisted of cigar-shaped naval mines of near-neutral buoyancy that would be floated down the river, guided by the frogmen.

The railway bridge party controlled two such mines, linked by 20 feet of rope, and the object was to straddle one of the bridge piers. The road bridge party had to control four such mines, also linked by rope, and again straddle a pier. Until then, they would stay on the surface; only the final placing of the cylinders required the use of breathing apparatus. Once this was done, they were to ride on down the river with the current until they were swept back into German territory again.

But, as at Caen, they had over-estimated the distance they had travelled—an easy mistake, particularly on such a wide river with featureless banks, quite devoid of landmarks—and so emerged too early onto territory being observed by part of 43 Recce Regiment and the "Free Dutch." Two of the frogmen were fatally wounded in the shooting that then occurred. Two others escaped.

The railway bridge torpedo-mines had been well placed, each containing 1,220 pounds of hecanite, and this had brought down the centre span. But the road bridge party had chosen the wrong pier to attack; instead of the north pier in some five feet of water, they had chosen the shallower southern pier. In order to make the mines "live," a special float chamber had to be released. The mines then turned vertical and sank, starting up a clock time fuse. There was insufficient water around the south pier and only one of the mines exploded, the others being stranded on the mud at low water, in a horizontal position, and the pier itself was not destroyed, only part of the decking above. This was quickly bridged by XXX Corps Engineers, while Dukws, storm boats, and raft ferries kept the traffic moving.

In his review, the chief engineer of 21 Army Group, Major- General Sir J. D. Inglis, reported the frogmen's attack as "successful" generally and for the railway bridge "highly successful" (it was out of action for the rest of the war). The public at home, however, were told in typically sneering fashion (*Picture Post*, January 27, 1945): "But we were ready, and the attempt failed. The heroes of the exploit were the British naval engineers, who dived to remove the fuses, knowing that they had been timed to explode."

In fact, far from being ready to meet attack by water, the British engineers found that the Rhine presented almost insoluble problems to any defence then known. Major-General Inglis wrote:

"This incident led to the provision at Nijmegen of a whole series of different types of booms varying from naval river nets down to balloon cables supported on jerry-cans. The problem soon became a vicious circle. The river nets were extremely difficult to moor in the fast current of the Rhine and would not stand up to large quantities of debris carried down by the floods. It seemed necessary therefore to provide some kind of boom upstream to divert the debris. This boom in turn required protection against floating mines and so on. In the end the solution appeared to be large numbers of light booms made of balloon cables on jerry-cans, so that a series of mines coming down and exploding on the boom would not penetrate the defences before fresh booms could be strung to replace those cut. For the rest, patrol boats, searchlights, and Bren-guns were provided to sink by fire any suspicious looking objects floating down the river. Fortunately for us the temperature of the water fell rapidly after the Nijmegen incident and produced conditions which no swimmer could stand. The possibility of ice conditions greatly complicated the boom problem. The only solution seems to be to remove all booms, except possibly the balloon cable type, as soon as ice conditions intervene."

The winter, now only a few weeks away, was to be an exceptionally hard one, locking Europe in snow and ice for month after month. To the soldiers, mostly men from the towns but now mostly living in the open, the casual phrase of the history books, "winter campaign," took on an entirely new dimension; their political rulers had no intention of allowing them to go into "winter quarters," the more civilised custom of former times. Their sufferings were to be shared by the civilian refugees also.

The van Dongeren family, having fled from their home for the second time and then been caught up in the actions of "Barrier Unit Harzer" to the south of Arnhem, then moved away from the battle to a farm near Angeren, on the eastern edge of the Betuwe, where up to now the inhabitants had only heard distant gunfire and did not understand the panic of the refugees at the sound. The family had hardly arrived when Field Marshal Model launched his offensive to re-take the Betuwe. They crawled into a big stone waterpipe for shelter, packed so tight they could hardly move.

"There was firing from Bemmel and Nijmegen and Pannerden—firing all day and all night" [said Maurits van Dongeren]. "Once, we heard somebody's boots walking over the top of us—a sound like clock—clock—clock—and we knew Germans sometimes threw hand grenades in such places, in case British soldiers were hiding there. Then, with my dad, I made a bunker by the side of the house. We worked three days on this hole, diving into it when shelled. Put pieces of plank over it, and cowstraw over the top, because somebody said, 'Very good for splinters.' We lived in the bunker most of the time. One night, when there was very heavy shooting, there was a cow by the bunker. About 10 p.m. it was hit by a splinter, and until 5 a.m. it was crying in pain. When daylight came, we saw it had a leg shot off, which was lying half a metre from the animal. The meat from the cow was blue and we couldn't eat it. About four days later, while we were sleeping there in the night, we found water had come into the bunker, up to 2 feet high. You don't feel it, if a little water comes in; you merely wake to find your shoulders under water. It feels very horrible."

The soldiers fared little better, except that their home was not their own. Dig a satisfactory hole, and you would be ordered off somewhere else. Herbert Kessler's company of the Hermann Göring Division, what was left of it, were taken out of Oosterbeek and sent to a rest area, to recuperate, on September 30.

"We built ourselves a little bunker and we slept for the rest of the day and on through the night until 2 o'clock in the morning; and then: 'Alarm!' Our troops are attacking across the river to form a bridgehead on the opposite bank, and we are their reserve. So we were marched to within a kilometre of the Neder Rijn, dug in under sporadic artillery fire, and rested. In the evening, it got livelier. We were ordered across the river. We marched to Castel Doerwerth and lay down 200 metres from the riverside. At midnight, I received the order to cross. The pioneers and rubber assault boats are supposed to be already on the bank, ready for us. We move forward. We can't find any pioneers and the rubber dinghies are all shot to pieces. Then up comes a messenger from the rear. 'No crossing! The moon's too bright!' We go back to the ditch and lie there until noon the next day, 2 October. Now, it's not bright moonlight, it's bright sunshine, and suddenly we got the order: 'Cross at once!' My group was the second to move forward. The first group, carrying two rubber dinghies, went towards the bank. One dinghy was immediately shot to pieces, the group also was shot to pieces, the group leader was severely wounded. Those 200 metres to the bank are under heavy artillery fire as well as flanking fire from machine-guns. As the wounded group leader is carried past me (he was a friend of mine), I received orders for my group to try it. I jump up, together with my soldiers (about a platoon), run to the rubber dinghy which is still intact, tear down to the bank, push it into the water, jump into it with three other men, and row it across the river. This all sounds so harmless, but as long as I live I shall never forget that rowing. The shots splashed into the water all round us like hailstones, and how we managed to get to the other side, I don't know to this day. But we did and, still under heavy fire, dug our holes. That crossing in bright daylight was nonsense."

And so, added Kessler, was the rest of the operation.

The war diary of 5 Dorsets records the same opinion, although there were British losses, too.

"The attack by the 7 Hamps did not go according to plan, as apparently the factory area had been reinforced during the night, and consequently suffered heavy casualties. During the morning the enemy again attempted to reinforce this area, but as this was done in daylight, met with little success, most of the boats being blown out of the water."

From then until October 11, Kessler was in the Betuwe, his group pinned down in hastily-dug holes.

"One day seemed just like another, a hail of artillery fire, snipers who shot into our positions day and night, attacks by enemy troops and by low-flying aircraft. One didn't dare to get out of the hole, for any reason. I think there were now about 20 of us, with only one heavy M.G. After we crossed, there were no more reinforcements, because there had been too many casualties. On 11 October we were ordered to abandon the bridgehead and came back by night in rubber dinghies. Then we were billeted in an Old Folks Home, given a little food, straw beds, and allowed to sleep. Next day, I received the Iron Cross. Today, I sometimes feel that I actually deserved it."

Similar infiltration attacks were taking place all along the northern edge of the Betuwe, but the main drive was with armour straight down the road from Elst towards Nijmegen bridge, which began on October 2, under the fire of about 150 German guns. They hit the Irish Guards, whose historian wrote:

"In their effort to get Nijmegen bridge they brought up everything they had and carefully stage-managed their attack. Squads of 'man-pack' flamethrowers advanced towards the embankment, squirting streams of burning oil. Just behind them came ten tanks, firing steadily to protect them, and behind each tank filed a section of fifteen men. Further back were more infantry in open formation. Our right-hand platoon was burnt and shot out of its trenches; it fell back on No. 4 Company and there re-formed. The tanks swung round, destroyed the 17-pdr. anti-tank guns and pressed on to encircle the embankment. It looked for a moment as if they were going to have a clear run through to Battalion H.Q."

But the attack was checked and by mid-day had clearly failed.

In the Dutch Staff College examinations, the approach to Arnhem from Nijmegen was a set question, and any aspirant who took the direct route via Elst was failed automatically. The Irish Guards had in fact taken that route to relieve the paratroops, and failed; now the Germans had tried it in the opposite direction against the Irish Guards, and they had failed. It rather looked as though the Dutch knew what they were talking about.

A few days later, the Irish Guards were relieved and Colonel "Joe" Vandeleur became garrison commander of Nijmegen. As they drove over the repaired road bridge, lit by a blue searchlight, bombs were bursting in the Waal and the night sky was alive with tracer shells. "The whole effect was quite lovely," said one witness. "The river was an incredible sight," said another. "The broken bridges standing gaunt like a surrealist picture in the blue glare. What a nocturne!"

Colonel Vandeleur wrote:

"The previous Commander had been more concerned about anti-aircraft defence. I persuaded him to give me six 3·7 A.A.

guns, six Bofors L.A.A. guns, and six multiple A.A. machine guns which were to be used purely for river defence. The top span of the bridge was in view from the Reichswald Forest; and the bridge and the roundabout just south of it came in for a good deal of shelling. A smoke unit kept up a persistent smoke screen to hide the bridge. Lighting effects upon the scale of Elstree Studios were established along the waterfront."

This was in addition to searchlights, tugs in mid-stream, a battalion of medium machine-guns, and Royal Marines with depth-charge throwers. They tried to anticipate the next form of attack—frogmen, midget submarines, E-boats, parachutists, floating mines.

"I gave orders that every floating object of any size or type should be immediately engaged by every gun and machine gun available. This included orange skins. I had at my disposal a light aircraft to reconnoitre up river. It discovered a large raft, rather of the Canadian pattern, being constructed about three miles upstream. The Germans never used it. It would have had a most destructive effect on the boom."

In his history of the Wessex Division, General Essame wrote:

"The enemy now displayed a sense of humour usually regarded as foreign to his nature, and entertained himself by floating haystacks and large logs down the stream. In the dark these were taken for more frogmen or even one-man submarines."

But it was no joke. The Germans did attach mines to floating tree-trunks and tried to detonate them under the bridge from one-man submarines launched from Emmerich. The difficulties proved too formidable, however.

These weird forms of warfare on the Rhine and Waal were matched by events along the Neder Rijn to the north, where in mid-October a body of 130 "evaders," mostly escaped airborne men, were being concentrated for a mass crossing of the river. They had to be moved through German territory for distances of between 8 and 15 miles before they could gain the bank of the Neder Rijn. One body of 40 men, commanded by Major Hibbert, rode down to the crossing-point in two lorries supplied by the Dutch and among much German traffic. As they were actually getting out of the trucks, soon after dusk on October 22, a German bicycle patrol came riding down the road straight into the mob of 40 Englishmen, plus Dutch guides shouting instructions in Dutch–English. The Germans slowed down and rang their bells angrily, for the milling mob to give them right of way, and then rode on.

The entire force, mostly armed and now totalling 147 men, had finally to reach the river across 1,000 yards of open ground, between two German posts, and then move 800 yards along the bank to the actual crossing-site.

"It would have been a hazardous move with a highly trained company" [wrote Major A. D. Tatham-Warter of 2 Parachute Battalion]. "But with a mixed bag of 120 parachutists, largely R.A.M.C. orderlies, 10 British and U.S. pilots, 2 Russians and 15 Dutchmen, all of whom were unfit and many of whom had never seen their leaders in daylight . . . our chances of slipping through unobserved were remote. Before we reached the river the party most closely resembled a herd of Buffalo, and I think it was this fact, which probably misled the Boche as to our numbers, added to the fact that the U.S. parachutists on the South bank had been patrolling very vigorously on previous nights, that got us through. Although the Germans were aware of our presence, they were obviously windy to take us on."

They were all brought back over the river early on October 23 by men of 101 U.S. Airborne Division, which had taken over part of the "Island" in the middle of Model's counter-offensive three weeks before. So ended the evacuation of the airborne from Arnhem, a month after the battle had ended.

About this time, the van Dongeren family escaped also, leaving the Betuwe in the east by the ferry at Pannerden that 10 S.S. Panzer Division had used in their attempts to relieve the German garrison at Nijmegen. It was still being used by the Germans as well at by the Dutch.

"We walked from Angeren to Pannerden" [said Maurits]. "There were a lot of people waiting by the ferry. Every ten minutes, a fighter plane came over, shooting at the ferry and at the people, and then we took cover by the side of the road, in the hedges. There was a Policeman standing on the ferry quay with two children holding his hands. I heard after that his wife had been killed and that they were his own children. Another plane came over, and from a distance I saw his two children shot, they died holding his hand, but he was untouched. After dark, our family crossed over by the ferry and on the other side my mum spoke to a German soldier, who tried to fix shelter for us. He took us to a German headquarters, about 25 men there. When we got inside, the Germans made the fire high, to dry our clothes which had got wet from the rain, and made places for us to sleep. We wanted to leave early next morning, but were not allowed to, because a German torch had been stolen and we had to be searched. Another family had stolen two of the Germans' pistols, but they threw them in the water before going in to be searched. The Germans asked my mum to cook them dinner, and afterwards let us go. We went to Apeldoorn and returned to Arnhem about three months after Holland was free. We found nothing in our home, it had been looted. No cups, spoons, no furniture, it was stripped. In some houses, guns had been placed inside the corner walls."

Part III

The Rhine

1945

About this time, the rain
In Brussels streets,
With shimmer and reflection,
Translucent pool and window pane,
Will show
The silken gaiety of girls,
Bizarre images; so silently
Down mirrored streets soft winds
Will blow,
And tenderness will cling and cry
About the places
That I know.

About this time, the leaves
In Antwerp streets,
With flutter, gesticulation
And gusty arabesques,
Will fall
From bare tall trees where blow
The first cold heralds of the snow,
And all
The distant voices of mind and memory
Will call.

About this time, the frost
By moonlight,
Will sparkle as a Queen's purple diadem
Upon all the old, forever lost
Black gabled roofs and spires
Of Tilburg and 's Hertogenbosch
Where die
The last stifled grasses of all the year,
Drowned in a sea of boundless, crisp-bright snow,
Where fly
The fast grey flakes of storm, and cold winds
Wail and cry.

About this time, the snow
Of Arnhem
Lies like a silken coverlet
For those embalmed below.
The crosses
Stand out of the white land, silently,
Where snow flakes flicker fast and flee;
These losses
The Wehrmacht owed long ago to me—
And now, only the snowed helmets and the skeleton crosses
May I, or any other, see.

About this time, the mist
Lies along the English coast;
And through the fog, the warm
And friendly windows glow,
And form
A faery picture that is home,
And all our memories are here;
And there it is that we shall go,
But not this year, not this year.

CHAPTER TWENTY-TWO

WINTER

"All through the winter we made an intensive study of the Meuse and the Rhine," reported Major-General Sir J. D. Inglis.

"The three main conclusions were, first, that icing conditions were liable to occur any time between December and the end of March, and that on the Rhine in particular they might prove very severe, so severe that no floating bridges could possibly stand. It was also evident that our plywood pontoons would not stand up to much less severe icing conditions, because even thin ice floating down the river would quickly cut through their thin wooden skins. The second conclusion was that although the winter and spring months would see the end of the floods on the Meuse, severe flood might occur on the Rhine at almost any time in the year, certainly up to the end of June. It did seem, however, that March and April were slightly less subject to flood than other months. From the engineer point of view, therefore, the end of March was the best date for the assault crossing of the Rhine.

"The third important conclusion drawn from our study of the Rhine was that, having failed to capture Arnhem and the island lying between the Waal and the Neder Rijn, we had lost control of the Germans' ability to cause very serious flooding of that island. It was clear from this, therefore, that the original plan for entering Germany on the Nijmegen–Arnhem–Zutphen axis was no longer possible, and that we must seek for crossing places upstream from the point at which the Easternmost arm of the Rhine Delta, namely, the Ijssel, begins. The built up area of the Ruhr was obviously to be avoided, and if the crossing was to be carried out by the 21st Army Group, crossing places must be found between the Ruhr and the Ijssel. This boiled down to Rheinberg, Wesel, Xanten, Rees and Emmerich. Emmerich was ruled out as an assault crossing because it was overlooked from

Hoch Elten. True to form, the Rhine gradually rose in January and February and flooded the island between Nijmegen and Arnhem through the breaches made by the enemy in the dykes. He also flooded a considerable area just east of Nijmegen on the south bank of the Rhine.

"At the end of February, within a month of the projected D-day for the Rhine crossing, a view of the valley from the neighbourhood of Nijmegen was indeed a depressing sight. The country was flooded Eastwards almost as far as eye could see, and one wondered, even if the floods were to subside, whether the flat ground on either side of the river would ever dry out sufficiently to allow the vast numbers of vehicles required for the crossing to deploy. However, once again the geologists proved right. The Rhine valley consisted of gravel covered with a clay loam which unfortunately at certain places was very thick, but the great thing was the gravel subsoil, and sure enough when the floods subsided at the end of February and a spell of dry windy weather intervened the ground dried rapidly."

Meanwhile, the equipment for an army group assault on Europe's major river was being brought up. It consisted of 22,000 tons of assault bridging equipment, including 2,500 pontoons, 650 storm boats, 2,000 assault boats, 60 river tugs, 650 outboard motors, 70 small tugs, 600 propulsion units, 260 miles of steel rope, 80 miles of balloon cable, plus 15,000 tons of material for the semi-permanent bridges that would take the place of the floating bridges once the assault had succeeded and exploitation into the heart of Germany had begun. This was done largely between December, 1944, and February, 1945, after Antwerp had been opened as a supply port.

In spite of the fact that the Market Garden axis had been repeatedly ruled out by the British, because of the fact that the Germans could flood part of that axis at will, the ghost of that failed offensive lingered in German minds long afterwards. Pastor Willi Schiffer, who had fought in the "corridor" battle with a parachute battle group in January, 1945, found himself on the "Island." They had been rested and brought up to strength and were now to relieve the badly equipped German units holding half the Betuwe. The German parachutists really were elite troops, probably better even than the Waffen-S.S., and their entry onto the "Island" was a measure of German uneasiness.

"During the Ardennes offensive, possibly the ill-equipped infantry units might have been sufficient," [wrote Pastor Schiffer]. "But at the beginning of January, the picture had changed completely and it was feared that the thrust into the German lowlands by way of Arnhem would be renewed. Shortly before our battalion went into action, Generaloberst Student came to see us and mentioned this possibility. (Later, after the war, I had the opportunity to discuss it with him at length.) In other words, we were to be thrown into a deadly trap which could snap shut at any time. We crossed the Neder Rijn by the ferry near Pannerden, but reached Haalderen without incident. The main battle line lay between Haalderen and Bemmel, with some wide stretches of no-mans-land. We knew that part of 49 Infantry Division lay opposite us, because some of our recce troops had brought back a few prisoners; and vice versa, we had lost a few men to them, including a Lieutenant who was taken prisoner on his birthday. (After the war, part of 49 Inf Div were on occupation duty in my home town of Lüdenscheid and their tablet of honour included the name 'Haalderen.') The artillery of the other side fired busily and sometimes very accurately, probably due to the fact that during the day there was always an artillery observer making his circles in the sky. During the day, we almost always remained under cover, and only patrolled at night. However, we very soon had the feeling that the dice would not be cast on this sector of the front. On 8 February we saw how on the other side of the Rhine, of which we had an excellent view, a fire steam-roller came up to the German lines, which exploded and were crunched to pieces. We ourselves lost eight dead that day, pulverised in their slit trenches. In mid-March, however, orders came to move off the 'Island' and infantry units took our place, mostly older men."

The elite parachute units were being pulled out to help defend the north bank of the German Rhine against the British Second Army assault that was due to follow the clearing of the south* bank of the Rhine by First Canadian Army during the Reichswald offensive that began on February 8.

The deliberate flooding of the "Island" by the Germans, which the British had foreseen, began early in December, by which time the levels of the Waal and Neder Rijn were rising anyway. At one time there had been three divisions on the "Island"—Guards Armoured, 43rd Wessex, and 101 U.S. Airborne. These had now been withdrawn and their place taken by two ordinary infantry divisions, the 51st Highland and the 49th West Riding; the former had served in the Western Desert, the latter more appropriately in Iceland (their divisional sign was the polar bear). Later, the 51st were drawn off by the Ardennes offensive, and the Polar Bear Division were left in undisputed possession of the title "Nijmegen Home Guard."

For three days, 2 South Wales Borderers had been holding Elst when, on December 3 at dusk,

"a shattering explosion was heard. Reports came in a few hours later that the water was rising in all the dykes at an alarming rate followed shortly afterwards by a report from our forward company, that the canal on their front had broken its bank and that water was pouring across the fields. It became evident that the enemy had blown the 'bund' and the 'island' was threatened with becoming submerged. The forward company had to be withdrawn—at least one section swimming out of their post. . . ."

The Germans followed up with a small-scale attack, which was beaten off. But their main, dangerous effort was made at Haalderen, held by 7 Duke of Wellington's Regiment for the last three days.

A witness described the march-in on December 1:

"We trudged up a filthy track that night in the darkness towards the right of the line at Haalderen, once a pretty village on the Rhine; all of us, I think, with an impending feeling of some future destiny around the scarred orchards, the unbelievable ruins of the street and church. For two days we

* On the east bank and west bank, respectively, for the course of the Rhine begins to curve south beyond Emmerich.

watched the waters rise—in the Rhine over the towering winter bund, or dyke, on our right, over the sides of our slit trenches. We formed strong-points amid the ruins and in the cellars. On the night of 3rd December I dragged my Jeep through the mud and darkness to Brigade for a conference on the evacuation of the 'island' in case of flooding. The Boche had blown several gaps in the Bund that day, and the rushing Rhine flood water had over-whelmed several posts on the north-west of the 'island' without warning. We expected every distant rumble to be followed by a tidal wave. Appropriately enough, the evacuation scheme was known as 'Noah.' I drove back through the worst storm I've known for many years. I called a short 'O' Group at midnight and decided to spend the night beside the phone in the cellar in case of swift flooding needing rapid action; or was it intuition?"

Whatever it was, the CO was in the command post by the telephone when at 0300 hours the first report came in of Spandau fire and shelling; then of a strong attack developing. It was in fact being carried out by II Battalion of Fallschmirmjäger Regiment 16, whose leading elements penetrated deeply into the British position, covered by the stormy night and relying on the floods to have disorganised the British, for if the British held on, the leading German company was vulnerable. Nevertheless, a break-through led directly to Bemmel and Nijmegen bridge.

The British CO ordered all his companies to hold where they were, then began to arrange for the artillery and mortar fire necessary to smash up the German reinforcements and any assault forces about to go in.

"There was indescribable confusion in the village—Spandaus, Brens, rifles, Stens and grenades being freely used in between houses and across the street. Boche cries in good English of 'Stop that firing' were frequently heard and ignored. One voice shouted out in perfect English, 'Stop that bloody Bren. We've got a wounded man here.' But as the British had not moved, daylight found the leading German company wedged into the middle of the D.W.R., under fire from three sides. 110 of them surrendered, in a hopeless position, and they had lost more than 50 dead. Losses to their reserve companies were not known. Some of the prisoners stated that Nijmegen bridge had been the ultimate objective, which a engineer unit was to have destroyed. The D.W.R.'s casualties were officially listed as: '10 killed, 19 wounded, and 2 missing (believed drowned).'"

The "Island" was now really an island, because the area to the west, from the Waal to the Neder Rijn on the line Andelst-Zetten-Randwijk was four to six feet deep under water, and only the houses and farms stood up out of the floods. All patrols were boating exercises, with the boats liable to run aground unexpectedly on uncharted obstructions, such as the tops of wire fences or the stone parapets of submerged bridges; and when the enemy was met, he was either in a house or boatborne, too.

But soon the winter froze much of the landscape under snow and ice, and the latter made silent movement difficult when moving across the eerie waste of old battlefields. "Everywhere there were the remains of the 1944 battle," recalled Reginald Dunkley, a private soldier of 7 Duke of Wellington's Regiment, one of the few who was to see 1945. An infantryman's life is a short one. Reginald Dunkley had been fourteen years of age when the war began in 1939.

"I remember seeing the posters the newsboys used to show then, carrying the declaration of war, and I little thought that it would still be going on four years later, and that I'd be pitched into it."

After Haalderen, his battalion went to Elst.

"Up on an embankment where we used to do 24-hour standing patrols, one of our lads saw a number of 3-ton lorries in no-mans-land. A party went out before dawn one morning and found them fully loaded with 'B' Echelon stuff—socks, shirts, boots, etc. I think they were Royal Artillery vehicles, for the jacket I 'won' had 'RA' stamped on it. We also salvaged a large W/T set and a Bren, both rusty, but in working order.

"We also had to do fighting patrols out of Elst: go as far as you can, till you hit something, then come back. I remember one in December, 1944, when we saw the 'hump.' A crisp, cold night with a brilliant moon, no cloud. We had donned white camouflage with our rifles wrapped in old sheets, and we went out along the main railway line between Nijmegen and Arnhem. It was easier to make progress there than on the frozen ground, by stepping from sleeper to sleeper as we went forward up the track. In some places the embankment was down, only the rails spanned the gap, and occasionally we had to go up on the embankment. We were doing this, when the patrol leader held up his hand, indicating 'Stop.' We waited. Then he whispered back, 'Somebody or something is lying in the middle of the track.' We waited, but still the figure didn't move. The patrol leader crawled up to it, looked, then beckoned us on. Well, the 'hump' was a body, but of what nationality we couldn't tell. It had no headdress, no boots, and was lying face downwards on the tracks. As it was frozen stiff to the tracks, we couldn't turn him over. Out of respect for the dead, we didn't want to disturb him. We didn't know if he was a British paratrooper, an American soldier, or a German. We assumed he was a private—no stripes or pips, but so covered in frost that you couldn't get hold of the clothing, to check whether it was khaki or field grey. No marks on the back, head not smashed, feet in good condition—we couldn't see where he'd been hit."

Nijmegen had now been taken over by First Canadian Army (which usually had at least one British corps under command) and was much less inhibited in its military signposting. At Grave bridge a whole series of welcoming signs had now been erected, starting with: SPEND YOUR HOLIDAYS IN THE NIJMEGEN SALIENT. This was followed by an elaborate list of attractions:

LUXURIOUS FLATS (MUD)
H & C (MOSTLY C)
BOATING & SWIMMING
SHOOTING
(BOTH WAYS)
BOSCH HUNTING IN THE WOODS

and concluded with an announcement for the future: TRIPS TO BERLIN ARRANGED FOR LARGE PARTIES VIA SHORT SCENIC ROUTE. Later, another large notice was to be erected, this one facing the German positions, which read: NO RUSSIANS PAST THIS POINT IN DAYLIGHT.

I had to go to Nijmegen on business several times in January, starting from Canadian Army headquarters in Tilburg. The road ran parallel to the Maas and covered the greater part of the northern front in Holland, which was a river-line front. I noted impressions in my diary.

"In some places the snow-covered fields look like cream, good enough to eat, and at others like the sea, or sands bared by the tide. The roofs of houses, white and heavy with snow, merge into the grey-white of the fog, so that they seem almost drawn up into the clouds. The fields and the rivers are frozen, we pass women towing their shopping behind them on sledges, and then a Don R's grave, where the bones of some Canadian lie beneath the snow and the ice-bound earth, a few feet back from the road and 3,000 miles from his home. We come up to 's Hertogenbosch; shell holes and bullet marks have scarred almost every house and the snow lies deep in the interior of roofless, ruined houses. We pass tanks in harbour, with a bright fire glowing amongst them, and the crews standing round it, warming themselves and brewing up; and then into open country again, where a Polish sentry stands by an anti-tank gun with field glasses to his eyes, staring out over the snow to the Maas, for the German patrols which infiltrate under cover of night or fog. On the right we come to a ruined windmill, its broken sails gaunt against the snow-laden sky, one side ripped open, the other peppered with small shell holes. Facing the side which has been shelled, a British tank lies, knocked out and tilted over, its gun pointing mutely to the ground at the base of the mill. We pass two more windmills, their sails turning lazily; it starts to snow, the flakes drifting diagonally across our windscreen. There are tanks guarding every bridge and anti-tank guns looking out over wastes of water or snow-streaked land. The Germans are a couple of miles from here, but there is no front line as such, merely an area which is watched and patrolled by both sides. The armies are in the towns, under cover from the vile and bitter weather, and concentrated to repel any breakthrough; it is as though the towns were mediaeval castles, from which garrisons made sorties. Almost parallel to this winding front, runs this road, the main supply line from Antwerp to the Nijmegen Salient, that fist clenched at the gates of the Rhineland.

"Looking at the crews of the tanks, the men at the guns, the Don Rs and drivers, all the miscellaneous personnel of a hundred different units, one wonders at their dissimilarity and yet at the way they are alike . . . a strange, hard army, more like a disciplined band of buccaneers than the barrack square, toy-soldiers of the pre-invasion years. There is a scream, half-human, half-animal, from an ambulance as it lurches over the shell holes in the road. Perhaps that is the answer. This is real.

"We drive up to the great nine-span bridge across the Maas at Grave, and rumble over it, the waters dirty and grey and troubled below us. We pass a tank harbour, cross the Waal-Maas Canal, and drive on into Nijmegen. The outskirts are pretty intact, despite the constant shelling. The centre of Nijmegen looks like the centre of any English town—it isn't there any more. It's snowing really hard now, and when the guns let go from somewhere round the corner, the snow nearly leaps off the rooftops. There are other noises, but rather more muffled in the snow storm, which might or might not be Jerry repaying the salvoes in kind. Business concluded, we return to the roundabout in the centre of Nijmegen and Driver Cullen, who's a bit short-sighted, takes the DIAMOND UP route instead of the MAPLE LEAF DOWN. At first, I thought we were going out merely by a different way, which is usual traffic practice, but when we pass through a barrier with a CMP standing by it, I become suspicious. Cullen insists that the BLUE DIAMONDS are MAPLE LEAVES, but I tell him to turn at a roundabout just ahead. This is barricaded and wired, contains a wrecked carrier and an 88 mm gun, and looks out over a snow-covered valley. There's a lot of ominous silence all round and a signpost pointing out over the valley which says KLEEF (presumably Dutch for Cleve, a town just over the German border). We circle the roundabout and go back into the shelter of Nijmegen."

This was in fact the "bridge roundabout" and the road we nearly took led to Beek and Wyler.

Our ultimate destination was Termonde in Belgium, which meant returning to Tilburg and carrying on through Breda and Antwerp. The latter was more of a front-line city than Nijmegen; even from 20 miles away, we saw "the horizon suddenly and horribly lit by a great red flash—a V-bomb falling into Antwerp," where "the docks are blazing with light as the unloading goes on." In October, we had seen the opening three weeks of a bombardment during which 3,714 V-1 flying bombs and V-2 supersonic rockets were to land in and around the great port, causing 8,500 casualties but doing little damage to the vital docks. From Tilburg at night, it was possible to see the other end of the process—the V-2s, like shooting stars, coming up from somewhere beyond the Maas and then curving over in a flat arc towards Antwerp.

On December 16, Eisenhower had paid the penalty for his "broad front" offensive, and in a drive reminiscent of 1940 the Germans had driven through the Ardennes, treating the Americans as they had the French, and using paratroops and "Trojan Horse" units. This was awkward for Montgomery's 21 Army Group, because it disrupted movements already taking place, that were intended to clear the Rhineland as a preliminary to crossing the Rhine. I noted in my diary:

"Our divisions have been caught on the hop, in the middle of being transferred northwards from Second Army to First Canadian Army for the attack into the Reichswald, and are now being switched back to the south again, towards the Ardennes, leaving behind them the vast stocks of munitions which were being accumulated around Nijmegen for the offensive."

The Canadians were not worried in the long term, for I noted on December 22:
"Rundstedt's offensive would seem to have as its aim the cutting off of 21 Army Group from the American Army Group (Bradley's), and in particular the isolation of Brussels and Antwerp by a drive to the coast. This appears to be rather an ambitious scheme."

What the Canadians were worried about mainly was the fate of their own headquarters, which at that time had under its command not merely all the Canadian divisions but virtually every British division as well, except for the "funnies" of 79 Armoured Division, and was busy turning them round from their own offensive to go and help the Americans stem the German offensive. If Canadian Army HQ was knocked out by paratroops or "Trojan Horse" units, there would be utter confusion at a time when control was critical.

Junkers 52 transport aircraft had been reported on airfields east of Nijmegen, and it was believed that General Student had three parachute divisions in reserve; and that an armoured force was ready to cross the Maas,* where we had only the thin screening forces I saw on my trips along the front, and little in reserve, as everything had been diverted to help the Americans.

This apparently ominous picture began to build up on December 23, when a teleprint warning was issued:

"There is a possibility that the HQ area might be attacked by small bodies of paratroops and of fighting patrols which have infiltrated SOUTH from the R MAAS [.] Also that small bodies of desperadoes and assassins might move into the area their object being to cause confusion and a diversion from their attack further SOUTH [.]"

This latter was apparently a reference to Otto Skorzeny's commandos and the Brandenburg Division in general, the successors to Special Battalion No. 100.

On Christmas Eve in Tilburg two German officers were reported caught in the town square, dressed as Canadians but with their gaiters fastened the wrong way round. Later, there

* This was the information available at the time. According to Colonel C. P. Stacey's official history, "The Canadian Army 1939–1945", the position was even more alarming. "Colonel-General Kurt Student, the experienced and formidable commander of the German Army Group 'H', has described the preparations he had made: the three infantry divisions, two parachute divisions and 150 armoured vehicles that were to attack across the Maas; the parachute battalion, led by an officer who had taken part in the rescue of Mussolini, which was to drop among our artillery positions; the minor naval units that were to assail our shipping in the Scheldt. The objective was to be Antwerp. But the great scheme depended on the progress of the Ardennes offensive, and that was shortly stopped dead."

was a brisk exchange of shots nearby which I assessed, accurately, as "probably drunken Canadians." But an "airborne attack imminent" warning was given during the night, and on Christmas Day salvoes of heavy shells began to fall into the town. The signal for "airborne attack in progress" was to be repeated bursts of five tracer shells from Bofors guns.

On the evening of December 26, I lay in bed reading a batch of newspapers, including an article about the Home Guard who waited for the parachutists who didn't turn up, and was very wide-awake, listening to the sullen growling of the guns on the Maas. Then there was a single burst of Bofors fire. Silence for some minutes, then repeated bursts of Bofors, mingled with the sound of planes—but no bomb whistles or explosions. A sentry came round, passing on the "stand-to" order.

"I dress properly, swallow a drink of water, put a slice of bread in my pocket, and go outside. Red tracer is streaming up into the moonlight over Tilburg in all directions; I strain my eyes for a sight of planes or parachutes, but there is only the sound of a distant aircraft. Someone lets off a shot. The swift searing balls of red tracer are very lovely as they curve past the twin spires of Tilburg church and float slowly towards the silver stars. There's frost on the spires and on the roofs which, touched by the moonlight, makes the picture one of silver and shadows, and perfectly Christmas. A U.S. Major comes up to us; he's pretty excited, so it must be the real thing and not a practice."

We marched through the streets to take up defence positions, but the only casualty was caused by a Canadian dropping his Sten, which promply shot a corporal in the foot. The Sten, undoubtedly the worst machine-carbine ever made, rarely fired when the trigger was pulled but was very liable to accidental discharge. We had dark suspicions that we had been got up for nothing, but this was dispelled by the breathless arrival of one of our staff sergeants, just back from a dance at a unit a mile outside the town.

"Three Germans had been caught there, skulking in a garden, and a German battalion was reported in the vicinity.

On the way back from the dance, a bullet went across the bonnet of their truck, but not knowing who might have fired it, they kept going. Then a Bren burst ripped up the front wheels, and the truck perforce had to stop. A sentry jumped over a wall and flattened a CSM in the truck, so the Staff Sergeant lay down and crawled out at the back, rifle loaded. A revolver was stuck in his spine and the owner said 'Drop it!' in a genuine Canadian accent. So he did."

This did illustrate the confusion that a "Trojan Horse" attack could cause, but apart from the Sten accident, I heard of no lethal results.

Next day the news was:

"Airborne troops dropped in battalion strength just outside Tilburg and Breda last night, but, so far as is known, none penetrated to the centre of Tilburg. The night before, however, 5 German paratroops were picked up in the centre—3 dressed as clergy, 2 in British uniform."

A young Dutch journalist whom I met a few days later had been picked up on the night of the 26th, during the Bofors firing, while going home late after preparing copy for the paper. He was taken by Canadians into a guardroom for questioning, before being released.

"In the guardroom" [he said], "were eight German parachutists—two in regulation parachutists' uniform, the rest in British uniforms or civilian clothes. The two in German uniform were wreathed in smiles and telling the others of the sticky end awaiting them, while *they* were now safely out of the war."

From this, he concluded that the disguised men were real Nazis, the other two just ordinary Wehrmacht. Weapons were Schmeissers and dynamite.

Next day, a parachutist was reported picked up in the local dancehall, known as "Hell's Kitchen," because if you wanted a dance, you had to mark your girl well in advance, and shove her out on the floor as the bandleader raised his baton; that way, you got in two steps before the mob became solid. Now, "Hell's Kitchen" was even funnier, because we all had to go armed and therefore handed in at the cloakroom one's rifle, pistol, or sub-machine-gun before entering the hall.

So far only sabotage troops had been dropped, and most of these had been seen off by Canadians whose offices were out along the Bredaweg near the drop zones; in bright moonlight, the attackers had an unenviable task in trying to penetrate the town. Our offices, in a central department store, were quiet; we fired no shots, we took no prisoners.

The headquarters, numbering about 2,000 men, was scattered all over Tilburg in unmarked offices, thus presenting a virtually impossible target to sabotage paratroops of the "Trojan Horse." If a full-scale airborne attack developed, each building was to be held individually, by its occupants, for a week. The reasons for anxiety lay not in the "assassins and desperadoes" but, as I noted in my diary on January 1, in the fact that "Not all the German reserves had been committed in the Ardennes offensive," and that Antwerp was wide open.

Canadian Army appreciations of the enemy, including this one, had almost throughout taken the correct slightly pessimistic line, in strong contrast to the invariable optimism of the British and the even more euphoric Americans, who until now had thought the German Army liable to instant collapse. Consequently, the effect of the "Trojan Horse" paratroops on the Canadians was negligible, whereas on the American front a "Fifth Column" panic of positively 1940 proportions, and just as unrealistic, developed. It was even rumoured that a plot existed to assassinate Eisenhower at his HQ back in Paris.*

As far as 21 Army Group was concerned, the effect of the Ardennes offensive was to delay the battle for the Rhineland by approximately one month. Once Allied armies were on the west bank of the Rhine, Germany was definitely finished, her main traffic artery dominated and the Ruhr itself in the front line, the Saar overrun. The actual crossing of the Rhine would be a formality. The British–Canadian drive had to go

* Well described in *The Battle of the Ardennes*, by Robert E. Merriam (Souvenir Press, 1958). The author was an historian on the staff of U.S. Ninth Army and saw these events at first-hand.

in from the Nijmegen area, parallel to the Rhine instead of towards it, because that was the pattern of existing roads. Consequently, although Nijmegen was the road and rail head for the offensive, the great Waal bridge played no part in it.

The build-up was restarted in mid-January, with trucks going through Tilburg at the rate of 800 an hour, and it was probably these movements towards Nijmegen that caused the Germans to suspect an attack towards Arnhem on the old Market Garden axis. As we have seen, in January they reinforced the "Island" with re-fitted and up-to-strength parachute regiments from General Student's command, in the mistaken belief that the British would drive north instead of east.

Possibly it was the existence of these uncommitted paratroops, plus the concentrations of Junkers 52s on nearby airfields reported as late as January 11, that were responsible for our "hold on for a week" orders, coupled with plans to retreat to Eindhoven. And very probably it was the Germans' fear that a new drive to Arnhem was intended that spurred them to make one last attempt to destroy the great Waal bridge at Nijmegen. This they carried out on the night of January 12–13, 1945. The history of the West Riding Division noted: "On 13th January the Division fought a naval 'engagement' against German torpedoes lashed to logs, and against two midget submarines!"

In all, 24 midget submarines set out from Emmerich for the attack. Unlike the one-man torpedoes, they were true submersibles, miniature submarines 25 feet long controlled by a single man who had to wear breathing gear and with an armament of either two torpedoes or two mines carried externally. Designed in February, 1944, and used against the invasion fleet off Normandy, the Germans called them Beavers.

The first wave of attack on January 13 consisted of 240 mines put into the Rhine and allowed to drift downstream with the current towards the booms guarding Nijmegen bridge; it was hoped they would break open at least some of the booms. The second wave of attack consisted of 20 Beavers that were to fire torpedoes into the resulting chaos; these torpedoes were fitted with hooks, so that they would catch in the nets suspended from the booms and so destroy them. The third wave of attack consisted of four Beavers, each towing a tree-trunk from which was suspended three tons of explosives. Photo-electric cells had been built-in to the tree-trunks, which were timed for release at dawn; when the shadow of the bridge fell across the cells, this would trigger the firing mechanism.

Although the British defences were not regarded by the Royal Engineers as being impregnable, they were sufficiently in depth to foil the elaborate three-stage German attack. The last attempt on the bridge failed in the thunder of gunfire and the roar of exploding mines.

I wrote in my diary on January 23:

"The world seems to have been forever under a carpet of snow and ice, gripped by winter for all time. The skies are sullen and snow-laden, the mail doesn't come through for days, sometimes weeks; but always the Doodlebugs go over, headed for Antwerp."

Few people had fires that winter, there was no coal, but no one seemed to catch a cold, perhaps because there was so little difference between indoor and outdoor temperatures. The infantry, of course, had the worst of it, as they did their work at night; and being forced to lie still for any length of time could mean being literally numbed into uselessness.

In the darkness, the opposing sides sometimes spoke to each other, sometimes in each other's language, to identify or confuse, and sometimes not. On January 15 a patrol of the Hallamshires out on the "Island" found a group of previously empty houses now wired in and occupied, the inhabitants apparently drunk, for one shouted at them, "English good soldiers!" To which another added, "German better still." This proved to be the case that night, as the Hallams had the worst of the encounter. On the 21st a patrol of the Hallams met another patrol in the open. To the challenge, "Who goes there?" came back the reply: "Schmidt."

On February 1 I wrote in my diary: "The snow is gone. The air is warm and mild. The snow-locked landscape and icy winds have vanished like a dream." It was the spring thaw. On the "Island" the repair and maintenance of roads now became a species of "marine engineering," noted Captain M.

Langley of 294 Field Company. The Hallams' war diary for February 15 read very differently from the entry for January 15.

"Two boatloads of enemy appeared in the village and proceeded to clear it with grenades and machine carbines. They were in two boats, one of which remained in the rear covering the front one. There were also two enemy in a canoe."

On the same day a boat from 4 Lincolns, carrying a Bren as main armament, defeated a German boat manned by eight men, but could not board and capture it, as the current swept it back to the German positions.

On February 21, the Hallams noted of a farm house they intended to occupy:

"The whole area is flooded—apart from a narrow strip of mud around the house itself—to a depth of 3 or 4 feet. The barns, for example, are used as boat houses, and boats can sail into them."

The Hallams duly sailed a 31-man patrol into the house, which was well in advance of their positions. That night, it was observed to be burning, and next day there was no sign of the 31 men who had occupied it. The first news of them came from Bremen radio the following night: "Troops of the Dutch S.S. eliminated an enemy strongpoint in Holland, capturing a number of PW from the 49 Div." The day after, propaganda shells were fired into the Hallams' positions. The pamphlets they contained were headed: "HELLO, YOU OLD POLAR BEARS" and mentioned: "You probably don't know it yet but the other day, 13 of our Dutch comrades captured 29 little Polar Bear cubs at De Hoeven." The Hallams' CO, Lieutenant-Colonel T. Hart-Dyke, wrote in his history:

"The loss of Sergeant Newman's platoon was a complete mystery until hostilities were over. The enemy had advanced quietly in boats and suddenly opened up with machine carbines at the windows and through the thin walls with bazookas, killing Sergeant Newman and seriously wounding Sergeant Potter and eight others. Before the remainder could collect their wits they had been rushed and taken prisoner. Revenge would have been sweet, but our men in their clumsy assault boats were no match for the Dutch SS working under conditions they understood only too well in their own craft and country. I therefore turned down the Brigadier's suggestion that offensive action should be taken."

There was indeed no sense in losing men for unimportant objectives. The bridgehead over the Rhine, gained at such cost in 1944, was only a backwater of the war now. All winter, on clear days, the spires and towers of Arnhem lay on the horizon to the north; not just another Dutch town, but the tide-mark of the invasion year, from which the invasion had receded.

On their road from Normandy, the British Army had yet to pass any new battlefield, any place without associations from the past. Their guns had shelled the birthplace of William the Conqueror, they had forced a crossing of the Seine as Edward III had done on his march to Crécy, they had motored past Waterloo and across the battlefields of the First World War, and now, even at Arnhem, could not escape the past; for it was there that Sir Philip Sidney, the courtier-poet of Elizabeth I, had died of wounds received at the battle of Zutphen in 1586, two years before the coming of the Armada. He had ordered his page to give water to another dying man whose necessity, he said "is yet greater than mine," a gesture that was still famous. But the saying was not recalled in connection with Arnhem; nor was the defeat of 1944 thought of in any narrow or petty sense. The broken towers on the winter skyline stood for the end of hope, for the continuance of the war.

CHAPTER TWENTY-THREE

RACE FOR THE RHINE BRIDGES

Reichswald and Remagen:
February–March

"It's a typical Monty set-up," I wrote on January 30.

"Bags of guns crammed on a narrow front, all your force at one point, and bash in. Unsubtle, but usually successful. Jerry knows you're coming, but he can't do very much about it. He can't thicken his front up too much, because the gigantic bomber formations we wield will sweep it like a broom."

On February 8, I noted:

"XXX Corps attacked at 1000 hours, to break the Reichswald pivot. There was 5 hours of counter battery work by 1400 guns (400 more than Alamein), then 5 hours barrage. One moment the night was black, the next as light as day from the gun flashes."

Later that day,

"Arnhem Mary joins in the battle and reels off the units taking part—she knows 'em better than we do! (We've lost 8 Armoured Brigade, and consider asking her where it is.) She also comes out with a crack that riles the Canucks: The Yanks are fighting hard down in the south, she says, the British are attacking through the Reichswald Forest, and the Canadians are eating hamburghers in Nijmegen . . . a spirited reference to the famous 'IT' joint."

21 Army Group now consisted of First Canadian Army (Crerar), British Second Army (Dempsey), and Ninth U.S. Army (Simpson). An army has no fixed establishment of fighting troops, and divisions are frequently switched from one army to another according to the needs of the moment. To the end, this puzzled and misled editors waging the war of words at home; and it is an odd freak of human nature that

ephemeral errors of battle reporting tend to raise a storm of fury at the front, and a positive hurricane at headquarters. The latter tend to rage for decades in the generals' memoirs, and the Battle of the Rhineland is probably the supreme example of World War II. While some of the generals were wrangling with each other on a level well below that of the average schoolboy, the front-line soldiers were engaged in a bitter winter battle across terrain that now most closely resembled the Western front of the First World War.

The object of the Reichswald offensive was to clear a springboard on the east bank of the Rhine in preparation for a 21 Army Group crossing of the river north of the Ruhr, in time to take advantage of the best predicted period—that is, when the flood plain had dried out and the danger of fresh floods was least. That period was the last week of March. This stretch of the Rhine, when crossed, gave access to the good tank country of the North German plain, where the best use might be made of superior Allied mobility, and where good roads and railways led to the German North Sea ports, the Baltic, and Berlin.

A glance at a relief map shows the geographical advantages of this route, which curves round to the north of both the densely built-up area of the Ruhr and the frequently mountainous stretches of the river to the south. The political advantages, at this stage of the war, were equally obvious. The question now was, not who was going to win the war, but who was to win the peace; and a successful drive on the northern route would block off the Russians from Denmark, which they might otherwise be tempted to occupy, and could also lead to the capture of Berlin.

21 Army Group had already made immense preparations for the crossing of the Rhine on the sector that would give these advantages, but the difficulty of the crossing depended on a German decision: whether they would chose to fight and be defeated west of the Rhine, or fight and be defeated east of the Rhine. Hitler decided that there was no point in "moving the catastrophe" from the west bank to the east bank; and Albert Speer, his war production chief, estimated that once the Allies gained the west bank in the region of the Ruhr, the resulting dislocation of Germany's main coal and steel

centre, together with its river transport lines, would mean an economic collapse within four to eight weeks. Hitler decided to buy time by fighting on the west bank, in the hope that the dissensions, both military and political, that were now apparent on the Allied side, would fatally split his enemies.

The northern end of the Siegfried Line, which had been extended to the Reichswald, was held by the German 84 Infantry Division, backed by about 100 guns. First Canadian Army attacked it on a six-mile front with four divisions—2nd Canadian, 15th Scottish, 53rd Welsh, and 51st Highland.

It was 2nd Canadian that smashed through the German border village of Wyler on the main Nijmegen–Kranenburg–Kleve road. From here, the Germans had attacked towards Nijmegen on May 10, 1940, and although the village had been captured in September, 1944, by 82 U.S. Airborne Division, it had been lost again to German counter-attacks from the Reichswald. Now it fell to the Calgary Highlanders, while 15th Scottish and 53rd Welsh advanced east of Grosbeek over the Dutch-German battlefield of 1940, which was still strewn with the wrecked Waco gliders in which Gavin's men had landed in 1944.

3rd Canadian Division, with amphibious vehicles, was to attack later, on the northern flood plain by the banks of the Rhine; the Germans flooded this area deeper still by blowing holes in the winter dykes. The tanks of Guards Armoured and the infantry of 43rd Wessex were in reserve. Supporting the attacking infantry were three independent armoured brigades, and the specialised tanks of 79 Armoured Division.

Surprise was achieved, because although the build-up in the Nijmegen area was too obvious to conceal, the direction of attack was unexpected, and the Germans, as we have seen, feared another drive from Nijmegen to Arnhem across the half-flooded "Island." As soon as they realised the true objective, they would of course reinforce the Reichswald instead; and in order to catch these reserve divisions in motion, Ninth U.S. Army was to enter the battle from the south, from its positions along the River Roer. It had not yet advanced across the Roer because the high dams controlling the water level of this river were in German hands, and the Germans could flood the assault area at will. This posed some awkward decisions for the American command, which was committed to attack on February 10, two days after the British and Canadian assault had begun and while the Germans were still moving up their reserves to the threatened point.

On February 10, the XXX Corps attack was going well into the Reichswald and hopes were high in some quarters. On that day I noted in my diary: "The Commander of XXX Corps (Horrocks) has a bet that he'll get one of the Rhine bridges intact. We doubt very dubiously." The German decision was to blow the Roer dams, producing a temporarily impassable obstacle in front of Simpson's men but failing to catch them in the middle of an inadvisable assault. That was the last card gone; once the "ace" was down, it could not be played again. The floods would subside and there would be no great physical obstacle to the American attack. But until the Roer floods did subside, XXX Corps would have to carry the brunt of the battle alone.

Their problems now worsened. On February 12, I wrote: "Battle area being flooded by the bursting of the dams, and by the melting of the snows; it's several feet under water in many places." And one by one, the Germans were committing almost the last of their good-quality divisions, many from the parachute army. Nevertheless, the British and Canadians fought their way forward through the maze of prepared defences, in the process taking another town from their history books: Kleve, the home of Anne of Cleves, fourth wife of Henry VIII.

How bitter the fighting was may be judged by the experiences of Karl Max Wietzorek, a German paratrooper who had fought both in Russia and in Normandy. He was wounded and taken prisoner on February 24 while holding the strongpoint at Kappeln. From the night of February 23 to mid-day on the 24th, he estimated that he used up some 50,000 rounds of belt ammunition for his machine-gun, which was emplaced among farm implements in a barn.

"Left and right I was protected by agricultural machinery, and that was my good fortune. All the other machine-gun nests were in the open fields, dug in, and when the tanks attacked, most of their crews were killed. Plagued by lice and by dirt, we had hung on to this last bastion for days, until the swinging barrels of the tank guns eliminated us."

What it meant to the attackers, the men who had to get up and go forward among the sleeting machine-gun fire and the whine and blasting shock of the shell and mortar fire, over the mines that maimed more often than they killed, was an equal savagery. The chance of survival was so small. For instance, B Company of 2 Gordon Highlanders had three men left out of the original 115 who had landed in Normandy some seven months before. That was on February 26, when I met one of the three, whom I had known when I was a member of B Company, 2 Gordons.

Even more indicative than the statistics of survival was a café incident in Tilburg at about the same time. A group of Scottish soldiers, none of them more than twenty years old, straight from the noise and shock of the Reichswald battle, were sitting quietly until the proprietress's baby began to cry—and cry—and cry. Their nerves were so on edge that one youngster jumped to his feet and shouted out that if the baby didn't stop its screaming he would bash its head in against the wall. The unfortunate mother went white, realising that he was quite capable of doing it, and rushed the infant out to a back room. I witnessed this incident, and judged that her fear was justified.

No reporter could expect to get clapped on the back by his editor by writing that sort of story; instead the British press was currently holding an earnest enquiry into whether or not the excellent leave club in Brussels was leading our soldiers morally astray. Nor could editors really be blamed in military matters for adjusting the size of the headline to the length of the advance. But when Simpson's Ninth U.S. Army attacked over the Roer on February 23, against comparatively light opposition, the press coverage caused irritation instead of the customary amusement, to judge by my diary note of February 28:

"Yanks advance 9 miles, our armour is about to be committed. The Yank attack was to go in as a diversion for us; but it was very late, and is going ahead fast because the German has slapped all his divs into the line opposite us. So the British and Canadians do the fighting, the Yanks do the advancing, and the press gives them the headlines. Cleve is Caen all over again."

The irritation, which I think was general in the Canadian and British armies, was not directed at the Americans, but at some dolt of a sub-editor. The Americans had already endured their Reichswald in the Huertgen Forest, which produced no headline advances either, only heavy casualties and bitter fighting in the snow. The Maginot Line may have been wasted, but the Germans were making full use of the Siegfried.

The irritations were reversed when on March 10 the battle ended with the fall of the Rhine town of Xanten to the Guards Armoured Division, after a desperate struggle. As the weary prisoners marched past, Colonel "Joe" Vandeleur ordered his staff to stand to attention and himself saluted them. The home newspaper commentators exploded in outraged fury. Perhaps they saw the gesture as an act of sabotage to their "hate" campaign, which was now reaching new peaks of obscenity.

The bitter last stand of the German rearguards enabled their commanders to evacuate a sizable part of their force, in defiance of Hitler's orders, and it also caused General Horrocks to lose his bet. Two thunderous explosions on the morning of March 10 signalled the fate of the bridge at Wesel, and an officer of the Irish Guards wrote:

"I'm afraid we wasted our time in Tilburg last February studying means of capturing the bridge intact by an armoured dash. They say the German armour is going south, so most of it will be facing the Americans for a change and not us, when we start again on the other side."

The abrupt change was the result of an American initiative on March 7, the news reaching Canadian Army the following day, for I noted on the 8th: "Yanks over the Rhine. Can't last more than 2–3 months now." I qualified the good news by pointing out, "Can already see the gentle jungle zephyr stirring the scorpions in the slime down Lashio way. . . ."

Naturally, at this time every commander carried at the back of his mind a picture of a Rhine bridge, beautiful and unblown. So, too, did Hitler. He had ordered that anyone who failed to blow a bridge in time was to be shot. But he had complicated an always difficult decision by adding that anyone who blew a Rhine bridge too early was also to be shot. "Too late" is easy to recognise; "too early" is disputable. And fears of blowing too early may indeed lead to being unable to blow the bridge at all. If a state of chaos can be achieved, the decision becomes even more difficult and the attacker may well be able to "bounce" the bridge. This, initially, had been Horrocks' intention; but the thawing of the previously hard-frozen ground at the very start of the Reichswald attack had prevented a swift drive by Guards Armoured.

In the first week of March Simpson's Ninth U.S. Army, on Horrocks' right, made a number of apparent attempts to "bounce" major bridges over the Rhine. Two of these attempts were made near Düsseldorf, one at least employing a "Trojan Horse" element of American tanks disguised to look like German tanks, with German-speaking Americans riding on them. One bridge was at Obercassel and the other at Uerdingen. Both attempts failed, and they may have been intended to fail. The matter is still partly "classified," but it seems probable that they were merely part of a large-scale deception plan.

Bridges at Düsseldorf were worthless, because on the other bank there were 80 miles of densely built-up area—the Ruhr—stretching eastward as far as Hagen and Dortmund. Stalingrad was just such an industrial complex bisected by a major river; and a crossing at this point would have meant a super-Stalingrad. These probes, which resulted in the blowing of the bridges, were made during the night of March 2–3; and on the night of March 4–5 another part of Simpson's army was ordered to storm the Rhine at Rheinberg, but met strong resistance. Rheinberg made more sense, as it was near Wesel, which carried main roads clear of the Ruhr complex, but was still very much a secondary choice.

On March 5, the Americans also captured Cologne, but with no real hope of getting the Hehenzollern road bridge, which in any event gave access only to the Ruhr from a different direction, with a choice to the south of the mountainous, wooded terrain of the Westerwald and Siegerland. It is very beautiful country, and I much enjoyed my three years there after the war, but would be no one's first choice for mobile warfare.

The actual feelings at the time are too easily distorted by historians, who know now much more than the soldiers themselves knew then, and can fall into the trap of rationalisation. Further, it is too often forgotten that soldiers are also individuals, as much if not more concerned with their own personal affairs as with the great issues occurring around them. Particularly illuminating are the diaries of those with a sense of history. A. J. Duplantier, Jr., now a chartered public accountant in New Orleans, Louisiana, and then a first lieutenant with 372 Field Artillery, 99th U.S. Infantry Division, used exactly the same history-recording technique as did Herbert Kessler of the Hermann Göring Division. He wrote his letters home in such a manner that when pieced together shortly after the war they made an orderly narrative.* During this period his artillery battalion was taking part in the advance towards Düsseldorf, on the right of the Canadian Army.

On March 3, he noted:

"Moving forward today. The attack is successful so far and with a minimum of casualties. The Heinies are apparently abandoning their position on this side of the Rhine and high-tailing it for the other side of the Rhine. . . . I have been thinking incessantly of Catherine these days. According to the latest prediction by the Doctor, the baby is due on the 4th or 5th of March, and that shouldn't be too far off. Only trouble the baby may already be here and I have no way of knowing. I keep thinking of Everett Mount who never found out that his baby was born, but then I'm sure that wouldn't

* Censorship must have been much less strict in the United States and German armies than it was with the British and Canadian. My own diary could never go home in letter form, because being at an army headquarters I knew what was going to happen before it happened. Even where other army groups were concerned, news was instantaneous; I heard the news of Remagen within half a day, and two days before Duplantier learned of it.

happen to me, I've prayed too hard for anything to happen at this stage of the game."

On March 4, he wrote:

"Left Bedburg at 1015 last night in one of the darkest nights imaginable, and naturally there were no lights, not even dimmers. About every 100 yards was a truck on its side or upside down. Thank goodness the ground is level and the roads are fairly straight, and thank goodness the Germans are not offering much opposition. . . . Have been going to sleep with the utmost of confidence these nights. I suppose it is because there haven't been any incoming shells to disturb a peaceful night's rest, and as long as there's nothing to be heard there's nothing to be frightened of. The doughs are advancing so rapidly that we are beginning to imagine the feasibility of operating from trucks rather than set up fire direction in every little town."

That night they moved into a country estate called Neukerchen.

"When we arrived we assembled the some 100 occupants into a huge barn and began interrogating in three languages, Russian, Polish and German (fortunately we have at least one who can speak these languages). After hearing the tales of some of the laborers who were forced into their predicament, I was amazed. . . . They acted as though they hadn't eaten at all in over a month. . . . We had a devil of a time convincing the Poles and the Russians that the Americans were here to stay and that after we left they wouldn't revert back to control of the Nazis. On one occasion, I saw a ten year old girl order an 18 year old Russian boy to get her a pail of water. He refused, timidly stating that the Americans had forbid him to work for her any longer. Ten minutes later we saw him carrying the water to her. They had been suppressed for such a long time that they knew no other way."*

On March 7, Duplantier wrote:

"Reached Uckerath, on the Rhine, at 2:15. The Germans

* Actually, as one discovered in due course, this was the Russian (although certainly not the Polish) character; most were simple peasants used to a medieval style of life, and would do what anyone told

made a beeline for the River and left no opposition after the first assault. We had clear sailing up to the River, with very slight losses. There were no casualties in our Bn., and very few in the Infantry. It was a curiosity motoring through the little towns along the way. Each house had a white piece of cloth sticking out of a window to symbolize their complete surrender to the Americans. There wasn't an ounce of fight in any one of them in spite of the propagandizing they had undergone. They're on their knees now, asking for mercy, which they weren't willing to give just a few months ago when England was so unmercifully bombarded. We can't feel much sympathy for them."†

On March 9, Duplantier was writing:

"Now the big question is how are the Armies going to cross the Rhine? It has always been a problem in the mind of the Generals, now that all troops are up to the Rhine, even down in the 3rd and 7th Armies, how will we cross? It's going to take a lot of casualties before we accomplish it, but the war will never end until we do. Wish I could hear some news about my wife, and whether or not the baby has come. It's hell sweating it out like this. Sometimes I believe I would rather be home pacing the corridors."

That night, the unit was routed out at an hour's notice and ordered to drive south, destination unknown.

Similar "hurry up" calls had been going out since the 8th, particularly for artillery, in the area of Lieutenant General Courtney Hodges' First U.S. Army, part of Bradley's 12th Army Group. But some of the movements in the area of Bradley's Army Group, which had Patton's Third U.S. Army on its right, in the Moselle area, had begun suspiciously early.

William C. Hendrix, of Bartlesville, Oklahoma, was then a corporal with the 467th Anti-Aircraft Artillery (Automatic

---

them. Canadian Army HQ employed as cooks Russians who had been captured by the Germans while fighting for Stalin and who had then fought for Hitler against the Canadians, for whom they were now working quite happily.

† Much my own reaction at the time; which altered when I saw what the R.A.F. had done to the German cities.

Weapons) Battalion, operating in a ground support role in the First U.S. Army. Their half-tracks carried either a 37-millimeter cannon and two ·50-calibre machine-guns, or four ·50s, all in turrets. In early March they had been supporting the advance of the U.S. 69th Infantry Division about 40 miles south of Remagen.

"On March 5 we were relieved of this assignment" [recalled Hendrix], "and told that we were to support troops who were to attempt a Rhine River crossing. We were not told where this crossing was to be attempted."

As they eventually arrived at Remagen, Hendrix assumed that this was the objective all along, but it seems more probable that it was one of two favourable areas—near Bonn and near Koblenz—where Bradley wanted to attempt an encirclement of the Ruhr, a move that would be complementary to that of his rival Montgomery to the north, provided it did not draw off too much force from the main thrust. As many of the "deception" plans of the period were designed more to deceive other Allied generals than the Germans, official records are not always to be taken at face value.

"In the afternoon of March 6 we began to encounter great quantities of amphibious equipment and U.S. Navy personnel," [recalled Hendrix]. "I asked one of the sailors, 'What the hell are you guys doing so far from the ocean?' He replied, 'We're going to take you across the Rhine!' I then asked if our engineers had surrendered or gone home, and he countered by asking if I had ever seen the Rhine River. I told him that I had not. He then informed me that the river was very wide and deep and that the crossing would necessitate an amphibious operation. I began to realize that this operation was going to be difficult. We reached our staging area later that afternoon and began to wait for further orders. About 5 p.m. on March 7 I heard a great cheer go up in the main part of the staging area and saw a great deal of activity. A few minutes later one of our officers, Lt. Wallace Gibbs, came rushing up to us in a Jeep and yelled for us to load up. He said, 'We have a bridge across the Rhine and by damn we're going to keep it there.' Approximately one hour later we were at the Remagen bridge. Someone had raised a large sign on the steel structure between the stone supports which read, CROSS THE RHINE WITH DRY FEET—COURTESY OF THE 9TH ARMORED DIVISION. The printing was not too well done but this was undoubtedly the most welcome sign I had ever seen."

Remagen was equidistant between the two chosen stretches for crossing—Bonn north towards Cologne and Andernach south towards Koblenz. However, the main road route on the opposite side, the Cologne–Wiesbaden–Frankfurt autobahn, was some distance inland from the river, and ran south not quite parallel to the Rhine. And the Ludendorff bridge at Remagen was a railway bridge only.

The route was a difficult one for an army, which moves in a mass of huge and unwieldy vehicles, including mobile workshops, tank-transporters, and towed guns among its necessary impedimenta. When the Americans first sighted the bridge on March 7, the Germans were still moving back across it, and their impedimenta included horses and cows. Their first reaction was not to the bridge but to the spectacle of the Rhine itself, winding broad between high cliffs topped by ruined castles and spires, and with the steep face of a 600-foot-high volcanic rock, the Erpeler Ley, facing them on the other side of the great gorge.

There should have been anti-aircraft guns emplaced on the flat top of that near-vertical basalt cliff, but most had been moved to Koblenz, where an American crossing seemed more likely, and only now were new guns being moved up. Indeed, the Germans had only just completed the four-day task of laying planks across the railway lines on the bridge, so that it could carry the road traffic of their retreating army.

The Americans' second reaction was to realise what a target the mass of men, vehicles, and animals made as they moved slowly across the bridge, and to think of bringing down mortar fire on them. But Lieutenant Karl Timmerman, commanding the company of mechanised infantry of 9th Armored Division that first saw the bridge, decided that the target merited artillery and tank guns as well, so he held fire. His colonel came up, but could not obtain permission to use artillery, so he ordered the tanks to go forward with their supporting infantry to sweep the bridge with fire and interfere with any attempted demolition.

The 9th Armored was commanded by Major-General John Leonard and divided into two large battle groups of mixed tanks and armoured infantry, known as Combat Commands A and B, similar in composition to Groups "Hot" and "Cold" of Guards Armoured Division. It was elements of CCB, commanded by Brigadier-General William Hoge, that had first sighted the bridge in the early afternoon and seen in it only a moving traffic target. But it was Hoge himself who saw the chance of capturing the bridge and urged his units on through the town of Remagen towards the bridge approaches.

There was an understandable reluctance to get on that bridge, because it looked like a trap, and even if it was not, the effect would be exactly the same if the Americans got on it, or even across it, and then the Germans blew it up. Indeed, as the leading infantry broke cover under the fire of their tanks, just after 1430 hours a considerable explosion shook the earth on the west bank. It was not a demolition charge, but a delaying charge, which blew a 30-foot crater in the approach road. Some of the charges and wires on the bridge itself were now visible, as were the German engineers working frantically to complete their preparations. The crater made a quick dash by tanks impossible; now only infantry could cross on foot, slowly, under fire from the bridge towers as well as from the far bank, and the bridge was over a thousand feet long.

Timmerman, whose caution had prevented an enthusiastically premature mortaring of the bridge, was now to lead the attack on it. Hoge, whose drive had got his units onto the approaches quickly, ready to attack under fire protection, now received an order from III U.S. Corps. That day's operation, to take Sinzig and Remagen, was cancelled; instead, he was to drive south along the river towards the good crossing-place at Koblenz, now being threatened by an unofficial advance of Patton's Third U.S. Army.

If Hoge let the attack on the bridge go in, he would be disobeying orders. If the Germans blew the bridge under his leading troops, he might lose a battalion for nothing, and contrary to orders; and would almost certainly lose his command and ruin his career. Only a success can justify disobedience, and the chances of success were not high. The Germans themselves were now firing on their own bridge, and it seemed likely to go up in the air at any moment. On the other hand, the prize was a great one, and might both shorten the war and save many American lives later. Hoge ordered the attack to go on. But as Timmerman was urging his company to get up and go forward, there was another explosion and, masked by smoke, the bridge seemed to sway and rise in the air.

On the German side of the river, the doubts and decisions were just as agonising. The German forces facing Bradley's 12th U.S. Army Group were in fact on both sides of the river, but those still on the west bank were concentrated at widely separated points covering the most likely crossing areas—Bonn and Koblenz. Between them was a 60-mile gap leading to Remagen that was almost uncovered because the German Army Group commander, Field Marshal Model, considered that the defects of the Remagen route made it an unlikely objective for the Americans.

The German Army commander defending the Remagen sector, General Gustav von Zangen, disagreed with his superior. The defences of the bridge were weak, and although Model forbade him to reinforce it, he also disobeyed orders; instead of trying to hold firm on an impossibly long line west of the river, von Zangen instructed his forces to retreat to the Rhine in a direction that would place them, on the west bank, between the Americans and Remagen bridge. This might delay the Americans long enough to strengthen the bridge defences.

All Brigadier-General Hoge stood to lose was his rank, his command, and his career. General von Zangen stood to lose his life as well, if his decision proved to be the wrong one; or if Hitler, now a nervous and physical wreck, thought it was. But the German command structure was now chaotic and first one general and then another was given direct responsibility for the defence of the bridge, and various liaison officers, unknown to each other, arrived at the bridge to confuse the junior officers on the spot. It was death to allow a bridge to fall intact into enemy hands; but it also meant a very probably fatal court-martial to blow it too soon.

Hauptmann Willi Bratge commanded the 36-man security company guarding the bridge, while Hauptmann Karl Friesenhahn led the 120 engineers whose task was to destroy it, if necessary. Bratge's force also included 500 Volkssturm (Home Guards), 180 Hitler Jugend (schoolboys), 120 Russians, and about 220 flak gunners and rocket-men. By March 7, the Volkssturm were fading rapidly, and only six remained; the artillerymen were also disappearing unaccountably, and the 36 men he could really rely on were all convalescent soldiers fit only for "light duties."

Model's headquarters was still telling him that he needed no more, because the Americans were driving for Bonn. There was no threat to Remagen. They refused to believe Bratge's appreciation, that the American tank-gun fire he was hearing was from a strong armoured force bound for the bridge; they passed it off as from a light force protecting the flank of the American drive towards Bonn and the good crossing-place there, north of the Drachenfels, the Dragon Mountain of the Siegfried legend. The "third man" on the German side this day was Major Hans Scheller, who arrived as liaison officer from LXVII Army Corps, with orders to supervise the defence or demolition of the Ludendorff bridge, whichever seemed appropriate.

It was Friesenhahn who had blocked the bridge approach on the west bank by blowing a 30-foot crater. He had waited until the very last minute, because a retreating German battery was due to cross, and when the Americans arrived first, he reluctantly fired the charge. He was blown unconscious by a shell from an American tank as he ran back across the bridge to the eastern bank, but eventually reached it with the two other survivors of the demolition party. He reported to Bratge, who was standing at the entrance to the railway tunnel on the east bank.

Bratge wanted the bridge itself blown immediately, but Major Scheller had forbidden it; not only was Scheller superior in rank, but he was some way inside the tunnel at that moment. So Bratge had to go a quarter of a mile over the railway tracks, forcing his way through a crowd of civilian refugees, to find the major; and when found, the major was still doubtful, because of Hitler's order that no bridge was to be blown prematurely. At length he consented, and Bratge had to struggle back to the entrance to give the order to Friesenhahn.

There were some 60 separate charges on the bridge, wired to a detonating device actuated by a key. Everyone dropped flat as the engineer officer turned the key—and nothing happened. The American tank guns were raking the bridge and probably one of their shells had cut the main circuit. Now it was impossible to blow the bridge scientifically. However, there was a small 300-kilogram emergency charge that could be set off merely by lighting a simple fuse, and an engineer sergeant ran the gauntlet of American machine-gun fire for 80 yards in order to set it burning. As he ran back, the charge exploded and debris shot up out of the welling cloud of smoke.

But the bridge still stood. The Germans were shocked. So too were the Americans. When they thought the bridge had gone, the feeling among the assault infantry was not dismay, but relief. Lieutenant Timmerman had some difficulty leading them out onto the bridge; they thought it was a suicide mission, and he knew it was. However, after some hesitation and at first in ones and twos, they got up and followed him. Once onto the structure, the fast water of the Rhine was 80 feet below them; the chance of surviving a demolition blast and a fall of 80 feet into the river in full equipment was negligible. While the rumour in Nijmegen had been that the Americans had already captured the north end of the bridge, the rumour in Remagen was that a German prisoner had stated that the bridge would be blown at 1600 hours precisely. Neither rumour was strictly true, but might have had the effect of speeding the operation for capture.

In any case, once on the bridge the American infantry were very anxious to get off it. Behind them came a group of engineers, who began dealing with the demolitions. The tanks and tank-destroyers (self-propelled guns) covered them and engaged targets that were holding them up, mainly machine-gun posts in the bridge towers and a barge lying in the river.

The right-hand tower was still resisting when the leading Americans rushed it. There were only seven men inside, all of whom surrendered. Those behind them came on so fast that the leading soldier, Alexander Drabik, lost his helmet, and because he didn't stop to pick it up, was first across.

One hundred yards from the east bank of the Rhine, the railway tracks entered a tunnel in the hillside, and Lieutenant Timmerman ordered a patrol to go inside, cautiously. They took several prisoners near the entrance where, logically, the defenders would be; and did not realise that, further in, the tunnel was filled with Germans. Most of these were civilians who had retreated from the American shells that had been aimed at the tunnel mouth until a few minutes before; and they were now trying to disarm the German soldiers and convince the officers that they ought to surrender. Major Scheller had disappeared, and only Bratge and Friesenhahn were left. Bratge asked if anyone wanted to fight, and as no volunteers were forthcoming, he decided to give up.

There were still German defenders on the heights of the Erpeler Ley, however, and Timmerman's men had to storm this before the bridge could be considered in any way secure. He was reinforced by two more companies of the 27th Armored Infantry Batallion, but they had little more than small arms, and the situation seemed so precarious that some of the men began to slip away and drift back across the bridge to the west bank of the Rhine. Meanwhile, the American engineers were completing the "delousing" of the bridge and were filling in the 30-foot crater on the west bank approach, so that tanks could cross to support the vulnerable infantry. They were also busy patching up the holes in the bridge flooring blown by the two emergency demolition charges.

It was dark when the first platoon of Pershing tanks began to cross; pitch-dark, in fact, and in spite of white tape laid to guide them, they could not see it, nor could they see each other. Like monstrous Dodgem Cars, bumping into each other with the thunder-clap of an armour-plated impact, the tank column crossed and drove off fast to find their infantry. The infantry they found were all German, and although some wanted to surrender, others opened fire.

Next to cross were the self-propelled guns of 656th Tank

Destroyer Battalion. The leading platoon was commanded by Forst Lowery, now of Minnetonka, Minnesota. While it was still daylight, Lowery recalled,

"One of my destroyers sank a German naval vessel. At least the commander, who was rowed ashore in his dinghy by sailors, was dressed in his full uniform, complete with epaulets, and carried his sword across his knees before surrendering it to me. Very formal note. The vessel itself looked like an ordinary Rhine river boat."

The tank-destroyers came across the bridge at a faster pace than had the Pershings, presumably because of the critical nature of the situation, and the lead destroyer slipped a track into one of the hastily repaired holes made by the demolitions; it hung there, part of it over the river 80 feet below, part of it blocking the hurriedly planked roadway. The whole platoon came to a halt, and there they remained for the rest of the night, in the middle of Remagen bridge, while engineers worked at the problem of how to extract the heavy and cumbersome vehicle.

Up to now, only a few of the troops who had got across had slipped back to the west bank. But now that the bridge was blocked to vehicles, rumour swept the troops holding on to their precarious positions on the Erpeler Ley, with only small arms to pit against 20-millimeter cannons. The principal rumour was that all troops had been ordered to withdraw, and it originated with an officer. One third of them "withdrew," although it was more of a panic flight than an orderly retreat, leaving the American bridgehead weaker still.

They were still stumbling back to safety when the first reinforcing battalion arrived. Its colonel, Lewis Maness, had been told that he would have no trouble, there was nothing across on the other side but "demoralization." But by dawn the engineers had extracted the tank-destroyer and covered the hole into which it had fallen. Vehicles and men began to cross in a steady stream.

The American press were in no doubt as to what to think of the affair. *The New York Times* quoted an instant-journalist who had written: "The swift, sensational crossing of the Rhine was a battle feat without parallel since

Napoleon's conquering legions crossed the Rhine early in the last century." In fact, it was necessary to go back only five and a half months for an even more rapid and successful crossing of the Rhine—the capture of both road and rail bridges at Nijmegen by Guards Armoured Division and 82nd U.S. Airborne Division. The capture of the Maas bridge at Grave by the 82nd had been at least as important and a good deal neater, owing nothing to luck.

The reactions at various levels of the American command were interesting. Brigadier-General Hoge was apprehensive, because he had disobeyed orders to attempt the capture of the bridge; but his divisional commander, Major-General Leonard, backed him and convinced III U.S. Corps; they in turn had little trouble with the commander of First U.S. Army, Lieutenant-General Hodges, who enthusiastically telephoned Bradley, the army group commander.

"Hot dog, this will bust him wide open!" was Bradley's reaction. He authorised Hodges to put in the 99th Infantry Division, as well as the 78th and 9th Infantry divisions, which had already been ordered to exploit the opening gained by the 9th Armored Division. But Bradley did not immediately inform Eisenhower, because Remagen meant a diversion of effort into unfavourable terrain and Bradley already had plans for a crossing by Patton far to the south, which was also not a part of the agreed Allied plan, for the main effort to be in the north towards Berlin. He probably had a bad conscience.

However, typically, Eisenhower blew hot when he first heard the news, and then, later, grew cold and forbade any large build-up across the Rhine at Remagen. The supreme commander then telephoned Montgomery, anticipating obstruction, but Montgomery was extremely pleased. "It will be an unpleasant threat to the enemy and will undoubtedly draw enemy strength onto it and away from the business in the north."

In fact, all Montgomery was worried about was that Eisenhower would try to close up to the Rhine all along its length, which meant cracking open new sections of the Siegfried Line, a slow and bloody business, before launching a crossing on the good northern route where the Siegfried

Line had already been overwhelmed at great cost by 21 Army Group. Eisenhower probably had a guilty conscience, too, because this was in fact his intention, Allied agreements notwithstanding.

Montgomery's prediction proved accurate, and the defenders of the Remagen bridgehead helped the northern thrust (and also Patton's unofficial southern advance) by drawing to themselves a frenzied German effort to wipe it out, using much of their reserves and including perhaps the weirdest assortment of weapons ever to be collected together in so small a space.

Forst Lowery recalled:

"After crossing, my platoon took up positions along the river in the Erpel area, firing on whatever threatened the bridge —boats, swimmers, floating objects, and a weird variety of aircraft which came over one at a time trying to bomb the bridge. We saw what must have been the death throes of the Luftwaffe. They must have collected enough fuel for one plane and then sent it out. Everything from the plywood jets which made their first appearance about this time through an old Ju 88."

"The dismal March weather and the use of smoke generators obviously helped in preventing enemy air attacks from destroying it" [wrote Lieutenant-Colonel William H. Anthony, who was then with the 809th Field Artillery Battalion]. "Although the near-misses and pounding that Remagen took sure must have helped weaken it. During that period Remagen was a real hot spot, and with the anti-aircraft batteries surrounding the place there was the greatest ring of conical firing one could ever hope to see."

The 99th Infantry Division, which had been the first to reach the Rhine north of Cologne, was sent all the way south to Remagen to make a crossing there. Roger J. Moore, a radio operator with a battalion headquarters, was another American soldier who kept a diary in letter form; and this reveals, not how much the ordinary soldier knows of the headline events in which he takes part, but how little at the time—because no one bothers to tell him anything. His unit were pulled out from the Rhine in trucks for an unexplained purpose, dumped in Ringen, and on the morning of March 11 began foot-slogging down the road in the belief that their destination was some minor town five miles away. After marching many times more than five miles, they came under shellfire on a road packed with trucks and tanks, went through a tunnel under a railway line, and found themselves facing a sign reading: "NACH DER RHEINBRÜCKE". Then, and only then, did they realise where they were and what they were going to do.

"We ducked along streets by dead bodies and shattered houses," wrote Moore. "After half-an-hour in a cellar, we walked some more to the bridge, which was a big surprise to us. Every couple of minutes a heavy gun fired a shell at it. Sometimes it hit and sometimes it missed, and engineers were at work repairing the damage. We were very tired from that long walk, but we had to go on. We climbed up the stairs in the stone tower at the end of the bridge and stepped on the bridge itself. Then we *ran*, breathlessly, all the way to the other side. I don't think my heart beat once all the way. Shells were flying over us and crashing into Remagen, and regularly, every couple of minutes, a large shell screamed down, over the top of the hill across the Rhine, down to the bridge. Oh, but that was a long bridge! I have never been so scared."

Armand Duplantier, of the 372nd Field Artillery, arrived on March 11 after that night drive to an unknown destination that had been lit only by the pyrotechnics of an air raid on Düsseldorf and the fires of blazing Cologne. He noted in his diary:

"The situation at the bridge was still indeterminable, and didn't yet look too rosy. The doughs hadn't been able to advance too rapidly in the face of the machine gun fire set up on the hills opposite the bridge. The Jerries are trying like hell to blow out the main bridge to thwart our attack before it becomes too powerful to overcome. Fortunately, Westum is about four or five miles from the bridge, and we aren't in too much danger from stray bombs, but brother, the jet-propelled planes are coming in about every five minutes. Each making a death dive in the face of a tremendous machine gun and anti-aircraft fire. This morning we stood atop a hill near 'C' Battery and watched the area of the bridge for several hours. There's a guard of P.38's (about 7 or 8 planes) on constant patrol to try to scare off the suicide jets as they come in, but without success. On one occasion as two P.38's chased a jet, they made miscalculations and crashed wing-tips. Both planes caught on fire immediately, but not before the pilots had a chance to bail out. Seemed to us like one made it on this side, and one on the other, but in either case we could see the tracer bullets going up after the pilot, and each one pulling at the drawstrings of his parachute trying to dodge the bullets. So far the Germans have been unsuccessful in knocking down the bridge. If they should make a direct hit now it wouldn't make a terrible lot of difference as we have two pontoons up now. The din caused by the antiaircraft fire when one of these jets comes in defies description. It makes a very interesting picture, the sky being literally covered with tracers, and to stop and think that for every tracer there are 10 steels makes one wonder how in the hell anything can survive such a saturation. But strangely those fast diving jets come charging in from the direction of the sun, and are usually about one fourth of a mile ahead of the nearest bullet (travelling at 600)."

On March 12, Duplantier forgot all about the Rhine.

"When I saw there was a telegram for me, my face flushed and a tingling sensation of pride began going up and down my spine. I'm the happiest man in the world. I've acted like a ten-year old on Christmas day. I didn't wait for congratulations, I solicited it. To make it nicer, I had a secret longing for a boy, but from the wording of the telegram, I wasn't quite sure what had happened. It read: 'SON BORN, ALL WELL, CHILDREN EVACUATED. WRITING.' That business about Children Evacuated had me guessing until I realized that the French had relayed the message, and naturally it would be confusing."

On March 14, Duplantier noted:

"We crossed the Rhine River today. Each man had to carry extra rations, and vehicles extra gasoline, in the event a German counter-attack spread us all over the country. But that doesn't appear likely, as reports show the rapid progression of all three divisions fighting. Crossing that flimsy pontoon bridge in between artillery barrages wasn't too healthful looking, and to make matters worse, just as we crossed, we saw 5 or 6 men lying dead near the head of the bridge, having been just recently hit by artillery. I doubled up on my prayers while crossing, hoping that just as I crossed the Heinies had to take time out to reload their guns. Not one round came in while I crossed; as soon as we hit the other side, we took off like a ruptured duck. It was humorous to watch those drivers pump the petrol when the chance arose. Our destination was Dattenburg, just a few miles inland, but on the other side of a mountain pass. This hilly country is terrific. What an ideal spot for a defense, and from the casualty reports the defense was utilized."

Next day, he added:

"I have found out that the going isn't as easy as the rumors have it. These doughs are having a rough time, and getting plenty incoming mail. I made the mistake of walking around a temporary Battalion HQ without taking precautions, and before I could shout 'cover' an 88 had landed squarely against the side of the house, scaring the hell out of me, two other forward observers, and most of the rifle company of the first battalion who had concentrated in the area to 'jumpoff' in a short while. That didn't delay the 'jumpoff' but it brought a new light on the subject. Later on in the day I came across two doughs coming in with 38 prisoners, who were too tired to keep their hands over their heads. Among them was a 12 year old boy in civilian clothes, who evidently had offered opposition when our boys walked into the town."

While Duplantier's unit was moving forward behind the infantry, "Bill" Hendrix's anti-aircraft battalion, with its fast-firing automatic weapons mounted in armoured vehicles, was still in the bridge area, where it had been since the evening of March 7, a few hours after the bridge had been captured.

"We were positioned on a hill which was much higher than the level of the bridge and our orders were to guard against paratroops. We were specifically ordered *not* to fire on *any* air-craft. We were told that the Air Force was to fly a twenty-four hour air cover above the bridge. And they did. Flood lights were installed and at night the area was as bright as day. Along both river banks up and down stream, troops were positioned with automatic weapons and ordered to fire on anything that moved up or down the river; consequently, there were many logs, pieces of paper, etc. that were shot to bits, as well as several German frogmen who attempted to swim the river and set charges on the bridge piers.* Then we began to get the rumors which are always started by worried or frightened men. We were told (1) that the Germans were attempting to move a huge cannon within firing range on a railway car,† (2) that a paratroop attack was imminent (this never happened), (3) we were to be attacked by buzz-bombs and V-2 rockets (we were), (4) the Germans had a new secret weapon to destroy us and the bridge. From our high position we were able to have a ringside seat for all that took place during the next ten days. We were able to see approaching buzz-bombs. The V-2 rockets would slam into the countryside and the explosions from these two weapons would make the earth tremble as though by an earthquake. Fortunately they did not have the pin-point accuracy of our modern-day rocketry. The Germans used jet aircraft to bomb the bridge. This was the first time we had ever seen this type of aircraft and when the first one flew over we dived for our fox-holes, thinking that the sound of it was the giant railway gun shelling the bridge. I personally believe that these near misses, coupled with the two demolition charges that the Germans had exploded, further weakened the bridge and were responsible for its collapse on March 17."

John E. Slater of New York, then with the 9th Infantry Division, recalled that moment vividly, for he was on the far

* Although the German frogmen had been successful at Nijmegen, and had succeeded also in blowing a pier of the Moerdijk bridge on November 15, 1944 (an ironic reversal of the German paratroop exploit of May, 1940), they failed at Remagen because the attack was expected and had to be carried out in freezing water conditions. Otto Skorzeny had insisted that the risks be explained and only volunteers should go. The target was a pontoon bridge, attacked after the collapse of the rail bridge.

† A 540-millimeter gun, the "Karl Howitzer," firing a 4,400-pound shell.

bank, on top of a hill, and had turned round at the precise moment that the bridge collapsed. "It had a stunning effect on the troops who had crossed," he wrote. Duplantier, however, was not impressed by the news. "The bridge had been hit so many times by shells and bombs that it could stand up no longer," he noted. "But it made little difference, because the front was some 28 to 30 miles wide along the Rhine, and there were about 4 or 5 auxiliary bridges across."

The loss of the bridge would have cost Bratge his life, had he not been taken prisoner; Major Scheller was shot, as were a number of people who had had nothing to do with it, including an engineer major who, after the Americans had captured the bridge, led a daring attack to blow it up, but failed. And, as Lieutenant-Colonel Anthony put it, "It's a cinch that finding that Rhine River bridge must have upset some preconceived plans, because, considering the terrain alone, it couldn't have been a picked spot for a river crossing."

Some of the American airborne commanders wanted "to get in on the show," but were refused by Eisenhower. This was to be symptomatic of the Rhine crossings as a whole. On the American side—and the Americans now had in Europe forces three times the size of the combined British and Canadian armies—the last stage in the downfall of the Third Reich was to be treated, not in mere mundane military terms, not in vital political terms, but as some stage show, with the actresses carefully examining their make-up and arguing about the relative prominence of their names outside the theatre, all with an anxious eye to the "first night" reviews next day. And in these terms it has been treated ever since, with the rival actresses' personal ambitions spoken of as if they were expressions of the purest American patriotism.

However, from what happened subsequent to widespread crossings of the whole river, it is clear that the rival American prima donnas were being "conned." There *was* a real political objective behind all the dressing-room tantrums, but it was at the level of SHAEF and the President of the United States; and it was to be achieved. Russian dominance of half Europe, including not merely half of Germany, but of many smaller states, such as Czechoslovakia, was to be ensured by the actions of future-President Eisenhower.

CHAPTER TWENTY-FOUR

"OLD MEN WITH OLD RIFLES AND HEARTS FULL OF HATE"

Oppenheim: March 22–23

On March 7 I noted in my diary: "Cologne is ours. Patton, farther south, instead of maintaining the defensive role as per instructions, has leapt forward 30 miles, and is still going." The spearhead of his advance was Major-General Hugh Gaffey's 4th Armored Division, which had made the break-out from St. Lo in Normandy and later relieved Bastogne. Unlike the 9th, which captured Remagen bridge, the 4th had an excellent reputation and was perhaps the best United States armoured division in Europe. It was also the only division to have no nickname, because its first leader, Major-General John S. Wood, had rejected such flamboyance and said, "They shall be known for their deeds alone." After Remagen, Brigadier-General William M. Hoge was promoted and transferred to command the 4th Armored.

Bennett H. Fishler, Jr., of Ridgewood, New Jersey, who was then serving with the 8th Tank Battalion of 4th Armored, wrote home to his wife on March 26:

"My three letters a week scheme sure went kaput for a while but that is not because I didn't want to write. We've been on the run some considerable bit, as you know from the papers, and it's been all I could do to eat, much less sit down to a letter. Today I've had a chance to brush up a bit and shave and that is some luxury, believe. Scarce recognised myself. Now that we are over the Rhine I at last feel as though I were really and truly in Germany. Before it was sort of quasi-Germany, if you see what I mean. The country is pretty, especially since the spring and the weather is near bearable (I thought winter was never going to end, myself, but I was never gladder to see a winter go. That old saw about can spring be far behind, is pure balony. It can, and it was.)

No German village is complete without the full set of white flags, although they are generally impromptu affairs such as table cloths, napkins, shirts, and grandpa's long winter underwear. If there are some German soldiers around who wish to contest our entrance, the reception is a little different at first, although later on it amounts to the same thing, except that the white flags fly from the rubble. Personally, I don't have a great deal of stomach for this town fighting business, even if they are kraut towns, because it means that there are plenty of non-soldiers involved, but what is necessary is, I suppose, necessary."

What had happened was that with the connivance of Bradley, Patton had made a deep penetration and then cut in behind the Siegfried Line defences of the Saar, then under painful frontal attack by U.S. Seventh Army in accordance with Eisenhower's desire "to close the length of his entire line to the Rhine." Eisenhower's stated reason was to avoid the possibility of a German counter-offensive; his real reason may only be conjectured.

Bradley's stated reason for encouraging Patton's drive was to avoid the possibility of his army group's being given a static role on the west bank of the Rhine, while Montgomery made for the Baltic and Berlin; and this may well be true.* His afterthoughts, that the British plans were "shrewd" and that he and other American generals were political innocents at that time, able to think only in terms of the current military situation and unable to grasp the fact that every military decision now taken affected the political and economic shape of Europe for at least the next 25 years, is a little hard to believe. Possibly the full truth still cannot be told.

Nor can even Patton be taken quite at face value, although his motive is clear—the simple military ambition, necessary to every successful general, assuming an intense and unnatural form. Cyril Ray described him as "tall, slim, under sixty, and the foul-mouthed bully looked like a rural dean." To others, he appeared not so much a bully as a "clown." Both these extreme views—one British, one Canadian—were really a

* See *A Soldier's Story*, by Omar N. Bradley (Eyre and Spottiswoode), pp. 515–17.

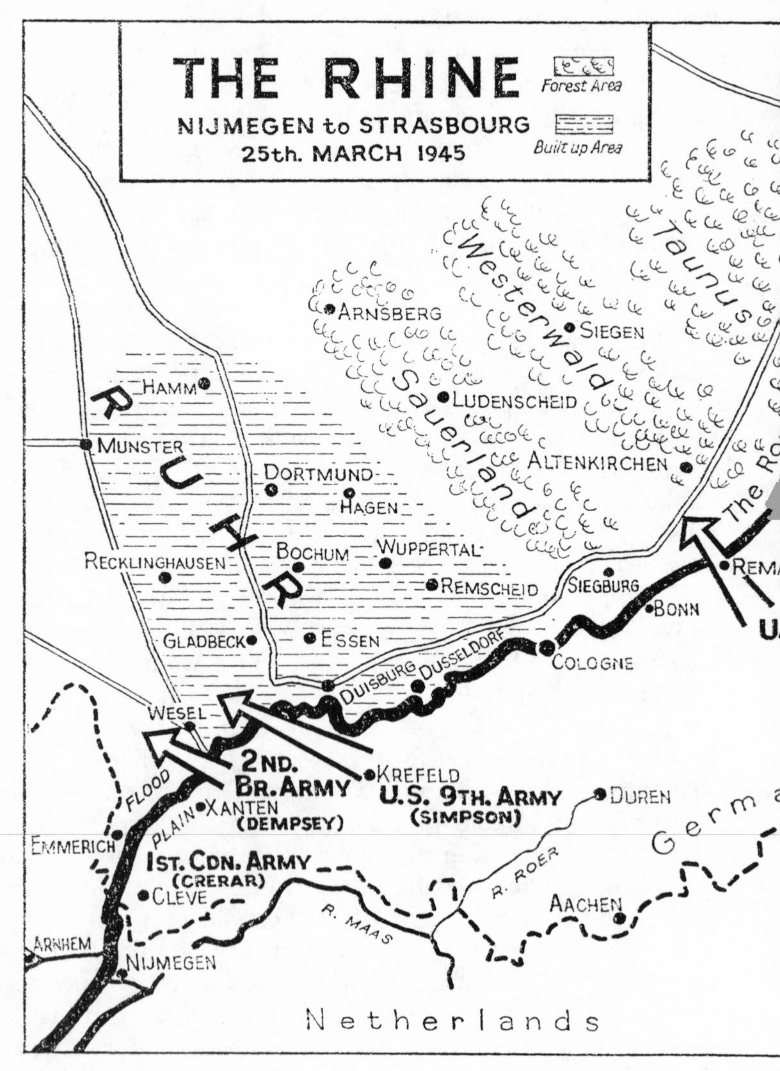

THE RHINE
NIJMEGEN to STRASBOURG
25th. MARCH 1945
Forest Area
Built up Area
Westerwald
Taunus
ARNSBERG
SIEGEN
HAMM
RUHR
LUDENSCHEID
Sauerland
MUNSTER
ALTENKIRCHEN
DORTMUND
HAGEN
BOCHUM
WUPPERTAL
RECKLINGHAUSEN
REMSCHEID
SIEGBURG
BONN
GLADBECK
ESSEN
COLOGNE
DUISBURG
DUSSELDORF
WESEL
2ND. BR.ARMY (DEMPSEY)
KREFELD
U.S. 9TH. ARMY (SIMPSON)
FLOOD PLAIN
XANTEN
DUREN
EMMERICH
IST. CDN. ARMY (CRERAR)
CLEVE
R. ROER
R. MAAS
AACHEN
ARNHEM
NIJMEGEN
Netherlands

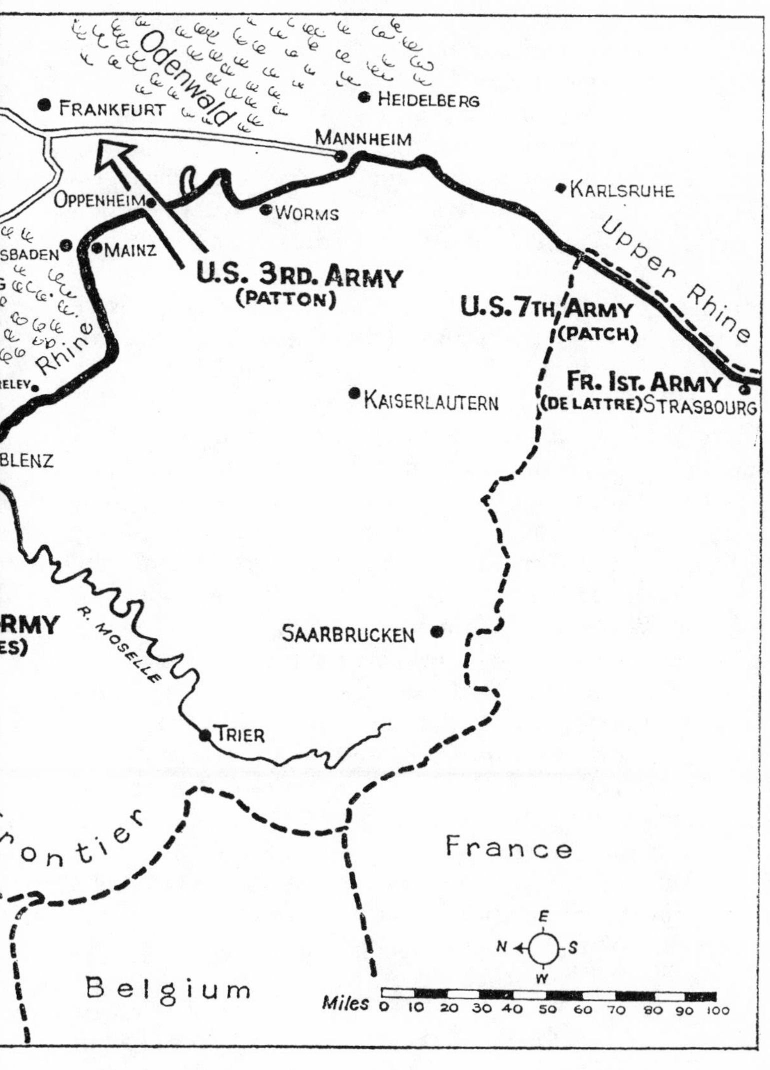

Odenwald
FRANKFURT
HEIDELBERG
MANNHEIM
KARLSRUHE
OPPENHEIM
WORMS
SBADEN
MAINZ
Upper Rhine
U.S. 3RD. ARMY
(PATTON)
U.S. 7TH ARMY
(PATCH)
Rhine
FR. IST. ARMY
(DE LATTRE)
STRASBOURG
KAISERLAUTERN
BLENZ
RMY
ES)
R. MOSELLE
SAARBRUCKEN
TRIER
rontier
France
E
N
S
W
Belgium
Miles 0 10 20 30 40 50 60 70 80 90 100

reflection on his style of command, which was indeed largely an "act" in the theatrical sense, rather than an appreciation of his generalship. The big talk and the twin six-guns were the exact equivalent of Montgomery's turtle-necked sweater and twin cap-badges.

In large organisations, civilian or military, the managing director has to "project" himself and/or the company "image," and both Montgomery and Patton were sufficiently up-to-date to realise that methods suitable for a battalion commander or the proprietor of a small garage in the matter of employer-employee relationships simply would not do where organisations with a payroll of hundreds of thousands were concerned. They were alike also in their ruthlessness towards subordinates, although Montgomery bowler-hatted at the top only, while Patton spread himself far and wide.

Typical of his method was a story I heard from Americans just after the war, concerning an occasion when Patton suspected that his armoured spearheads were not getting their replacement tanks because the crews of the tank-transporters were "whooping it up with the local damery." Some, my informants admitted, were doing just exactly that; but most were simply held up by blown bridges. However, Patton did an aerial reconnaissance of his own area, saw tank-transporters laid up under trees in every direction, and ordered the "busting" of every sergeant commanding a tank-transporter that day. This was gross injustice, because if a tank-transporter is held up for any reason, good or bad, it makes such a target that it is common prudence to take it off the road and under cover.

However, the principle of "no excuses accepted" is one valid method of driving men on; and in addition Patton was extremely quick to find and exploit enemy weak spots where these existed. When these did not exist, and his command came to a sudden halt, there frequently occurred ill-judged outbursts of temper, as one of his biographers, Ladislas Farago, points out. In the final drive to the Rhine, what Patton scented was not just a weak spot but the imminent collapse of most organised opposition and thus a good chance of "taking the river on the run" and thereby wiping Montgomery's eye. In British parlance, he intended to "bounce" a crossing.

Although one would never suspect it from reading most

ARNHEM AND THE NEDER RIJN—mid-1945

In foreground, two Bailey pontoon bridges built by engineers of First Canadian Army. In background, the ruins of the demolished road bridge, showing (*right-hand bank*) the end of the bridge onto which the author climbed while the left bank was held by the Germans.

RHINE BRIDGING—EMMERICH, 1945

Bailey bridge partially completed by Canadian engineers on the west bank, the day following the author's visit, when this area was still under observed shellfire from Hochelten. *Photo:* W. L. Lugrin.

Am 6. Oktober 1944 fiel bei Arnheim, kurz nach seinem 18. Geburtstag, unser braver WILLI —

Panzer-Grenadier in der Division „Hermann Göring"

Willi Wohlfahrt

So anständig, wie er gelebt hat, erfüllte er seine Pflicht bis zum Letzten.

Wir können seinen frühen Tod kaum fassen, unser sonniger Bub hat uns allen ja nur Freude gemacht.

FEUERBACH, WIEN, NEUKIRCHEN a. W., 2. November 1944.

In tiefer Trauer:

Hans Möchel
Schwager.

Butzi
Neffe.

Josef und Aloisia Wohlfahrt
Eltern.

Krempl und Wohlfahrt
Großeltern.

Herbert Wohlfahrt
Gretl Möchel
Geschwister.

WILLI WOHLFAHRT
Obituary Notice. A fr
of Kessler's, he was k
in the abortive and us
counter-attacks laun
out of Arnhem into
Betuwe, after the defe
the British paratro

BEFORE THE RHINE—
1945
Three men of the H.L.I. of Canada just before going over the Rhine. Lt. J. Ferguson (*right*) was to be mortally wounded.
Photo: H.L.I. of C. archives.

BEFORE ARNHE
1944
Major Tony
bert (*left*), Bri
Major of 1
chute Brigade
the airfield b
take-off.
Photo: M
Hibbert's collec

American authors on the subject of the Rhine crossing, the concept—far from being a Bradley-Patton patent—is as old as warfare, and no one owns the rights to the idea. Actually carrying it out is a different matter, however, and as we have seen, Horrocks' attempt to "bounce" the Rhine bridge at Wesel with Guards Armoured Division foundered in the floods and fierce opposition. How Patton's army fared is best seen through the eyes of junior witnesses.

Max Gissen, now of Weston, Connecticut, was then an infantry first lieutenant.

"We, the 26th Infantry Division (from Massachusetts)" [he wrote], "approached the Rhine after breaking through the Siegfried Line in the Saar. What happened there, the intensity of the fighting, the casualties taken, were all of much more importance to us than anything that happened at the Rhine or after. We broke through at Serrig, Beurig, Merzig, not far from Trier and we drove alone a line that roughly paralleled the Saare River, capturing places like Reimsbach, pushing on through Dottweiler, Furth, Landstuhl, etc. We had jumped off on 13 March and the initial progress was slow. The Siegfried was said to be roughest at that point and I can easily believe it. Once it cracked, though, about the third day of the attack, prisoners began coming in in larger numbers. In one place we took six 88s intact and 190 prisoners. This was near Thalexweiler and at dusk of the 19th we were approaching Furth. The 20th was a crazy day. What had been a stubborn retreat became a real rout. The Air Force had a field day, the infantry no longer walked but mounted everything on wheels and pushed on as much as 25 miles a day, leaving behind pockets of Germans to be mopped up or taken prisoner without resistance. Some, of course, fought on and raised the devil with the few rear-echelon troops. But after the Bulge, and before that the dreary, muddy, inch-by-inch crawl through Lorraine, the few days before we reached the Rhine seemed a lark. I came into Kaiserslautern at night with only two men and couldn't find any enemy troops at all. Only Polish and Russian forced laborers, cadavers wandering aimlessly about and suddenly become creatures to be feared by the terrified civilians.

"During the entire preparation for the crossing, I was the liaison officer between the 104th Infantry and 26th Division headquarters. During this brief period I reported to GI, II, III, and IIII, and to the division chief-of-staff and the division commander. I have no doubt that from the standpoint of Corps, Army and Eisenhower, all was going according to plan, but to me there seemed to be one hell of a lot of confusion. On the way from the Siegfried Line, the supply-road situation had become badly snarled because our Seventh Army had come up to our right flank and, in country where the roads were inadequate at best, the competition for even a dirt track was fierce. The men, however, were relaxed. No one dreamed that we would cross with the suddenness that we did. The natives in the Oppenheim area around which we sprawled were surly. But many of the young people, especially the girls, did not seem to be crushed by the presence of conquerors and many liaisons were quickly formed even when one discounted the routine boasting."

He added:

"With Patton, it was always attack, attack and (no barbs across the sea here) he never waited around to 'tidy up' as Montgomery did. He was a driving commander, quick to make the most of the slightest opening allowed by the enemy and twitching to force one if it wasn't there."

The final decisions were taken at a conference on March 19 when, with Eisenhower's approval, Bradley authorised two Rhine offensives—the first to be made out of the Remagen bridgehead by Hodges' First Army, the second to be a crossing near Mainz by Patton's Third Army; both armies would then link up in a 12th Army Group drive that would rival, or excel, that of Montgomery's 21st Army Group in the north. Once 12th Army Group was committed, it would no longer be possible to detach divisions from it to aid the northern thrust, if that should be required.

Militarily, it made sense only in terms of U.S. Army, and particularly U.S. Third Army, prestige. Politically, it made sense only if the ultimate objective was to free Czechoslovakia before the Russians arrived there with their own peculiar brand of "liberation." But Eisenhower must have had strict orders from his political masters to ensure, at all costs, that it was the Russians and not the Americans who occupied Czechoslovakia. And although he would never rein in Patton in the over-riding interests of Anglo-American offensives elsewhere, he was to find no difficulty in stopping or diverting any number of U.S. armies when Russian interests were threatened.

But Patton, apparently, did not realise this. He saw the Rhine only as a glorious opportunity to score off Montgomery and steal some of the limelight from Hodges, whose Remagen coup had temporarily snatched the headlines for First Army. As Montgomery's crossing was planned for the night of March 23–24, it was necessary (from the propaganda point of view) for Patton to cross not later than the night of March 22–23. On the 19th he therefore ordered forward from Lorraine the men who never got any headlines at all—the engineers and their bridging convoys.

Concentration on the deeds of the fighting troops obscures the fact that the actual crossing of a major river by the initial assault units is a mere fraction of the real effort involved. First to sustain a major blitzkrieg by army groups, then the prolonged occupation of an immense area of conquered territory, which was the prospect in view, requires rather more than a handful of rubber boats or even a few pontoon bridges. Arrangements had to be made, not merely to bridge the major river but all rivers to be encountered beyond, and also, within a short space of time, to erect semi-permanent high-level road and rail bridges that would be immune to floods and bad weather.

The problems in the Mainz area were not of the magnitude encountered on Montgomery's front opposite Wesel, and Patton had prudently collected sufficient bridging material some time previously, although as its origins were dubious, he was less inclined than Montgomery's publicity machine to stress the vast amounts of material involved. Having ordered up his bridging train, he then began "to tramp around and shout" at his commanders, in order to get them to cross the Rhine a day or two earlier than was administratively convenient.

In particular, he pushed the XII Corps commander, Major-General Manton S. Eddy, to get across at Oppenheim, near Mainz, on the 22nd, whereas the 23rd would have suited Eddy better. So Eddy passed on the bad news to Major-General S. Leroy Irwin, commanding the 5th Infantry Division. The news was bad only in the sense of the timing. Oppenheim was topographically an easier proposition than two other areas, both along the "Romantic Rhine" downstream from Mainz in the Koblenz area, which Patton had also selected previously as crossing-points in case the Mainz area proved to be more heavily defended than appeared probable.

In fact, there was nothing the Germans could do at Mainz. The 50 miles from Mainz to Mannheim was held in theory by the German Seventh Army, but this "army" consisted of one actual corps HQ, another corps HQ in process of formation, no regular divisions, but only a hotch-potch of depot and line-of-communication troops incorporated in the disorganised remnants of four former divisions. Their armoured reinforcements consisted of five S.P. guns. Had Patton waited another day, two more would have become available, making a total of seven. Even these were there only by chance, part of a unit re-fitting and earmarked for use at Remagen, in Hodges' area.

Late in the evening of March 22, six battalions of the 5th Division began to cross the Rhine in assault boats at two places near Oppenheim, were opposed by what was probably a platoon, and by dawn had formed a small bridgehead at a cost of 28 men killed and wounded. Next, it was the turn of the engineers to build temporary bridges and rafts, and then the infantry of the 26th Division and the tanks of 4th Armored began to cross, a procedure that took several days.

"The crossing, when it came, surprised us all" [wrote Max Gissen, who was with the 26th Infantry]. "Through my binoculars I had seen an occasional German soldier on the far bank and I assumed, as we all did, that they were dug in on the other side. Some, like myself, knowing that Rhine was a holy word to most Germans, and especially to the wretched little house painter, expected a terrific battle and even a crossing under intense fire. It seems, from my subsequent reading, that Allied intelligence was aware that the area was lightly defended, but to those of us who were in ignorance of what the Germans had there, it was a certainty that all hell would break loose once we started across. There was no 'jostling in the queue' to be first into the attack. There were commanders who couldn't wait to be committed and our own first Colonel was one. But the men and junior officers? Nonsense. Everyone was exhausted by the time we reached the Rhine. We had suffered heavy casualties in the preceding week and nothing would have pleased us better than a longish leave (say about a year) in Paris or Biarritz or even what was left of St. Lo. Of course there was great excitement when we saw the Rhine. Even the deepest dyed half-wit in the outfit knew that we'd be crossing, and in addition to the natural apprehension there was a sense of history in the situation that no one tried to laugh off. But forget all that about being wild for the chance to have the first go.

"What we did not know as we started for the treadway bridge (it seemed close to a miracle to us that the engineers, the real unsung heroes of the war, had thrown the bridge so fast as they did) was that Lt. Gen. Sir Miles Dempsey's Second British Army had crossed at 2100 hours on the night of the 24th and had established bridgeheads at Wesel and two other places. And, of course, there had been Remagen. Obviously the German forces had been pulled out to meet these threats and Patton made his jump. I should not forget to tell you that the Rhine looked as wide as the mouth of the Amazon to us when we thought about the crossing. Actually, by U.S. standards, it isn't wide at all. This past summer, I took my family on a cruise from Basle to Rotterdam (one of those four-day trippers' things). I herded by wife and children over to the rail so that they could see just where father had made his historic crossing. Their only comment was that the river didn't look nearly as wide as I had led them to believe, and it was a shattering anticlimax for me when I realized that our apprehension at the time had made the Rhine appear so vast. Then, as we started over, I had inwardly crouched and waited for the first German 88's to open up. Nothing happened. We crossed on the night of March 24–25 and not a shot was fired. So there it was, the great crossing, a cinch compared to our crossing of the Cumberland River when we were back in the States on the Tennessee manoeuvres. There we lost 22 men by drowning in just such a crossing."

Bennett H. Fishler, Jr., then commanding Company B of the 8th Tank Battalion of the 4th Armored, who crossed at much the same time, was disappointed by the river.

"In the first place, I was surprised by the smallness of the Rhine. We had had drilled into us for a long time by superior officers and by intelligence that the Rhine was a great water barrier and that probably the Germans would make a strong stand. I fully expected to see something as magnificent as the Hudson River with which I was familiar at home which in the busy port of New York is over a mile wide. I do not know just precisely the width of the Rhine at Oppenheim but I would be surprised if it were more than 300 feet wide at that point. The far bank opposite Oppenheim is a meadow with an open expanse of flat land leading up to Wolf's Kehlen. The escarpment on the west bank (I guess that is the left bank) is approximately 100 feet high at Oppenheim and there are vineyards on the terraces. My recollection is that we were on the escarpment for at least a day and maybe two days waiting for the pontoon bridge to be built by the engineers of the Fifth Infantry Division. There were a couple of barges tied up on the right bank of the Rhine at this spot which we sank at our leisure with gunfire from the top of the escarpment. While there we were not fired upon nor was any contact made with the enemy nor could the enemy be seen anywhere from our position. A small Piper Cub airplane attached to our division circled the crossing area constantly acting as spotter for artillery in the event we got any fire. None ever came. My recollection is that the Fifth Infantry Division engineers built the pontoon bridge during daylight and night hours without being fired upon and that it took them about a day and a half to complete it. Once the bridge had been completed, my tank company crossed the river and proceeded to Wolf's Kehlen which we did not attempt to take but surrounded and later by-passed. The most interesting moment of the day for me was approximately one hour after the securement of Wolf's Kehlen. I was resting in an orchard southeast of the town when I was accosted by a Captain from Intelligence, 3rd Army, who turned out to be my first-year roommate at law school. 'A' Company moved through our position to the next objective, and my recollection is that we got to Darmstadt by nightfall. The opposition was very scant at the crossing and did not really pick up until we got into the Darmstadt area. But there was very little opposition from the time we crossed the Rhine until the war ended in May. What opposition there was came from old men and young boys who had hand grenades and old rifles and hearts full of hate."

Events at headquarters made a strange contrast. On the morning of March 23, Patton made the first of a series of widely quoted telephone calls to Bradley. "Brad, don't tell anyone but I'm across!" he fired off.

"Well, I'll be damned. You mean across the Rhine?" queried Bradley.

"Sure am. I sneaked a division over last night. But there are so few Krauts around there they don't know it yet. So don't make any announcement—we'll keep it a secret until we see how it goes."

But he couldn't wait. That evening, he was again telephoning Bradley, this time at the top of his already unnaturally high voice. "Brad, for God's sake, tell the world we're across! We knocked down thirty-three Krauts today when they came after our pontoon bridges. I want the world to know that Third Army made it before Monty starts across."

But for Patton's sake, the world had already been told. At the morning 12th Army Group briefing, a Third Army representative had stated: "Without benefit of aerial bombing, ground smoke, artillery preparation, and airborne assistance, the Third Army at 2200 hours, Thursday evening, March 22nd, crossed the Rhine River."

That is, 23 hours before Montgomery was due to cross, with such assistance.

Shortly after, Bradley himself announced that the U.S. Army could cross the Rhine almost at will, almost anywhere, without air bombardment, and sometimes even without artillery. His subsequent criticism reveals the motive: "Had Monty crashed the river on the run as Patton had done, he might have averted the momentous effort required in that heavily publicised crossing."

In short, what was biting both Bradley and Patton was the heavy publicity. When the future of a continent was at stake, this may seem an oddly irrelevant outburst of professional jealousy. But publicity is more important in America than in Britain, and the whole affair sharply recalls the American General Mark Clark's action in Italy when he disobeyed the British General Alexander's orders and allowed a German army to escape from a British–American trap merely in order to seize the headlines for being first into Rome, an undefended city, albeit a most famous one.

The Patton–Bradley gambit at least had no unfavourable military effects, but regrettably no political point; the end of Patton's Rhine run was a compulsory halt, waiting for the Soviet to take over Central Europe.

Bradley's boast proved to be not quite correct. The "Romantic Rhine" was better defended and offered an imposing physical obstacle, the Rhine gorge, where the river has cut deeply into the rock so that the sides are high and steep. The Lorelei feature, for instance, is a mass of rocks rising 430 feet above the river level, with its base 76 feet below the river surface. The width of the Rhine at this point is only 650 feet, but nevertheless one is forced to admire the assault troops who placed the American flag on top of the rock.

Two assaults were made near Rhens on the night of March 24–25, and both failed, the few men who succeeded in crossing being withdrawn. An assault at Boppard succeeded, as did opposed crossings made at St. Goar and Oberwesel on the 25th. Nevertheless, one can only conjecture why they were ever carried out, because the narrow twisting valleys that lead down into the gorge were unsuitable for the deployment or even the passage of the mass of heavy vehicles that is a modern army. However, American generals were notoriously less careful of the lives of their men than the British generals, who, as junior officers in the First World War, had received an unforgettable lesson in appalling waste.

On March 26, the U.S. Seventh Army, part of the 6th Army Group, crossed at Worms, between Mainz and Mannheim, but took heavy casualties from shell and mortar fire;

they were not able to assault until some 10,000 rounds of counter-battery fire had been shot away in the space of little over half an hour. The last crossings of the Rhine were made by the French First Army near Speyer and Strasbourg. The preparations were pitifully inadequate and the losses heavy, but the objective, which was political and not military, was gained. This was to establish a French "presence" over the Rhine inside Germany, as a bargaining counter for the post-war period.

Important though this was for France, it was a minor matter compared to forestalling the Soviet on the Baltic at the gateway to Scandinavia, the ultimate objective of 21st Army Group's stage-managed crossing and the only one with a vital political aim as the prize. It was also the most critical as regards the time factor. Eisenhower was unique in his insistence on "broad front" policies of advance. The Russians were not sweeping into Europe on a broad front, with all the armies keeping step; instead, they were making their main drive for the politically most vital objectives—Berlin and the gateways to the Baltic. Their line bulged out here towards the west, leaving Czechoslovakia and Austria uncleared to the south-east, hundreds of miles in the rear of the Red armies driving for Berlin and the Elbe. Montgomery's real target was not the German Army, now a secondary matter, but the attainment of a geographical line that would deny to the Russians any further foothold in Europe.

CHAPTER TWENTY-FIVE

THE FLOOD PLAIN OF THE RHINE

Rheinberg to Rees: March 23–24

"But still the enemy parachutists fought back grimly," wrote the historian of the Lincolnshire Regiment.

"Snipers fired from first-floor windows, and Spandaus shot through loopholes made in the walls at ground level. Now the light was going fast, and the infantry and tanks went into the village in billows of smoke, punctuated by the orange flashes of the enemy 88's, and criss-crossed in all directions by lines of red tracer. It was a great and terrible spectacle."

So the 2nd Lincolns took Winnekendonk, the last village but one on the road to Xanten and the Rhine. That village and those few hours cost the battalion 87 officers and men—a tenth of their numbers, had they been at full strength. In this manner the British had had to fight every foot of the way to the Rhine.

And the Canadians also. The war diary of the Highland Light Infantry of Canada for March 6, the day of the attack on Xanten, noted:

"Weather—dull. Visibility—limited. Morale—poor—coys have taken heavy punishment and are all far below strength. Officer and NCO casualties were heavy."

The result of the bitter fighting on the British and Canadian front was that shattered towns and torn-up roads, half-cleared minefields and blown bridges stretched from the German border in the Reichswald to the banks of the Rhine. But, as we have seen, the vicissitudes of that battle had allowed the Ninth U.S. Army, also part of Montgomery's 21st Army Group, an almost uninterrupted run to the river near Rheinberg.

Indeed, the Americans had so little opposition in front of them, and the physical obstacles to a crossing seemed to them so small, that they thought an immediate assault over the

Rhine on the heels of the fleeing Germans would have succeeded. This did not suit Montgomery, who specialised in "set-piece" battles such as Alamein and the D-Day landings; and the Americans were told to wait.

In Montgomery's view, the area would allow only one division to be used, three weeks in advance of the planned date for the assault—March 31, soon after brought forward to March 24—and the unpredictable results might upset the carefully orchestrated battle he had been planning since December. There was in fact no hurry, because the Rhine itself at this point dictated the dates of attack by its flood record, and the 21 Army Group scheme was geared to that.

If an American division had got across and then had its bridges destroyed by one of the periodic floods, or otherwise got into trouble before the entire army group was ready to cross, a calamitous rescue operation would have had to be mounted. In the circumstances, with the war definitely won, it was hardly worth risking, militarily; apart from the risk of unnecessary casualties. The war correspondents might not mind; the widows would. Make it sure and keep the losses small, was no great error at this stage of the war.

Although Montgomery has been criticised for it, the 21 Army Group crossing had to be a "set-piece" assault, for three reasons: the topographical nature of the Rhine at that point; the type of battle that had preceded the approach to the Rhine by the British and Canadian armies; the quality and quantity of the opposition that the Germans were capable of offering to a crossing at that point.

The forces available to Montgomery also favoured the "set-piece." These included the specialised landing craft, amphibious vehicles, and amphibious (D.D.) tanks accumulated as a result of the D-Day landings; the great superiority, both in quality and quantity, of the British, Canadian, and American artillery over the German artillery; and the availability of a two-division airborne corps. Immense power could be harnessed to ensure rapid and certain success, provided a waiting period of two to three weeks was allowed in which to bring it forward and deploy it.

And, as will become apparent, an early and ill-organised assault at this point would almost certainly have failed; even if it had succeeded, thousands of men would have been killed and maimed who otherwise might have survived. The fact that a delay would enable the Germans also to bring up reinforcements mattered little, because Montgomery's resources were greater. On balance, a delay favoured the 21st Army Group most decidedly.*

Therefore, there was a pause, during which the whole front of the 21st Army Group was screened by smoke in order to aid the deception plan. That the attack was coming on the sector Rheinberg to Emmerich—from just north of the Ruhr to just south of Nijmegen—could not be concealed; and that Wesel, the best road and rail communications centre, must be the most vital objective was as obvious as the fact that London is the capital of England. All that could be achieved was to pretend that the frontage of the attack was longer than it in fact was, and so spread the German defenders unnecessarily thin.

Emmerich was threatened when in fact assault at Emmerich was ruled out by Montgomery on account of the pimple-shaped hill nearby on which the mediaeval village of Hochelten stands. In the basically flat flood plain of the Rhine delta, this feature commanded the whole of the Emmerich area back to the Reichswald. This deception was successful, and the German armoured reserves were stationed here. Montgomery had achieved one of his standard gambits—to put the enemy "off balance," while remaining himself "balanced."

It was also necessary to prevent German patrol activity across the Rhine, which might reveal the deception. The British measures were successful and the 2nd Lincolns, for instance, captured a complete patrol of 11 men from 7 Fallschirm Division. As the regimental historian wrote,

"This provided, together with other information already acquired, proof of the presence of the major part of the 1st

* This would be quite obvious, and it would be unnecessary to stress it, but for the fact that all the more superficial American writers on the subject have, willy-nilly, assumed that the Rhine itself was uniform along its entire length (which is like saying that the geology and scenery of the North American continent is uniform) and that because few German troops opposed Patton, there can have been few German troops opposite Montgomery. They merely assume it, they never bother to find out if it was so.

Parachute Army on our front—a fact of no small interest to the 51st (Highland) Division who were destined to carry out the crossing."

This German parachute army, together with the two armoured formations that were its reserve, represented almost the last best the Germans had. Why it opposed 21 Army Group and not Bradley and Patton may best be left to conjecture.

Patriotism did alter some of the details of Montgomery's plan. Originally, the assault was to have been made entirely by the British Second Army, with the Canadian First and the American Ninth crossing later in the pursuit role, the former into Holland. But the American commanders definitely objected, and it seems possible that someone in Canadian Army may have asked for representation. Whoever it was, it was certainly not the troops concerned. However, this time there were no dark suspicions of Montgomery's motives, or any belief that the British were trying to hog the "glory" of the assault, or any hypersensitive suspicions that omission equalled aspersion.

The Canadian Army was at least as good as the British Army and, in some respects notably the assault, probably better. It was left out because that pimple at Hochelten overlooked its sector. Therefore, the plan was very slightly amended to allow General Crerar to raid Emmerich if he thought fit, or even cross independently if he thought fit; and if he did not think fit—and of course he did not—then allowance was made for the Canadian Army to cross via the British bridges, turn left to take Emmerich and Hochelten from the far bank, and then build their own bridges at Emmerich. This was what actually happened.

To give Canada representation in the actual historic crossing, a Canadian Scottish brigade was attached to the British assault formation, the 51st (Highland) Division. A Canadian parachute battalion was due to drop with the British 6th Airborne Division in any case, which was to go in side-by-side with the 17th U.S. Airborne Division in any case, so there were no squabbles there. However, as Simpson's Ninth Army HQ did not like being left out of the assault, the front was reshuffled to allow them to attack at Rheinberg; but because Rheinberg did not count but Wesel, being the main communications centre, did, this was to be transferred to the Americans as soon as the British had secured an adequate bridgehead, for the passage of the bulk of the American forces.

In short, the whole army group line shuffled to the left, rather like a squad taking up their dressing by the right on the parade ground, with the Americans taking over part of the British sector in stages, and the Canadians extending the line left to Emmerich in theory only for the first stage, because this was the deception area, but in fact for the second stage.

Some aspects of war may well be like chess, but not where senior Allied commanders, egged on by their home editors, are concerned; in chess, the senior pieces cannot talk back. Of course, no one cared to enquire of the pawns whether or not they appreciated the honour of leading the historic assault—or they might have got a very dusty answer.*

The "star" of the Rhine crossing was in fact the river itself. British and Canadian engineers had been studying the topography, hydrology, and history of their section of the Rhine—Ruhr–Nijmegen—since early October, 1944. Firstly, with the winter in view, and then with the spring campaign in mind.

The history of the Rhine in the delta area was complicated and disputed. The river had changed its course a number of times, not merely in geological time but in historical time. One of these changes had occurred about A.D. 150 (late Roman times) and another about A.D. 1275 (mediaeval), although archaeological evidence since discovered points to a somewhat earlier date, of around 1200. In most cases a loop of the river

* So much has been made of these sheer, screaming trivialities by previous writers, that some mention had to be made; in particular, one has even alleged that Montgomery's plan was for the Americans to build all the bridges. With the British and Canadian Engineer plans in front of me, I cannot imagine how this idea got about, except by quoting Max Gissen's note on an American work of military history: "I would expect the dullness of the thing, cranked out as it was by an academic hack, but I was quite unprepared for its show of ignorance."

had been cut off and abandoned, the Rhine tending to straighten somewhat. These old loops of the Rhine, of varying ages, were now marshes or winding lakes occurring on both sides of the river, on the approaches to the near bank and also on the approaches to the far bank. Large-scale maps show them clearly, but not the maps one can normally include in books of this or similar format; and therefore it has tended not to be realised that to talk of a "Rhine crossing" in this area meant in fact crossing, or better still going round, many older Rhines, which made the approaches to the present Rhine bad or impossible going to vehicles of any sort, let alone the extremely heavy impedimenta of a modern army.

It is possible that this erratic behaviour of the river in the low-lying delta area (a former seabed) was due to later but slighter changes in sea-level, as the dates tie up with coastal inundations elsewhere. This is hardly surprising, because the Rhine is fed at source by mountain snow melts, a basic cause of alterations in sea-level, and in its lower, flatter reaches would inevitably be affected by the results of a rising or falling sea-level, but more especially by the former.

And, of course, in the long term what the river was doing was carrying down sediment from its upper reaches to deposit them in its lower reaches, thus helping to create the flat lands of Holland and the neighbouring areas of Germany. Here, the Rhine is not very deep, averaging only about 10 to 15 feet according to statistics, but it is wide—normally about 1,000 feet (at Cologne 360 metres, at Düsseldorf 310 metres, at Emmerich 400 metres).

Its peculiarity is that in times of flood, that simple average of 1,000 feet in width suddenly increases to as much as three miles in width. Similarly, the current speed varies from a mere two to a full five and one-half knots. The latter figure can best be appreciated by thinking of a solid wall of water moving at a speed twice that of man walking briskly. The force exerted by only two knots of moving water roughly equals that of the wind force of a hurricane. The river at full speed may be roughly considered as applying to bridges, pontoon or otherwise, and to rafts and to boats, a force three times more powerful than a hurricane. Any army attempting to cross when the river reached its peak speed or width was bound to be foiled; and if a sudden flood occurred when the crossing was actually underway, with everything depending on the anchors of the frail pontoon bridges, then catastrophe was in sight. In short, although in normal conditions the Rhine was only a medium-difficult obstacle, from the purely physical point of view, it was as potentially treacherous as a known hurricane area in the hurricane season.

The crossing of the Rhine by a handful of men in a few rubber boats would be no great feat; but modern armies are like juggernauts, and therefore it was with the approaches to the Rhine that the engineers were principally concerned. It is difficult to construct a bridge to which no approach roads lead, and pointless to construct a bridge where there are no good exits on the other side.

A modern division consists of a small body of fighting troops—around 3,000 men—out of a total number of about 15,000–20,000. Some of the 3,000 walk; the rest ride. But only a tiny proportion of the vehicles are personnel carriers, because a modern army has to be self-contained, and this means carrying along in vehicles the food supplies, the fuel supplies, the ammunition supplies, the bridging supplies, the workshops, the hospitals, the administrative centres, the concert parties, the newspaper and radio representatives, the graves registration units, dentists, and Lord knows what else; and at corps, army, and army group levels there are additional units, many of them farmed out as required to divisions for specific tasks.

All this quite apart from the armoured fighting vehicles, the armoured self-propelled guns, the towed guns, the tank-transporters, and so on, which move behind the few thousand walking troops of the leading infantry companies.

A Russian army of the time was not like this; it was a human sea, all mixed up with animals and carts and a few Lend-Lease American trucks, sweeping forward across the countryside, living on the countryside, and not bothering even to bury, let alone mark the graves, of its own dead. As for informing the relatives; well, the Russians don't like paperwork.

But the Western nations insist on such things, and even with these complications the mobility of their armies did give them a crucial advantage, in 1945, over both the German

Army and, if it came to the pinch, the Red Army. Unfortunately, this is no longer the case, as the Russians have modernised, too, but it was so then. Therefore, the crossing of the Rhine, anywhere, was not so much the problem of assault, as of the construction of adequately robust roads and bridges and the regulation of traffic.

The peculiarity of the 21st Army Group sector of assault was that there were considerable physical obstacles, not to the assault itself, but to the traffic on the approaches. It is, naturally, absolutely impossible for the average newspaper reader or TV-watcher to conceive of an army group advance in any terms other than that of yelling heroes brandishing bayonets, because this is the newsworthy bit, that also chimes with their boyhood reading matter. As the actual assault-crossing, being motorised, would occupy no more than four minutes, whereas the build-up and break-out from the bridgehead could take up to a week, and the building of semi-permanent bridges up to three months, this is a distressingly naïve view of the affair. For those more interested in the techniques of river-crossing, however, it will be well to quote the engineer appreciation of the problems of spring assault.

"On each side of the river are low lying areas forming the flood plain. Natural flooding is contained within a flood bed by a system of dykes. The surface of the flood bed is pasture land with a clay surface on sand and gravel. It is intersected by innumerable ditches and by abandoned meanders of the river. Some of the latter have stretches of stagnant water and others consist of peat bog. These form obstacles to cross-country movement. At abnormally high river levels the entire flood bed is under water. Flooding occurs after either heavy rainfall has swolled the Rhine and its tributaries, or a period of frost and heavy snow. In the latter case the flood reaches its peak approximately three weeks after the thaw has set in. The dyke system consists of the following: (a) Low Banks enclosing open polders; (b) Summer Dykes about one foot above summer high water level (these run along the edge of the normal river course and have easily sloping faces); (c) Winter Dykes about 6 to 10 feet high which are normally sufficient to contain the winter floods; (d) Main Dykes, about 10 to 16 feet high with sides sloping at approximately 30 degrees, which are designed to control the fullest extent of flooding (they are continuous on each side of the river in the area between the Ruhr and Nijmegen). Breaches of these main dykes could result in very extensive flooding of the flood plain."

This was the appreciation on which Montgomery's careful plans were based. It proved to be defective in one respect only.

"The winter 1944 to 1945 had been true to form. There had been two major floods, which reached their peak level on 30 November and 17 February. Luckily, the thaw came sufficiently early to allow the floods to subside before Operation PLUNDER (the ground side of the Rhine crossing) was launched. The weather during March was good, with the result that the flood plain and winter flood bed dried out quickly. Excellent air cover and maps were available for planning, and the merits of possible assault crossing sites were readily assessed. First Canadian Army and Ninth United States Army cleared up to the West bank of the Rhine from Neuss to Nijmegen by 11 March, and it was decided that the assault across the river would take place on 24 March. A postponement of up to five days would be accepted if weather delayed the airborne operation. The only serious difficiency in engineer intelligence had been the lack of an accurate cross-section of the river bed. Some, over fifty years old, had been obtained, but proved to be inaccurate. The deepest part of the river was, in fact, ten feet deeper than expected. This was immaterial in the assault crossing, but subsequently necessitated the use of spliced and extra long piles in the construction of the semi-permanent bridges."

To further destroy the public picture of an army group commander as a modern Marshal Ney waving his men on to the attack in person with a glittering sword, the decisive decision by Montgomery, based on a SHAEF estimate of supply tonnages of 540 tons per day per division, was to order the construction, in order to cross the Rhine, of eight more bridges over the Maas. In short, in order to bridge the Rhine, further bridging operations had to take place over a major river in the rear of the crossing-sites; and, further, since there were many small rivers ahead on the northern route on the other side of the Rhine, provision had to be made to bridge these also.

Indeed, the British built more bridges between the Rhine and the Baltic than they did between Normandy and the Rhine. They were mostly small, but they consumed bridging material, and that material had to be available in the rear and then brought forward at the right time. Despite the newspapers and television, war always has been like this. The really exciting bits are only a small part of the whole, affect very few men, and most soldiers are merely workmen, technicians, and clerks.

This was to be brought home to me in person, because, as a hitherto non-fighting cog of supreme unimportance, doing a decidedly dreary and boring job, I was able to get up to the battles of the Rhine and the Neder Rijn and appreciate something of the immense effort on the part of the non-combatant troops that is, was, and probably always will be the major part of an operation of war.

With the benefit of the latest briefings, the up-to-the-minute large-scale operation maps in the operations room, our own order of battle in detail and the enemy's order of battle so far as currently known, I was further able to appreciate how little the ordinary soldier sees of the immense canvas of events unfolding around him.

I was also able to appreciate perfectly that up at the "sharp end," a war in progress looks rather like a butcher's shop, and that this moved me far less than stumbling on the odd, unburied corpse left over from the battles of the previous year. It was undeniably exciting, but also most serious; and I still believe that the best short summary ever made was that of the American Civil War general who mused: "It is as well that war should be so terrible, or men might get to like it too much."

In one respect it is true that the 21 Army Group planners had over-estimated the size of the German forces that would oppose a Rhine crossing, because these estimates were made in January, 1945, before it was clear that the Germans would stage their biggest effort on the west bank of the Rhine, in the

Reichswald, and before the capture of Remagen bridge by the Americans, which was to divert further reinforcements from the dwindling German reserves.

Both the Reichswald and Remagen contributed substantially. In January, it had been estimated that, apart from the German field army, some 58,000 German troops would be available to man static defences along the Rhine. On March 15, this estimate was written down to only 30,000 men, apart from the field army.

When the time for the crossing came, the German field army opposing 21 Army Group consisted of 13 divisions, mostly good ones: between Cologne and Essen—four infantry divisions; between Essen and Emmerich—four parachute divisions and three infantry divisions; and in reserve north-east of Emmerich—one panzer and one panzer grenadier division. It was estimated that the Germans on this section of the Rhine deployed 720 field guns, and that some 114 heavy and 712 light anti-aircraft guns were available, mostly in and around the Ruhr, and these, being dual-purpose, could be moved up for use in a ground role, as many of them in fact were.

The Ninth U.S. Army was to make its assault at Rheinberg, largely for prestige purposes and the pleasing of home editors, although this was now dignified by the role of "protection of the right flank of Second Army." But as soon as the British had secured a sufficiently deep bridgehead at Wesel, all American bridging was to be concentrated there, and this would then become the main axis for Ninth Army. The British Second Army was to assault Wesel, Xanten, and Rees, and build bridges at Xanten and Rees.

The First Canadian Army were to pretend to be about to cross at Emmerich, hold securely the immensely long river-lines of the Rhine, Waal, and Maas down to the sea, and when Emmerich had fallen to assault from the bridgehead on the far bank, to centre their bridging operations on Emmerich, preparatory to swinging left into Holland for an assault-crossing of the Ijssel and the capture of Arnhem, after which they would bridge the Neder Rijn at Arnhem for an advance to the Zuyder Zee (i.e., the objectives of the ill-fated Market Garden operation of September, 1944, although the axis of advance would be that of the successful German attack of May 10, 1940).

The Second Army was ultimately directed towards the Baltic and Berlin, the Ninth Army was to seal off the Ruhr, and the really vital early objectives were Wesel and Bocholt. These would be the keys to open the route to the Baltic.

It would be anything but an unopposed crossing. For example, Horrocks' XXX Corps, which shared the initial assault in Second Army with XII Corps, consisted at this time of three British infantry divisions, one Canadian infantry division, and the Guards Armoured Division. They would be opposed by 8 Parachute Division, parts of 6 and 7 Parachute divisions, supported by the German armoured reserve—15 Panzer Grenadier Division and 116 Panzer Division.

In an assault river-crossing, as indeed in most attacks, the accepted best technique is to attack in column, and not on a "broad front." The initial assault would be carried out by a single division, and the success of the operation in part depended on bridging the river quickly and so being able to pour across the rest of the "column," which, pencil-like, would drive clean through the enemy before he could concentrate sufficient force to stop them.

The chances of success in this instance would have been negligible, had it been merely division against division, for the problems were not dissimilar to those involved in the D-Day landings; and the same solutions were used. The basic idea was to harass and confuse the enemy so that he could not concentrate sufficient force in time to stop the establishment of a secure bridgehead. The methods boiled down to air power, artillery, and airborne divisions.

In Phase I, the air forces isolated the Ruhr; in Phase II they isolated the battle area; in Phase III they bombed the battle area for the three days prior to the crossing; and in Phase IV they attacked German airfields and flak positions on the day of the crossing, kept the area clear of enemy fighters and bombers, blew Wesel to pieces with 277 heavy bombers, and supplied the invaluable Typhoons for close support.

The artillery programme, which was to begin at 1700 hours on March 23, was to be fired by 600 American and 1,300 British and Canadian guns. The first part of the programme was counter-battery, with special emphasis on knocking out the German flak batteries for the benefit of the airborne troops; followed by a drenching fire on the German infantry positions.

The leading units of the assault divisions would cross at 2100 hours and half-way through the following morning, when the German flak should have been quietened somewhat and the Germans would be bringing up their reserves and making various counter-moves, the two airborne divisions comprising XVIII U.S. Airborne Corps would drop onto the enemy's rear areas, within range of British artillery support, and make his disorganisation total.

This novelty in the use of airborne divisions clearly owed a great deal to the awful lessons of Arnhem. The Luftwaffe appreciation of Arnhem had indeed forcast in almost exact detail the nature of the next Allied airborne attack:

"Objectives for airborne troops must not be as far from the front lines as Arnhem was; instead of spreading a landing over three days, it should preferably be completed in one day, with forces concentrated as much as possible; another such full-scale assault is to be expected, the lessons of Arnhem being utilised to produce more concentrated landings."

What the Germans did not expect was that the airborne landings, instead of being synchronised with the assault of the ground forces, would take place half a day later. That was playing safe with a vengeance; but it would also come as a surprise and at a time and place most awkward for the Germans, as well as being the most expedient time as far as the German flak position was concerned. Even so, this daylight drop was to make Arnhem look like a Sunday picnic. The trouble was, of course, the immediate availability of flak guns from the formidable defences of the Ruhr, tuned to concert pitch after five years of fighting R.A.F. Bomber Command.

But guns were a Montgomery speciality, and this time, including the light pieces which added a "pepperpot" to the bombardment, he had about 4,000; the heavier guns being radar-directed. Gunner Ted Reeve, formerly sports columnist of the *Toronto Telegram*, had already commented on this fact, as well as giving a lifelike impression of authentic British Army dialogue.

"The further we go the more we realize how Monty loves an artillery set-up. Any time he can manage it he packs in the guns"[wrote Gunner Reeve for the *Maple Leaf,* adding:] "Get more than three Limey soldiers together at any time and one of them will be an amateur Tommy Trinder or Max Miller. It was all very jolly anyway to hear them on the 2 a.m. shift yelling:

'Hie there, Sawgent Grigg, what are you firing from that gun now, fresh air?'

'Keep a civil f———g tongue in your head, Bombardier Pawsley, and don't forget to put something in the breech this time.'

'We shall be ready to fire again in three minutes St. Panacras Time, Sawgent!'

'Right, Bombardier Pawsley, shall I start counting now or will you let me know at the minit hinterval?'

Then somebody would whistle a few bars of *Underneath the Arches* or *The Anniversary Waltz* with the tune carrying good through the dark wet air, and all of a sudden—wham—guns open up for miles around."

On March 23, at zero hour, it was like that, only more so. "The noise was so terrific that conversation in Battalion Headquarters became almost impossible," complained the historian of the Lincolns. "Our targets were pre-selected and the guns lost the paint from their barrels," recollected R. G. Saunders, then with 103 Regiment R.A. Mobile Radar Site. "Well behind us were big guns, in front an S.P. was having a go. An hour later I was off duty and couldn't go to my hole to sleep, the noise was too much."

All the previous day, motor transport convoys had been passing through Nijmegen nose-to-tail, and I had been astounded to see tank-transporters carrying assault landing craft, with navy men sitting on them, playing guitars, and grinning at our amazement. The actual crossing was to be literally like D-Day, carried out mainly by armoured and armed amphibious craft, not frail storm boats or rubber dinghies with paddles.

All day on March 23, there had been gunfire, mixed with the noise of bomber and Typhoon formations; and this was reciprocated shortly after sunset by numbers of German reconnaissance aircraft dropping flares over Nijmegen and the main routes out of it, MAPLE LEAF and RUBY. But the noise of tank convoys roaring along the roads to the Rhineland sometimes drowned the sound of the German aircraft engines. At any one instant, hundreds of tracer shells from the Bofors guns were streaking up the night sky, so that when Montgomery's bombardment began, the thunder of continuous gunfire ran along the Rhine for almost 50 miles, from Nijmegen to the Ruhr.

In the American assault sector, eight miles long, 1,500 bombers attacked German airfields, and American guns fired 65,000 shells in 60 minutes. On March 24, at 0200, the U.S. 30th Division was to put three battalions across as the first waves of its three regiments; at 0300, the U.S. 79th Division was to put two of its three regiments across. The total casualties in the initial assault waves of these two divisions amounted to 31 killed and wounded.

Apart from 1 Commando Brigade, which was to assault Wesel at 2200 hours on March 23 after the night bombers had dropped more than a thousand tons of bombs on the town, the British assault was a Scottish affair. XXX Corps nominated two brigades of 51 (Highland) Division to assault on the left at 2100 hours on March 23, while XII Corps ordered 15 (Scottish) Division to attack on the right at 0200 hours on March 24. Attached to the 51st as follow-up was the Canadian 9th (Highland) Brigade.

The two assault brigades of the Highland Division were 153 and 154 and they were ferried across in Buffaloes of 30 Armoured Brigade. These were tracked, armoured, armed amphibious vehicles. Their ferry service began at 2100 hours on March 23, 23 hours after Patton had crossed far to the south, and in 154 Brigade their first customers were the 1st and 7th battalions of the Black Watch, followed by the 7th Argyll and Sutherland Highlanders. The 1st Battalion of the Highland Light Infantry of Canada, attached to 154 brigade in order to secure Canadian representation in the river-crossing, went over at 0400 hours on March 24.

Losses were light, just as they had been in Normandy on D-Day, except on one American beach where the assault was made by men instead of machines. A properly conducted beach assault or river-crossing should in fact result in only slight casualties; the losses occur when the real battle begins. That is, when the enemy has identified the areas of penetration and has brought up his reserves to meet them.

Affairs like Winston Churchill's adventure at Gallipoli are unusual and were not likely to be repeated because the British soldiery had had enough of his wild gambles with other men's lives. Whatever may have been Montgomery's faults, he had started his initial climb to fame on the right lines—by refusing to obey Churchill's order to attack at Alamein before he was certain of success and forcing Churchill to accept that refusal. The Prime Minister was indeed present at this crossing of the Rhine, but fortunately he had had no hand in its planning and execution. Militarily, he was rather like a George Patton, but without Patton's sense for the battle and flair for picking the weak spot.

Just like a coastal assault, a river-crossing is essentially a struggle to build up a bridgehead faster than the enemy can bring in troops to corral it off or wipe it out; and the losses therefore normally occur later, inside the bridgehead during the build-up phase. How severe this struggle would be, in the case of the Rhine, depended on the success of the air, artillery, and airborne strikes on the German rear areas; and on such a long front, this was bound to be variable.

Although the quality of the static troops was poor—many were elderly Home Guards of the Volkssturm—the German field army was a good one, and the parachute regiments were particularly good; they fought heroically, and, of course, skilfully, not always the same thing. Parties held on in the ruins of Wesel and Rees for longer than had been expected, considering the preliminary punishment they had taken, and caused delay to the bridging and rafting operations that should have taken place at these points. While at most points the defenders had either been obliterated or rendered hopelessly "bomb happy" and incapable of serious resistance, on the left of the American sector and on the left of the British sector, aided by favourable open ground, some German units remained intact and in the last defence of their homeland put up a fight that, for once, may truly be described as "fanatical."

It was 154 Brigade of the Highland Division that, after a fast and easy crossing on the British left, bumped into serious trouble in two towns lying back from the river, Speldrop and Bienen. The Black Watch were driven back from Speldrop, less two companies cut off inside the town, which very shortly ran out of ammunition but refused to surrender. The Highland Light Infantry of Canada were launched to their aid and experienced their toughest fighting since Normandy, where the battalion had been virtually wiped out. They had also lost heavily in the Reichswald, but had now been rested and brought up to strength. The entry in the war diary for March 23 concluded: "Weather—clear, warm. Vis—unlimited. Morale—100 per cent."

Point company of the H.L.I. was B Company, commanded by Major J. King; and 12 Platoon, led by Sergeant Cornelius Jerome Riedel, was point platoon of the company. And point man of the point platoon of the leading company was Private Malcolm B. Buchanan of Kapuskasing, Ontario, acting as number one of the section Bren gun mounted in the bows of the assault boat.

"The whole sky seemed to light up as the guns commenced firing" [he wrote]. "At 0400 hours we were scheduled to cross. On coming down to get into the boat assigned to my section, I almost ran over a newsreel cameraman, who was taking pictures of the men as they came down the bank. As number one of the Bren, my position was in the front of the boat. At that point the river looked awfully wide, foggy and lonesome. I asked the operator of our boat why we had been singled out to have our pictures taken. 'You,' he said, 'will be the first man to hit the shore. How do you like *that*?' Well, to tell the truth, that answer kind of stunned me. Here I was loaded down like a horse. I thought, *'Boy! How am I going to move fast?'* We had been told it might take some time before our vehicles got across the river, so we had to take enough food and ammo for two days. In addition to my regular load of Bren gun and mags, I had 48-hours rations, 8 bandoliers of ammo, six '36' grenades, 1 anti-tank mine, 1 blanket, I shovel and 2 water-bottles (1 water and 1 liberated fluid). As the boat pushed off for the other shore, I thought that every other man probably felt the same as I did. My number two man, Percy Wagg, said he did, anyway. While the shells screamed overhead and exploded on the other bank, we roared across wide open. Although it was about a four-minute crossing, it seemed like an hour."

Corporal Sam Dearden of Brownsville, Ontario, was in the fourth H.L.I. vehicle to cross in one of the Buffaloes.

"Bulldozers cut through the earth embankments and the way was open for the water-buffaloes, as we called the amphibious craft" [he recollected]. "The area behind us was flat farm land and it was starting to get daylight as I loaded the command carrier and six 6-pounder anti-tank guns aboard them, plus six gun-towing carriers. As I moved towards the opening German shells hit a vehicle behind me. There were many good-sized shells falling in the water and around. The lieutenant in charge of the craft asked me to man the weapon on the right hand side, a 20-mm cannon. As I sat up there looking at the Armada of craft crossing the Rhine, the Lieutenant commented, 'Better wear your steel hat.' I said, 'From the size of the shells falling near, I'm afraid it would be of little use.' We arrived at the other side with very few losses. We quickly hooked guns and vehicles together, and moved out into the fields. We were none too soon, as heavy fire was poured into the bridgehead we had just left. But we were safe and dug-in. A few hundred yards inland we came upon a tank that had hit a mine. It was amphibious and manned by men of the Royal Marine Commandos. They were busy getting a track back on it, to get it back in action. Infantry was spread out in front, while the enemy had tanks and an S.P. out in front. The commandoes made repairs to the tank and, nosing back into action, after less than quarter-of-a-mile it was hit in the side by a mine fired off a trip wire. It broke the driver's legs and the tank caught fire. They later passed me, carrying the driver in a blanket. They said to me, 'Goodbye, Canada, we done our bit,' and headed back for the bridgehead. There were now many planes in the air, flying over carrying paratroops, and gliders in a great steady procession."

Buchanan with 12 Platoon was out in front of the carrier-towed anti-tank guns of the battalion.

"On hitting the bank we had been told to spread out and move in. Sergeant Tuttle, who was in my boat, moved us inland about 50 yards, where we went to ground in some shell and 'Jerry-dug holes.' When all the Regiment was across, we moved inland under an artillery barrage to our assembly area. On the way, and in the area, we picked up a few prisoners, many of whom were 'bomb happy.' None of these prisoners had any fight left in them. We stayed in our area for several hours, taking the opportunity to eat and sleep. We saw paratroopers drop to the south of us, which made us feel a lot better. Around noon Major King came up with a roll of maps under one arm and a tommy gun under the other. As he approached, we saw a big smile on his face, which caused one of the men to comment, 'If Major King looks that happy, they must have dug up something real nasty for us to do.' We found out soon enough."

It was to take Speldrop and relieve the two companies of the Black Watch, which had been cut off by a German counter-attack launched with determined infantry, tanks, and self-propelled guns.

Meanwhile, the paratroops were not having a very good time, and the gliders of the airlanding brigades were being shot to pieces. But, again, the lessons of Arnhem had been learned. Both British Typhoons and American Mustangs were not only on call, but more than adequate arrangements had been made this time to control them from the ground, so that the air-land battles were fully integrated and not just private wars.

Sergeant Leo R. Gariepy, who had spearheaded the Canadian assault on June beach in Normandy in an amphibious (D.D.) tank of 6 Canadian Armoured Regiment, and also taken part in the seaborne assault on Walcheren, part of the battle to clear the approaches to Antwerp, was chosen as a specialist in D.D. tanks. By removing the breech of the 75-millimeter gun and clearing the turret, space was made for the specialist wireless sets used to communicate with the Typhoons. Of the crew, only Gariepy and his driver remained; the other places were taken by a wing commander of the R.A.F. and a leading aircraftman to operate the radio. The only armament the tank now had was Gariepy's collection of personal weapons—revolver, tommy gun, and liberated Mauser rifle, which he kept "for personal shooting of snipers."

The wing commander was delighted with his mobile, amphibious, armoured command post; and the only question was, the Rhine current at Rees being faster than the speed of the D.D. tank, could Gariepy get it across and ashore in the right place near Rees? Gariepy went up and inspected the place before the assault, noted the groins and jetties jutting out from the far bank at intervals, and was convinced that he could cross the current at an angle and touch ground beside a jetty, out of the main current stream. This sounds very simple, but quite a number of real D.D. tanks fitted with guns failed to manage it or landed where the far bank was too steep or too muddy to climb.

Gariepy chose his own exit point on the near bank, and wrote briefly,

"We did not have too much difficulty in making the other shore, some 80 yards obliquely from our dunking. The Wing Commander then got in touch with his squadron and told them of being across on the enemy shore. Targets were picked here and there, and we had a grandstand show of what the rockets could do. Afterwards, we moved as far as Munster, not firing a single shot, because we could not. But the Wing Commander was enjoying himself like a little boy; he said this was the best observation post he could have had—we could get so close to the targets."

Indeed, Gariepy had more trouble getting back to the Rhine afterwards, with what was still a secret tank, than from the Germans, once 21 Army Group had broken out of its Rhine bridgehead. The hammering from accurately directed Typhoons served to break initially dangerous German resistance to the airborne forces, although it could have no effect in Speldrop, where H.L.I., Black Watch, and German paratroopers were fighting each other, literally, from a range of a few feet.

CHAPTER TWENTY-SIX

"LOOK, THE AIRBORNE DIVISION!"

Air Drop over the Rhine: March 24

Distressingly, just as an army advance is basically a traffic problem and a river-crossing basically a bridging and rafting problem, so even the dramatic arrival of soldiers from the sky is mainly an air marshalling and organisation problem. The airborne side of the Rhine crossing, Operation Varsity, was, wrote General Gavin, "the most complex simultaneous airborne-troop carrier life of the war." This is best realised by considering first the end product—the delivery to the German-held areas just in the rear of the Rhine of 17,222 soldiers, 614 jeeps, 286 guns and mortars, and hundreds of tons of fuel, food, and ammunition in the space of some two hours.

One-half of the combined procession, the American, was two hours and eighteen minutes long; that is, it took that space of time for the massed formations of troop transports and gliders to pass a single given point. A general who, by using his brains, could shorten this time by, say 15 minutes had made a critical contribution to victory. And ever since Arnhem—five days to deliver one division—the decision had been made to make the landings both as rapid and as concentrated as possible, and close enough to the ground troops to be within gun range of the medium artillery.

Overall planning was the responsibility of General Brereton's First Allied Airborne Army, and the assault force was designated XVIII U.S. Airborne Corps, commanded by the American Major-General Matthew B. Ridgway, with the British Major-General R. N. Gale as his deputy. This formation was placed under the command of the British Second Army for the operation. It consisted of the comparatively inexperienced 17th U.S. Airborne Division, commanded by Major-General William Miley, and the experienced 6th

British Airborne Division, commanded by Major-General E. L. Bols. The parachute troops flew in American transports of IX Troop Carrier Command, while the airlanding troops flew in British gliders towed by British aircraft of 38 and 46 groups, R.A.F.

The American division when airborne consisted of 913 transports and tugs and 906 Hadrian gliders; the British division of 683 transports and tugs and 444 Hamilcar and Horsa gliders—a total of 1,596 aircraft and 1,350 gliders, of which the British component would start from 11 airfields in England, the American component from 15 airfields in France, to merge together in a single operation, side by side, just over the Rhine. A supply mission was to be flown within two hours by 120 American Liberators. In addition, the battlefield and neighbouring German airfields were to be attacked by more than 3,000 bombers, while more than 5,000 fighters would protect the armada and attack ground targets. That is, some 11,000 aircraft and gliders, mostly in mass formations, would be travelling to and from the target in a matter of a few hours.

It was the last great airborne operation of the war, and one of the most costly. Fourteen Liberators and 53 transports never came back, while 440 transports were badly damaged. Glider losses were much heavier. About 100 British glider pilots were killed, of whom 60 were R.A.F. men who had hoped to fly fighters or bombers and were not very enthusiastic about the "matchboxes." Unlike the Americans, who did not use their glider pilots in combat, the British had hitherto insisted on the pilots being army personnel—trained soldiers—expected to fight on the ground, but Arnhem had taken a very heavy toll and the R.A.F. men filled the gaps.

The gliders presented an especially difficult marshalling problem in the air, and this was the last time they were ever to be used on operations. The marshalling was difficult anyway, because the two airborne divisions started from 26 different airfields in two different countries, and the armada, in Gavin's words, "contained at least five elements of different characteristics and speed." Timing was rendered even more critical by the stubborn fact that a tug aircraft towing a glider had one fixed speed, variable only by a few miles per hour either way. It could not slow down, nor could it speed up. R. S. Trout, then a flight sergeant flying a Stirling tug of 38 Group and towing a Horsa glider containing men of 12 Devons, commented:

"You were too near stalling speed to slow down, while opening the throttles made the tow dangerously violent without increasing speed more than a few m.p.h. Cross-country exercises, therefore, were not only map-reading practices but often involved deliberately early arrival at a given point so that tug-pilot and navigator could work out a slow turn to use up exactly the excess minutes and seconds. The immense importance of timing will be realised in considering the hundreds of combinations in the glider trains of the big operations, squadrons taking off from different airfields and, in the case of the Rhine Crossing, from different countries."

For the planners, the variables arose from the fact that the American transports were of two different types, the old C-47s and the newer and faster C-46s; and that there were three types of glider, including the monster Hamilcar, which could only be towed by a Halifax bomber, and many types of tug aircraft, all of them under-powered for the job, with a towing speed of about 140 miles per hour.

The glider got airborne at about 70 miles per hour, so that on take-off it rose above the tug, struggling for altitude at a speed that meant a certain stall if one engine cut out, and inexperienced glider pilots would occasionally fly wing-tip to wing-tip with the tug or, worse, try to help the tug by increasing the glider's altitude, which pulled up the tail of the tug at the moment when the tugpilot was trying to get his nose up. Pilots who had survived enemy fire to earn decorations died in this manner at the hands of helpful glider pilots. The British bombers used as tugs had most of their armament removed to save weight, and the value of what remained was problematical, if German fighters got in among them. On the Rhine crossing, none did.

While the world's first assault by glider-borne troops at Eben Emael on May 10, 1940, had involved a stealthy long-distance motorless flight at dawn by 11 small gliders carrying seven or eight men each, the world's last glider attack was

JOHN WILSON
21 Independent Company, 1 Airborne Division.

SGT JAMES CRAMER
Royal Ulster Rifles, 6 Airborne Division.

M. B. BUCHANAN
H.L.I. of Canada.

SGT P. T. ROBINSON, DCM
2 Grenadier Guards, Guards Armoured Division.

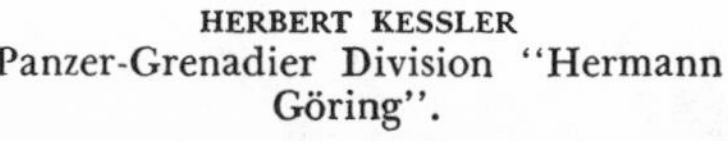

HERBERT KESSLER
Panzer-Grenadier Division "Hermann Göring".

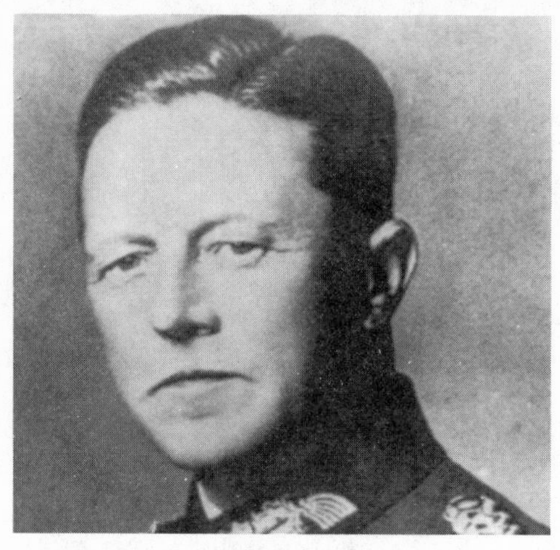

Generalleutnant Graf Sponeck, commander of 22 Airlanding Division, 1940.

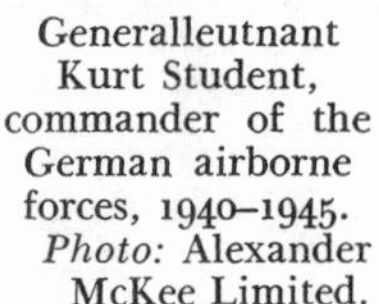

Generalleutnant Kurt Student, commander of the German airborne forces, 1940–1945. *Photo:* Alexander McKee Limited.

AUTHOR driving motorboat in Neder Rijn, 1952.

carried out by 1,350 gliders, some large enough to hold howitzers and tanks, arriving in full daylight in the middle of the morning in the middle of a battle. The concepts were totally different, because while the German experiment had involved landing key personnel—specially trained engineers—to demolish key parts of a key fortification, the Rhine landings on March 24, 1945, constituted a mass assault by storm troops. The rapier and the bludgeon, in other words.

But, given that 1945 was not 1940, and that the enemy, instead of being an unsuspecting neutral, was thoroughly expert in the techniques of airborne landings, and that there was no key point that would cause the fall of all the rest, this probably was the best solution of how to use existing airborne resources. As Gavin wrote,

"The enemy situation was more favourable than it had been for some time. Their units were taking special precautions against an airborne assault. Gunners had to sleep at their posts at all times. Selected and specially organised anti-airborne forces were covering all likely drop and landing areas."

The target, broadly speaking, was the German gun area on the hills and in the woods behind Wesel, which was the key point of the river-crossing. As with the ground troops, the Americans would be on the right and the British would be on the left. All landed correctly, except for one American regiment. The techniques, both for paratroops and gliders, were different from those of Arnhem and other previous operations where time had been lost by concentrating at a rendezvous after landing and before moving off for objectives, some of them many miles away. Now, the units would land in concentrated tactical groups on or very near their objectives and go straight for them without further ado.

Just like an old-style battle, Waterloo or the Crimea, the Rhine crossing produced a crop of grandstanders, all of whom were warned, "Don't miss the big event—airborne drop starting punctually 10 a.m." Latecomers missed it, because the star attraction started nine minutes early, at 0951 hours on March 24. Gazers ranged from Winston Churchill (an embarrassment to Montgomery's staff), through General Gavin and the

Y.M.C.A. to a lieutenant from my own unit. I, an underprivileged walker, had to be content with a visit to a quiet sector of the Rhine on the fringes of the big operation, able only to note that *this* time the Tactical Air Force Typhoons were being used to the full.

General Gavin undoubtedly had the best ringside seat because, his division not being involved, he was free to take an aircraft and fly along with the armada, keeping station some 2,000 feet above.

"It was a new experience to fly an airborne mission but not jump it" [he wrote]. "It was an indescribably impressive sight. Three columns, each nine ships or double-tow gliders across, moved on the Rhine. On the far side of the river it was surprisingly dusty and hazy, no doubt caused by the earlier bombing and artillery fire. On the near (west) bank of the Rhine clearly visible were panel letters to guide the troop-carrier pilots. Yellow smoke was also being used near the panels. It was hard to see how any pilot could make a serious navigational error. The air armada continued on and crossed the river. Immediately it was met by, what seemed to me, a terrific amount of flak. A number of ships and gliders went down in flames and after delivering their troops, a surprising number of troop-carrier pilots we saw on their way back were flying planes that were afire. The crew I was with counted twenty-three ships burning in sight at one time. But the incoming pilots continued on their courses undeterred by the awesome spectacle ahead of them."

Thus the expert, in the ringside seat. Near Gennep on the Maas, where the Germans had taken the bridge with an armoured train in 1940, many new bridges were being built to support the thrust across the North German plain, and the great dumps of bridging material for the Rhine itself were being completed. Y.M.C.A. Mobile Canteen No. 699, staffed by Margaret E. Chettle and Marjorie Whiteside, had been over into Germany, handing out last cigarettes, chocolates, and biscuits to the elderly men of the Pioneer Corps who were to help the engineers bridge the Rhine. Now they were going back to Holland for fresh supplies, when Majorie called out, "Look, the Airborne Division."

"Stopping the van, we jumped out" [wrote Miss Chettle in an account published in 1946]. "Squadron after squadron of aircraft, some towing great gliders, some probably carrying parachute troops, flew over in perfect formation. Nothing has ever impressed me more than this endless invincible armada, passing relentlessly overhead. All our thoughts and prayers and good wishes went up into the sky, to the men of the airborne division. For over half an hour we stood and watched, and still they were coming."

They needed those prayers. Most men's memories were of burning planes, sometimes their own, and burning gliders, and gliders falling like shot birds, and tug aircraft diving straight into the ground. The 513th U.S. Parachute Infantry Regiment had flown from Amiens in 72 of the new C-46s, some two dozen of which were shot down.

The plane carrying the regimental commander, Colonel James W. Coutts, was on fire as it crossed the Rhine. The formation was flying what was called the right-right stream and was supposed to catch up with the slower C-47s en route and then pass in front of them; but the timing was just a little wrong. Port engine blazing, Colonel Coutts's plane led the American formation for three minutes, while jagged holes kept appearing in the fuselage and from 500 feet it was possible to hear the German guns firing; then the green light glowed and out they went. Once on the ground, they came under instant small-arms and mortar fire.

"I started looking for orienting terrain features that I had memorised, but couldn't find them" [reported Coutts]. "I noticed more and more British paratroopers, their cherry berets. I saw British Horsa gliders landing. Either the British or we were in the wrong place. Through an interpreter we learned from a very scared German family that we were northwest of Hamminkeln rather than southwest. The British were in the right area, we were wrong."

For Private J. A. Collins, sniper scout of 1 Canadian Parachute Battalion, this was his first drop in action, although he had served with the battalion in Normandy. He had had twenty-one practice jumps and now a daylight drop in mid-morning over the Rhine.

"We were somewhat apprehensive; many of us remembered our sister Div at Arnhem and the mauling it had taken. I lost some of my friends in that action" [he wrote]. "As I looked thru the small port, I could see plenty of land fog. This was haze from the heavy bombing of the area. We jumped from Dakotas flown by American pilots; I was 19th man of a 20-man stick. I was quite calm by now and it seemed like a normal exercise jump. The aircraft bounced a few times and I could hear the anti-aircraft burst quite close. The most vivid thing I remember on the descent was a burning Dakota passing me, going back towards the Rhine. I always hoped he made it, because these fellows deserve a lot of credit. As I looked to my right, I could see a sudden flare of small arms fire—I learnt later that this was an assault by the 8th Battalion on Suicide Woods, so nicknamed for the heavy losses in taking the area."

Collins landed just short of the trees, the twentieth man, Sergeant Hartigan, landing in the trees.

"As I hit the ground, I moved fast clearing my chute. I had practised this move along with securing my rifle, so that I did it instinctively. As I loaded my rifle, which I had left with the 'scope attached in spite of regulations, I saw my first enemy soldier. I lay right down and fired at him. He just thrashed sideways, and I never waited, I ran straight for the trees."

Ray Newman, of the Vickers machine-gun platoon of the same battalion, was more heavily loaded, one of 10 men in a 20-man plane because of the gun tripod and ammunition. They came out of the plane slowly, because each man had a heavy kitbag attached to him, which hit the ground first. He had no time to look round but from the noise of gunfire—which was clearly German from the sound of it—he could tell they were in for some action. "As I was getting out of my chute, one of our aircraft came over very low. It was on fire and the men were still jumping from it, but it looked much too low for any of them to survive." Newman should not have been there, he was A.W.O.L.—from hospital. Now he gathered his load out of the kitbag, and "feeling like a pack horse" started to walk half a mile past "Suicide Wood" to the rendezvous.

"These woods were loaded with German soldiers, with so many targets they did not know who to shoot at. Some officers were calling men together and they would charge into the woods only to be thrown back out again. Our C.O., Jeff Nicklin, landed in this wood and was killed hanging in his chute. As I passed the end of it, a German fired in my direction and a soldier near me fell. I jumped into a shell hole and someone with a Bren fired into the area where the German was; then someone else threw a smoke bomb, and I was off again. At this point the whole DZ was loaded with men all going about their own business. The Vickers platoon stayed on the DZ and protected the rear of the battalion as it moved off to meet the men coming up from the Rhine."

Private Collins took up position in a brick building by the road and sniped at targets appearing on the open ground towards the Rhine. This was after they had flushed a German sniper.

"A few minutes later he came running out with his hands locked over his helmet. Fortunately, or maybe purposely, he had missed us. But one of the boys lifted him with a butt stroke of his Sten. He was hit so hard we just left him there and moved on."

Two hundred yards away two platoons of his own C Company had taken a village and were holding it against tank attack, knocking out two of the tanks. Then German 88s opening up, killing or wounded some of Collins' best friends alongside him.

"It was during this time that Corporal Topham with our Company got the Victoria Cross. Toppy saved many lives that day. He had two Germans going around with him, carrying casualties. He was everywhere. All this time he had been shot clear thru the nose. We kidded him, and little did I know the same fate awaited me on April 13th. It seemed the enemy now had made his final attempt to oust us from our positions."

In the middle of this heavy shelling there occurred a most extraordinary fight.

"I did not actually see the whole thing" [recalled Collins], "only the landing of the German pilot. He was one of the few daring ones that took to the air that day. He landed right in the middle of the D.Z. in front of our position. Both sides wanted him. He did not know where to go. Three of our fellows ran out and made him prisoner. During the first stages of capture he was very cocky. One of our Sergeants challenged him to a fist fight, and the German pilot took him on. He gave an excellent account of himself, but the Sergeant knocked him down at last and he did not wish to continue. This was all going on during the shelling of the village. Next day we moved out and passed thru the Glider Fields of the American troops. They had it pretty rough, I understand, as they landed smack on anti-aircraft positions."

While Topham was winning his V.C. in aiding the wounded, the 6th Airlanding Brigade of 6th British Airborne Division were coming in to their landing zones nearby.

"At this time the gliders started to land" [recalled Ray Newman]. "This was a kind of sorry mess, for as soon as most of them landed they were destroyed by German gunfire with many casualties. The fight for our DZ was severe, but after about two hours the most of it was over."

The men of the airlanding brigade had a shrewd idea of what they were in for before they ever took off. Staff Sergeant James Cramer, now a retired police inspector, was then with C Company of 1st Battalion Royal Ulster Rifles, a unit composed of about 65 percent Ulstermen and about 35 percent Southern Irish (i.e. neutrals). His company commander was Major Huw Wheldon, later to become well known in the television world.

"We were driven through the night to the airfield" [recalled Cramer]. "All of us had a premonition. We had gone into D-Day light-hearted. But we had since been in the Ardennes, had seen what happened to other people, and were sure we were not coming back. There was a gloomy feeling. We had the Arnhem affair on our minds, as well, and it seemed hazardous, on the surface, crossing the Rhine. We had a fat-free breakfast and then I remember nothing until we were coming up to the Rhine—a glimmer through the smoke. Our smoke, German smoke, houses burning. Just a mass of smoke and flashes. We weren't aware of the A.A., though it was there (a terrifying film was made of it—you can see gliders in flames, gliders going upside down, with troops and guns falling out, gliders crashing into houses). Our glider was a Horsa carrying C Company HQ—Major Wheldon, myself, five riflemen, a trailer with stores and ammo, and two very upset parachutists (their first glider lift). As we went over the Rhine, there was a lot of shouting up front, in the cockpit, something obviously wrong there. I don't know if we were cast off, or if we cast off, but we were going down at the rate of knots. We levelled out —terrified!—then there was a terrific crash, something broke open the floor of the glider and a spray of fine earth came in. Wheldon was yelling, 'Get out! get out quick!' for this was the vulnerable moment, but the door was jammed and had to be forced open. Fortunately we had landed in a kind of hollow, which was dead ground, and skimming just over us was 20-mm tracer. We ran to the nearest line of hedges, and I confess we were in so much of a hurry that I had to go back for my Sten! As I returned to the hedge, we saw the outline of camouflage-netted helmets which we thought were coal-scuttles, so we all threw ourselves down. Then a voice called out, 'Christ, we're glad to see you boys!' They were a group of eight or nine paratroopers from the U.S. 17th Airborne Division, miles from their DZ. So the parties joined together (we were three miles off our LZ) and made for the British landing zone. Even in that distance we could see our gliders being released and going towards the LZ in quite heavy German flak."

One of the last gliders to land was that towed by the Stirling bomber flown by Flight Sergeant R. S. Trout.

"The troops were men of the Devonshire Regiment and before they embarked I went over to speak to our intended passengers" [wrote Trout]. "A little Major was most irate to find that he was to be towed by a Flight Sergeant when some other tugs were being flown by officers. I sent my navigator, a Flying Officer, across to reassure him. If the troops were edgy, they had my entire sympathy—*I* hoped to be back in England by tea-time. The twelve take-offs were uneventful. I had a modest rear place and so benefited from a few more yards of runway than the press-on types ahead. The gliders were fully loaded and we lost two of the twelve by breaking towropes before we reached the coast and one more in the Channel. At 1,500 feet we could clearly see the different tributaries closing in and progressively forming one long stream. We never saw a German fighter and assume the only casualty we saw before the Rhine was an accident—a Horsa not far ahead of us disintegrated in a sudden explosion, leaving the towrope snaking in the sky.

"As we came up to the Rhine we could see Allied guns evenly spaced along the field hedges firing across the river. The dropping zone on the eastern bank was a blanket of black smoke shot through with red flashes. Some two miles north on the eastern bank a German ack-ack battery was firing at the aircraft over the zone. Just before we reached the river, a Halifax coming out on a reciprocal course banked into a gentle diving turn to port. We could see no sign of damage or fire, but it went straight into the ground and blew up. As we continued across the dropping zone our gunner gave the glider pilot a green on the Aldis just in case he didn't know we'd arrived. It was impressed on us that the glider pilot decided when to cast off and that we should never release the towrope from our end. We were near the end of the stream and obviously the glider pilot could only see the unbroken pall of black smoke where he had hoped to see the landmarks of the briefing photographs. He hung on and so did we until we were clear across the battle over apparently peaceful country once more. I remember thinking that if he'd decided to go on to Berlin I was honour bound to try to get him there, but after what seemed an age he cast off. We were briefed to turn left after release; I forgot Berlin, pulled the Stirling hard round and came back north of the dropping zone in a full-throttle dive, acutedly conscious of the ack-ack battery close by. We dropped the towrope before we got to the river. When my gunner last saw our glider it had turned on to a lonely reciprocal course, flaps still up, stretching its glide to come in under the far edge of the smoke. We were not surprised to be the last of the aircraft from Matching to get back to base. The fates of our various gliders were reported to us within a few days. Ours had been hit in the cockpit by a shell which had seriously injured the second pilot, but had disembarked its passengers safely."

Meanwhile, Major Wheldon's party of the Royal Ulster Rifles were being joined by more and more lost Americans from the 513th Parachute Infantry Regiment.

"Eventually Wheldon commanded about eighty at the front, so he told me to take over the rear" [said Cramer]. "The noise of S.A. fire, mortar fire and artillery was increasing all the time. We saw many American dead and wounded. It appeared that the American infantrymen were not trained in 'battle noises.' They seemed to drop to the ground and fire, whenever shots were heard close by. When passing a burning farm-house, there was a sound of what appeared to be a machine-gun; no one could have been in the house, because of the flames, and it was obviously ammunition burning; but it took some time to get the Americans up and on again. As we got to the LZ, I saw a figure in a long German greatcoat rise to his feet from the centre of a field, and walk towards us with his hands up. The man was Volkssturm, about 50 or 60 years of age, a long, thin chap. Before we could do anything about it, three Americans let fly with their carbines and the figure fell. God, we were angry. So was Major Wheldon.

"We left the Americans with their unit and found our battalion digging in outside the village of Hamminkeln. I was with seven or eight men passing a deep ditch overgrown with bushes, when I heard a rustle. We parted the bushes, and out came two of the vaunted German Army, tearing through the brambles, shouting, 'Nix schiessen!' One was a young chap, not Volkssturm, the other was middle-aged, and obviously both victims of the German propaganda which always called Airborne soldiers 'Murder Troops' (this used to please us, I don't know why it should). These two threw themselves down on their knees and the older one was nearly crying. He offered me a silver watch (which I've still got—a French watch, so he probably got it the same way). They were in baggy uniforms, trousers reinforced at the seat, and instead of lovely jackboots they wore thin canvas gaiters, like us. I was impressed by the German soldier as shown to us in poster form, contrasted with these specimens. When we handed them in to the Battalion POW cage, the glider pilot in charge said, 'Christ, can't you do better than this!' We were most upset.

"Back at Battalion, I was shocked by the casualties (16 officers, 243 other ranks). But the Typhoons, my God they were good. We were very jumpy, from our heavy losses and having no ground troops near. Then the Tiffies appeared and sorted out the enemy armour. They operated only two or three hundred yards in front of you. When we advanced later, we saw the terrible damage they had done; the Germans were terrified of them. In a field in front of us, between the two armies, a light observation plane came down smack. The Germans fired at it and we fired at them. We saw the door open and a young American officer come out. He ran the hundred yards in four seconds, to a roar of cheering from us. But there was a sad affair during the landing. Sergeant Major McCutchan, M.M. was caught in the centre of the road by a German tank. He couldn't get away, so he went on firing at the tank until it hit him and ran over him. I had his rifle afterwards, you couldn't get the bloodstains off. There was a horrible sight in a field nearby—a wounded American with the flesh of his chest torn away and all the rib cage exposed. One thing I did notice. The Americans will bunch, whereas we go up two sides of a road. It was purely a matter of lack of experience. They were shouting at each other and firing at nothing. They're still doing it in Vietnam. There was a film of them at place called Hue, and it was just the same. One thing I'll say for the Germans; they were better than we were with enemy dead; buried them properly and neatly with their equipment (which had their numbers on) over the crosses."

As the strength of a British battalion is just over 800 men, the Royal Ulster Rifles had lost one-third of their strength in killed and wounded between 1000 and 2400 hours on March 24. In the entire campaign they lost 804, or roughly the complete battalion. This is light compared to an ordinary infantry unit, in action most of the time.

Colonel Coutts, commanding the 513th Parachute Infan- reported,

"By dark we were on our objectives and all defenses buttoned up. We had about 2,000 prisoners which was more than the infantry strength of the combat team. But there was no doubt that the Kraut defensive set-up was shot to pieces and he was badly beaten. The greatest single contributing factor to our tactical success in this odd situation (landing in the wrong place) was the fact that the troop carrier pilots put us down together in tactical groups despite the heavy flak and battle haze that made finding pin-point DZs almost impossible."

Major General Ridgway summed up the whole operation:

"The impact of the airborne divisions at one blow shattered hostile defence and permitted the prompt link up with ground troops . . . permitting Allied armour to debouch into the North German plain at full strength and momentum."

This was true, generally, but the airborne assault was concentrated ahead of the *Schwerpunkt* on the drive over the Rhine—Wesel. At other points, it had little or no effect, and this was particularly true of the extreme left flank, where the 51st Highland Division met unbroken units of the German field army, of much higher quality than the static troops and elderly Volkssturm, badly shaken by the tremendous bombardment and the sight of an armada of paratroops and gliders descending on them. The main defence had clearly been put up by the veteran flak gunners of the Luftwaffe, veterans of the Ruhr, and the Allied air forces' attempt to knock out the 20-millimeter flak positions had been largely unsuccessful.

CHAPTER TWENTY-SEVEN

"HELL'S LAST ISSUE"

The Highland Light Infantry of Canada at Speldrop and Bienen: March 24–26

Montgomery's decision to cross the Rhine on March 24 was taken at 1530 hours on March 23, on the basis of a good weather report, because clear visibility and light winds were essential for the airborne side of the operation. And indeed it was almost like summer. By later afternoon, the armies of Scotland and America had substantial forces across and were expanding their bridgehead to link up with the airborne troops on the following day.

The width of the Rhine at the point of main effort, Wesel, was twice that at Oppenheim but this fact was nearly immaterial as far as the fast-moving and mostly armoured assault waves were concerned; its effect on the subsequent bridging operations was naturally far greater. How important these were can be judged from the numbers of engineers and pioneers brought up to the near bank areas of the Rhine—22,000 on the American front, 37,000 on the British front.

Bridging went well except at Rees on the left, where the Germans still held part of the ruins on the far bank and kept the crossing-sites under fire; and their resistance on the extreme left, at Speldrop and Bienen, would delay the capture of Emmerich and the subsequent building of the Canadian bridges there. Which meant that the capture of eastern Holland would be delayed.

It was in late afternoon of March 24 that Major Joseph Charles King had come up to B Company with a tommy gun under one arm and "a big smile on his face." As 12 Platoon had suspected, they had indeed "dug up something nasty for us to do."

Speldrop and Bienen had been attacked by 154 Brigade of the 51st Highland Division. The divisional commander, Major-General T. G. Rennie, was dead, killed by a mortar bomb. The 7th Battalion of the Black Watch had made three attempts to capture Speldrop, and been driven back by determined infantry, supported by tanks, S.P. guns, and 88s. Some of their men were believed cut off in the town, short of ammunition.

Between Speldrop and the start-line for the attack, which began at 1730 hours, was a broad open field swept by German machine-gun fire and pounded by artillery and mortars. The attack was to be made from the reserve brigade, by the Highland Light Infantry of Canada, with Major King's B Company in the lead. The fact that the H.L.I. belonged to the 9th Canadian Infantry Brigade of the 3rd Canadian Division but were attached to the British 154 Brigade was cause for concern to the H.L.I.

General Bradley, suspecting a slight, had been furious that during the Ardennes offensive Montgomery was reluctant to mix British formations with American formations, but kept his forces concentrated on the flank, ready to strike the German panzers if they should force the Americans to continue the rout. The old, old stories about Montgomery's "tidiness" and "caution" got an airing again.

But Malcolm B. Buchanan, rank private, perfectly appreciated the point, because he was the one most likely to get shot if things went wrong. "In change of command situations like this," he wrote, "the chances of a Snafu were greatly increased." The stresses of command, which are undoubtedly serious, and were responsible for most of the inter-Allied bickering, are of a quite different nature to the brutal facts of the front.*

Some of the men who went forward with the leading platoon in that attack are still alive, including the platoon sergeant, Cornelius Riedel (now of Curnel Riedel Draperies); Buchanan, the Bren gunner, and Sam Dearden, the corporal

* NATO once initiated a short-lived and clearly foredoomed attempt at "integration" by mixing sailors of different navies in a single ship, for political, not military reasons. A child could have told them it would not work. After the war, I worked often in units with a large German staff, particularly in Forces Broadcasting, but highly competent though the Germans were, there was sometimes just that fraction of critical delay due to language and background being different.

in charge of a carrier supporting 12 Platoon. Riedel, who was to receive the Military Medal, stressed the part played by Major King (who was killed in an air crash some years ago).

"Major King displayed great courage in the Speldrop operation" [he wrote]. "Two of his platoon officers were killed and one was wounded. With the exception of myself, all of the B Company sergeants were out of action as a result of a jeep accident a few days before. Major King was responsible for the success of this engagement. The enemy were well-trained and tough."

Buchanan remembered that moment as follows:*

"After the O Group, we got word from our platoon officer, Lt. Donald Isner. The Black Watch had tried to take the town of Speldrop and were in bad shape. They had two companies cut off in the town and were unable to withdraw or relieve them. It was our job to take the town. The plan called for a rolling barrage from our guns across the Rhine, with B Coy as assault Coy. We were to follow 100 yards behind the barrage, which was to roll over the town and stop on the other side. After a 3 or 4 mile march to the start line, we waited for the attack to go in. A group of Black Watch officers and men gathered behind us to watch the attack. I asked one of them how their men in the town were making out. He replied: *'All dead or captured. Shoot anything that moves because it will be a Jerry. Don't take any chances as too many have died there already.'* During this time the ranging shots of the guns had been coming in. There was about 800 yards of open, flat coverless ground between us and Speldrop. When the Army spotters were satisfied, we lined up, took last drags of our

* The witness's accounts give far more detail than either the H.L.I. war diary or their regimental history, but it was hard work for them—they had to go back mentally 24 years to picture the scene. "I am sorry to take so long in getting the material to you," wrote Buchanan. "When I first started to put it down on paper I thought it would be easy, however it wasn't. I found myself having trouble in getting the events in their proper place." The reader may judge for himself how successful Buchanan was, eventually, in picturing a typical infantry attack of the Second World War.

smokes, a good belt from number two water bottle, and away we went."

"We crossed the open in staggered intervals" [wrote the carrier corporal, Sam Dearden]. "I rolled out into the open knowing it would be rough even if the roads were mine free. Immediately we came under fire from some 88s and S.P. guns. You could hear them shells crack, as they passed overhead and beside you. Calmly, Lieutenant Isner said to me: *'I don't believe they like us here,'* as we bounced madly forward. He showing no sign of fear. Overhead a Typhoon was circling and it was looking the situation over. He then went into a steep dive, his guns going, to bring him onto the target, and then he released his rockets. He had seen an S.P. backed into a brick house firing at me, and in one swoop he had destroyed it. It made my job much easier" [an understatement, as the tiny Bren carrier was merely bullet-proof, not shell-proof, and open on top].

"We caught up with the barrage and had to go at a fast trop to keep up to it" [wrote Buchanan]. "Everyone was loaded down with equipment, but managed to keep in line. About 200 yards from the town we began to pass Black Watch dead. There was one complete section of 8 or 10 men who had apparently been cut down in a cross fire. As we came to about 150 yards of the town, the barrage *stopped*" ([i.e. stopped moving forward—the expected Snafu had occurred]. "We pulled in as close as we could and went to ground. Soon shells and mortar rounds were dropping behind us. Jerry had opened up with his own barrage and was walking it right up our backsides. In the meantime our barrage had died down a little so Lt. Isner jumped up and yelled: *'Come on! If we're going to be killed, I'd sooner get it from our guns than theirs.'* Due to his action, 12 Platoon resumed the attack. We crossed the barrage as fast as we could and at this point began to take casualties. Lt. Isner, about 25 feet to my right and forward, was blown into the air by a shell burst in front of him. At the same time I was knocked off my feet by a blast of hot air. I was stunned for a minute, unable to catch my breath or move. Rolling over, I managed to get up and found to my surprise

I was all right. Grabbing my Bren, I ran over to Lt. Isner. He hadn't been as lucky as I. He was finished.

'While moving up again I saw many gaps in the line. The smoke, explosions, and noise of the shells was hellish. On reaching the first house, which was made of brick, I fired a few bursts at the cellar window facing us. This window, as most of the windows in the town, was more of a firing slit for a pill-box than a window. It seemed these houses were constructed with defence in mind. Kicking open the kitchen door, I fired the remainder of my mag around the room. Stepping back to change mags, I saw several dead Jerrys against the wall. I went back into the kitchen with a grenade and was ready to drop it down the cellar steps, when someone shouted: *'Don't shoot, for God's sake! Black Watch here.'* Putting the pin back in the grenade, I warned the men outside to hold their fire. Covering the door from the corner, I yelled for the men in the cellar to come up one at a time. First up was a Sergeant. He was a brave man to stand on those steps in the face of Bren gun fire. He said: *'You've shot three of my men.' 'My God, I'm sorry, mate,'* I answered. *'But your officers told us you lads were all dead or captured.'* He told me they had run out of ammo and had held the Jerrys off with bayonets, shovels, and by throwing their own grenades back at them. As I left to join the section clearing the western part of town, one of the boys coming up from the cellar said it was a grand sight to see us coming through the barrage. They knew that help was on the way, and I wasn't to worry about the men I had shot up, as it wasn't my fault. We left our stretcher bearer with their wounded."

This may or may not have been the house held by Lieutenant J. R. Henderson of the Black Watch for 12 hours, unsupported. Speldrop had been captured early on the night of March 23–24 and then lost to battle groups of the Panzer Grenadiers. Henderson had led in a patrol to find out the extent of the penetration, had been cut off with many casualties, and found refuge in a burning house, which he held against at least six attacks, some supported by bazookas. There were a lot of Black Watch cut off but still holding, in and around the village. Sam Dearden contacted others.

"After we had crossed the open ground, I pulled up alongside some of the houses on the street to wait for the rest of the vehicles to run the gauntlet and catch up with us. I noticed good-sized holes through the houses, and some of the Black Watch soldiers who were cut off and were in slit trenches, said: *'Don't stop here, he shoots through these houses any time he feels like it. Leave your vehicle and join us in the trench.'* Which we did, while our other vehicles gathered. Then we went forward on foot to recce the position, and there were many machine-guns so that it was very deadly for us, plus snipers that actually hit me in the pocket; it was very active. Quite often, we'd dodge from door to door, being fired on most of the time. The town was burning uncontrolled in some areas. This lasted part of the day and the night. By morning, only isolated resistance remained, but in the confusion of the dark we had lost men to the Black Watch and them to us, not knowing we were there.'

"We began the house and barn clearing on the edge of the town" [wrote Buchanan]. "Not many prisoners were taken, as, if they did not surrender before we started on a house, they never had the opportunity afterwards. We had spent many hours training for this job and we had it down pat. First a '36' into a room, then a man with a Bren or Sten going full blast in through the door. Room by room. And always a grenade down the cellar steps. I saw one man throw a grenade into a house, but before it exploded one of the new men went through the door. He was blown right back out. He had gotten excited and it had cost him his life. When Lt. Isner was killed, Sgt. Reidel took command of the platoon. He had switched his faulty Sten with a wounded man, and now led us in a bayonet charge on several machine-gun posts and a 20-mm gun position in a small orchard at the edge of town. Again, no mercy was shown the enemy. Gathering 12 Platoon, he pointed out a group of buildings about 75 yards beyond the orchard, from which heavy fire was coming on the rest of the Company. We could see muzzle flashes from heavy guns coming from three points. *'Get that objective, and we have done the job,'* he said. Crawling around one side which did not seem covered by fire, we got in close and then, leaping up, we raced in. Throwing 36's, firing all our weapons, and doing a lot of yelling, we were into them before they could turn their M.Gs. around on us. It was over in a few minutes. They threw up their arms and yelled: *'Kamarad.'* We disarmed them and put them in a barn. When we had them all in, I shuddered. There were twice as many of them, all paratroopers, than there were of us. Going outside, to look around, I found that the muzzle flashes had been coming from 75-mm guns. There were three of them and beside each was a stack of HE, AP, and what one man said was Cannister. No wonder the Black Watch had been cut to pieces."

B Company was followed by A and C companies, with D in reserve, supported by Wasp flame-throwing vehicles. The enemy were well dug-in with machine-guns, and a number of houses had been turned into strongpoints. While the other companies tried to clear through the town, forcing the enemy into the open, the remnants of B dug-in for the night.

"Two of our platoon commanders had been killed and a third wounded" [wrote Buchanan]. "One young lieutenant, a recent replacement, wanted to know the location of our forward Bren position. On being told, he started across a barnyard to it. A corporal stopped him and told him the area was under sniper fire and stay in the shelter of the buildings. Disregarding this advice, he started off on the run. About halfway across, he was hit and went down with a yell. He began calling for a stretcher bearer to come and get him. The stretcher bearer yelled back: *'Stay there, you stupid bastard, till after dark. You were told not to go out there.'* He was picked up after dark. He had been shot in the butt.'

Digging-in was difficult, because this was the flood plain of the Rhine; after three feet, they hit water, and so they were compelled to build up the sides of their trenches. Buchanan and Wagg put a barn door over part of their trench and piled earth on top of that.

"It was now quite dark and, owing to the number of dead and wounded, we were on 100 per cent watch for the night. We could still hear the firing of A, C, and D Coys, as they continued to clear the rest of the town. Now and again we saw the flash of fire as the Wasps were used to clear strong points. Through all this came the heavier thud of the carrier section M.Gs."

Then they heard another sound—the noise of enemy tank tracks. They called up one of the six-pounder anti-tank guns belonging to the battalion, and as it was being towed by carrier along the dyke road towards them, a Focke-Wulf 190 lit a flare that illuminated them all. Every gun in the company let go at the plane, plus the Bofors sites. Meanwhile the carrier was streaking along the dyke, towing the gun, and as the Focke-Wulf pulled up out of the tracer and was coned by searchlights, Buchanan could see that the six-pounder was airborne. "I could plainly see the sky under it." His impression was that it had bounched six feet in the air, so fast was the driver going.

"By now it was after midnight and a light rain was falling. It seemed it always rained when we were dead beat and on guard for the night. All at once we began to come under very accurate shell fire. These air bursts seemed to be concentrated on the B Company area, about 100 yards square. At the first burst, I dove under the roof of our slit trench to join Wagg, who was having a smoke. I got halfway in when my tunic caught on something. To keep from thinking about my predicament I started to count the shell bursts and I reached 80 before the shelling stopped, and I freed myself from a large spike in the door that had tangled in my tunic."

Tired as were the Canadians—for the nervous drain of battle is far, far more exhausting than mere lack of sleep—the Germans had taken a hammering, too. Next morning, a D Company patrol sent out beyond the town captured several German machine-gun crews who were asleep at their guns, oblivious to the enemy or the sounds of battle. At 1200 hours on March 25, the depleted battalion was withdrawn, having recaptured and secured Speldrop.

They went to a "rest" area, where they were heavily shelled, until 2200 hours on the 25th, when the weary men were roused again. Another rescue operation was to be undertaken. Two battalions, the North Nova Scotias and the Argyll

& Sutherland Highlanders, had proved insufficient force with which to capture the larger town of Bienen, about five miles away. The H.L.I. of Canada would complete the job.

"We went in around midnight under fake moonlight" [wrote Buchanan]. "The platoon officers still had not been replaced, so Major King led us in, again with 12 Platoon on the point. Reaching the centre of the town, we ran into one of our own tanks, burning and giving off a lot of light. We passed many dead, both ours and the enemy. After going one block, I reached an open space which I started to cross at a run. Halfway across, I realised it was a small barnyard. All of a sudden, I ran into something at waist level. It was very dark, but looking to the right and up I saw the turret of a Tiger tank and realised I was draped over its barrel. All I could do was drop to the ground and yell to the others to get back. There was no movement from within the tank and I could see the hatches were open. The tank had bogged down, almost to its turret, in a manure pile with its barrel three feet off the ground. In case there was anyone in there lying 'doggo,' I dropped a 36 down the front hatch and left the tank smoking."

"As we moved in to the streets of the town bitter fighting was raging on every street" [wrote Corporal Dearden, who was covering the advance from a carrier]. "Progress was very slow. You tried to know friend and foe by the sound of his weapons. German machine-guns fired faster than our standard Bren. It grew darker and as we moved further into the town it was a nightmare trying to know who was firing at who and vice-versa. I was using a 50-calibre machine-gun I had taken off a knocked-out tank and welded on, as it gave me more fire-power at greater range. I seemed to be drawing a lot of return fire because of the heavier sound of the bigger gun. I nosed the carrier by the last building and all hell broke loose. Fire, tracer and everything was criss-crossing the streets. I backed up the carrier a few feet and into a deserted building on the corner with a Bren gun, which I set up to cover the streets."

Not until next morning did Dearden know that he had parked his carrier on top of two dead German soldiers.

The war diary recorded:

"Progress was very slow as the enemy fought like madmen. Isolated houses had to be cleared and proved most difficult. The enemy artillery and mortars poured shells into our troops continually. Again, single paratroopers made suicidal charges at our advancing troops. They were consistently chopped down but sometimes not before they had inflicted casualties on our sections."

"Our platoon objective was a brick house beside a large road block" [wrote Buchanan]. "With a barrage of grenades through the windows we cleaned the Jerries out in short order. We found an old German lady, about eighty and paralized, in the basement. She was very frightened, but one of our boys who spoke German told her she would be OK. About half the platoon was in the basement and the other half upstairs, when a shell came in through a window and exploded in the back room. When the smoke had cleared, we counted noses. One man thought he was blind, but his eyes were only filled with plaster and dust. Another had the funny bone on his elbow clipped off. We found one of the men laying under a pile of shelves, bleeding from the nose and ears. The stretcher bearer said he was dead, and to lay him outside against the back wall. After a short time we heard someone stumbling down the stairs to the basement. By the light of smoky old lanterns we saw the man we had left for dead outside. He had been knocked unconscious and the rain had revived him.

"Now it was beginning to get light enough to see a short distance, although there was a ground mist. We went out and started digging our slit trenches. When Wagg and I had dug in, and I was stripping and cleaning my Bren, a man standing on the back step of the house, shouted there were some Jerries. I saw two of them come out of a camouflaged pill box, about 150 yards down at the bend of the road. The man immediately opened fire with his rifle and brought down the two Germans at the door of the pillbox. By the time the rest of the men had taken up positions, we came under heavy machine-gun fire. As the pill box was out in the open with a good field of fire, Sergeant Tuttle asked for help from the

Wasps. After a short while, two Wasps appeared, moved past the road block in front of the house, and made their runs up the road as fast as possible. Coming up to the enemy position, they swung off the road and around the pillbox to the door side. Going past, each Wasp gave it a long burst of flame. The M.G. fire stopped and no one got out. The pillbox was emitting a lot of smoke, and we could hear the ammo popping off."

As the mist cleared still further, an 88 began to bring down fire on the road-block outside the house from an orchard about 1,000 yards away.

"It perfectly covered the road block. We radioed back for an S.P. to take it out. A Priest came up half-an-hour later and manoeuvred beside the road block. It fired two rounds and the shelling stopped. The 88 ammo supply may have been hit, as a lot of heavy explosions and smoke came from that direction. The town seemed to be cleaned out now, and our jeeps were coming up for our dead and wounded. After they had been taken care of, Sergeant Tuttle sent the old lady back to casualty clearing station on a jeep, as there were no civilians left in the town to take care of her. She was terrified when we put her stretcher up on a jeep, but one of our German-speaking boys held her hand and told her not to worry. Later, they said the M.O. was sure in a rage when he saw the old lady we sent back.

"We had had very little sleep since the morning of the 23rd (it was now the 26th), as we had been fighting and on the move almost continuously. Looking around at the men, I thought: *We sure look like our regimental nickname suggests —Hell's Last Issue—taken from the initials H.L.I.* That afternoon B Company held a parade. Looking around, I was shocked at the number of men missing. The CSM reported to Major King: *'54 men on parade—all the rest accounted for.'* Examining the faces of the survivors, I found it was mostly the new replacements taken-in in the Reichswald that were missing. The old saying of surviving a week at the front and your chance of living went up, seemed to hold true. Unfortunately, they had been through two days of the bloodiest fighting that the Regiment had been through in a long time."

B Company had lost half its strength on the far bank of the Rhine—and they were all "accounted for" as killed or wounded. No prisoners. "The Regiment was proud of the fact that they had never had a man taken prisoner, no man posted missing, and no ground once taken was ever lost," wrote Buchanan.

In the afternoon, a British battalion, believed by Buchanan to be the Dorsets (and it was probably the 4th Battalion, which had fought at Arnhem), passed through the H.L.I., who were hoping for a rest.

"A short time later we heard a fierce fight going on. About an hour later, we saw a group of about 30 or 40 Jerries coming down the road on the run, followed by two Tommies. One, on a bicycle, had a sten and a rifle slung over his shoulder; and the other was running with a long whip urging the prisoners on. As the Tommies stopped for a minute, I asked one how far they had run them. He answered: *'Three or four miles.'*

'What happens if one of them can't keep up?' I asked.

'If the whip doesn't encourage them to keep running, I leave him to my mate, and he stays there for good. We haven't had to leave too many behind so far. These boys like to run.'

I don't think I've even seen men that looked so terrified as these paratroopers—Hitler's Supermen. Changing places with his mate on the Bike, the Tommy took off again with the Jerries in their long coats flopping and sweat running down their faces. With cries of *'Schnell!'* and whip-cracking, they moved down the road. I wondered how many of them they would deliver to the POW cages, as it was another four miles."

Next day, the H.L.I. were issued with grenades and ammunition, reinforcements filled the gaps, and they were off again.

CHAPTER TWENTY-EIGHT

"WORST-HIT AREA OF THE WAR"

Erlekom to Emmerich
March 24–April 3

On the day of the Rhine crossing, March 24, 1945, the headquarters of First Canadian Army was south-east of Nijmegen in the hilly wooded area captured by Gavin's Americans the previous September, some three miles from the nearest German-held sector of the Rhine and just downstream of the junction where the broad German Rhine becomes the wide Dutch Waal and the narrower Neder Rijn branches off north-west by Pannerden to join the Ijssell at Arnhem. That is, within easy walking distance of the war, for the first time. And at this time, we had very little to do and were given one day off in seven.

This was a result of Montgomery's policy of battle-planning. HQ First Canadian Army had planned and controlled the battle of the Rhineland (which is why I had immediate, precise, and accurate knowledge of events), while HQ Second Army, with no divisions to command, was planning and preparing for the Rhine crossing. Now, HQ Second Army was controlling the current battle, while the Canadians were planning for the conquest of north-eastern Holland and the third Battle of Arnhem, while at the same time absorbing into their ranks I Canadian Corps, being transferred from Italy, so that for the first time First Canadian Army really would be all-Canadian, or nearly so.

The policy of putting an army headquarters within easy artillery range of the enemy was new, and I believe the idea may have been that no one would suspect the offer of such a tempting and vulnerable target, although the Allies were better at knocking them out than were the Germans—in Normandy the HQ of Panzer Group West had been obliterated at a critical moment, and two days before the Rhine was crossed, the HQ of the German First Parachute Army was attacked by fighter-bombers and the army commander, General Alfred Schlemm, severely wounded. HQ Second Army had once been dislocated by bombing, but up to now the only attempt on HQ First Canadian had been the abortive drops by parachute saboteurs back at Tilburg.

The first entry in my diary for Saturday, March 24, 1945, reads:

"It was a hot and hazy day, the Typhoons droned over and the guns roared continuously. It also happened to be my day off, so I checked over my rifle, and armed with 40 rounds, 2 bars of chocolate, and some tobacco, set off for the Rhine. I followed rough paths by ruined houses, where yellow butterflies played in the sun, heading always for the SE tip of the island at Nijmegen, where the map* showed the Germans to be. The road to Beek and Persingen began to fall steeply in great curves between wooded hills, with the haze-dim countryside along the Waal and the Rhine and up to Arnhem in view ahead, basking in the heat.

"I came into Beek, dusty and shattered and abandoned, except for a handful of inhabitants and a few soldiers taking a bath. The traffic for the Rhine crossing rattled along the broken road, and an ambulance came through headed for Nijmegen, with Naval wounded as well as soldiers. The road to Persingen led down onto a flat plain, criss-crossed by waterlogged ditches. A few people were cultivating their gardens. A dead cow, with its head missing, lay by a telegraph pole. Two hay-carts rumbled slowly past me towards Beek. This plain lay at the foot of a long line of wooded hills, which reached up to Nijmegen, where the twin bridges rose up in clear view on the left, silvered by the haze. The sunlight was golden on the fields, from which the spring wind blew the sweet scent of the clover. The sun beat down in warmth on one's face, and it was good to be living. It was very peaceful. The birds still sang as the guns roared and the shells went

* The ops room wall map, which showed that the crack parachute regiment to which Pastor Willi Schiffer had belonged had moved from Haalderen several weeks previously and been replaced by elements of a mixed division drawn partly from the German Navy. I was in fact seeking the worst German unit within easy walking distance of the office.

screaming away into the haze on the heels of the brittle crack of the discharge. Nothing moved on the road now, not a vehicle, not a soul. One was alone with the sun and the scent of the clover, the sudden scream of the shells, and the lonely spire of Persingen rising from a clump of willow trees from out of the plain. Just beyond, black smoke was writhing like serpents in the haze, from the bursting of the shells which one heard going over. Rusty coils of barbed wire littered the fields, and papers and magazines were floating in the ditches. At a road fork there was a white tape and a large notice: NO ENTRY—ROAD MINED AND IMPASSABLE.

"From here on nothing was intact, nothing. I passed through a broken village, cracked open to the sun, and beyond I walked where a shattered farmhouse cast its twisted silhouette into the clear and quiet waters of a lake, and a turret-less tank leaned crazily against the sky. Three men walked along the skyline, a Belgian patrol. Somewhere a machine-gun rapped angrily in the sunshine. A dead horse lay half buried in a pile of litter, its skull showing through, and the skin of its body stretched so tight that it looked like wood, as if it had never lived and never died; and not at all horrible. I went along a track not marked on my map, past some Belgian soldiers and an abandoned Buffalo containing an RE Bren carrier of 49 Div. I asked a Belgian how far the Boche was from here. '500 yards,' he said.

"It was not in the least like going to war for the first time, for I had five years of stukas and blitzes and V-bombs behind me; but I was still new to bullets, and I walked cautiously into the brickworks which lay ahead, in case I came too suddenly into view of the enemy. Through the brick kilns and past a small street of ruined houses I walked, to where a Honey tank was heeled over on the bank of the Rhine, half buried in the end house. Remembering snipers and telescopic sights, I kept low as I walked up, then slowly peered over the edge. Ruined buildings lay on the far bank, and willow trees blown by the soft spring breeze, seemed unreal in that bright sun. The Rhine was silver-blue with sun and haze, and very still. Nothing moved on the river or in all that waste of countryside in front of me. I searched out the Company Commander of the Belgian unit holding the brickworks. He was a Lieutenant of about 22, a pleasant youth, speaking good English, and just signing some papers in the little room which served as his office. A series of explosions jarred the house, as we spoke. This, he explained, was Erlekom, and he had no objection to my having some rifle practice on the Boche on the other side of the river. 'They know we're here,' he said, with a grin.*

"I went back to the abandoned tank, took the breech cover off my rifle, cocked it, and placed my jacket on the embankment to make my elbows comfortable. The river was still blue with sun. Some of those apparently deserted buildings three hundred yards away† across the shining water were part of a brickworks, similar to the one at Erlekom. Our one was being used as a Forward Observation Post for the guns which had been firing; possibly those other brick kilns held the German FOP.

"My first shot goes ringing over the river, followed by four more, as I tickle up each building in succession. I'm just a trifle tense, I change my position a couple of times, and move my position a couple of times, and move slowly all the while, even though everything is so peaceful, because if there's a sniper with a telescopic sight over there, and he sees me, I've had it. I keep remembering the scene in *All Quiet on the Western Front*, when the soldier reaches out of the trench to pick a flower, the sniper fires, and you see the hand holding the flower slowly unclench. It must be more than a dozen years since I saw that film, but it seems very real now. The echoes of my shots die away upon the river, and all is as it was, quiet and warm under the sun. Rather annoyed that I haven't got a field gun, something that would really make the fur fly, and disturb somebody, I come down from the bank and bask in the sun while I eat chocolate and then smoke a pipe. I crawl up to firing position again. The river is as still and lovely as the unruffled Serpentine, and those shattered buildings, raw and bare among the willow trees on the far

* I chose a Belgian unit and was in future to visit only Belgian or Canadian sectors, as I knew the British would tend to be stuffy and sticky about visits from casual tourists; in their army, that sort of thing went out with Waterloo.

† Twice the width of the Rhine at Oppenheim, I knew the distances approximately, because I had to set the sights of my rifle, therefore I saw what I expected to see.

bank, seem somehow unreal, a jarring note in the peace of afternoon. To zero my rifle, which has never been fired until today, I aim at the water just in front of the centre of a barge moored against the opposite bank. The rifle roars, the bullet whines across the water, a spurt of spray leaps up in the right place. I aim next at a building, and hear the thud of my shot going home. *Tap tap brrrrrp brrrrrp* comes from the far bank, as a German machine-gunner cuts into action against me.

"There's a crane on the far bank; a likely place. I swing round and let him have it. He replies instantly, in short bursts, and I fire back. The sustained burst of an LMG is easier to track down than the single, aimed shot of a rifle, and though I can't see anything, and that distant bank is just as deserted as before, I feel that my bullets are going pretty near him. On the abrupt crash of my rifle, he suddenly stops firing. Perhaps I got him, or maybe he just got bored."

The target for my final shot had been what looked like a low mound of earth in front of the crane, which I thought might be a slit trench, although I could see no sign of helmet or gun. The LMG was definitely firing from that area, its approximate position given away by the bursts, professionally short though they were. The German, however, had no idea where I was—I didn't even hear the whine of the bullets, let alone the whipcrack of a near one. This was because I had made careful use of the daylight under the front sprocket of the tank, bringing up my head and right shoulder very slowly into position under and in front of it, and so merging imperceptibly with the tank. Anyone who saw me, let alone hit me, would have been a very sharp man indeed.

"I lie back once more in the sun, contentedly munching chocolate, and laughing to think that after five years of being a target, I've fired back, and it was all so easy and undramatic. I watch an Auster spotting for the guns, which are still sending salvoes over the Rhine, and see the Typhoons come back in pairs out of Germany at 2,000 feet, the German high-angle heavy MGs hammering away at them ineffectually."

Frustration was not my only motive. Probably there was

some sense of shame, that I was playing so poor a part in so great a drama. And definitely, my career having been smashed by the war, I knew that my only chance of a new one was to succeed as a writer, and as I would probably be including the war among my subjects, I had better find out what it was like at first-hand.

If I'd had to pay for my ammunition, I'd certainly have charged it up to "research expenses." But if I was going to write about the war, I had to survive it; hence the cautious first choice of a mediocre German division, and the very careful attention to professional detail; the tank, for instance, was the perfect answer to the "cover from view is not cover from fire" warning.

Very satisfied with the results of the "duel," I returned by way of Nijmegen, with the sounds of an unseen dogfight above the town coming down through the haze; then, unknowing, I went for a walk along the Waalkade, past the ship chandler's where Philip van Heerde had lived, and had watched the Germans enter in May, 1940.

"I walked down to the waterfront along the Waal, where quaint Dutch characters lolled about, wearing exactly the sort of clothes one sees in photographs, and which, during five months in Holland, I've never seen before. On the right the road bridge spanned the Waal; on the left, one span of the railway bridge was down into the water, where it had been blown by the 'frogmen.' The road bridge, still intact, was guarded by netting and a boom. I read a description of the feat in *Picture Post* a week ago; it described the affair as a total failure. I dropped into the Corner House for some grub, but didn't bother with the flics, as Arnhem Mary says they're not very good here, and something ought to be done about it. . . . Back at camp, there's an American flying film on in the Knights of Columbus, and the sound of machine-gun fire comes rattling out of the Nissen Hut, and it's very much more real and exciting than that German Spandau this afternoon; I get really thrilled, and put my head inside the door, but the audience is up the walls, and hanging from the room, so I go to bed. Len and Vic are having a quiet game of draughts on one of the beds, and I am just drifting into sleep, when an aircraft which has been circling the camp begins to dive. The roar of the dive become a howl as the plane comes thundering down to about 300 feet; there's a sudden, harsh, sharp burst of machine-gun fire. Len leans over flat beside his bed, Vic is recumbent alongside his rude couch, and the draughts are performing ungraceful arabesques in the air. The plane goes storming down the valley, with no shots fired at him. Even this doesn't sound so realistic or terrifying as the Zeroes in the film at the K. of C. All the same, I'm glad he didn't hit our tent, because the bullets might have come through. The tent was dug-in and I had gracefully arranged an ex-Coldstream Guards tank track round my bed as additional protection.)

With the events of the afternoon, *hubris* had set in and I sallied forth in greatcoat and long woolly pants ready to take the thing on with my rifle (as I had been a pilot, I actually had a chance of hitting him), but I was implored not to. The plane was so low, it was visible in the moonlight, but apart from bombing and setting on fire the camp fuel dump it did little damage and fled "with all the LAA between hell and Nijmegen" after it.

Odd though it may seem, this was in fact typical of the "war" as experienced by all but the few fighting soldiers during the Rhine crossing. For 50 miles, the fields were packed with troops and dumps; and the Luftwaffe came out by night to harass them, so everyone dug-in a little deeper. With plenty of field cinemas to entertain the troops, it was like peace, only more so, except for the shaving in cold water in the open air at dawn.

The gulf between war as we knew it, and up at the sharp end on the other side of the Rhine, was immense. In the space of time between my walk to Erlekom and the machine-gunning of our camp, some of the airborne units had lost one-third of their strength; and the H.L.I. of Canada were fighting from room to room in Speldrop. But Erlekom had been merely a deliberately mild "battle inoculation" in a quiet sector; I now intended, if I could, to attend the remaining real battles for the Rhine—Emmerich and Arnhem. In personal terms, the parachutists and the Waffen-S.S.

My diary recorded briefly the British break-out from the Rhine bridgehead. March 28:

"7 Armd Div went into the bridgehead last night, and just went clean through the Germans and out of sight. No-one knows where they are now."

March 29:

"7 Armd Div and G's Armd Div, who followed them over, are on the loose and out of sight, God knows where. The Recce vehicles of 7 Armd Div were coming up to Munster, when the main body of the Div was crossing, that's the sort of war it is. But the Parachutists still fight fiercely in the north."

It was a repetition of the break-out from Normandy, but this time with the British spearhead driving for the Baltic, the American 9th diverted (by Eisenhower) to cut off the Ruhr, and the Canadians in their left-flank, hard-fighting role nearest to the coast. But before the break-out could begin, the engineer work had to be done. On March 26, "Waterloo" bridge (class 9) and "Lambeth" bridge (class 15) were completed; at 2400 hours on March 26–27, "London" bridge (class 40); on March 28, "Blackfriars" bridge (class 40); and on March 29, "Westminster" bridge (class 40). Engineer casualties were 155 killed and wounded.

But the Germans still held most of Holland. During an evening walk on March 29, I climbed the highest hill I could find, which gave an extensive view.

"I can see right out over western Holland, with Canadian and German territory alike bathed in blue haze, sparkling with gold and crimson. Here the people are free; there the Gestapo stalk the streets; but the sunset knows no distinction, and casts no dividing line."

The Canadian drive westward along the far bank of the Rhine, from Speldrop and Bienen, was intended to cut off the several hundred thousand German troops still in Holland; but the drive could not gain momentum until the Canadian engineers had built their bridges at Emmerich; and before that could be done, Emmerich must fall. This was to be almost the last battle of the German Rhine, apart from the French crossings far to the south.

Although I made meticulous notes of what I saw, the atmosphere of the time is almost impossible to recapture—a mixture of normality and abnormality, which, because it had been going on so long, had become normal. On March 30, for instance, I noted three events. A visit to Grave for a bath, a visit to the Y.M.C.A. in Nijmegen, and a bang near the camp office, followed by a cloud of smoke. The soldier who had trod on the mine walked 10 yards out of the smoke, put his hands to his stomach, and fell on his face. It was a "jumping" mine, actuated by a spring, which exploded at waist level. All these three events were of much the same order of importance, as long as you did not know the casualty.

On the following day, Saturday, March 31, my "battlefield tour" would be semi-official, as I was to write an article on Kleve for the *Beaver*, the unit magazine; and I was told merely not to get myself shot, as that particular type of wound would be hard to explain away as being the cause of death for HQ personnel. I wrote:

"Vic Taylor comes along as well—being RAMC and unarmed, he carries the grub and water; I carry my rifle, 50 rounds, and my 'shooting jacket' (a German sniper's cloak, picked up in the woods). We also take field dressings—the Island opposite Erlekom was held by an ordinary German div; but Emmerich, where we're going, is held by units of the First Parachute Army, just about the best troops the Germans have got. The latest news is that the Canadians are fighting inside Emmerich, which was not the case when we made our plans."

All this seems very odd now, but was by no means unusual. For instance, Lieutenant-Colonel E. H. Capstick, who was then a lieutenant with 32 Field Company, RCE, in the area we were going to, recalls that

"During our wait, we went out and bribed the British gunners with cigarettes to let us fire a few rounds; and one of my sappers assisted a cow giving birth to a calf!"

And R. G. Saunders of 108 Regiment R.A. wrote: "But the one thing which annoyed me most were the cows crying to be milked; they were even standing on top of the mangle wurzel clumps and eating so much that their udders were touching the ground—some we destroyed as we couldn't find farmers."

The incongruity of killing men and being sorry for animals struck no one at the time; indeed, one had to erect one's own code of morality, none too successfully; but at least not so illogical as that of the press, the priests, the politicians, and the B.B.C., whose theme then (with certain honourable exceptions) was: Kill, kill, kill! Once the killing was over, they began again to deprecate all forms of violence and hatred, with what sincerity I know not. From the German border onwards into the Rhineland, I personally was in a state of shock and unable at the time to find the right words.

"We get onto MAPLE LEAF and hop a truck. We go roaring into Wyler, just over the border—the place has just been ploughed into the earth. Then through Kranenburg, a fair-sized town—not a house intact anywhere. German signs glare down at us and the quaint church steeple lolls drunkenly. On and on for mile after mile—the whole countryside devastated, swept bare of buildings and of all human life. The empty, ruined, looted interiors of houses gaze upon one like the stony eyes of the dead, arrayed for miles along the road. This is war . . . hate and the love of destruction . . . the fury of vengeance . . . this is the fate we escaped in 1940 by so narrow a margin. On the right of the roadway lay the dark mass of the Reichswald forest, and, upside down in a field, right wing gone, and one wheel sticking pathetically in the air, like the leg of a dead sparrow, lay a fighter; and on the left, smoke swirled viciously from the long barrels of a battery, and the horizon shook with the roar of their firing.

"We dropped off the truck, and made our way up the hill on which Cleve stands. About half the town was flat, the rest of it, bar perhaps 5 per cent, was still standing, but damaged. Somehow, because the ratio of damage was greater but the area of total destruction less, Cleven did not seem so obliterated as Caen. But there was life in Caen, people lived in basements, and moved in the streets, and looked at you sullenly; here nothing moved, only a cat; it was very quiet. No-one had bothered to clear the side-streets of debris, no-one had cared to lift the fallen masonry, to release those trapped in cellars or ground-floor rooms. And the rooms of the empty houses were stripped clean, except for piles of junk upon the floor; Cleve had been looted and pillaged like a town of the Middle Ages . . . and there in the streets, mixing with the debris of the bombing, were the large articles of furniture, the red mattresses, and the splendid toys that German children had—and all of them smashed to pieces by the hand of man. The streets are choked with debris, books, postcards, religious emblems, stockings, underwear, toys . . . the contents of the houses lying in the street, a thing I have never seen before, because blast is impersonal, but human hate has no limitations. A terrible destruction, with the marks of rage stamped clear upon it. A Nazi flag, attached to a stick, flies from the lip of a crater where a German house has been, just as Union Jacks flew from the blitzed ruins in East London and Southampton all these long years ago. A good souvenir, that . . . I lean down to pick it out of the ground, then withdraw my hand as if it had been a rattlesnake and not just a little swastika flag."

This was part of the atmosphere, that if you were not wary, you were likely to be dead. I got the flag, though, by pelting the stick with stones from a safe distance, and knocking the flag off the stick, which bends but will not budge an inch out of the ground. Clearly, it was attached to something.

The absence of civilians was because they had been moved (by our side) to camps in Holland as part of the preparation for crossing the Rhine. The Germans had already done the same thing with the Dutch civilians in Arnhem; and these two clearances of important battle areas explain a German order of 1940 for removing the male population from England to the Continent. Obviously, they could not have meant the entire male population (although every book I have ever read assumes this), but that in the immediate beachhead area, which would be a logistic possibility, as well as being militarily desirable.

I felt an immense sense of depression in Kleve, whereas in

Caen I had been ashamed; ashamed to belong to the side that had done such a thing to its friends. And I had felt hatred, too, at being confronted for the first time with a real war atrocity (as opposed to those concocted daily by the newspapers). So widespread was this feeling—the value of my impressions is that they were so very average—that the man actually responsible, Winston Churchill, subsequently forbade the mass obliteration of Allied towns and populations. However, once the German border was crossed, this afterthought no longer applied.

But the most peculiar feeling was to be here in Germany at all. And this was because, living on the English south coast, the real war had begun as a real threat of a German invasion of England; not necessarily a successful one, but at least it was not impossible to imagine German soldiers marching through English streets. The one thing that seemed really impossible was to find oneself as an English soldier inside a ruined Germany. But it had happened.

The Battle of Emmerich was taking place inside a box about a dozen square miles in extent. The bottom line of the box was the Kranenburg–Kleve–Kalcar road, some five or six miles distant from the Rhine and running roughly parallel to it. This road was plumed with dust from the vehicles rolling towards Xanten and Rees, and shaken by the ear-cracking salvoes of the heavy and medium guns drawn up in the fields on the Rhine side of that road.

The road from Kleve to Emmerich runs north-east through Kellen and Warheyen to the near bank of the Rhine, with Emmerich on the far bank. There was no bridge, but there had been a number of ferry sites; and some of the piers were to be utilised for the bridges that the Canadian engineers wre about to construct. The first two, "Melville" and "Contractor," were to be 1,348 feet and 1,757 feet long respectively.

Construction of Melville bridge was to start simultaneously from both banks of the Rhine, the moment the far bank was clear. The equipment necessary for the far bank, which included bulldozers, was to be ferried across. Three rafts for this purpose had been constructed during the night, and then hidden round an upstream bend of the river. 32 Field Company were responsible for the far bank, 33 Field

Company for the near bank, while 34 Field Company was to construct and bring into position the floating bays of the bridge.

The signal to indicate "Go ahead with your bridging" was a large blue sign marked with the number "32," which would be erected in Emmerich by an engineer officer accompanying the leading brigade of the 3rd Canadian Division into the town. This signal was made at about mid-day on March 31, which was about the time Taylor and I were walking past Kleve castle and the railway station into the marshalling area of the bridging convoys, which were destined for a great many different units and bridges apart from those already mentioned.

We scrounged a lift in one of these vehicles and had to wait only 10 minutes before the convoy started off for the Rhine. Speed noticeably increased when we passed the first signpost, which read: ROAD UNDER CONSTANT SHELLING. After a few miles, we came to a crossroads, where every vehicle stopped briefly while a soldier with a wireless set checked it in and out. Here I got out, because the driver said he was going up FIN route and that MAGGS route was the road to Emmerich. Unfortunately, Taylor was on the back of the truck, and the driver was off so quick there was no time to tell him. "He just went round the corner, all mixed up with bridges, looking indignant."

The principal traffic on MAGGS at that moment was an old horse-drawn carriage occupied by three soldiers enjoying themselves immensely at their modish form of transport, while others were getting free rides from horses. Animals of all descriptions were running loose in the fields, and despite the two-way shell traffic, a fine German bull was trying to mount a cow.

The next sign read: NO MOVEMENT PAST THIS POINT IN DAYLIGHT. Beyond was a dead Buffalo of 79 Armoured Division, which had taken a direct shell hit; and further along a cow that had also taken a shell. "It looks like the contents of a butcher's shop that had been left out in the rain for some time."

The next scene was six soldiers filling in two newly made shell holes in the road, just short of the final sign, which ordered: HALT! ROAD UNDER FIRE. "The waterfront of Emmerich is in plain view, with an Auster circling over it, and the smoke of bursting shells coming up from the ruins. It overlooks the road to Cleve for miles." In fact, a few vehicles were using the road—at breakneck speed—so I presumed the sign was an hour or so out of date.

"I walk up past some lorries, and look down on the Rhine, moving fast, cold and agitated under grey skies and a strong wind. The waterfront of Emmerich across the way is just a single scar . . . churches, factories, houses all torn and mangled. Away on the left, white smoke swells up continuously from woods at the base of a hill upon which stands a town, surmounted by a church. Once, I saw the flash as a shell burst, and once I heard a machine-gun, but the wind blows most sounds away. There on the left, the infantry must be going forward, covered by the guns; you can see the bursting plumes of white smoke go slowly up the slope towards the village on the hill. Here, opposite Emmerich, which has just fallen, the bank of the Rhine is packed with Engineers, only about 5 per cent wearing tin hats, who are methodically preparing to bridge the Rhine, so that masses of material may move up. It's all very slow and everyday and unexciting. There's a loud bang, and a black cloud of smoke leaps up from the opposite side of the Rhine and drifts slowly past the square tower of a shattered church, but after the smoke has rolled away, the far bank of the Rhine looks just the same as before. Then the Engineers fall out for tea, lining up at a house on the Rhine bank with their mess tins in evidence, but not their tin hats. Naval craft fuss about in the river and Brigadiers watch the operation with satisfied eyes. I wander past a farm building. A dead fox lies within. A dead pig lies outside. Twenty yards ago two Engineers are at work; one sweeping the ground with a mine detector, the other prodding the ground with his bayonet. They take their time at the nasty job, and look rather cold. Our guns are hammering away like fury at a church about a mile from Emmerich, and smoke is bursting up all around it. Jerry replies and a dense cloud of black smoke drifts away over the flat plain where his salvoes fell. A soldier is walking along with his supper in both hands—a couple of German fowls. This is war, this unspectacular operation, as commonplace and logical as digging a garden."

The church near Emmerich was probably Huthum (my map was too small-scale to be sure), the church on the hill of Hochelten was the twelfth-century convent church of St. Vitus, which had been destroyed before, in the sixteenth century, during the Dutch wars of liberation. Both were the objectives now of the Régiment de la Chaudière, a French-Canadian battalion of 3 Canadian Division. Of this action, their historian wrote: *"Le Régiment capturait un secteur qui fut peut-être le plus bombardé dans l'histoire de la guerre."*

There are probably many contenders for the title of "most bombarded area of the war," from Cassino to Stalingrad, but in proportion to its size Emmerich was the most badly damaged town I was to see. It had already been heavily bombed before the battle, and when my unit crossed the Rhine at Emmerich on April 19 and I was able to see more of the damage, I noted "Not one house intact."

This was clearly going to be true of Hochelten, too, for within half an hour of my reaching the Rhine on March 31, I wrote:

"The shells are now bursting about halfway up the hill that looks down on our side of the Rhine; you can see the red flame as the shells burst among the houses and the puff of white smoke that goes billowing up. The guns are letting go almost continuously, and the air is full of steel that sings. It isn't all one-way traffic, either."

And about half an hour after that, "The shells are bursting like envenomed fireflies almost at the crest of the hill now. The Canadians have almost got that town." At this moment, I got up off the dyke on which I had been lying, about to walk away, when—*wheeeeeeyou!*—a bullet cracked past an inch or so from my head. Like almost everything else on that grey, depressing day, it was anti-climax.

I had walked with sore feet some distance along the bank of the Rhine, to be sure of having parachutists opposite me, but the flood plain on the far side west of Emmerich was so extensive that the range was virtually impossible; however, I was firing a few rounds for luck, lying down inconspicuously in my "shoot suit," and merging with the top of the dyke in my best professional manner, when I was disturbed by three Canadian infantrymen, walking along the top of the dyke upright, in full view of the other side, highly casual, one not even wearing uniform but merely denims, and with no equipment at all, only rifle and bandolier, and searching, so they said, for a boat in order to cross the Rhine.

Could I join them? Certainly, so that made four of us walking along the dyke looking for a boat. If only my feet had not been so sore, it would have been great fun. A fourth bridgehead over the Rhine established! Remagen, Patton's, Monty's, and Mine! But we had gone no more than 50 yards, and found no boat, when a Don R roared up to the house they were using as a billet, and a shout recalled them. They were being pulled out to cross the Rhine the official way, further up stream.

I lay down again to fire a few disconsolate last shots, and was getting up to go home in disgust when that large-calibre bullet cracked past my ear and I nearly dived for the ditch. Apart from being blown 20 feet through the air by an anti-personnel bomb during a night raid on London in 1943, this was my closest shave to date, easily. It missed by only an inch or two. The cause of the trouble was a large-size calf, which two Canadians were trying to shoot with revolvers, a notoriously inaccurate weapon.

"They pump lead into it; it prances about, falls to its knees, gets up, runs a bit more, slips down, kicks, rolls over, kicks again, lies still. I almost offer to shoot the thing myself, if they don't feel able to despatch it. One of them grabs the corpse, and starts to drag it home, whereupon it kicks like mad. So they put a gun to its ear, and start blasting away again. It does seem pretty dead after that."

Of course, this was much more logical than the war; they were killing it because they wanted to eat it.

On my way back, I walked through the village of Warheyen.

"I stop for a moment in the door of its shell-riddled church. Instinctively, I take off my hat. Inside, there's a soft wind, which ruffles my hair and stirs the dust of the debris in the nave; almost a refuge from the bitter wind without, and a sanctuary, shattered though it may be, against that desolated countryside inhabited only by roving herds of cattle and the birds that shriek at the firing of the guns."

From there I hitch-hiked. "It's getting dark as we pass the horrid ruins of Kranenburg and Wyler, and night as we ride into Nijmegen, with the searchlights by the bridge playing upon the river."

I still had not really taken part in a battle, and had principally been impressed by what the Canadians had told me: that the bridge into Emmerich would be built during the night and would be completed by the next day. This seemed to me enormously impressive, particularly when I recollected that Portsmouth City Corporation had taken 10 years to build a 100-yard bridge across a ditch by the airport. Canada went even higher in my estimation.

I did not understand all the technical difficulties—the effect of the high wind on the floating pontoons, for instance—but the width of the river, the speed of the current, the mass of material that had to be moved, and the work that had to be done on the approaches was clearly immense. What I had witnessed were parts of the first stages of the building of Melville bridge, a 1,348-foot-long class-40 floating Bailey named after Brigadier J. E. Melville, a former chief engineer of the Canadian Army. It was opened to traffic at 2100 hours on April 1 for a total building time of 33 hours, nine hours ahead of schedule.

FINN route led to the rafting site, and MAGGS route was named after Major Percy J. Maggs, OC of 32 Field Company, R.C.E., responsible for the far bank. Maggs had been up all night on March 30–31, building and then concealing from view two class-40 rafts and one close-support raft. He returned to his billet at 0630 on March 31 and before he could get any sleep a Don R arrived with orders from the CRE to cross the river and recce the far bank. "We arrived back at noon just as the signal came through to commence bridging," he wrote.

The naval craft I had seen were in fact helping to get his equipment over.

"The Class 40 rafts were powered by four 8 H.P. Petter engines driving props through flexible shafting. Since the Rhine current was about 5 knots it was felt this might prove inadequate, so an LCV(P), manned by Royal Navy Personnel, was lashed into each raft and we soon set off with the first load, which was a bulldozer. Mine sweeping on the far bank got under way, the bulldozer was put on shore and it proceeded to build a ramp to get the bridging lorries up on to the bank. Once this was completed the two rafts began shuttling the stores across the river and in due time construction got under way."

Eighteen bridging lorries had to be ferried over and unloaded, without help from pioneers, and the area checked for mines—30 Riegel mines were found under the roadway and removed. Buildings were pulled down for use as rubble, but this hardly made any difference to Emmerich. As Colonel Capstick, then a lieutenant, commented: "The whole city was a shambles. The rails at the railway station seemed to be tied in big knots."

The work on the near bank was easier, because there was no rafting to do before bridging could begin; but putting in the floating pontoons in a fast current and a high wind was difficult. They had to be manoeuvred into place by power boats and infantry landing craft, and then anchored.

"For anchors we used a Bailey panel with 3 big anchors wired securely to each one," [wrote Capstick]. "This would make about a 900 lb. anchor. 300 feet of rope was tied to each anchor. And I remember figuring it out that we used 18 miles of rope for all the anchorage in the Class 40 bridge. From the morning of 30 March until 1400 hours on 1 April—55 hours—we slept only for a couple of hours in the morning of 31 March."

There was only one mishap, even so.

"We lost one pontoon, the knot gave way. I ran down the bank, removing my jacket, belt, hat, etc., with the intention of swimming out to retrieve it, as the rope was trailing; but the CO ordered me to let it go. It certainly would have alerted the enemy, but since further upstream British Army Engineers had thrown a bridge across, they might have assumed it came from that operation."

While searching for a boat with the three Canadian infantrymen, I saw "a black barge floating down the Rhine out of control," and this may have been Capstick's lost pontoon. I am afraid I fired a shot at it, as I was suspicious of floating objects.

Further up stream, other Canadian engineers were preparing a class 70 and also laying anti-mine cables. One of them, George I. L. Reid, recalled,

"The Germans sent bombs down the river and we had to pay cables across to pick the bombs off before they hit our bridge. The fast rising and lowering of the river was a hazard to us, also the river rose as much as two feet overnight. There was also a terrific undercurrent which made it very hazardous for the boys working."

34 Field Company, building the floating pontoons for the class-40 experienced the same trouble. Sapper E. H. Isley wrote,

"We started to build the Bailey pontoon bridge about 5 o'clock the first night. We had quite a few pontoons built when the tide came in about midnight; they were all damaged but one. There were about 35 men holding on to it and we had pikes drove in the ground, but we thought it was going to get away from us. I thought the whole bridge was going to go out."

But it did not, and Melville bridge was completed nine hours earlier than planned.

Traffic at this stage was one way only: UP. That is, if you got over the Rhine you didn't get back until a return DOWN bridge had been built. So for the engineers there was no respite. After completing Melville late in the evening of April 1, Maggs recalled:

"Some time was spent in clearing up, mooring the rafts and getting back to HQ. I crawled into a sleeping bag just in time to be roused by a Don R with a message for me to report to the CRE. We were informed that another bridge, only a class 15 instead of a class 40, was required to serve as a return bridge, so we started organising for this second effort. By 0800 on April 2 the men were back on the job but they were tired after a long spell with little sleep and there had not been time for the detailed planning which went into the first bridge. The weather worsened and in the wind and rain an LCVP pushed a floating bay too quickly and it sank. The wind continued to rise and was blowing directly upstream. The floating bays as they come into bridge drop their upstream anchors and pay out until they are on correct line. But this time wind pressure rose about the drag of the current and as the bridge was built it formed a great arc upstream. So it was necessary to get out quickly and lay the downstream anchors and the bridge was slowly warped into line. This Class 15 bridge was 1,757 feet long between banak seats and was finally opened to traffic at 1800 hours on April 3. I slept well that night, having been 4½ days without sleep."

Lieutenant W. W. Gemmel, who had been on the Arnhem rescue operation with 20 Field Company, was now with 30 Field Company, which had helped build the even longer Blackfriars bridge upstream at Rees for British traffic. This 1,865-foot-long class-40 bridge was built in 40 hours. British engineers had previously built the class-15 Lambeth bridge just upstream. "This was an assault bridge and we heard that they had heavy casualties," wrote Gemmel.

There would have been heavy casualties at Emmerich, but for the continuous counter-battery fire in general and in particular the barrage that drenched the heights of Hochelten during the assault that coincided with the start of the bridging operation on May 31. Technically, Emmerich was the reverse of Oppenheim. There, the near bank consisted of a terraced escarpment 100 feet high, which overlooked and dominated the far bank, and which the Americans lined with tanks. But at Emmerich, the entire plain back to Kleve was overlooked and dominated by the Hochelten feature on the far bank. Hence, the need for a smokescreen early on and considerable artillery support. But the work of the engineers, here as elsewhere, was without glamour.

As Major Maggs explained:

"The normal deck of a Bailey bridge consists of 2-inch thick planks laid loose across the steel stringers and held down at the ends by timbers called ribbands which were bolted down. However, when a bridge was likely to be in use for some while and especially when it was to carry tank traffic a second layer of 2-inch plank, cut so it could be laid in herring bone style, was nailed on to the regular planks. This was called a skin deck. It meant driving quite a few nails to skin deck a bridge like the Melville, and one of the Sappers at Emmerich looked up from his work and said, "*They sure got us pepped up about this crossing of the Rhine, but I never thought I'd cross the ruddy thing on my hands and knees.*"

CHAPTER TWENTY-NINE

ARNHEM THE UNATTAINABLE

"Fortress Holland"—April 2–13

Four weeks short of five years from the day the Germans launched Operation Yellow, on May 10, 1940, the situation was almost exactly the same—but with the roles of defender and attacker reversed. The irony was unconsciously stressed by the German command, which in the first week of April re-designated the area held by their Twenty-fifth Army as "*Festung* Holland"—Fortress Holland. Once again, the Netherlands were to be defended on river lines—the Ijssel and the Grebbe. Unfortunately for the defenders, these defences had been reconstructed since 1940 to face the other way—westwards, against an Allied seaborne invasion.

The forces available to Generaloberst Johannes Blaskowitz probably did not amount to more than 120,000 men. This was not the German Army of 1940, and their quality was variable—they included Volksgrenadier divisions and Dutch S.S. The commanders and staffs, on the other hand, were far better than in 1940; immensely experienced and skilful after nearly six years of war, during which Germany had conquered almost the whole of Europe, from Norway in the north to the African desert in the south, from the borders of Spain to the mountains of the Caucasus.

They were faced by an almost entirely volunteer army, General H. D. G. Crerar's First Canadian Army, composed now of II Canadian Corps, which under Lieutenant-General G. G. Simonds had landed in Normandy on June 6, 1944, and I Canadian Corps, which under Lieutenant-General C. Foulkes had just been moved to Holland from Italy where it had been fighting since the summer of 1943. In their view, the change from the mountains and strongly built stone houses of Italy to the flat lands of Holland was a military improvement from the attacker's point of view; and the facilities, both in the latest weapons and in hitherto-unknown luxuries at the front, were far superior.

Of the British divisions that up to now had always formed part of the Canadian Army, only the "Polar Bears" of the 49th West Riding Infantry Division now remained under command; although the 79th Armoured Division still farmed out its specialised assault vehicles to all three armies—American, British, and Canadian—forming Montgomery's 21st Army Group. There were also a few Belgian and Netherlands Resistance men organised in light infantry battalions, and, of course, the Polish Armoured Division.

Only the political command bore no relation to that of 1940. Instead of a single source of political power—a somewhat nervous Adolph Hitler, apprehensive about his southern front and anxious to finish off matters rapidly in the north—there were innumerable pressures on the military command, ranging from the foolish to the downright devious. The move of I Canadian Corps from Italy, although it has never been admitted, was clearly aimed at giving more strength to Montgomery (and specifically British objectives in Europe for the post-war period), thus making him less vulnerable to American pro-Russian manoeuvres ordered by Eisenhower but clearly instigated by Roosevelt and his advisors.*

The main pressures on Mongomery at this time cancelled each other out. On the one hand, the Dutch government-in-exile, which had left Holland very swiftly in May, 1940, in April, 1945, was anxious to get back just as quickly. They produced "harrowing stories of misery and starvation" coming, quite truthfully, from the Netherlands as a reason for a campaign by the Canadian Army into western Holland and a speedy liberation of such 1940 objectives as Rotterdam and The Hague. But, as Colonel C. P. Stacey, the official Canadian historian, wrote:

"It was questionable if it would be a kindness to the folk of western Holland to turn their country into a battleground

* In some circles in the United States, it was said, the principal threats to the U.S.A. were regarded as being Roosevelt, Stalin, and Hitler—in that order.

. . . and the Germans were likely to flood still more land as a measure of defence or spite."*

Indeed, "liberation" had become a bitter joke among all Allied soldiers. While the verb "to liberate" meant simply to "loot," the word "liberated" used as an adjective to describe a city, town, or village implied a totally devastated former population centre through which roads had to be cleared with bulldozers and the stench of death hung sweet and sickening on the air.

By now, very few European and Russian towns and cities remained that were not in this unenviable state. What Rotterdam had endured in 1940 would be a bagatelle compared to what was now in store, not merely for that city, but for The Hague, Leiden, Haarlem, and Amsterdam, among other places, according to a Canadian order issued on April 12, as a result of pressure from the Netherlands government-in-exile. This was cancelled at the last minute, as a result of orders filtering down from the top that were themselves the result of an American decision of April 4.

On that day, the vital northern thrust by the 21st Army Group to secure the North German ports and reach the Baltic before the Red Army was endangered by the transfer of Simpson's Ninth U.S. Army to Bradley's army group with a new role that would ensure non-interference with Stalin's ambitions, thus weakening Montgomery's drive. Consequently, he had insufficient forces remaining with which to carry out his main objective, the political denial of Denmark and the route to Scandanavia, to the Soviet, as well as the militarily non-essential clearing of western Holland, the political aims of which were known only to the Netherlands government-in-exile and formed no part of British policy.

The political considerations were simple in comparison with the military problems. Many plans were put forward and studied by the soldiers, but foundered on engineer objections, based on the nature of the Rhine delta and the fluctuations,

† *The Canadian Army* 1939–1945 by Colonel C. P. Stacey (Ottawa, 1948); see also *The Victory Campaign,* Chapter XXI, by the same author.

natural or induced, by which the river might or could be made to frustrate them.

The last suggestion for a completion of Market Garden in 1944 came from Montgomery in early November. This was to be in two stages: first, the clearing of the "Island" between the Waal and the Neder Rijn; then, an assault over the Neder Rijn near Arnhem aimed at the high ground around Apeldoorn, and including a bridgehead over the Ijssel. The German action in partially flooding the "Island" effectively blocked this idea in its initial stage, as the base of operations then became even more subject to the winter weather pattern of flooding and icing.

The next suggestion put forward by Lieutenant-General G. G. Simonds (II Corps) and worked out by Lieutenant-General C. Foulkes (I Corps) had an identical first stage; but in the second stage, instead of driving for Apeldoorn, the Canadians would immediately turn eastward into Germany and drive along the far bank of the German Rhine towards Emmerich. This was in February, long before Remagen. But Foulkes's appreciation showed that both weather and the enemy, including enemy-controlled flooding of the Ijssel, made success unlikely.

When the Rhine crossings became imminent, and it was clear that Emmerich would be captured before Arnhem, two alternative plans were considered. The first plan was basically Market Garden, except that the Neder Rijn would be crossed at Oosterbeek, west of Arnhem, thus avoiding a built-up area in the early stages, but nevertheless risking disaster from the German-held high ground at Westerbouwing that overlooked the bridging site. (A suggested amendment was to cross at Renkum, five miles west of Oosterbeek.)

The alternative plan, to be employed if the state of the ground combined with enemy resistance made the first unlikely to succeed, was virtually a duplicate of Operation Yellow. It is unlikely that the Canadians had studied the German operations of May 10, 1940, but in spite of many minor planning fluctuations, which it would be tedious to recall, this was to be what actually happened. Basically, this depended on the capacity of the Rhine bridges at Emmerich, so the two battles were immediately connected.

Further, the fruits of success at Arnhem would be, not the premature clearing of the western Netherlands, but the opening of an additional supply route, from Nijmegen railhead via Arnhem and Zutphen, which would in its turn assist the great drive to the north from the Rhine bridgehead towards the Baltic. This would make full use of the existing road bridge at Nijmegen, although the Neder Rijn would have to be bridged, as Arnhem road bridge had been damaged in October, 1944, by air attacks and in February, 1945, had finally been "blown" by the Germans.

But as Lieutenant E. F. Burkart of the 49th Division wrote:

"At the risk of being though frivolous, I would remind readers that this was a battle that very nearly did not come off . . . Higher Authority seemed quite unable to decide how to attack Arnhem."

Doubtless the planners were recalling the Roer dams and the effect the consequent flooding had had both on the British-Canadian offensive through the Reichswald and the timing of the American attack.

Stage one of the third Battle of Arnhem began on April 2, 1945 (code-name "Destroyer"), stage two on April 11 (code-name "Cannonshot"), and stage three on April 12 (code-name "Anger" or "Quick Anger"), followed by the drive to the Zuyder Zee (code-name "Cleanser"). The last was a latter-day Market Garden, the others were vitually a second Operation Yellow.

"Destroyer" was the clearing of the "Island" between Nijmegen and Arnhem; "Cannonshot" was a drive out of Germany into Holland across the Ijssel far to the north of Arnhem, directed at the high ground of Apeldoorn on an axis that drove into the Netherlands between Zutphen in the south and the Deventer to the north; and "Quick Anger" was an assault on Arnhem across the Ijssel to the east, from Westervoort, on the same axis and in the same place and with the identical initial objectives of May 10, 1940, down to and including the capture of Fort Westervoort.

"Cleanser" would be the breakout from the bridgehead in the Arnhem area secured by the 49th West Riding

Division by the 5th Canadian Armoured Division, with its axis directed to the Zuyder Zee, 30 miles to the north—with, in effect, the 49th Division taking on the role of 1st Airborne and the 5th Canadian Armoured taking on the task of Guards Armoured. But now, in 1945, this drive to the Ijsselmeer would link with other Canadian forces driving out of Germany into Holland towards Apeldoorn, a plan that was a mixture of Market Garden and Operation Yellow.

The parallel with the latter was most striking, in that the Canadians would be attacking Holland out of Germany, from bases that were mainly in the Reichswald. Now they held Nijmegen, but then the Germans had held most of Nijmegen by 0445 on the morning of May 10, less than an hour after they had attacked out of the Reichswald and roared down the road from Wyler. There was therefore only an hour or so's difference, apart from the fact that, this time, the attackers had previously taken the bridges at Nijmegen.

As far as the "Island" was concerned, the Canadians started by occupying the southern half of it; but then the Germans had taken the eastern part of it, from Pannerden and Doornenburg to Angeren and Huissen by late afternoon or early evening on May 10, with the Dutch falling back.

On the Ijssel front, east of Arnhem, the Germans had left Germany at 0355 hours, following the road that nearly parallels the railway line leading to the Ijssel bridges, and had reached Westervoort by 0440, where blown bridges prevented their armoured trains from crossing. Nevertheless, they had put Fort Westervoort out of action, crossed the Ijssel, and were in the western outskirts of Arnhem by 1100 hours, heading for Oosterbeek and, eventually, the Grebbe Line, where they were halted.

This parallel was to be precisely re-enacted in 1945, but more slowly and with immense fire power and masses of armoured vehicles. The Germans had simultaneously attacked well to the north of Arnhem, another gambit that was to be repeated. As numbers of Dutch S.S. troops were to fight with the Germans in 1945, so even some of the defenders were still Dutch; and, it must be admitted, they fought well, even desperately.

The line-up in 1940 had been two regiments of the

German 207 Infantry Division, storm troops from the S.S. Standarte "Der Führer," an armoured train, a passenger train, and detachments of Special Battalion No. 100. They were opposed by a weak force consisting of 22 Frontier Battalion and III Battalion of the 35th Regiment of Infantry.

In 1945, the attack along the equivalent axis from Westervoort was to be carried out by the 49th (West Riding) Infantry Division, attacking initially on a narrow one-battalion front; supported by the Sherman tanks of 11 Canadian Armoured Regiment (Ontario Regiment) from 5 Canadian Armoured Division; with specialised aid from the 79th Armoured Division, which provided a squadron of Flails from 1 Lothians & Border Yeomanry, a squadron of Crocodiles from 1 Fife & Forfar Yeomanry, the Buffaloes of 11 Royal Tanks, and the Avres of 617 Assault Squadron, Royal Engineers.

The Flails (or "Crabs") were gun-Shermans fitted with a rotary chain on booms for exploding mines; the Crocodiles were gun-Churchills with a flame-gun in addition; the Avres were gunless Churchills fitted instead with a large mortar. The last two were appropriate for dealing with concrete defences, such as pillboxes, at close range. They had materially helped the cracking of the Siegfried Line pivot in the Reichswald.

Gun support was fairly lavish. It included the 49th divisional artillery, the 5th Canadian Armoured divisional artillery, 1 Army Group Royal Canadian Artillery, 11 Field Regiment, R.C.A., and 1 Rocket Battery, R.C.A. The latter would engage Fort Westervoort initially. R.A.F. Spitfires and Typhoons would ground-strafe before the attack, and some of the assault troops would be brought up river from Nijmegen in landing craft belonging to Force "U" of the Royal Navy.

The days were past when 20 cyclists in faked uniforms and wearing cardboard helmets could open the attack with a ruse; and prepared defences were no longer to be cracked by a covey of motor-cycle combinations aided by a couple of tanks backed by armoured trains and troop trains. With rivers on two sides and hills on the other two, Arnhem was a geographically difficult nut to crack. But that it was going to be cracked, there was little doubt.

As Colonel Stacey remarks, the composition of the

defending forces "remained something of a mystery to our Intelligence before the attack." At the time, we were told that it was 34 S.S. Division "Nederland," the Dutch S.S., but it seems to have included many miscellaneous units of which the largest was the 858th Grenadier Regiment of the 346th Infantry Division.

No gun-state is available, but they certainly had a fair supply of artillery and also rocket batteries, the so-called Nebelwerfer, nicknamed "Moaning Minnie" by the staid British and "Screaming Meemie" by the more uninhibited Canadians and Americans. Although called mortars, they were really multi-barrel rocket projectors on wheels, fired electrically from a distance. Six barrels to one piece was a popular arrangement, and the calibres were large—150, 210, and 300 millimetres. The projectiles needed only a very thin casing and had maximum blast effect, whereas a shell, which has to withstand the shock of discharge from a rifled barrel, has a thick casing and proportionately less explosive content; although accuracy and range are much greater, The unanimous choice of female nomenclature for something so noisy and so deadly to the male may be of interest to psychologists.

The German military historian, Paul Carell, has complained that "the achievements of this splendid branch of the army have not so far had the acknowledgment and publicity they deserve." That omission will be rectified.

"Destroyer," the clearing of the "Island," was carried out on April 2–3, with the Germans simply falling back to the Neder Rijn and retreating across it to the far bank. This attack was carefully timed to coincide with the advance of 3 Canadian Division out of Emmerich, and was carried out by the West Riding Division with Canadian support in infantry, tanks, and guns.

The plan still was to cross the Neder Rijn in the Driel area, but embarrassing events occurred. The smokescreen laid down to conceal the preparations was ineffective and on one occasion left a number of senior inspecting officers in clear view of the Germans on the hills beyond the far bank of the river.

Therefore, on April 7, the plan was altered for the last time, and General Foulkes decided to move the 49th Division to the east, across the Neder Rijn near Doornenburg, and thence to Westervoort. This was yet another striking parallel, for this had been the German crossing-place onto the "Island" on May 10, 1940, when they had captured the fort at Doornenburg after an assault-crossing.

No assault-crossing was necessary here, as both banks of the Neder Rijn were held at this point by the Canadians, and after a rafting operation had proved unsuccessful because of the steep banks of the river, 294 Field Company, Royal Engineers, built the class-9 folding boat bridge called "Gremlin" near Doornenburg. "Practically the whole of the 49th Division passed over the bridge in two days, nearly wearing a hole in it in the process," wrote their historian.

The dykes of both the Neder Rijn at Driel and the Ijssel at Westervoort presented an impassable obstacle to vehicles. 756 Field Company, Royal Engineers, had already prepared the bund at Driel in three places, by boring down 35 feet and filling the holes with explosives. About 400 tons of soil needed to be removed in this manner before vehicles could approach the river. These charges were blown anyway, just prior to the real assault, as a diversion. The same unit had to prepare the bund at Westervoort for blowing in three places, but this was not to prove a success, partly because of damage to the cordtex and electrical leads caused by Typhoons, British shelling, Canadian shelling, and German shelling, but also because of the sticky nature of the bund clay.

The engineers were to move into Arnhem close behind the assault with a bulldozer, a half-track, and a three-ton winch lorry, as well as carrying out miscellaneous tasks that included both mine-clearing and barricade demolition as well as attaching green lights to the groins as a guide for a prefabricated pontoon bridge that would be floated up the Ijssel to Westervoort. A class-40 bridge was necessary to take the armoured vehicles that would follow the assault infantry. Everything was very carefully prepared and timed, and nearly everything went wrong.

The 56th Infantry Brigade (2 Glosters, 2 South Wales Borders, 2 Essex) were to carry out the assault and gain an initial bridgehead in the area of Fort Westervoort, the silk factory near the "Spit," and the "Spit" itself—the name given to the apex of land where the Ijssel meets the Neder Rijn; then they were to clear the southern sector of Arnhem. 146 Infantry Brigade (4 Lincolns, Hallams Y. & L., 1/4 KOYLI) were to pass through the assault brigade and enlarge their bridgehead. 147 Infantry Brigade (7 D.W.R., 11 R.S.F., 1 Leicesters) were to secure the high ground west of Arnhem and then exploit west and north-west.

Arnhem lies in a half-circling bowl of wooded hills that overlook the low dykeland, bordered by the Ijssel and Neder Rijn, to the south-east; and the battle would not be over until the attacks had taken not merely the streets but the heights as well. It was basically an artillery and infantry task; there was no chance of deploying armour until the battle was won, and a few tanks were there merely to support the Infantry at this stage. The bulk of the armour was held back for the break-out later, to the north.

On Thursday, April 12, I wrote in my diary: "The guns on the Island before Nijmegen begin to beat away at nightfall. 49 Div, for so long the 'Home Guard' of Nijmegen, are going in to take Arnhem."

D. B. Hollins, who was with 2nd South Wales Borderers, part of the assault brigade, recalled:

"On the evening before the attack, the S.W.B. assembled near the river, and then embarked on amphibious vehicles by platoons under cover of darkness, to cross the river. It had been a beautiful evening, and we stood and watched the terrific barrage that our guns put up from every direction on Arnhem. It was so inspiring and yet frightening, that I remember that we could not talk but just stood and watched."

"Searchlights cast an eerie light over that night of the assault" [wrote Captain R. D. Marshall]. "Rocket-firing Typhoons of the West Riding squadron of the R.A.F. joined the artillery barrage, and salvoes of ground rockets fired at 350 a time. Sweating gunners on 25-pounders kept up the last ten minutes at five rounds a minute. Buffaloes and stormboats came in to ferry the attackers across the 120-foot span of the fast-flowing Ijssel."

Colonel R. H. Tierney, commanding a field gun battery covering the initial assault by 2 Glosters, recalled that his eight-gun battery fired 640 rounds in the first 10 minutes.

Lieutenant E. F. Burkart, then intelligence officer of 2 Glosters, wrote a narrative that was published in the regimental magazine three years later.

"During the day of 12 April, Typhoon attacks were made by the R.A.F. on various targets connected with the operation, including the area of the fort, which was shot-up with rockets. At 8:40 p.m.—H hour minus two—the timed artillery programme began, reaching a crescendo during the last hour. The artillery support itself was provided on a reasonably heavy scale—not as great as during some previous operations—but two especial features were the use of 'mattresses' and the 'pepper-pot.' The 'Mattress' was a land-based version of the multiple rockets fired from naval craft during the Normandy invasion, and one 'mattress' had a very much greater effect than a normal shoot by a regiment of artillery. The 'pepper-pot' was the use of all spare weapons under divisional command—in this case including heavy mortars, machine guns, A/tank, tank, and A.A. artillery—in a harassing role on the back areas of Arnhem. The purpose was to frustrate any movement or concentration of reinforcements, ammunition or supplies and was aimed at likely targets, rather than confirmed centres of enemy defence. In this way too it was possible to bluff the enemy as to the direction of the attack, without at the same time sparing any of the targets essential to its prosecution."

Arnhem had been heavily fortified by the Germans after the airborne battle, but these defences mostly faced the Neder Rijn, where indeed both the British and the Canadians in turn had originally planned to attack.

"An integral part of the assault plan was the blowing of a gap in the bund by the sappers," [Burkart's narrative continued]. "This was necessary to allow the Buffaloes of A and C Companies to take to the water directly opposite their objectives, only being exposed to hostile fire at the latest possible moment. Charges were laid during the day, yet while the long procession of Buffaloes was moving from its assembly area close alongside the line of the Emmerich–Arnhem railway, news was received by the C.O. that in fact the earlier confidence of the sappers had been misplaced, and that the charges had failed to do their part satisfactorily, due it was thought to wires being cut in the earlier Typhoon attack. Thus it was that at 10:40 p.m.—H hour—under a cold and clear night sky, lit by the artificial moonlight of searchlights, the carefully laid plans went wrong. It is to the credit of the careful briefing and determined responsibility of platoon commanders that the assault was made at all. Shortly after the first intimation of A and C companies' check, it was learned at Bn.H.Q. that B Company were having trouble with the engines of their assault boats. In fact the simultaneous assault by four companies proved to be an assault by D Company, followed some half hour later by B Company. Then A and C Companies made the crossing, ferried in only three Buffaloes, which had been manhandled over the bund, after emptying their loads to reduce weight over the muddy incline."

But pushing on fast through the minefields, all four companies were on their objectives by 0300 hours on April 13. They had Fort Westervoort, the "Spit," and the outlying part of the silk factory area. Some hours later, Captain R.V. Cartwright, who was exploring the inner cells of the fort, discovered 60 armed Germans hiding there; they surrendered. Meanwhile, first South Wales Borders, then 2 Essex, had passed through the limited bridgehead gained by the Glosters.

D. B. Hollins was with the South Wales Borderers, who followed immediately after the Glosters.

"When we were crossing the river, we came under enemy fire, but to the best of my knowledge, none of the vehicles was hit. The current pulled us away from the point we were to land, and the vehicle I was in had to endeavour to climb a steep bank, which it failed to do. As the doors could not open, we were forced to jump from its bows, which were half up the bank, a distance of some 12 feet. We assembled and proceeded towards Arnhem, but my company was held up at the outskirts by an enemy platoon the other side of a railway embankment. However, after a small amount of LMG fire these retreated. I was in the leading section of the leading company, and as we came under a railway bridge, with open ground on our left and a row of houses on our right, we were pinned down by LMG fire, and took refuge in the houses, where we remained all day, coming under heavy fire from 88s, which were sited on high ground to the left. Our tanks were brought up, together with another infantry battalion, but these, too, were held up."

There would have been no tanks at all, but for a piece of good luck to offset the bad. The initial timing of the assault had gone wrong in two places—the Glosters were late in getting their full strength across, whereas the pontoon bridge that was to carry the tanks had started off ahead of schedule and appeared likely to arrive opposite the German machine-gun positions on the far bank before the infantry. In fact, the Glosters got there first, with about one minute to spare, and by 0930 on April 13 a class-40 bridge spanned the Ijssel at Westervoort.

The tanks, specialised armour, and 146 Infantry Brigade began to cross. That is, 10 hours and 40 minutes after the assault. The Germans had taken 11 hours and 20 minutes to get their assault bridge across at the same place in 1940, and their first wave of rubber assault boats had been broken up and driven back by the Dutch. In 1945, the armoured amphibious Buffaloes had carried 260 loads across the Ijssel for the loss of two vehicles and a dozen crewmen killed or wounded.

The leading battalion of 146 Infantry Brigade was 4 Lincolns, and they suffered more heavily than the assault battalion, the Glosters, particularly in the clearing of the "factory" near the two railway embankments just outside the town, which lies well back from the Ijssel, with many factories on its south-eastern outskirts. This delay meant that the battle for the built-up area of Arnhem did not begin until early evening, and less than half the West Riding Division was engaged throughout the greater part of the 13th. The OC of the Glosters had reasonably expected to lose about 100 men, but in fact had only 32 killed and wounded, in spite of the plan going awry through no fault of his.

The Lincolns, however, lost 55 men killed, wounded, and missing that day, and there has been some criticism of the battalion plan. The basic problem was the flood plain of the Ijssel—a large expanse of open, water-logged ground, virtually devoid of cover, which lay between Fort Westervoort and the built-up area of Arnhem proper. The complex of fortified railway embankments (carrying the Emmerich–Arnhem line plus a branch line to the goods station), backed by the fortified outskirts of the built-up area, backed by artillery and mortars on the high ground beyond that, was likely to take heavy toll of any attacker who came on in a hurry.

The author of a private newsletter, *4 Lincoln Activities for the Month of April, 1945*, wrote:

"We had about a two mile march to the position where the Coys were to start passing through the leading Bde. The Country was very flat and open and one felt very naked from the high ground and church spires of Arnhem. The Bn formed up under cover of a large railway embankment and at 1200 hours started to move forward with D Company in the lead. The plan was for this Coy to pass straight up the Bn axis to seize an important cross roads about 800 yards from the start line. C Coy was to follow and mop up behind them. The start line was a railway embankment, a hundred yards beyond which was another railway embankment. The axis passed under these two railways. Beyond the second railway was a very large factory. There were signs of enemy on the second embankment and the road underneath it was blocked. D Company was therefore forced to push on without their tanks. At first all went well."

D Company was commanded by Captain R. V. Francis, with Captain J. R. Ainger as second-in-command. The latter, now Major Ainger, M.C., recalled:

"The original plan drawn up by the new C.O. Lincolns was talked out by the very experienced Company Commanders as being far too risky as it meant ploughing through boggy ground, very open, before reaching the cover of the railway. It was eventually decided to go left along the road to the bridge immediately in front of the factory with D Company leading. Anybody would have realised that the bridge would be blocked and covered by machine-guns. We attempted to clamber over the barricade before being driven back and had to wait for the 'odd' tanks (of 79 Armoured Division) to break up the barricade before we could move forward. Consequently we lost some very good men who had fought with us all the way from Normandy and had even been in Norway. I remember being pretty sour about the whole plan of attack, and the scheme proved as bad as anticipated. When eventually the barricade was cleared a factory manned by mixed unknown troops who fought to the last had to be cleared. There were long lines of shelving running up and down the factory and the opposition went from one to another making life very difficult. The factory was eventually cleared due to some excellent leadership by Francis. I was so disgusted at losing so many good men at such a late stage of the war, that I concentrated on my own job rather more than usual and kept away from the rough stuff in the factory."

Now, after the specialised tanks had destroyed the barricade under the railway bridge, the first troops of fighting Shermans from C Squadron, 11 Canadian Armoured Regiment, came up. The first troop was led by Lieutenant (now Lieutenant-Colonel) F. S. "Steve" Wotton, the second by Lieutenant (now Captain) H. W. Macdonald, who won his Military Cross this day. Wotton recalled:

"C Squadron took the right hand road through the factory area and did its initial attack over a railway embankment with the British infantry clearing a large factory which I understand was in the cellulose business and was, in peacetime, a competitor to a British firm which employed the Company Commander who I was working closely with. I can recall some interesting comments by the Company Commander prior to the battle that we should ensure a very thorough covering fire for his men as they cleared the factory."

Very soon, two companies of the Lincolns were struggling to clear the factory, which had been turned into a fortress, so it is not clear who made that grim joke.

Immediately the covering fire had ceased, Francis led D Company out of its toehold in the factory to begin clearing the whole building. "This was no easy task as the factory was a labyrinth of passages, stores and sheds, while the roofs were alive with snipers," wrote the author of the newsletter. "The enemy fought back very hard, for the most part at very close range indeed." One of the snipers was shot off the roof by tank machine-gun fire, "and his body fell somersaulting grotesquely to the ground" in best Hollywood war-film style. C Company had to join D Company by advancing to the factory while being raked by German fire both from the factory and from the railway embankment.

"The two Coys Comds then divided up the factory between them and set about the final expulsion of the enemy. This was a hard and costly business. In places the enemy resistance was fanatical. One enemy officer received five bursts of bren through him before he was finally stopped, another wounded Bosche tried to throw a grenade at anyone trying to approach him. By the evening, however, the factory was clear, although the enemy was still managing to hold out on the outskirts of it. A quick check up in the failing light revealed 32 enemy dead."

The Lincolns had lost only five killed, but had 50 wounded, in "some of the hardest fighting the Bn had met during the campaign."

Meanwhile, the Canadian tanks and the rest of the Lincolns were trying to by-pass the factory and get forward into the town. The Canadian war diary noted:

"Lt. Wotton managed to force his way North of the factory but was unable to strike East because of an anti-tank gun covering the corner. Lt. Macdonald was then ordered forward. By-passing Wotton's troop, he made a lightning move across the corner to knock out the gun, thus opening the way for the advance. Employing by-pass and block tactics, Macdonald's troop had soon cleared well to the east of the factory, where he was obliged to hold firm, while the infantry mopped up the factory area. The situation was now immensely relieved, and by 1600 hours the remainder of C Squadron had crossed into the town."

Macdonald was by far the most experienced of the two leading troop commanders and he was not impressed by the battle.

"We were kept mucking about at first. Example of how *not* to win a war—two to three miles of armoured fighting vehicles, many of types I'd not seen before, all on one road. There was so much stuff there, that all you had to do was line it up and let it go. The Germans couldn't have stopped it. Why attack Arnhem at all? Go over the Ijssel elsewhere and cut it off. Artillery are hopeless in streets, all blood and guts, like Stalingrad. And in streets, only the leading one or two tanks can operate. You can't deploy the rest."

Macdonald's troop of four Shermans now had two with the normal 75-millimeter guns, two with the long 17-pounders.

"These 17-pounders were held back from Italy" [he explained], "because after Normandy, we were second-class citizens. It was a beautiful weapon, you could thread needles with it at 3,000 yards. We used to practise-shoot at barrels marked with white crosses at that range. So the first job I had to do at Arnhem was to knock off some spires, where OPs were thought to be. I was told: go along the dyke and clear those spires with a 17-pounder. Afterwards, about 2 p.m., the battle had been going on since dawn, but hadn't got very far. The Brigadier was dissatisfied. So he married us with an infantry company. The company commander, a major, was a real soldier.* One in a thousand. One of the best I've ever served with. I was with every Div in the British Eighth Army and some in the U.S. Fifth Army, and I knew only two like him. Working his men through the streets, then on during the night, and didn't have many casualties. The Germans didn't stand a chance against guys like him."

It was this combination of two experienced infantry and tank commanders that late that afternoon finally broke the

* Major J. O. Flint, D.S.O., M.C., commanding B Company, 4 Lincolns. Such personal identifications are difficult, but Mr. Macdonald, who travels widely for his firm, Canadian Forest Products Oversea Limited, gave me an interview during a visit to London, and from his hotel we were able to ring Major Flint, with whom I had also been corresponding, and they very soon confirmed the identification, principally because one of Flint's platoon commanders had just been killed when the tanks came up.

German "crust" and took the attack right into the town and beyond.

"By 1945, we were the professionals and the Germans were the amateurs" [commented Macdonald]. "They were using boys of 16, and so on. They were not what they had been, and they knew the war was over, too. The Germans here were not as good as in Italy, where we fought the Paras—they were pretty rough people. We didn't take 200 prisoners in the whole campaign. In Arnhem, the crust was broken on the first day, to the centre of the town."

The slight delay in breaking the "crust" was to cause me, personally, a good deal of puzzlement. If I got up to Arnhem at all, which was doubtful because there was a check on unauthorised persons going over Nijmegen bridge onto the "Island," I expected to find myself on the left flank of the 49 Division advance; instead of which I found myself on the right flank of the German defenders, and very uncertain about it.

Further, I went up unarmed because if by luck I managed to make Arnhem, I saw little difficulty in picking up a weapon of some kind in the wake of the attack, thus saving all the bother of carrying a rifle round the cathedral at 's Hertogenbosch, which was my "diversionary target" for a sight-seeing visit on this particular day off. I particularly wanted to see the stone carvings there, which I had hitherto studied only in photographs. But I missed my chance for good as, after swallowing some buns and a cup of tea in the shell-battered Nijmegen N.A.A.F.I. canteen, I had no trouble at all in "hitching" over the bridge, through Elst, and to within two kilometres of Arnhem.

The mist had given way to a sunny morning, with bright blue skies and cumulus clouds, and a maze of spring blossoms hiding the ugliness of sandbagged houses and wrecked vehicles. Beyond Elst, until a week ago the front line, the road was lined with newly shattered vehicles and tanks, and the bodies of dead cattle lay thickly in the fields, the sweet and sickly smell of death mingling with the scent of the blossoms. The sound of the guns was now a continuous roaring, like a waterfall overhead, as I walked up the road towards a smoke-screen that blanketed Elst and the Arnhem road from the view of the Germans in the town and on the hills behind. At one point, however, the road rose so high on an embankment that it gave me my first distant view of Arnhem.

"It lies before me, a mile away, on wooded hills across a river, rather like Bath" [I wrote in my diary]. "On the left is a great dome, like the Albert Hall, with four shell holes in its green roof; and near this, great tongues of fire leap and play at the base of an immense column of black smoke. From among the houses on the hills other columns of smoke stand sharply up against the blue sky; towards the centre stands the ruin of a great church, one side of the tower alone standing, with blue sky bright through the bare windows. Black church spires surmount the houses, and from those houses black windows gaze out like eyes across the plain.

"Sudden and sharp among the sighings and sobbings of the shells and mortars comes now and then a fierce burst of machine-gun fire, answered immediately by the rolling rattle of another machine-gun, so that it sounds like two crazy xylophonists trying to out-do one another on tin trays. But because one can tell the slower, sweeter note of the Bren from the sharp, angry, irregular rattle of the Spandau, these eloquent little duels amid the houses seem so very much more vicious than the thundering and shrieking of the guns, which dominate the battle."

When I had walked up to within a few hundred yards of the smokescreen blowing across the road, the picture presented by the battle was peculiar. At ground level, the smoke-screen billowing whitely; above and behind it rising the shattered tower of the great church in Arnhem; behind that, the arabesques of the cumulus clouds seeming to conform in shape and colour with the dense white smoke; and all projected against a gigantic blue backcloth, burnished by the high sun at noon.

The cross-roads before the smokescreen had a signpost: MONCYPLEIN: ARNHEM 05 KM. The house where Maurits van Dongeren had been taken by his parents after the bombing of Rotterdam was just to my left, but I did not know this, and walked thankfully into the smoke, feeling much safer for a brief moment. Approximately, this was the time when 4 Lincolns, leading 146 Brigade, began to advance on the railway bridge; and 2 S.W.B. had been held up and pinned by LMGs and 88s; 2 Essex were probably advancing along the waterfront road.

I emerged from the smokescreen to find Arnhem very near and the road rising up on a very steep embankment leading to the even-then famous bridge, but from my viewpoint even the southern end was not visible, let alone the northern end, which had been held so long by Colonel Frost's paratroops.

"I walk more carefully than ever, ready to drop for cover if the whining and singing of the bullets should come any nearer. It does, and I make my way down the embankment, and up to another embankment which runs parallel with the river. From here, I can see into Arnhem's ruins in great detail, and if I can do it, so can they, so I come down and walk along to where some Belgian soldiers are lying flat behind the embankment, watching the show. I say, 'Good morning,' and flop down beside them. Arnhem is burning in many places, but they don't know whether Jerry holds the opposite bank or not. After a bit, being unarmed, I pick up a rusty Jerry bayonet, and make my way towards the bridge, to try and cross the river."

I expected the bridge to be "blown" of course, but sometimes the structure just collapses into the water and is negotiable on foot.

"I am in the open now, ready to dive behind the nearest pier of the bridge, if anything should come too close. But nobody takes any notice of me (*sic*) and I climb, un-shot, up to the highest part of the bridge, giving a grand view of the burning city. Nothing moves over the way, and the singing in the air does not come nearer, so I walk out along the actual bridge itself, which is twisted and shattered. It ends abruptly, in a maze of twisted girders and splintered planks . . . the river runs between . . . and about fifty feet away is the German half of the bridge, stretching out maimed girders like appealing hands. Distorted by the explosion, they dip soothingly in the blue waters of the river. It is not very wide, about 200 yards only, and from out here I can look down onto the German side less than 150 yards away. Along the waterside is only ruin, with the single tower wall of the great church very plain. There is a green-painted vehicle in a street over the way, but nothing moves. Lulled by the peace of it, I take out my note-book and start sketching."

To cut a fool's story short, the green vehicle was German and I had indeed been seen, but had been taken for something much more important than a casual tourist-*cum*-would-be-historian with a notebook. Possibly an engineer officer, or the preliminary to a new assault direct across the Neder Rijn, for no one on the German bank could tell what lay behind the smokescreen I had just emerged from. I do not know whether they were 150-, 210-, or 300-millimeter, although some were probably 88s. I quite lost these in the appalling sound of the Nebelwerfer.

"Among all the whistling and sighing in the air comes a new note, like a Typhoon in a dive . . . there's a sound like thirty express trains going through a station . . . a column of water stained by smoke leaps out of the river 100 yards on my right, and smoke rises sullenly from the buildings straight in front of me. The sound of the explosions rolls downs the river like thunder."

I got up against a twisted girder on the right and flattened myself against the planks underneath, then peered over the end of the bridge.

"Almost immediately comes the sound like Typhoons diving, mixed up with a high, fluttering scream, and more smoke and water leaps out of the river, and more smoke and dust roll away from the buildings. White tendrils of smoke, like fire-works, come curving out of a house directly opposite my precarious perch, and go bouncing among the rubble. What in hell was that? Fascinated, I watch. Soon, black smoke is pouring up from the house directly opposite me, and also from our side of the river. Flames show at the windows, then in a great blaze they burst through the roof, and roll up to the sky. And all the time the shells and mortars are bracketing the river alongside the bridge. Shrapnel goes bouncing about my end in crazy curves. Red flashes run along the river bank, and smoke blows away. Smoke of all colours goes up from the houses, black with HE, or pink where buildings have been hit. Thank God they hit the same spot almost every time. I get out my note-book for a quick sketch. Now, how did that water look as it spurted out of the river. Bang! Bang! and Jerry supplied the answer in two places at once. Thank you!"

The sketching was one way of relieving tension, because by now I was trembling with a curious mixture of fright and fury. For 20 minutes I was pinned to my perch over the Neder Rijn, unable to retreat, dreading an alteration of aim that would bring the mortar bombs onto the bridge, instead of all round it, and yet so wound up with the urge to hit back that during a few seconds' lull I got to my feet and shook my fist at the people on the other side; although I could see none of them.

Unlike a genuine soldier, however, I could retire nearly at will; and as soon as the bombardment stopped, and I was sure it had stopped, I clambered down from the bridge and walked along the embankment to the west. That did it, and in trying to walk 150 yards to a house, I had to dive flat four times, once grazing my elbow on the ground, I hit it so fast, and even then hearing the sound of metal hitting the fence just above my head. When that stopped, I walked back to the east of the bridge, where the roads were torn up by the shelling and four rows of houses were crackling away noisily. "Very soon these rooms as yet untouched, and all the furniture will be burnt black like the rest. The heat from the burning street is too much under that hot sun, and I veer away."

It never occurred to me at the time that I was responsible for four rows of houses being burnt to the ground, I merely saw a toy clog that was going to burn with the rest, and took it as a souvenir for my daughter.

My next intervention was even more questionable.

"There's an abrupt burst of machine-gun fire from the opposite bank immediately ahead, and I make tracks for it. Burst after burst sounds, sharp and abrupt. To look at it, one would never guess that there were human beings over there. I come on a Bren gun position dug into the embankment, manned by two casual Belgian soldiers—one of them has his boots off . . . I flop down beside them, with a 'Good afternoon.' The Bren is pointed down a street in Arnhem, about 300 yards away. There's a big building, probably a store, on the left hand corner of the street. After watching for a few minutes, and seeing nothing, a man in greenish uniform comes out of it, and lopes down the street with a rifle in his hand. That's a damn queer shade of khaki he was wearing. 'Was that a Bosche?' I ask. They reply: 'Yes, it was.' Another greenish figure comes out of the house, and lopes swiftly down the road, rifle in hand. I could hit him if I had brought my rifle. 'Damn it, why the hell don't you do something about it?' I ask. They grin sheepishly, not understanding, and try to fire the Bren, which jams, before the cartridge goes into the breech. They take off the magazine, and prod at the cartridge in leisurely fashion. About half-a-dozen green-clad forms come out of the house, and walk down the street, bunched together. I rather think one of them has his hands up, and there certainly is a white streamer flying from the house—but it might be a curtain, and the first two had rifles."

At this moment the Belgians cleared the jam at last, but did not fire—I thought, because they were windy of bringing retaliation. I had two seconds or so in which to decide, and what I did was to move in behind their gun.

"I slap the Bren into my shoulder, cock it like lightning, without thought, at a speed I could never equal in training. The six green-clad forms are square in the ring-sight. The foresight is dead centre. A five year memory of stukas, blitz and V-bombs goes into the squeezing of that trigger. The gun is shaking at my shoulder, but I am only half conscious of the sound, because the tracers are leaping the river, they're going in slap amongst those fieldgrey forms. Brrrrrrp. Brrrrrrp. Brrrrrrrrr! The streaks of red light soar across the water. The green forms dive for the dirt in all directions, tracer shining amongst them. Spurts of dust kicked up in the street. Brrrp. Gun jams. Re-cock. Brrrp. Tracer slashing into the street and kicking up. Gun jams. Clear it. Brrrrp. Gun stops. Mag empty. The street is empty, except for a few uneven bundles which might be dead men or just bits of rubble."

I regret, but it is true, that both I and the Belgians were laughing our heads off. A Belgian sergeant then appeared. He thought that the Germans were trying to surrender to a Sherman tank that was sitting in front of a house on the waterfront to the east, its gun pointed towards the German-occupied building. His guess was that the first German came out to negotiate with the tank commander, the second one joined him, and then, surrender having been agreed on, the rest of them walked out in a bunch, at which point I mowed them down.

Actually, none of the Germans went near the tank; on the contrary, they moved up the street, away from the waterfront, and out of view of the tank altogether; and the first two quite definitely had rifles and were running, as if to continue the battle. As for the bunched group, I could not be sure. Normally, I might have let them go, just in case, but with my nerves screwed up after being pinned helplessly to the bridge by the bombardment, I felt only the urge to hit back. Recollection of what I felt during this incident was later to prove valuable when, as an actual war historian, I had to appraise "atrocity" stories, particularly those committed by the S.S. According to the Belgians, the troops in that corner house were S.S.

The battle directly in front began again, almost immediately. A rash of dust-spurts kicked up along the front of the house next to the corner building, and the heavy rattle of the Sherman's machine-gun rolled across the river.

"It changed target to the corner house and the Belgians, having scraped some of the rust off their Bren, join in. Spurts of dust leap along its wall in irregular lines; tracer goes flying through the windows, or ricochets off the walls at all angles; a cloud of grey-white smoke blossoms sideways out of its front wall, as the tank lets drive with the turret gun. Black smoke wells up among the houses, on the heels of a sound like thirty express trains gone crazy, as the Germans shell their own troops and the tank with impartiality. The Bren is blasting away at my side, and the air if full of crimson tracer. Every time the Belgian gets off a burst he says, 'Iss gut?' and the others babble back, 'Ja, ja, ja.' Other Belgians bring up fresh ammo; smoke leaps again and again from the front of the house, as the tank gun lets drive; and everything is a proper madhouse. Things die down. The echoes roll away across the river. To the right another tank comes crawling through the ruins along the waterfront, like an enormous remorseless insect. A German shell envelops the first tank with black smoke, but after the smoke has drifted away, the tank moves forward a few yards, and stands motionless, watching. It starts up again, goes round a corner, and out of sight; the second tank follows it round the bend, a block away from the houses which are the object of attention. Out of our sight, they start to blast the house next to the corner building. Dust spurts along its front wall, smoke blossoms from it as shell after shell goes home. It almost disappears in the blossoms of smoke and the rashes of machine-gun fire. Soon it starts to blaze, black smoke wells up and fire comes out of the windows.

"Small figures in khaki move jerkily among the ruins of the water front, the colour of their uniform making them appear more clear-cut than the greenish hue of the Germans. They walk slowly towards the corner house. One of them is carrying a Bren, and looks tired. As they near the corner house, the covering fire stops and they walk up to it, well-spaced, not running. One of them goes inside. One by one the others follow. The burning house is blazing furiously, flames rolling through its roof now, and black smoke drifts away over Arnhem in a dense stream. All is quiet inside the corner house. Five minutes later, the infantry walk out. There are no prisoners with them. They go into a huddle outside—'O' Group, apparently—and then wait while one of them walks cautiously along the river side of the corner house, ducking as he passes a gap in the hedge which covers that side of it. There's a high wall beyond that, enclosing some fairly large buildings, which a Belgian map reveals as the Electric Centrale. Behind that is the gas works. The rest of the infantry section pass the gap in the hedge one by one, running and ducking as they pass it, and then walk very cautiously after the bloke in the lead. He looks around, peers through a gap in the high wall, and returns. They hold another conference, walk back to the hedge around the corner house, pass through, appear just once more, moving even more cautiously, and vanish. About a minute later there's a burst of Tommy-gun fire from the Electric Centrale. A machine-gun goes into action. Odd rifle shots ring out flatly over the river. A tracer bullet comes leaping out of a window. Fifteen minutes later the infantry re-appear, and gather by the corner house, undecidedly. Jerry beat them back from the Electric Centrale, apparently. The tanks can't cover them there, and from the map it's a pretty rambling place. The burning house is spewing flame and smoke almost down to ground level now, and it blows flatly away over the town."

I then went down, forward of the dyke, to the bank of the river, looking for a boat; all I found were the remains of a British night bomber, amid a lot of bomb craters, and some of the whistling and moaning in the air got so pointed that I dived into a large circular pit holding a house-boat. When I was actually at the water's edge, some infantry on the far bank began to wave frantically. I could just hear their shouts, and took the hint. So for the third time I had a river between me and the enemy and for the second time had failed to cross. Arnhem was still burning brightly in the evening sunshine, funeral pyres of smoke drifting past its shattered towers and spires, as I walked back over the embankment and set off for Nijmegen. What I had seen was part of the climax of the battle. Up to the time I left, the "crust" was either still holding, or merely going back by one house or one street. But before dark, it had collapsed; and there was nothing much behind it.

The South Wales Borderers had been pinned down in houses on the outskirts all day, and even when tanks were brought up and another infantry battalion joined them, they were unable to advance. Then, suddenly, recalled D. B. Hollins,

"Towards evening, which was again a bright sunny one, enemy opposition collapsed, and we were ordered to climb on all the available vehicles, when we swept through the town, meeting only light sniper opposition. The tanks simply blew all opposition away. We rested comfortably that night in deserted shops, clearing the rest of the town the following day."

"We were Army Troops" [said Macdonald of 11 Canadian Armoured Regiment]. "Our job was to crack the crust—then the Armoured Divs would go through. Ours were usually set-piece affairs, seven to ten days of training with the infantry beforehand. But I'd never seen these guys [4 Lincolns] before, I just had ten minutes with Flint. We met in a house in a built-up area, with a slight incline. One of his platoon commanders, Lt. H. V. Burns, had just been killed. He told me where the start line was, and the avenue of advance. I told him: I'll be in the lead tank; the other tanks will be behind me; I want flank protection from your leading platoon; no infantry to get in front of me. This was going to be the tough part, going through the built-up area."

Macdonald led in a Sherman with a 75-millimeter gun, followed by a sergeant in another 75-millimeter tank. They had five-man crews with both a turret and bow machine-gun. The two Shermans with 17-pounder guns had room only for a four-man crew and had no bow machine-gun, so they brought up the rear. Only the first two tanks could fire. The machine-guns of Macdonald's lead tank would fire continuously, going down the street, the bow gunner raking the lower rooms left of the road, the turret gunner taking the lower rooms right of the road. The machine-guns of the sergeant's tank immediately behind would do the same, but raking the upper rooms of the houses. Unlike Italy, where house walls were often of stone a foot and a half thick, machine-gun bullets would probably penetrate.

Macdonald's main concern was being picked off by snipers in the top levels of the houses. Even in daylight, a tank is virtually blind, and in order to control the battle Macdonald had to be able to see over the top of the turret. He had the turret flap up behind him, so was protected from the rear; he had infantry sections walking along the sides of the road level with the three tanks behind him, so that they protected him from the sides; and even so, he was careful not to keep his head up, but to pop up and down for rapid checks on the situation. So they rolled forward through the streets of Arnhem, machine-guns spraying continuously, with no regard for the rifling, which was ruined.

There was a very slight delay on the 75-millimeter fuses, and Macdonald used this to occasionally slam a high-explosive shell at the road surface and burst it in the air ahead of him. The German defenders were in deep dug-outs between the house-fronts and the pavements. When Macdonald saw one, he stopped, switched the 75-millimeter gun until the muzzle was practically in the dug-out, and then his gunner pulled the trigger.

"Whenever I came to a street corner, I stopped the tank, got out, and told the infantry section commander: 'I'm going to blast the corner house. Then, when I wave my hand, two infantrymen go lickety-spit into it. OK?' Next morning, when the machine-guns had cooled down, there was no rifling left, and the bullets were coming out sideways."

But the technique took the tanks and the Lincolns through to their objectives that night. At midnight, they halted the advance. Macdonald told Flint: "We got to gas up (takes two hours), then go on again at 5 a.m. Can you guard the Shermans, and let us sack up?" Aware of the vulnerability of tanks at night, Flint had patrols out all night, plus a close guard on the armoured vehicles.

A sketch by the author looking into Arnhem from the south end of the road bridge

CHAPTER THIRTY

"A DAY OUT WITH A BRIGADE OF INFANTRY"

Arnhem to the Grebbe: April 13–May 4

The Hallamshire Battalion of the York and Lancaster Regiment was to pass through the Lincolns, and from the eastern part of the built-up area launch an attack on the wooded heights beyond the town, from which heavy fire had been coming all day. But as Major-General M. G. K. Halford wrote in a contemporary account,

"The Lincolns met much stiffer opposition than expected and their anticipated rate of advance was much slowed down. The result was that the Hallamshires' attack, which was planned for daylight, was only able to start at 1930 hours. The plan was for one company to attack at a time, each leapfrogging through another company in turn. Each company attack was preceded by a short, concentrated artillery programme and a 'mattress.' This latter was a massive concentration of about 400 rockets firing into a limited area on the objective. It was believed that nothing could remain alive at the receiving end of this weight of high explosive. On the slopes of the high ground which was the Battalion's objective there was a thick wood, beyond this some barracks, and beyond them again a road junction. Starting its advance at 1930 hours, B Company under Major Grey reached its objective halfway through the wood with little difficulty. C Company under Major Lonsdale-Cooper then passed through, but took a long time getting up the hill through the thick wood in the dark. Nevertheless, by 2200 hours it had captured the barracks, its objective. D Company under Major Mackillop then made a night advance through the woods to the west of C Company and reached their objective at 23 hours, without meeting any major opposition. Both these advances were carried out with some skill as the woods were thick and it was a dark night. During the day seventy-four prisoners were taken. At this time the commanding officer decided to wait until first light before continuing operations."

Next morning, opposition had stiffened, but the objective, plus 43 more prisoners, was taken.

The 147th Infantry Brigade, coming into the bridgehead last, met generally much lighter resistance; but to understand what some of them saw in the town, it is necessary to consult Dutch sources. Paradoxically, the inhabitants of Arnhem have virtually no knowledge of what happened there during the third and most destructive battle of all. As the archivist of Arnhem, Mr K. Schaap, kindly explained to me:

"You may know that, at the end of September, 1944, immediately after the British airborne assault had failed, the inhabitants had been evacuated by the Germans; consequently, at the time of your arrival, the town had been almost completely deserted but for German troops and Nazi civilian 'rescue squads' (i.e., looting organisations) for about 7 months. This accounts for the substantial gaps in our present knowledge as to what really happened. From Allied air photos, taken at irregular intervals between September, 1944, and April, 1945, and from reports and diaries of Dutch civilians who, most of them illegally and at great risk, had visited the town a rough notion can be formed of the damage already done at the moment of this last battle. (There is not much to tell, I am afraid, about what happened in May, 1940; Dutch resistance in and around Arnhem had been but little, and only a few buildings had sustained slight damage.) We are able to draw the following conclusions: (a) During the September action considerable damage had been done to houses and buildings in the actual battle zones (near the road bridge and in the Oosterbeek 'perimeter'), along the western approaches to Arnhem, and in some parts of the town centre which had been deliberately set on fire by the Germans, allegedly to wipe out the last British resistance. Summing up, the damage had been severe but limited to relatively small areas. (b) Due to several heavy air raids and, especially from December onwards, to artillery fire from the Nijmegen area, destruction took place on a much wider scale. Moreover, the

Germans, who now had the town practically all to themselves, plundered and raised fires at random. In early February, the Germans blew up what was left of the road bridge. (c) The Allied advance on Arnhem, in April, was preceded by a heavy artillery barrage which went on for several days and resulted in considerable additional damage; as there was no fire-brigade left, and the Germans did not care at all by now, fires spread freely and rapidly, causing much destruction that could have been prevented. From the military point of view it may be doubted whether such a heavy artillery supporting programme (including rockets) was really necessary under the circumstances, as the German forces in the area were only small and weak; no doubt the Allies were understandably intent on limiting their risks as much as possible, but on this particular occasion it took the form of senseless waste."

One of the targets was the Arnhem zoo, and the author of an article in *The Yorkshire Pud,* the magazine of 7th Battalion, the Duke of Wellington's Regiment, noted that C Company became "involuntary custodians" of the animals, "but the day before our arrival an elephant had succumbed to shell shock as result of the heavy bombardment of the immediate area of the Zoo."

Private Reg Dunkley, who had been fourteen years old when the war started, was with A Company of 7 D.W.R.

"We were to take the high ground behind Arnhem. Just street clearing for our platoon, flushing out trouble when we found it. It was all high ground (for Holland!), a suburban area, undamaged. Not even windows broken. Walk into a room of a house you had to clear, and you'd find cutlery still in the drawers, everything untouched. There was no sign of looting in the houses we investigated, they were just like this room here, with carpets, curtains, furniture. It was ghostly, being in an empty town. You felt that you had no right to be there and that someone was watching you, in case you did something you shouldn't. You were looking over your shoulder all the time. The other lads felt it, too. But the only sign of looting we saw was in the street where the road curved gently left. On the left-hand side was a farm cart, with clucking coming from it. We were doing it, four men to each side of the street, so I lay down with my Bren, taking up a covering position. But it was all right, there were no Germans there, only the hens which were in a sack on the cart, in which was also a litter of German equipment and weapons, and a big wooden box, locked, full of paper money, brand-new, done up in elastic as if from a bank.

"At one point we came to a round house in a lake, an ornamental lake with lilies. Someone in the leading files saw movement behind the widows of the house and loosed off a few shots. A white flag was waved from a window, and we went forward over a causeway across the ornamental lake to the house. Inside were some German medics, who surrendered. It didn't strike you very much at the time, but it's surprising how you can be involved in a little battle on a platoon sector. It was quiet with us, but away on our right there was what sounded like mortars and loads of MG-fire down in a little hollow which we couldn't see."

The final advance was made uphill towards a wood, with D Company leading, A Company following behind. It was actually a "tongue" of woodland—trees with small saplings and high shrubbery in between—some 200 to 300 yards beyond a road that ran at right angles across the line of advance of the D.W.R. In the verges of the road were many convenient round holes (presumably those dug by the Germans as funkholes for the occupants of vehicles under air attack); and A Company went to ground in these holes for the night. But there was no sleep for anyone. D Company in front were counter-attacked all night by what were believed to be Dutch S.S. troops ("Landsturm Nederland"), and there was a 100 percent stand-to.

Next day, D Company attacked in their turn, supported by Canadian tanks; and the enemy countered with his own tanks—three little French Renault vehicles, armed only with two-centimeter cannon, which were quickly knocked out. The D Company attack was made parochially famous by a battle picture taken by Lt. K. M. Evans, M.C., who always went into action with a camera round his neck. The "action" picture he took on this occasion was so good that it was reproduced a number of times in *Polar Bear News*, the weekly newspaper printed by the division when it was occupying part of the Sauerland where I happened to be stationed at the time and was used to illustrate a commemorative article on Arnhem, which also included a poem written by me. The coincidence was that, before the D Company attack took place, Dunkley's section from A Company were sent forward to reconnoitre that precise "tongue" of woodland shown in the photograph.

"The following morning there was a call for a section to recce the wood in front from which the German counter-attacks had been coming all night" [Dunkley told me]. "This was our section of A Company. We were the oldest serving members —we had been with the Battalion since France—while the rest were mostly reinforcements, and this was why we were chosen.

"So off we went, seven of us in line abreast, mostly armed with automatics. Two Brens (I had one), three Stens I think, and two with rifles. Object, to pinpoint any German positions dug-in in the wood. We had gone about 150 yards into the wood—out of sight of our people, from whom we were hidden by lots of shrubbery—and probably the Germans had an OP in a tree; anyway, the stonk opened just like that. It was not tank fire. Nor was it 88s. A distinct whistle of shells. No word of command was given to retreat—but, and this is funny—we just turned through 180 degrees and ran like the dickens. The sergeant in charge (Sergeant Roden) was hit and killed by the same shell, which fell very close to both of us. I heard it coming for perhaps three or four seconds, then it burst, fairly close, I suspect, for I can recall, when I was back in hospital, picking out tiny bits of shrapnel.

"I knew I was wounded. There was a singing and ringing in my ears. I knew my right kneecap had gone. You know, at the dentist's, you can feel the grating of the instrument on the bone—so I could feel my kneecap grating; and it wouldn't go where I wanted it to. I couldn't speak, and I thought I'd bought it, because they were still shelling. I saw one of our chaps, only the length of our small garden away from me, bending down. I shouted to him, but I could make no sound. So I scrabbed myself along to a sapling (this was where the kneecap wouldn't obey), and propped my back against it, so that I was partly upright and visible to anyone walking near by. My one regret, as I lay there, was that I might have been hit in a bigger operation than this.

"How long it took for the stretcher bearers to come, I don't know. Not long, perhaps ten minutes. I didn't know that the Sergeant had been clunked behind me, until I heard the stretcher bearers say: 'Let's get Dunkley away first, the sergeant's obviously gone for a chop.' We were the only two hit out of the seven. I felt no pain, I was so numb or senseless, but when the stretcher bearers put me on the stretcher, I lost consciousness.

"I came to in the RAP (now in a farmhouse captured by D Company). I assume I had been doped, but I can remember the MO saying: 'Would you like another cup of tea?' I tried to speak, but couldn't, so he said: 'Don't strain, nod.' So I nodded. The tea was very sweet. Morphine? At the RAP they just cut off your clothes and bandage you. The ambulance seemed to be there already, revving up, and I was off in no time. Flown back from Nijmegen in a Dakota, landing perhaps at Blackbushe? Anyway, I was in one of the two hospitals at Basingstoke. I lost my right leg, above the knee.

"Now, I get a 90 per cent disability pension. About three or four years ago, I suddenly suffered two epileptic fits. There was no history of epilepsy in my family. My wife was terrified, the first time. I just went mad in bed. The second time was not so bad, because then we knew what it was. I had seen the doctor and had an X-ray. You see these depressions above my left eye? They found I had two bits of shrapnel in the brain there, which had been dormant for more than twenty years. They didn't take them out, because they said the damage is caused by the shrapnel going in, and then the damage is done —there's no point. But you'll have to take tablets for the rest of your life, they said. I take three a day."

Another battalion of 147 Brigade, I Leicesters, also found little resistance left in the town, and their advance was harassed mainly by German shellfire.

"It wasn't pleasant" [wrote Bob Day, a twenty-one-year-old private in the carrier platoon]. "But this was nothing compared with the hell which was let loose on our company when we were advancing beyond Arnhem—and this came from our own fire. As you know, other ranks and indeed junior officers, have little idea about the general strategy of a battle at the time in question. But we all understood that one of the officers in our battalion became over-confident, following our advance through the town, and, against orders, decided that our company should press on through a wood on the high ground just out of Arnhem. We eventually came to a halt in the wood, presumably to consolidate our position, and about half a dozen of us were in a dell. The Bren gunner and I were side by side against a bank of the dell, pointing the gun at a house which, we thought, probably contained a German sniper or two. Suddenly, there was a dreadful shrieking sound followed by a tremendous bang.

"I immediately lay down flat as these sounds were repeated over and over again in rapid succession for what seemed like hours, although, in fact, it was probably only a minute. Great jagged bits of metal were flying all over the place and it was far worse than any mortar fire I had encountered (I had been wounded by a German mortar bomb at Salerno). When, mercifully, the firing ceased, I looked up in a daze, scarcely believing I was alive. Then I heard screams coming from the other side of the dell, and I could see a young officer with one of his arms nearly torn off. The poor chap was obviously delirious and several of my section did what they could to comfort him before he was taken away on a stretcher. I turned to have a word with the Bren gunner and saw that he was still leaning against the bank, with his head bent forward. He appeared to be asleep, so I nudged him. But he was dead. There was a tiny hole in his back and he must have been killed instantly by a piece of shrapnel or splinter from the British rockets which had rained on us so furiously. I cannot remember his name, but he was a quiet, pleasant fellow who had told me only a day or so previously that his wife had had a baby. Others were wounded in that rocket barrage."

This was the actual effect of a "mattress," deadly enough, but falling short of the complete devastation one would expect on seeing the rockets fired.

On April 14, the battle was taking place round Arnhem, rather than in the town, and the thrusts were being made in a number of different directions. In the morning, for instance, Macdonald's troop of Shermans was again married up with the Lincolns for a drive over the flatland south-east of Arnhem, between the town and the Ijssel, which here curves away north-east; while in the afternoon he was driving north-west. The morning attack was "just a day out with a brigade of infantry," because it took the German defenders of the Ijssel Line in the rear and in country where the Canadian tanks could deploy.

The distinction between Canadian armoured and infantry divisions was somewhat arbitrary.

"The Canadian Army was designed to be the Most Armoured Army in the world" [pointed out Macdonald]. "All the armoured divs had infantry, of course, and the Infantry divs had one tank brigade each (to begin with), so the difference was merely of how many tanks they had. If you lost a tank, you indented for a replacement, and it was there the same day or night, in a matter of hours. We were always up to snuff. Usually, we had a regiment of SP guns given to us, broken up one battery per squadron. They were Priests, a tank chassis making a stable base for a gun. This gave a feeling of power, because you could call them up if you were in trouble."

In the morning drive, there was no trouble. There was an embanked road, not then completed, leading out across the flood plain towards the Ijssel between Arnhem and Velp. Leading to the embankment was a wood-covered approach with the last 600 yards open ground. As Macdonald's troop of four Shermans rolled out of the trees, with British infantry mounted on the backs of the tanks, Macdonald could see the German positions.

"They'd dug in on the wrong side, facing us. We charged, the four of us, lickety-spit, all guns blazing. When we got there, the Germans were in a state of severe shock, with many wounded. They couldn't control themselves; they rolled down the embankment, faces grey-green in colour, and it took ten minutes for them to regain the use of their faculties. They all just fell into the bag. We took a map off them—it showed their brigade HQ—and we radioed the position back. We took their money off them, then sat down and played cards. In the middle of the game, a machine-gun opened up. Four tanks were facing it, but they were all empty. A sergeant jumped into one with his crew, and went over and despatched the machine-gunner. Later, we were faced with a house near Velp. We put six rounds into [it], plus MG, then I raised my hand and dropped it, for the infantry to go in fast. They took thirty prisoners, many wounded."

This was the nadir of the German Army. Macdonald and his accompanying infantry took more prisoners that day than he had seen in the whole of the Italian campaign. It was not merely a matter of inferior equipment, but of junior leadership. The best men were dead or wounded. This is always the result of prolonged heavy fighting. As Macdonald pointed out, the people who count are the commanders at company and battalion level. If too many of these become casualties, the division becomes weaker, even though the high command, with increasing experience, gets better.

"In Italy, to begin with, the British Eighth Army pulled the whole show" [he said]. "The line inclined forward where the Eighth were. Then, after actions where, for instance, all four company commanders in a battalion became casualties, the British divisions became weaker, and the American Fifth Army pulled the Eighth."

Having destroyed the defenders of the Ijssel Line, the force was switched back to the western outskirts of Arnhem, the same day. Here the Germans had many flak guns firing in a ground role at the British infantry trying to clear beyond the built-up area of the town.

"The built-up area was cleared" [said Macdonald]. "It just stops dead, and open country begins. Flak guns were firing over the open area at British troops to the south-west. The flak guns were exposed, so I asked for artillery. I was not believed, or perhaps they were used to infantry OPs, not tank OPs. The 88-mm flak gun will knock out a tank in seconds, if you show.

In a built-up area you are not worried about anti-tank guns, but you are worried when they are in open ground with a full field of fire. This flak, they may have been 88s, I don't know, were just pumping out shells across our front. Our defence overproof sheets were wonderful, they had all the German positions on, even machine-guns. They showed everything. So we wheeled out a 17-pounder tank and fired four rounds. that stopped them, they knew their goose was cooked."

Had the Germans had tanks, it might have been a different matter. The German tanks had thick armour and big guns, and were good in the defensive role; whereas flak guns were virtually immobile and unarmoured. A combination of the two had proved deadly in the past, but guns alone were a poor defence.

Now the way was open to bridge the Neder Rijn and make the long-delayed armoured drive right through to the Zuyder Zee. Canadian engineers put two Bailey pontoon bridges across the river a few hundred yards to the west of the massive ruins of the road bridge, and the rest of 5 Canadian Armoured Division rolled across. Their drive to the north began on April 15, right into the flank of the Germans defending the Ijssel Line against attack from the east around Apeldoorn, and on April 18 the Canadian tanks had reached the Ijsselmeer. Thus the final phase of the ill-fated Market Garden operation was carried out successfully seven months after the airborne landing, and the time taken to do it casts doubt on the practicality of the 1944 time-table.

Even in 1945, with the German Army so weakened as to be unable to strike back, it was not all easy going. Macdonald for instance, had been roaring along, with the infantry packed on the back of his tank using it as a mobile shooting gallery, when a bazooka shot blew them to shreds all over the armour plate.

"We were going a fair clip, and had seen German infantry get up and run" [he said]. "But one had the guts to stay behind with his bazooka near a railway embankment. He hit the infantry on top of my tank, not the tank itself. Holy catfish."

The projectile, designed to disembowel an armoured vehicle, had a devastating effect on unprotected human flesh.

This drive helped open up the road to Hamburg, but Montgomery's insistence on the importance of the northern drive left too few troops to attempt the capture of western Holland; and therefore there was a semi-official truce on the Grebbe Line, and after the 49th Division had cleared the bank of the Neder Rijn to that point, all serious fighting ended in Holland, two weeks before the war itself came to an end with total German surrender. Quite apart from avoiding much suffering and loss to the Dutch population, this tacit cessation of hostilities saved many soldiers' lives. The Hallams held this position at the end and described it in the war diary:

"The position was the original Grebbe Line, constructed by the Germans when they anticipated an attack on West Holland from the west. The ground was low lying and wet, and the position consisted of vast defence works raised up above the ground. In front of them lay a vast glacis, formed by the fens bordering the River Grebbe. Beyond the river lay a high feature from which the enemy could dominate the whole position. No movement was possible in daylight, and the position could have been most uncomfortable. Fortunately the truce to admit the taking of food into Holland was now being observed by the enemy, and there was no interference from them. The enemy consisted of 34 S.S. Div (Landsturm Nederland) and the remnants of 346 Div. No patrolling or harassing fire was permitted. There was nothing to report."

On the night of May 4, 1945, on learning that unconditional surrender of all enemy forces facing 21 Army Group would take place next day at 0800, "victory was celebrated forthwith." A double issue of rum was distributed, all the Véry lights were fired up into the darkness to create a celebratory fireworks effect, and rifles and revolvers were fired into the air. Thus the 1945 drive past Arnhem ended at the same place and in the same month as had the German drive to the Dutch-held Grebbe Line in 1940. Ironically, half the defenders were still Dutch. There was a difference only of five years, less 10 days, between the Dutch surrender and the German surrender of Holland.

CHAPTER THIRTY-ONE

ECHOES OF ARNHEM

April–May

The final stages of the campaign from the Rhine may be marked by a few decisive dates. April 4 was the day that Simpson's U.S. Ninth Army was returned to Bradley's 12th Army Group, diverted by Eisenhower from the main drive to the north in order to complete an encirclement of the Ruhr in combination with a break-out from the Remagen bridgehead. An encirclement in such strength of the largely immobile German forces was quite unnecessary, and the object must have been political. As a result of this diminution of strength, it was formally decided by Montgomery and Crerar on April 12 that only two divisions—the British 49th and the Canadian 1st—could now be allotted to western Holland, where they were opposed by some 120,000 men of the German Twenty-fifth Army. This was the day before the third Battle of Arnhem began.

A few days later, about mid-April, with Arnhem fallen and the break-out to the Zuyder Zee begun (which would cut off the German Twenty-fifth Army from Germany) contact was made with Dr. Artur Seyss-Inquart, Hitler's Reichskommissar in the Netherlands, and the first wary discussions for a semi-official armistice commenced. On April 22, these had progressed far enough for Montgomery to forbid any further move westward of his forces, in return for which Seyss-Inquart had agreed not to carry out any demolitions in or flooding of Dutch territory, and to allow in food supplies for the starving population.

On April 28, an unofficial truce came into operation. The wariness was largely a result of a desire not to arouse Russian suspicions that they were being excluded from a "deal" with the enemy; and there could have been American suspicions as well.

In the case of western Holland, there was every reason to

halt the troops and cease fighting, on purely humanitarian grounds; and there were no valid arguments, military or political, for continuing.

In the case of Czechoslovakia, it was otherwise. Bradley's forces waited for nearly two weeks, until April 25, for the Russians to "liberate" that unfortunate country. And just to make sure that the Americans would not be able to forestall the Red Army in Central Europe, SHEAF concocted a story of a mythical Nazi "national redoubt" based in the mountains of southern Germany and Austria. On April 22, the enthusiastic Patton, like a bull with the red flag waved in front of him, went charging off in that direction; and there was then no further chance of any unhappy thwarting of Marshal Stalin's ambitions for Europe.

The incautious Bradley, while claiming to have been "naïve" at the time as regards the critical political issues now being decided, admitted in his autobiography that "Because Czechoslovakia had already been earmarked for liberation by the Red army, we were not to advance beyond Pilsen, a few miles inside the border."* That there was a mutual U.S.A.–U.S.S.R. agreement that Russia would dominate Central Europe after the war, and that this agreement is still in force, was made quite clear by official Washington reactions to the second Red Army "liberation" of Czechoslovakia in 1969.

On the other hand, the drive by Montgomery's 21 Army Group to deny Denmark and the North Sea to the Red Army was successful; and he put sufficient pressure on Eisenhower to obtain, not the return of Simpson's army, but at least the loan of the XVIII U.S. Airborne Corps, three divisions strong. The British 6th Airborne Division went all the way from the Rhine to the Baltic, and when the first Russian tanks rolled into Wismar, near the old Hanse port of Lübeck, they were startled to find the town already in possession of British and Canadian paratroops. Strategically, the Russians were not merely barred from Denmark, but locked inside the Baltic, with no easy access to the North Sea for their warships in time of war.

* *A Soldier's Story,* by Omar N. Bradley (Eyre and Spottiswoode edition, page 549).

On the American front, however, all was thrown away; by no fault of the troops, Austria, Czechoslovakia, and large parts of Germany fell under the control of one of the most notorious mass-murderers in history and a regime every bit as contemptuous of human life and freedom as Hitler's.

There was no military reason why this should have been—the forces of the western Allies were stronger then than those of the Russians, and although some parts of the agreement to divide up Germany and Austria after the war into zones of occupation had been signed, the Russian treatment of their pledges on Poland was sufficient to show what their real intentions were, and excuse enough to occupy and hold the greater part of Central Europe.

Instead, it was allowed to become an outpost of Russian empire, as a result of a war supposedly fought for liberty and the rights of small nations. The number of deaths during the Second World War cannot be computed accurately, and estimates range from a "low" of 25 million to a "high" of 50 million. For this travesty of a future, they had died.

When the war ended, not all of them had been buried. In almost every great ruined city of Europe, tens of thousands of bodies lay under the wreckage; men, women, children. And on the merely military battlefields, soldiers still lay where they had fallen months before. After the third Battle of Arnhem, 4 Lincolns were put into reserve and billeted in the old Oosterbeek "perimeter," where 1st Airborne had made their last stand. "The ground was littered with containers, burnt-out jeeps and tanks, and British and enemy graves." Near the Hartenstein Hotel, Urquhart's former headquarters, there was now a knocked-out Sherman tank, which had arrived seven months too late.

The scene of the American airborne landings between Nijmegen and the German border had been hardly touched; the winter front-line had run across it, and it was still mined and booby-trapped. As it was more or less on the doorstep of Canadian HQ during March and part of April, I made several expeditions into it with friends.

The remains of Gavin's gliders lay in a valley about three miles away, by the German border, and on April 9 three

Canadians who went to look at them were fired at from the woods. On shouting out who they were, the firing redoubled, and they had to make use until dark of abandoned slit-trenches. The HQ defence platoon was called out to comb the area (which was vast), but although they found traces of recent firing, there was no trace of the culprits, or clue as to who they were.

Next day, April 10, rather carelessly, I went out with Taylor to see the American gliders for myself. Carelessly, because Taylor was in the R.A.M.C. and therefore could not legally carry arms, and the magazine spring of my own rifle was defective and I had not yet had sufficient cause to get a new one. This evening's walk provided it.

The first group of gliders was on a hillside surrounded by earthworks that had been roofed in with glider wings covered with soil. A main road lay a few hundred yards away, and tank tracks led ominously down from it across the grass towards the gliders. We then turned and walked north, towards the German border, with a wood on our left that was a confused mass, inside, of slit-trenches, dug-outs, and pits for tanks or S.P. guns. To the right, ahead, on the brow of the hill, were farm buildings, the only buildings in sight at that moment. Just before the farm lay two dead cows, "so long dead that a filthy green liquid has formed underneath them, upon which flies are feeding."

It was sunset as we walked up the path to the farm, passing there a man in civilian clothes who gazed very keenly at us and only grunted when Vic said, "Good evening." Beyond the farm, a rough track led downhill between tall trees bare of foliage, but with a green parachute caught in the branches. Sunset was turning to twilight as we made a rapid inspection. The track was lined with lifted mines and mine-warning signs; there were six graves marked: UNKNOWN GERMAN SOLDIER: BURIED 23 MARCH 1945; and on the left, more gliders, suspiciously intact, and others to the right.

I picked up a U.S. paratrooper's helmet, with bullet holes both ends, one entry and one exit, the latter being the wider; and it was at about this point that the key question occurred to me: *If you lived on a farm, would you leave two long-dead cows, unburied, on your doorstep?* With a click,

I put a round into the breech of my rifle, and we turned back.

As we approached the farm, it was last light and we were miles from any help, so I was ready to fire as soon as I saw the hard-faced civilian again. Alas, I was still as green as grass. Before we even came level with the scarred building, there was a soft *wheeeeyou* as a bullet whined over about 20 yards in front. It was fired from the wood, which now lay on our right, beyond a probable minefield, and unless the man was a very bad shot, seemed meant as a warning. There was no point in firing back, as the shot could have come from any part of the wood; and to advance on the wood, through the minefield, with a defective rifle, was suicide, even if he was a poor shot.

I noted that night in my diary: "It's all very fishy, and there's a bad atmosphere about the place—not just the atmosphere of death, which has ample reason to be there—but a live atmosphere of living things." In brief, it was the living I was afraid of, not the dead.

All the same, it was an eerie place, and the events were most curious, so next day after tea I went back, this time in earnest, with a borrowed magazine spring and Corporal Hudson of the Reconnaisance Corps with a revolver. This time, we 'put one up the spout' as soon as the gliders came in view, calculating that, presented with two armed men, the strange civilian would not shoot, because even if he got one, the other would get him. But the farm was completely deserted, except for the decayed cows, so we turned off left to search the wood.

After interrogating two obvious Dutchmen collecting timber for firewood, we came across some recent military artifacts, which indicated a defence position built at the edge of the wood by American paratroops, with anti-tank mines out in front, facing the German border; the Americans driven back towards Nijmegen, the minefield added to by the Germans; and the position later re-taken by Canadian troops. The critical distinction between British and Canadian was made by noting the reading material scattered about among the ammunition and equipment.

The edge of the minefield was clearly marked with white

tape. The lure was in the parachutes lying in the fields that stretched bare and open on the hillside for about a mile. The encouragement was that the mines seemed to be anti-tank, not anti-personnel, although rust could have sensitised the fuses.

"Hudson is impetuous, and wants to go in; I hate the thought of maiming, though not the thought of dying, and I am not so keen. We walk in, slowly, carefully, watching the ground, avoiding suspicious patches of soil. The next step may mean a lost leg. Then I take over the lead for a bit, pushing on fast in my anxiety to get through, and have done with it."

Within 20 yards, I came on German slit-trenches and German equipment, mixed with German, United States, and Canadian ammunition in quantity; and also some good parachutes. Shortly after this, we noted more happily that raw areas of earth showed clearly in the grass, making the position of the mines obvious; and the competition now was the right colour of parachute, the red being more tempting than the camouflaged. Then on to where the ground was still cut up by zig-zag swathes—machine-gun bursts—and into some more German slit-trenches.

"There's a ribbon of the Iron Cross, a Jerry's paybook (joined up Osnabrück), a Hun helmet, and plenty of German haversacks. Somebody has had the Iron Cross, but Hudson has the ribbon. But it's sunset now, and walking is beginning to get dangerous."

It was dusk when we came into the village.

"A German mortar, all rusted up, with the bomb sticking out of the muzzle, stands by one of the ruins. I step on the charred remains of a cow or horse—it's too dark to see properly. And we follow on between the ruins, which have been shelled almost to the ground in most cases, there's a horrid, sickly-sweet odour; somebody needs burying, and quickly. We pass several more areas where there is this same smell. We go along a line of earthworks, shadowy with night, so that they almost resemble a trench of the last war. Then we come to a sign, facing away from us: 386: A COMPANY:

THIS AREA NOT CHECKED. This refers to the area we have just crossed."

We got onto a track leading to the House of the Suspicious Character, and so to bed; but one of a Canadian party also out exploring that evening was killed in the minefield. We saw their jeep going along a path in the distance.

On April 17, still keen to get the suspicious character, I went out with Taylor; this time he got himself a revolver.

"We follow the tank track uphill for several miles. On either hand are the deep, dark woods, pitted with slit-trenches and dug-outs, literally thousands of them, and strewn with abandoned equipment. It would take a Brigade of infantry all their time to search them, and many men could hide there indefinitely. Somewhere in there are many sights like the one that the Liaison Officer's driver saw—the burnt skeleton in the wrecked plane."

When I came to study Gavin's battle later, it was quite clear why at all costs, Nijmegen bridge or no Nijmegen bridge, he had to hold the Germans in the open and prevent them from establishing themselves in the woods; and why, although he has been criticised for it, I have not followed suit.

We moved fast and by a more direct route, so as to examine all buildings in daylight. In all, out and back, it had been about a 12-mile walk with Corporal Hudson. We went straight for the farm where the suspicious character had been standing on the first night.

"A glider pilot's jacket lies on the left of the path; that horrible half of a cow, with the maggots crawling inside the hide that seems stiff as cardboard, and the filthy pool of green liquid underneath it, where the flesh is decaying into the soil, lies on the right hand side. I am holding my rifle in both hands, ready to fire. Building by building, barn by barn, we go over that farm. We go into wrecked rooms; down, cautiously into dark cellars; or clamber over hay in shell-holed barns. Beneath an upstair window is a pile of used cartridges, but there is no human being there, and no signs of occupation at all."

We then went down the rutted path where the fragments

of parachute, hung up on the trees, moved slowly in the wind, towards the ruined village.

"On the right are the fallen-in remains of a trench system, clotted with the foul debris of battle—the shattered rifle butts, the battered spandau, the cases of mortar bombs, the riven helmets, and tatters of equipment. And the odour of battle comes from both sides of the path. On the right, amid the mines, where a dead cow and two wrecked German AFVs are lying; on the left, where nothing is visible but the field and the odd wreckage; and from the front, where the shattered roofs of shelled and fired houses point splinters against the skyline. And over all the weird and evil feeling of menace. The menace of the living. A red parachute lies on the path by the first house of that fated village. The house is part of a farm, and dank and musty, and wrecked. It has no door. In the short patch of garden is the sign: 'This Area NOT Checked.' I walk carefully up the path, looking for a man or a booby-trap; watching the floor of the interior and also the corners at the same time. I am inside the door. I move slowly and cautiously up the passage. There is a room on the left with no door. Rifle first, I look inside. There is a German there.

He is lying face downwards, away from me, his field boots pointed to the door, the putrid body half fallen in and horrible, covered with flies. It is not a man, it is a thing. There is no telling flesh from uniform, except for the boots; it is just one weird, horrible mess, rigid and stiff and surprisingly small, and grey and filthy like the light inside the room. A young man, too, I think, and now he is like a putrid, rotting ghost, lying beside wreckage upon filthy floorboards among spilled grenades. The smell is sweet, sickly, poisonous and pervading, like some disease. Did he once cheer the Führer at the Sports Palast? I come out of the house, after Taylor has had a look, and walk on, rather hushed. Taylor, being RAMC, is not much affected.

The entire place being clearly mined, we do not explore as thoroughly as we might have done, in that deserted village; but we counted some thirty German helmets, half-a-dozen Canadian helmets, and two American. Quite a mix-up, and many lives, for this small corner of Holland, if it was Holland. In daylight, the mortar with the bomb rusted in its mouth stands rather foolishly outside a ruined house; and the burnt horse in the wrecked building opposite is not so horrible as the night I stepped into it at dusk."

But now it was beginning to get dark again, and we turned back.

"We pass again that dreadful house, and some freak of morbid curiosity impels me to walk again up that path, and to look through the window into that twilight room of the long-dead. He's wearing a sniper's coat, I can see that now— the tough fabric has stood the decay better than the uniform, of which there is no sign; and his head is covered by rubble . . . if he has a head. The thing seems to have been mashed about, perhaps by grenade. I creep cautiously round the corner. The shock wasn't so bad this time, though I nearly stepped on him. He's hideous, all huddled up outside a window of the room where the corpse of the German is lying.

It's small, and like a mummy. All huddled up. The boots and gaiters are of British pattern, shiny and mildewed, and the only recognisable thing about it. The rest is just a mess. It has no head—the bones of the spine protrude from its mildewed collar; the thigh bones are visible, and bare of flesh; but his legs, where his trousers have been torn away or ripped by rats, have a cold, mummy-like, sickly covering that once was human flesh. The odour of putrescence is an atmosphere about him. This is flesh, along the putrid limbs . . . that is bone along the thigh . . . that must be a battledress, and yes! I can make out an army-issue jersey . . . but there is no beginning or end to these things . . . no demarcation line where one can say: that is flesh, and this is bone, and that is but cloth . . . it all merges into a decayed mass, smelling of evil. The rats jump about the corpse of the German three feet away inside the room.

"Attached to the thing's decayed right knee, and exposed by the tearing of his trousers, is a black metal object, obviously a booby-trap, once cunningly concealed by the cloth. Now the rats have revealed the ghastly device.

"Six feet away from this huddled, decayed ruin of a man,

sprawled face downwards on a heap of rubble, is a great, bloated thing, so unhuman that it's hard to distinguish him from the earth and the wreckage on which he lies. It's greenish, and shiny, and the boots alone proclaim for what he died; that he, too, was once a Canadian infantryman. Dust to dust, they say . . . if they had seen this . . . It is not dust . . . it is disease, the antithesis of dust. Dust is clean. This is foul.

"These decaying, putrid things merge into the dusk in their surroundings. The Wehrmacht boy fits into the grey, foul twilight of that deserted room so that he seems almost another bit of debris, only more foul; the two Canadians outside his window merge with the soil and the rubble so that we failed to see them as we passed by the first time, though they lay but a few feet away. These are the glorious dead, the politician's speeches.'

This, though I did not know it then, was where the war in the west began. And this is how it ended.

But not quite. For we reported the ruined village, so that these things could be de-mined, identified, and buried. The booby-trap on the leg of the decapitated Canadian was identified as a German contact grenade, neatly placed. Another search party, not guided by one of us, failed to find these corpses; instead, they came on the bodies of two German infantrymen killed on patrol in the woods. I do not know what happened to the skeleton in the burnt aircraft, which I did not see personally, and only the Dutch may know how many bodies there were in that area.

When I wrote to Herbert Kessler, for an account of his experiences at Arnhem, he added a note:

"There is one thing I should like to mention, before I close. I don't know your books, but I sincerely hope that they are not serving the glorification of war. I have no wish to contribute to anything like that. Having been called up at the age of 19, and finishing up as seriously wounded, I nevertheless, thank God, came home again, whereas many good people on your and [my] own side had to die. I should like to think therefore that my notes will rather contribute to show the senselessness and tragedy of these incidents in the past, so that they may not be repeated."

I have done my best to present as balanced a picture as possible within my own limitations and the scope of my theme; and the moral of it, if any, I must leave to others.

But I cannot leave my theme without mentioning a recent description of the Rhine between Emmerich and Cologne as "a complete anthology of new bridges." The rapidity of recovery from perhaps the most devastating war in history was the most surprising aspect of the "peace" for those of us who saw its appalling beginnings at first-hand. Even while the armies were still driving for the Elbe, the first of the semi-permanent high-level bridges were going up, built to withstand winter floods and ice. Within a few weeks of the end of the war in Europe, and while the war in the Far East was still going on, Field Marshall Mongomery's job included the surely civic task of declaring open the first high-level bridge over the Rhine in what was now the British zone of Occupation— the twin-track "Tees" and "Tyne" bridges near Rees. Measuring 1,660 yards long, they were built in less than two months, during April and May, 1945.

Mobile Canteen No. 699 was still serving out the tea to bridge builders, on the near bank, a sore point with the Misses Chettle and Whiteside, for the staff of static canteens were allowed over; and it was a victory for them when on June 7 HQ sent a teleprint reading: CVWW MOBILE CANTEENS MANNED BY WOMEN ARE NOW ALLOWED TO CROSS RHINE WITH ARMED ESCORT. But before they moved on, Margaret Chettle took the opportunity to visit the scene of the most famous airborne battle, beside the Neder Rijn. She wrote to me:

"My visit to Arnhem was only very brief, one day when we had 24 hours leave in Nijmegen, and we drove over there. This was after things had begun to settle down, and what I remember so vividly was how moved I was by the British Military Cemetery. It was very quiet that sunny day, and nature was beginning to cover the scars of war, and the birds were singing. I remember the colour of the flowers and the beauty of them—the blue sky and the trees in leaf, and the feeling one sometimes experiences in the quietness of a great cathedral. But I cannot tell you anything worth putting in your book."

INDEX

Armed Forces